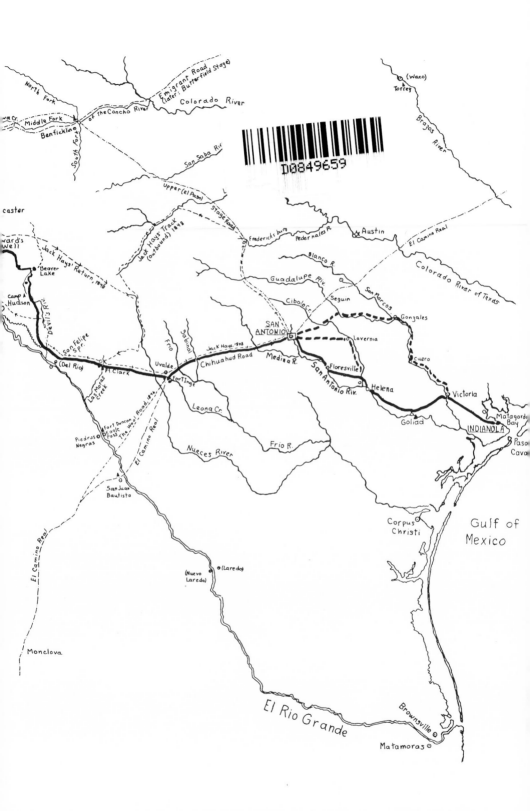

Three Roads to Chihuahua

Three Roads to Chihuahua

Chihuahua

THE GREAT WAGON ROADS
THAT OPENED THE SOUTHWEST
1823–1883

Roy L. Swift
and Leavitt Corning, Jr.

EAKIN PRESS ☆ Austin, Texas

Library of Congress Cataloging-in-Publication Data

Swift, Roy L.
    Three roads to Chihuahua.

    Bibliography: p.
    Includes index.
    1. Southwest, New — Description and travel. 2. Roads — Southwest, New — History —
19th century. 3. Southwest, New — History. I. Corning, Leavitt. II. Title. III. Title: 3 roads
to Chihuahua.
F799.S94 1988   979'.02   87-30497
ISBN 0-89015-640-9

To the late Dean D. L. Vest,
St. Mary's University,
San Antonio,
who, in the 1950s, first reopened
study of the Chihuahua Road.

CHIHUAHUA'S SIX GREAT SILVER-MINING AREAS IN LATE 1800s

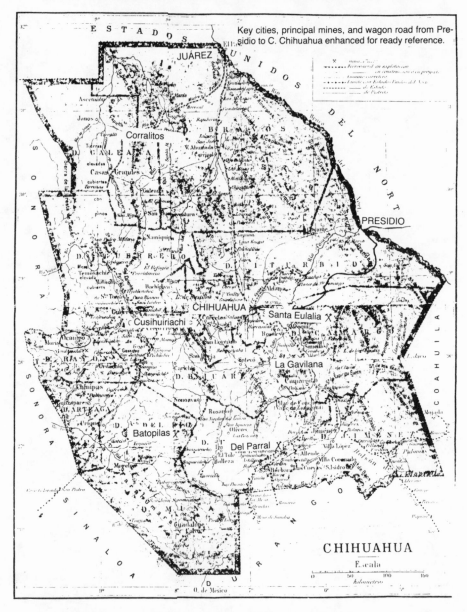

Key cities, principal mines, and wagon road from Presidio to C. Chihuahua enhanced for ready reference.

Adapted from La República Mexicana: Chihuahua (1909), *this map indicates the six silver-mining areas most productive in Chihuahua during the latter years of the nineteenth century. The railroad shown from Juárez due south to Ciudad Chihuahua followed closely the route of the old Santa Fe Trail. The Chihuahua Road from Indianola and San Antonio in Texas may be seen running southwest from Presidio around the Sierra Grande to the capital.*

Contents

Preface

In the early 1970s I met Leavitt Corning, Jr., retired petroleum geologist with a new career as instructor of history at San Antonio College. He had published a book, *Baronial Forts of the Big Bend,* and that struck a common chord, for the Big Bend country has been a passion of mine for sixty years. Leavitt appeared with me on a public service television program I was then conducting at a San Antonio station. He told me about a new book he was starting, to be called *Three Roads to Chihuahua,* dealing with the old wagon-freight roads into northern Mexico. I told him it was an exciting subject and a splendid title.

Leavitt Corning and his wife did a great deal of research and exploration on the project, and although ill health had already beset him, he drafted a couple of tentative chapters. He died of cancer in 1972.

I thought often of that beguiling title and of Leavitt Corning's concept for his book. Finally, I got in touch with Mrs. Corning. She graciously authorized me to go ahead with the work, asking only that I give her husband credit for his inspiration and research, and that if a book were published, it should be under his title.

As I undertook over the next decade to develop the subject, I traveled many thousands of miles throughout Texas, New Mexico, and old Mexico, and through museums, archives, and libraries from Washington, DC, to Mexico City. I met scores of wonderful, helpful people. Essential new materials, along with tantalizing adventures only tangential to the original concept, kept offering themselves, until the "book" reached unmanageable length. The text herewith presented will, I hope, reflect the considerable discipline that my advisers have urged I should impose upon it.

I take this opportunity to give grateful and affectionate acknowledgments to the late Leavitt Corning's initiative and to his title, *Three Roads to Chihuahua.*

In deep appreciation, also, I wish to pay tribute to Travis Roberts, of Marathon, Texas, whose encyclopedic knowledge of Brewster County and the whole Big Bend country gave immeasurable assistance in tracing the lore of the several key roads in that area.

And I thank Mrs. Marie Berry of the History and Reference Department, San Antonio Public Library, and her staff, for their unfailing patience and diligence as they helped me gather material for this volume.

Introduction

In the middle years of the nineteenth century, three widely separated wagon roads snaked out of the United States and made their laborious way to Ciudad Chihuahua, capital of the Mexican state bearing that same name.

The first of these was known in this century only as the Santa Fe Trail, because many of the wagon trains stopped in that old New Mexico town. The fact was that Santa Fe represented only the point of exchange for American and European goods freighted down from the States, to meet the wealth of Mexican mines as it found its way by cart trains up from the south. A substantial number of trains did go all the way to Chihuahua. As a whole, however, the Santa Fe Trail took a long way around from the markets of the east, through Independence, Missouri, and that state's full width, across all of Kansas and part of Colorado, then south in New Mexico through a wild, mountainous region into Santa Fe. And from there, it was still 500 miles to Chihuahua City.

The second road came into being when Dr. Henry Connelley, an American trader long situated at Chihuahua, became dissatisfied with the inefficiencies of the Santa Fe Trail. He seized on the idea of a more direct route which would go down the Conchos River from Chihuahua to the present location of Presidio on the Rio Grande, then strike out across the uncharted wilderness of northern Texas, to gain access to eastern markets at Fort Towson, beyond the Red River.

It was a bold plan, and the story of the party's adventures and hardships, on a round trip which lasted from April 1839 through August 1840, merits a book in itself. Dr. Connelley did establish the feasibility of this second road, but for some reason it did not catch fire, and the route was eventually abandoned.

By the end of the Mexican War in 1848, the elements were falling into place for the inevitable opening of the third road, the most direct route from the Eastern Seaboard and Europe: through the Gulf of Mexico, across Texas, and into the treasure troves of northern Mexico.

Along this great artery, known properly as the Chihuahua Road, moved more traffic and commerce from the 1850s through 1877 than the Santa Fe Trail experienced in those years, and it carried, as well, a tide of immigration that opened up the Southwest. Yet the route was not widely recognized as an entity during its own day, and it had been almost totally lost to history in the succeeding century. Its several parts are known variously as the Indianola Road or Goliad Cart Road; the Old Spanish Trail; the Government or Military Road; and, in Mexico, El Camino del Rio Conchos.

This road wound across the Southwest from a port town on Matagorda Bay — Indianola — which has literally disappeared, washed into the ocean by successive hurricanes; through San Antonio and out along the great springs of the Balcones Fault to the Rio Grande; then in a surprising loop northward for hundreds of water-seeking miles, until it finally turned back to the Rio Grande at Presidio del Norte; then into Mexico and up the Conchos River to Chihuahua City. This bald itinerary suggests little of the wide variety of terrain which that route traversed: the lush, flowered prairies of the Coastal Plain, the magnificent pecan and cypress-shaded springs along the Fault, the desolate reaches of the Trans-Pecos and the Chihuahua Desert.

The rough little towns along the way; the lumbering trains of great freight wagons and the boot-tough men who drove them; the innumerable desert campfires tended by weary freighters, taut with vigilance against the perpetual threat of Indian or bandit attack — these elements develop as the story of the Chihuahua roads unfolds. First, however, some examination of the early attitudes, the lusts and motivations that opened the roads, is necessary for an understanding of this artery of commerce and culture.

What was the talisman? Whence sprang that silver flood which put a thousand wagon trains on the long, dry roads from Independence and Indianola during the mid-1800s?

It came from the most prolific array of silver mines that the Western Hemisphere has known. Beneath the hills of Chihuahua lay an incredible lode that was found and tapped by the ancient Indians, rediscovered by the Spaniards after they had given up their dream of the Seven Cities of Gold, and even now, after three centuries of exploitation, is still yielding a constant flow of silver.

Chihuahua silver reinvigorated the Spanish colonial rule after the golden wealth of the Aztecs ran dry. It provided the hard basis of Mexican currency throughout the turmoil of nineteenth-century revolutions and the Pax Porfiriano of the Díaz regime. The peso's silver cartwheel stayed at par with the United States dollar until the holocaust following the 1910 revolution broke its integrity.

Dr. Francisco Almada, venerable historian of Chihuahua, lists more than 200 mines in the state which had been exploited for profit. A few of these were gold mines; a considerable number were for copper, zinc, and lead; but the overwhelming majority were silver mines.[1]

In the years when the wagon freight lines were most active between the United States and Chihuahua, the principal silver-producing lodes were distributed in six major areas of the state: Santa Eulalia, known also as Aquiles Serdan, a few miles outside the capital city; Cusihuiriachi, sixty-odd miles southwest of the city; Corralitos, 180 miles northwest; Batopilas, in the southwestern extremes of the state; La Gavilana, seventy-eight miles south of the capital; and those mines directly under and about the city of Hidalgo del Parral.[2]

Of these, the most generous throughout three centuries, and the most significant in the development of the city of Chihuahua, western anchor of the three roads, has been Santa Eulalia. So romantic is the history of this great mother lode that it deserves a place as background for the entire story.[3]

More than 300 years ago, in 1652, when what is known now as Ciudad Chihuahua was no more than a mission outpost of the church in far Nueva Viscaya, Capt. Diego del Castillo first stumbled upon raw silver outcroppings in the jagged hills less than sixteen miles east of the settlement. This Spanish adventurer tried to work his discovery, but was forced to abandon the project because of Indian harassment. The great discovery was forgotten for fifty years. Around the turn of the century, the lode was rediscovered.[4]

Only the names are known of the three men who made the find: Nicolas Cortes de Monroy, Eugenio Ramires Calderon, and Juan Holguin.[5] From one of the famed MacManus brothers of Chihuahua, Lew Wallace derived his story that these three were

[f]ugitives of justice, hunted out of the haciendas about Chihuahua . . . [who] took refuge in the fastnesses of what is now known as Santa Eulalia. You can form an idea of what precious scoundrels they must have been, and of how desperately they must have sinned

against civilization . . . by asking yourself what kind of men they were who chose to face Apaches rather than fellow-Christians.

In the course of this desperate sojourn, however, they camped in a great ravine and one day made there a "rousing fire" for cooking, in a fireplace made from the boulders lying about. To the astonishment of those outlaws, as the fire heated the stones, a shining white metal trickled out. The men "recognized the metal as silver, prospected, and . . . their fortunes were made." [6]

The refugees sent word by a friendly Indian to the *padre* heading the Chihuahua mission

> that if he would absolve them, and obtain their pardon from the offended authorities, they would put him in the way of getting enough silver to build the grandest cathedral in New Spain. The offer was accepted. They were absolved and pardoned. The mines were opened. Their fame went rapidly through the country. Miners flocked to . . . Chihuahua. The mission became a city of seventy thousand, a growth and prosperity attributable to Santa Eulalia alone.

The proposal made by the three discoverers, to finance the building of a cathedral, was consummated in substance by the bishop, Don Benito Crespo, when he visited the area of the mines in 1726 and saw how rich they were. He struck a bargain with the miners and allied industries that they would donate one *real* (fifty cents) out of each mark ($8.50) of silver produced from the mines, toward building a great cathedral. Within a few years this produced a fund of $900,000 for the church, sufficient to build not only the cathedral but also a church in the village of Santa Eulalia. The first stone of the cathedral was laid by Bishop Crespo in 1727, and the towers were completed between 1757 and 1759. Though hardly the "finest cathedral in New Spain," it still graces the Plaza Mayor of Ciudad Chihuahua, handsome, sturdy, and revered. [7]

While Sir Henry George Ward was England's minister to Mexico from 1825 to 1827, he wrote an extensive treatise on the country, with emphasis on its mining industry. In this he also tells how the cathedral was financed by the one-*real*-for-each-mark donation; elsewhere he says that during the eighty-six years from 1705 to 1791, the mines produced a little over $100 million in silver. These riches brought some 6,000 inhabitants to the district of Santa Eulalia, where there were seventy-six *haciendas* for reducing metal and 180 smelting furnaces. [8]

La República Mexicana: Chihuahua, published in 1909, substantially confirms the figures cited above for the eighteenth century. It then proceeds to show that though the mines produced over $11 million from 1825 through 1834, income from their riches fell drastically after the collapse of Spanish rule: only $1 million from 1825 through 1834; $3.5 million from 1834 through 1868; and not quite $3.5 million from 1868 through 1884. The last two citations cover the era of the United States wagon freight trade.[9]

Lew Wallace emerged from the Civil War as the Union hero who defended and held Washington against a far superior Confederate force, earning him at age thirty-eight the two stars of a major general. Wallace had gone to Mexico immediately after the close of the war, ostensibly as an agent to raise a corps of former Yankee soldiers who would fight on the "liberal" side of the post-Maximilian skirmishing. Nothing much came of this mission, but Wallace was irresistibly a journalist, always stirred to take up the pen when he encountered a romantic subject. And, next to gold, what more alluring subject could he have found than the silver mother lode of Santa Eulalia?

Traveling with a friend by private carriage, Wallace crossed the deserts after leaving Monterrey. In one monumental sentence he recorded conditions, giving an insight to what the wagon freighters and most other travelers of the time endured without comment:

> . . . after so many days of drouth, heat, and dust, and so many nights spent in unsuccessful struggles with fleas and vermin; after so many leagues, pistol or carbine in hand; after a watch so constant against robbers seeking valuables, and Apaches hungering for scalps; after a wearisome repetition of such incidents as dismounting to convert valises, trucks, "paja," and boxes of bread into barricades, which fortunately were never attacked; passing whole nights in sleepless expectation of war-whoops and arrows; finding ranchos deserted; traversing passes which seemed formed for ambuscades, and lined with crosses, significant of murders already committed — after all this I imagine there need be no hesitation in confessing that it was with relief and positive happiness that we at last passed through the shadow of the Sierra Grande, and caught the first glimpse, leagues away, of the tall spires of the Cathedral of Chihuahua.[10]

He had come so far, enduring such hardships, because ". . . if common opinion can be relied upon, Chihuahua is the great silver state of Northern Mexico, and Santa Eulalia the richest of all the silver districts in Chihuahua."

Once established in a *meson* fronting on the cathedral plaza of the capital, Wallace and his companion were further encouraged to visit the legendary mines by Secretary José Iglesias of the national cabinet of President Juarez, the secretary being then on business in the city. "Do not leave without visiting that district," Iglesias said. "In my opinion its mines hold the grandest fortune in Mexico. All they need is to be possessed by a company which will work with them with proper management and enough capital." [11]

Thus stimulated, the travelers placed themselves in the hands of three Americans, "wealthy, generous, hospitable; shrewd as Yankees ought to be when in foreign lands . . . The three constitute the firm of M_____ Bros." Though General Wallace followed the irritating habit common among nineteenth-century journalists of coyly giving only the initial letter in the names of significant men he mentioned, these three could only have been the same MacManus brothers, Frank, George, and Edwin, prominent at Chihuahua when Alexander Doniphan reached the city in 1847, staunch friends of responsible wagon freighters, and mentioned often by Texas newspapers.

So it was that the party of five Americans, including one of the MacManus brothers, and six Mexican servants moved out on one early November morning. Either of two routes might have been taken to the mining district. One went directly through the plains to the east and across the River Chuviscar, then ascended steeply into the jagged "silver mountains of Santa Eulalia," as Wallace captioned one of the many sketches that illustrate his report. The other route wound southward past the fine stone aqueduct which the old Spanish engineers had originally projected to bring water all the way to the mines. From there the road ascended into the Sierra and turned back north into the mining district. This was the one the party took, though Wallace felt, from stories he heard, that the first way might have been more picturesque:

> I call it the more interesting because there are those yet living who remember the day when it was lined with houses and *fundiciones*, to a point far down the river. They speak of it in melancholy tones: of the business that used to pass down it; of the coming and going of long trains of burros, laden with sacks of ore, of the shouting of drivers, of the column of dust which, like a yellow curtain, stretched perpetually across the valley, from mountain to mountain, for it was the road established by the Spaniards in the glorious days of Santa Eulalia, when thousands of men found occupation in her "pockets," when the annual profits of the various owners summed up millions,

when the *Real de Santa Eulalia* was a city of seven thousand souls, and Chihuahua, with her far-reaching suburbs, a mighty metropolis of seventy thousand.

At the mention of such greatness, strangers are generally astonished; looking over the capital as she now appears, her population reduced to fifteen thousand, and with not so much as a chimney of a furnace left standing to speak of mining operations present or past, he naturally concludes the pleasant picture to be a baseless tradition. The ancient inhabitants solemnly repeat the history, and silence doubts with equal gravity.[12]

By these caveats is the reader forewarned that the old mines had fallen on hard times when Lew Wallace visited them and were being only feebly worked in the most primitive manner. The decay had resulted from the breakdown of economic entrepreneurism in the decades of revolution. Nevertheless, the MacManus brother who accompanied the party subscribed to the fact that Santa Eulalia still possessed vast undeveloped riches, for he had the word of a distinguished French scientist (unnamed in Wallace's narrative) who had surveyed the mountain during the reign of Maximilian:

After thorough examination of the district, including explorations of the interior of most of the mines, he expressed the opinion that Santa Eulalia consisted of silver strata in the nature of vast deposits of ore, not so rich as abundant and inexhaustible; that the oblong mountain in which we will find the San José, Parcionera, Negrita, and Santa Rita mines, was a kind of mother mountain of silver core, from which the metal radiated in all directions, growing less rich according to its distance from the center; that five thousand men might dig, and pick, and blast away at it for a hundred years, and at the end of that time the yield would be as rich, if not richer, than when they began; and that if it were possible for an able and wealthy management to concentrate all the mines of the mother mountain under its single control, there would be treasure enough taken out each year to pay the cost of the work plus all the cost of the army in Mexico.

And so the travelers came at last to the half-ruined village of Santa Eulalia, and from there commenced explorations that took the better part of three days. They were struck, first of all and throughout their inspection, by the utter primitiveness of the operation and the abject poverty this imposed upon the peons who were doing the work. On the very outskirts of the village they saw huge piles of slag, residue of the richer days of the Spanish Empire, now being combed through to extract pebbles and grains of silver which had been let pass in the hastier exploitation. This residue had gradually, over the years, settled to the bedrock at the bottom of the slag piles. It was dug out from there by miners, each working on his own initiative and for a beggarly percentage of the yield; they then washed out the precious metal from the sand and other pebbles by a primitive kind of "placer" process. As Wallace described it

> . . . nothing could be simpler. The operator provides himself with a crowbar, a shovel, and a cowskin. The latter he fashions into a water-tight basin by stretching it into a wooden frame. Filling it with water, he stands over it rocking his little tub containing sand and grit, from which, washed free of clay and earth, he separates the worthless pebbles and selects the valuable particles. Other, somewhat more pretentious placers were dug into the hard clay and kept fed with water by little boys bailing water from a reservoir integrated into the device. But even here the scarcity of water controlled and limited the operation . . .

Moving on toward the mines on a narrow path skirting precipitous cliffs, the travelers met a train of burros, conducted by a peon, and carrying out leathern bags of raw ore as they stepped carefully in single file. Wallace then saw how generations of such burros, in a century and a half of carrying out "the millions which had thus gone to swell the currencies of the world," had worn into the rock "hoofholes large as washbowls." Arriving finally at the ancient mine Santo Domingo, in the side of a deep gorge, they found "a hole cut in the face of the solid rock, large enough to admit a man well doubled-up." They learned, though, that Santo Domingo was not a silver mine; its product was a lead ore taken in great quantities and required in order to blend with the silver ore in the chemistry of the smelting process. As the visitors watched,

> out of the black door of the mine comes a figure [who] steps out quickly, lightly, although weighted by a sack containing a hundred and fifty pounds of ore. A broad rawhide band attaches the burden to his forehead. He is as naked as when born. His neck and limbs are like Heenan's. The perspiration streams from his sooty face and body, and his breast heaves spasmodically. And why not: For two hours he has been down in the hydrogen of the mine — down two hundred yards perpendicularly . . .

The man had climbed with his burden for half an hour up a winding and slippery path, with hazards of jagged rock and places where he had to bend over double under his load to pass beneath low-hanging ledges, lighted only by a tallow dip stuck upon his forehead.

> His first act on stepping into the daylight is to snatch the little tallow dip from his forehead and blow it out. It cost him a *claco* only; but it was such a friend down in Tarturus; without it could he have ever risen to the light? . . . He proceeds next to the door of a roofless house. A man meets him at the threshhold, helps unload him, takes the sack to a rude contrivance and weighs it, giving him a ticket of credit. Not a word is spoken. Resuming the now empty sack, the naked wretch turns, walks quickly to the entrance to the mine, lights the friendly taper; looks once to the sky, as if to bid the glad sunshine goodbye, re-enters the rocky jaws, and wades back into the darkness. Yet he is not alone; he is a type; he has comrades whom he will meet on the way, comrades in the extremest pit, wherein the sounds of rueful labor are blended with peals of laughter. What is there to which men can not accommodate themselves?

Wallace's party made an abortive attempt to penetrate the depths of that gas-laden mine. They gave up after a few hundred feet. Mac-Manus suggested they would find better traveling in the San José mine, across yet another mountain. This they traversed, coming down into the half-abandoned houses of an old adobe village where "within the radius of a mile are the mines San José, Vieja, Negrita, Santa Rita, and Parcionera, reputed the richest in the *Real.*"

MacManus, an older man, chose not to join his guests in exploring the inner recesses of the great mines. He advised them to enter, first, the Parcionera, whose gateway was directly above that of San José. Here with a guide they would make their way through a succession of galleries down into the San José and then back to their starting place. This the party did, marveling at the huge irregular voids of darkness surrounding them as they ventured along with the feeble light of a few tallow candles.

> In running these slopes and galleries, if such they may be called, the early miners set no value upon the common ore; in preference they sought the pockets of soft yellow clay, which . . . were sometimes of immense extent, requiring years to exhaust. Rich with silver, they were cleaned out carefully, and when cleaned left immense chambers with arching roofs, like those of a natural cavern.

The stone comprising these natural caverns, still rich with ore, Wallace found to be sandwiched between strata of limestone seldom more than twelve or fifteen feet thick. Only here and there the miners had blasted through these layers. One result, Wallace felt, of this particular stratification was that "the great mines, San José, Parcionera, and Negrita, for instance, run horizontally into the mountain . . . The great man for whom the *Real* is waiting will find himself at liberty when he takes possession to convert the mines already opened into initial galleries, and operate from them upward, downward, or laterally as he pleases."

Solitary miners were scattered among the burrows of stone, each at his favorite spot. The Yankee travelers, attracted by the glow of one light, drew near:

> The moment we came upon him he was bending forward to examine closely the ore he had broken off. In the uncertain light his naked, crouching body seemed that of an animal . . . We spoke to him; the voice was kindly, yet it sounded in his ears, so long attuned to silence, like a pistol shot. He started up and turned upon us in an attitude of defense. Is it possible *he* is one of the masters through whom all the silver is introduced into the world? . . . It will be long before I forget that poor solitary. He may be squatted at the base of the same wall now. Pity for him wherever he is! Pity for all his class!

Once outside the entrance to San José, after two miles of stumbling through the caverns, the party proceeded, in the last twilight of that long day, back into the town of Santa Eulalia, to accept the hospitalities of their local host, who was operator of one of the *haciendas* in the *Real*. Next day he took them on a tour of these facilities, proudly exhibiting the elementary working of reduction.

Wallace had stopped at each mine the day before to sketch the entrance and its surroundings, as well as to make separate renderings of the near-naked men who sat with small hammers crushing chunks of ore to make it ready for the furnace; the peons staggering under great leather panniers of ore to bring it to the smelters; and of the primitive furnaces themselves. These on-the-spot drawings by the author were eventually translated into dramatic etchings by staff artists at *Harper's,* as was the wont of nineteenth-century publications in order to adapt the art to the mechanical requirements of printing at that time. Allowing for Wallace's own romantic inclinations, plus the further enhancements of the staffers, the reader today who pores over that musty and near-forgotten exposition remains convinced that by word and pen Lew Wallace captured a sense of the harsh majesty of the mountains in the mother lode, the riches they contained, and the dreadful squalor investing the labor which produced Chihuahua's silver.

As the visitors jogged back into the capital on the ancient Spanish road via Tabalopa and the Junto, they tried to come up with answers to two obvious questions: why the mines were not better worked, and what would be the best plan to work them.

As to the first point, MacManus and his guests from the States agreed with Yankee condescension that

> Santa Eulalia really ceased to be worked in any magnitude when the Spaniards were driven out of Mexico. In different ways the mines fell to owners who had little capital and still less energy . . . As miners the Mexicans are, in some respect, without superiors; they can tell at a glance the quality of ore, and in the mere manipulation they excel; but when extensive management is required of them, they utterly fail . . . As to foreigners: Frenchmen, Englishmen, and Americans have often sought to obtain the control of the mines of Santa Eulalia, but in vain . . .

For information on how the *Real* could best be worked, General Wallace blithely referred the reader to his partner in the exploration, "who actually did survey and map the whole district." Unfortunately, even to the last, this young engineer was identified only as "my friend G_____."

As a matter of history, however, during the final twenty years of wagon freighting before the railroads came, the mines of Chihuahua gradually increased their output. Data already cited showed that in the eighteen years ending in 1884, they produced $3.4 million in silver as compared with $3.56 million in the thirty-two preceding years. During August Santleben's years of freighting out of Chihuahua, he considered the mines of Santa Eulalia to be among the most valuable in Mexico. Nevertheless, silver bullion from Hidalgo del Parral and from Cuisihuiriachi often had to be brought in to help pay for the huge amounts of merchandise the American traders were delivering to Mexico's hungry markets.

American enterprise and the Yankee dollar did finally move in on Chihuahua's mining potential. Santleben related that "when San Antonio first became the terminus of the Galveston, Harrisburg & San Antonio Railroad, in 1877–1878, the firm of Froboese & Santleben freighted from the railhead over 500,000 pounds of machinery to the Knox Mining Company of Parrall [*sic*], to the Santa Eulalia Mines, and to the mines of Cuisihuiriachi." He noted also that Cuisihuiriachi had been sold in 1876 to a San Francisco mining company for

$500,000, that the Corralitos mines were sold to an American mining company for $400,000, and that Wells, Fargo & Co. bought the Botapilas mines. La Gavilana, he said, was sold to the Chihuahua Mining Company of Logansport, Indiana, while the Knox Dry Mountain Company of Chicago, in which Santleben was a shareholder, had bought mines four miles outside del Parral as well as those which extended far under the city itself.

Lew Wallace's cheerful conclusion that the intervening strata of limestone in Parcionera and San José assured their strength was apparently too optimistic. According to the *Republica Mexicana: Chihuahua,* the overlying strata and the roof of the main chamber in the old mine caved in about 1885. It seemed for a while that the old treasure house was dead, but in 1895 American mining engineers from the Randolph Hearst enterprises made explorations under the original chambers and in virgin areas to the north. This led to findings that seemed even richer than the ancient ones.

It was said then, according to the publication, that in order to exhaust these new findings, one would have to extract fifty tons a day for fifty years. Don Luis LeJeune is quoted in his writing of Santa Eulalia: "We are not talking about a Leadville; we are talking about the largest lead-silver deposits in the whole world. The Comstock Lode, Eureka, Broken Hill, those mines best known for their abundance, are but 'pygmies' (the expression used by Professor William Adams) when you compare them to the giant which is Santa Eulalia." Tracing the exact history of Santa Eulalia during the next decades is difficult, but the same journal quoted above shows that a new mine in the Santa Eulalia *Real,* "El Potosi," operated by the Potosi Mining Company, produced $8,510,467 in silver and zinc in the one year of 1906 — far ahead of any other mine in the state of Chihuahua.

Working on his memoirs with I. D. Affleck in 1909, the same year that *La Republica Mexicana* was published, Santleben summarized his views on Chihuahuan treasure:

> . . . through the facilities offered by railroad transportation, the old mines have been opened by American capitalists and are worked by modern machinery under the direction of skillful engineers so as to yield enormous profits. Many new mines have also been opened in other localities, and American enterprise, backed by unlimited capital, has introduced new methods, and the mineral resources of that region are being developed into enormous proportions . . .[13]

But then came Madero, Carranza, de la Huerta, Zapata, and Pancho Villa, inciting and leading the massive uprising of the poor. One day in 1916, Villa's hired exterminator stood seventeen American mining officials up against an adobe wall and shot them down.[14] What happened to the mines through destruction, neglect, and expropriation during those fifteen years and the reconstruction of the last fifty would make another later story.

Turn now to the means whereby the American roads to reach that silver were opened.

"Commerce, not the invader,
after all is the conquerer."
— William Elsey Connelley,
War with Mexico, 1846–1847

[1]

Spanish Explorers
Along the Roads

Alvar Nuñez Cabeza de Vaca and his three companions were the
first men from across the Atlantic to travel on the Chihuahua Road, as
they struggled through the Trans-Pecos country of Texas in 1535 and
came upon an organized settlement.

Before these first Europeans intruded, the town had stood on the
high western banks of the Rio Grande for century upon century. It was
not a single town, precisely, but a loose grouping of at least five *rancherías*. Its earliest aboriginal citizens had recognized the significance of
the Junction of the Rivers *(La Junta de los Rios)* where they settled: the
strong, limpid Stream of the Shells *(Rio Conchos)* rushing down out of
the southwest from the Mother of Mountains *(Sierra Madre)* to join the
turgid Great River of the North *(Rio Grande del Norte)* that drained all
the huge basin above. From the east came the lesser creek of the Little
Cottonwoods *(Los Alamitos)* that gave access, beyond its farthest pass
and on distant shimmering plains, to the precious salt of commerce.

The three valleys provided natural thoroughfares for the restless nomadic tribes, the traders who moved among them, and the
raiders who preyed upon them all. A town at that junction was as
natural as Babylon where the Tigris and the Euphrates swung close
together, as predictable as St. Louis at the mouth of the Missouri.

1

And the location was all the more propitious because of the sun-drenched river-bottom loam that provided a laboratory for primitive peoples learning the art of agriculture. This may have been the entrance point of maize and beans to what is now the United States; almost certainly the area has sustained the oldest continually cultivated farm plots in the Southwest.

By the early years of the sixteenth century, the people there were basically Jumano, though the Patarabueye of the middle Conchos had also filtered down to La Junta. Others believe the Jocome of northern Mexico were present also.[1]

Until the *conquistadores* terrorized them with slaving expeditions, and the priests evangelized them, and the Anglos later occupying their lands harried them into the mountains, these industrious, hospitable Indians tilled the soil, cultivating maize, beans, and a wide variety of squashes and melons. They built solid homes of wattle plastered with adobe.

Into this precariously balanced society, in November or December 1535, stumbled the last four survivors from the glittering expedition launched by Gen. Pánfilo Narváez against Florida seven years before. After a series of disasters along the gulf, 242 surviving adventurers had been cast ashore on the Texas coast when their five makeshift boats broke up in the surf. One by one, through harrowing exposure, hunger, and abuse by Indian captors, they died along that desolate shore during the next three years. In the workings of the law of survival, four men emerged and triumphed. They were Alvar Nuñez Cabeza de Vaca, who had sailed from Spain as treasurer of the expedition, Capt. Alonzo del Castillo Maldonado, Capt. Andrés Dorantes de Carranza, and the latter's slave, Estevanico the Moor. Estevanico was one of the more antic figures to prance across the pages of American history, but he shared with his masters, the three Europeans, incredible resources of endurance.[2]

Perhaps Castillo and Dorantes were personalities in their own right; we shall never know, for their only testament was a dessicated "joint statement" reported in paraphrase by the chronicler Oviedo.[3] Cabeza de Vaca, though, throughout a long and crowded life, wrote reams and reams of *relaciónes* which reveal him to have been one of the most sensitive and perceptive souls among all the hosts of adventurers who opened up America.[4] This man from Jeréz, who came down out of Texas to La Junta de los Rios, was no ordinary fellow. The Southwest was fortunate to have him as its first messenger. Indeed, the Chihuahua Road might well be his best monument, for the burden of evidence weighs toward the conclusion that he and his fellow wanderers trudged right down the valley of Alamito Creek — the immemorial Salt Road of the Indians which 300 years later became a crucial link in the freight artery from Indianola to the silver mines of Chihuahua.

A separate volume would be needed to trace the torturous road followed by Cabeza de Vaca in the years of privation that led him and his companions at last to the Rio Grande del Norte and to their objective: a haven with fellow Spaniards. His own narrative is illuminating, however, from a point when he and his fellows, accompanied by an adoring group of Plains Indians who considered him a *shaman,* were but three days' journey, as it turned out, from that river.[5] Assuming that they were making their way through the Big Bend down Alamito Creek, where dependable water can be found in frequent small springs, one can see how Cabeza de Vaca's own words give us European man's first picture of that already-old settlement at the Junction of the Rivers:

> We ordered those who had been sick to remain, and those who were well to accompany us . . . Next morning all those who were strong enough came along, and at the end of three days journey we halted. Alonso del Castillo and Estevanico, the negro, left with the women as guides, and the woman who was a captive took them to a river which flows between mountains where there was a village, in which her father lived, and these were the first abodes we saw which were like unto real houses . . . Castillo returned to where he had left us, bringing with him five or six of the Indians. He told how he found permanent houses, inhabited, the people of which ate beans and squashes, and that he had also seen maize. Of all things on earth this caused us the greatest pleasure, and we gave endless thanks to our Lord for this news . . . we started, and after going a league and a half met the negro and the people that came to receive us, who gave us beans and many squashes to eat, gourds to carry water in, robes of cowhide, and other things . . . We went on . . . and six leagues beyond, when night was already approaching, reached their houses, where they received us with great ceremonies . . . Here we remained with them one day, and left on the next, taking them with us to other permanent houses, where they subsisted on the same food also. There was nothing they would not give us. They are the best formed people we have seen, the liveliest and most capable; who best understood us and answered our questions . . . We wanted to know from where they brought the maize, and they said it came from where the sun sets, and that it was found all over that country, and the shortest

way to it was in that direction. We asked them to tell us how to go
. . . They said we travel up the river toward the north, on which
trail for seventeen days we could not find a thing to eat, except a
fruit called *chacan,* which they grind between stones.[6]

At least two clues in the truncated passage above offer compelling
reasons to identify these settlements with those at La Junta, later
known as Presidio del Norte. First, no other area on the Rio Grande
offered such an easily traveled and well-watered road leading west to
the Rio Grande, with settlements there and bottomland farms, just
above a point where the river "flows between mountains" — a most apt
description of La Junta's vicinity. Second, the mention of "beans,
squashes, and calabashes" appears recurringly. (Fanny Bandelier ac-
knowledged in a footnote to her translation of the explorer's memoirs
that the word she renders "squashes" was *melones* in the original, which
might be any or several of the rinded variety of vegetables.) Throughout the 400 years since the explorer's *Los Naufragios* was written, travelers reaching La Junta have exclaimed at the abundance of pumpkins,
squashes, or more recently, canteloupes, onions, and chíles, always
found in that immediate area.

Biographers and geographers have debated the issue of why the
four travelers when they left La Junta did not go up the Rio Conchos,
which one might feel instinctively should come in from the west,
while the Indians declared that the land of corn lay "where the sun
sets." But a glance at a modern map shows that the main course of the
Conchos runs out of Mexico from deep to the south — southwest,
rather than from the west — while the valley of the Rio Grande runs
upriver almost exactly northwest from La Junta to beyond El Paso del
Norte. Therefore, to get "where the sun sets," travelers would more ef-
ficiently follow the Rio Grande Valley than that of the Conchos. As
these Indians said, about seventeen days' journey would take them up
the difficult terrain of that valley to the rudimentary agricultural settlements beginning to appear in the area of the Pass of the North.[7]

By this route, then, hastened Cabeza de Vaca, Castillo, Dorantes,
and the exuberant black, Estevanico, toward their several destinies.
They had made the first record of a road from the east into Chihuahua
— the river crossing at La Junta.

In the century and a half after Cabeza de Vaca's passage, northern Mexico and what became California, Arizona, and New Mexico
were intensively explored, the indigenous people subdued, and con-

siderable settlements established. At about the same time that Viceroy Don Antonio de Mendoza appointed twenty-eight-year-old Francisco Vásquez de Coronado as governor of the west-coast province New Galicia, he gave permission to an adventurous churchman, Fray Marcos de Niza, to head up a small scouting expedition to check out reports of the fabled Seven Cities somewhere in the deserts of Arizona and Nueva Mexico.

Estevanico the Moor had been the source of much of the rumor concerning these Golden Cities; he suggested persuasively that he and his masters had either seen or been close to them and their riches on their trek across the Southwest. Dorantes had sold the Moor to the viceroy, who turned a cautious but fascinated ear to the stories his new slave told. As a result, Mendoza sent the tiny party headed by Fray Marcos out into the wilderness, with Estevanico as its guide. The expedition departed Coronado's new capital in March of 1539, only four years after Cabeza de Vaca had been rescued. Shortly afterwards, Fray Marcos sent the Moor ahead with a few natives to scout briefly for information and report back.

Thereby released from authority, though under the viceroy's orders to obey Fray Marcos in every respect, Estevanico seized his own initiative. He continued ahead of the pursuing Fray Marcos and ignored the priest's orders, sent by messenger, to wait for the main party. All the while he was sending messages back to his exasperated chief, telling of the imminence of their reaching the Seven Cities, which he now for the first time called *Cíbola*.

His huge limbs decorated extravagantly with ornate clusters of feathers and bells, his broad chest covered with amulets and necklaces, Estevanico created an imposing presence and carried his new leadership with great aplomb. He had gathered admirers at each Indian village they passed, until at last he headed an entourage of 300 Opatas and a harem of adoring girls.

Estevanico the Moor (sometimes called Esteban, or Black Stephen) played out his remarkable string at a new kind of settlement in the high mountains of western New Mexico. This stronger village of Hawikuh on the Zuñi River was the home of the Zuñi chief, who was not impressed when Estevanico sent ahead by messenger the same sacred medicine rattle which had opened doors to Cabeza de Vaca. When Black Stephen strode up before the gates of the town in all his magnificence, the chief ordered him imprisoned. Accounts vary as to how he died, but the only contemporary report, that of Fray Marcos, says that he and most of his followers died under a shower of arrows as they tried to escape.[8] A story persists that the Zuñi cut the Moor into small pieces, distributing bits of him to all the towns of the Cíbola cluster to prove that the strange visitor was mortal, not a supernatural.

One year after Fray Marcos set out on his abortive probe, Coronado started north along the Pacific Coast, equipped and provisioned as none other had been, armed with the authority of the viceroy himself. The story of this young man's feverish search across the entire Southwest, from Sonora through Arizona and New Mexico and onto the high plains of Texas (the *Llano Estacado*), has often been told. He found no new riches: the fabled Seven Cities of Cíbola turned out to be six tiny pueblos of mud and stone, with two to three thousand people altogether, subsisting on primitive agriculture. But in his desperate, doomed quest to gain new wealth such as that of Cortés and Pizarro, he pioneered the searches that opened up vast areas to the more peaceful conquests of trade, settlement, and evangelism. Seventy years would pass before the founding of Santa Fe, and two more centuries then before Yankee traders would open their first road from the Mississippi through Santa Fe to the silver-rich markets of Chihuahua.

A handful of probes into Texas in the first 150 years did blaze the way, bit by bit, for what much later became known as the Chihuahua Road from the Texas Gulf Coast through the Trans-Pecos country and the Chihuahua desert into the new capital city. The following jump across three centuries does not purport to review the opening of the whole Southwest but to highlight only those expeditions and establishments which bear upon this story.

First was Espejo. A wealthy cattleman from Santa Barbara in Nueva Viscaya, which comprised what is now the northern Mexican states of Sonora and Chihuahua, Antonio de Espejo offered in 1582 to lead an expedition for rescue of two friars believed stranded in New Mexico. No doubt he wanted to improve his standing with church and Crown, for he was under sentence for capital felony in the death of one of his cowhands.[9] Fray Bernardino Beltrán of the Franciscan monastery at Durango was to represent that holy order on the search, for the missing churchmen were also Franciscans. With only dubious permission for the search, Espejo and Beltrán, a dozen soldiers, some servants and other churchmen, started out from San Bartolome on November 19, 1582.

They came down the Conchos River, as other traders and priests had done in the past half century, but they kept better records of what they saw and heard. They found primitive people in grass huts along the Conchos, but as they reached La Junta, they found better-built houses inhabited by Jumanos, just as Cabeza de Vaca had found. Furthermore, said Espejo, these "gave us to understand that three Christians and a negro had passed through there" and Espejo was sure they meant Cabeza de Vaca and his companions.[10] The expedition moved up the Rio Grande, learning in the province of the Tiguas, beyond what became known as El Paso del Norte, that both of the priests they sought had been killed.

Excited by stories he had heard of rich mines, Espejo pressed on, exploring across northern New Mexico and into western Arizona. Father Beltrán and about half the party left him there, starting back to Nueva Viscaya, but Espejo continued his search — north along the course of the upper Rio Grande, then east to the long open valley of the Pecos River in northern New Mexico.

The Indians they had met had become increasingly hostile, so Espejo finally and reluctantly set his course southward for a return to home base. He traveled for hundreds of miles down the Pecos Valley until, in the vicinity of Toyah Lake, northwest of today's Pecos, Texas, he met three friendly Jumanos. When they understood that Espejo wanted to reach La Junta de los Rios, they offered to guide him.[11]

Though Espejo in his report cited no landmarks at all on this passage to La Junta, logic and tradition concur in the conclusion that the Jumanos took him up the Toyah Valley to the huge San Solomon Springs, at today's Balmorhea State Park, then across or around the Davis Mountains and down into the Alamito Creek valley, familiar to all indigenous Indians — or possibly down Pinto Canyon to the vicinity of Ruidoso on the Rio Grande.[12]

By one of these routes they reached La Junta, at the mouth of the Conchos, in twelve days' journey, and were back at last in familiar territory. That last hundred miles had, in the majority opinion, established Antonio de Espejo as the first European knowingly to use the Alamito Valley to reach La Junta — granted that Cabeza de Vaca's route is still in lively controversy. The Alamito Valley 250 years later would become a key link in the Chihuahua Road out of South Texas.

Next was Gaspar Castaño de Sosa, another man in trouble with the law. A successful but unscrupulous miner and rancher, he had incurred the displeasure of the Crown through his blatant engagement in the slave trade. In 1590 he was settled in Monclova. Failing to get permission from the authorities for his cherished plan to explore and settle

northern New Mexico, he took the initiative illegally. By August of
1590 he had organized most of the population of Monclova into an expedition to establish a mining camp in territory where he claimed to
have knowledge of rich silver lodes. With about 170 men, women,
and children, a train of two-wheeled *carretas* for provisions, and two
brass cannon on wheels, Castaño took his party across unknown territory — the Bolsón de Mapini — toward the Rio Grande. He crossed
somewhere near Eagle Pass, came up the east bank of the river, and
may have been the first European to see and use the tremendous
springs of San Felipe, where Del Rio was founded 300 years later.

Somehow he took those clumsy *carretas,* the two cannon, and all
his people down into Devil's River Canyon and up across that dreadful
country between it and the Pecos, which would utterly baffle Jack
Hays and his small horseback party in 1848. To accomplish this, Castaño almost certainly must have moved up the valley of the Devil's
River as far as water lasted, to Beaver Lake, and then somehow have
traversed the almost waterless passage through the Johnson's Run
country to the Pecos River. This heroic trek may have given rise to the
tradition that early Spanish explorers discovered what is now known as
Howard's Well, a spring long used by the Indians and essential to any
such crossing. On this route they would have reached the Pecos River
in the vicinity of present-day Fort Lancaster and Sheffield — the first
place the Pecos Valley opens up enough that a party with wheeled vehicles could conceivably have moved up it. And up the Pecos River he
did go, hundreds of miles, into northern New Mexico. Eventually, in
1591, he crossed westward once more to the Rio Grande Valley and
began to establish his mining settlement at a pueblo called Santo
Domingo.

But the long arm of the law reached him there; a company of sol-
diers had followed his trail. Armed with warrants from the viceroy,
Capt. Juan Morlete arrested Gaspar Castaño de Sosa, herding the de-
spairing settlers all the way back to Monclova, and took Castaño on to
Mexico City. Viceroy Don Luis de Velasco ordered him deported to the
Molucca Islands on the other side of the world. [13]

Castaño's ill-fated expedition was significant to this story in two
important regards: he brought the first wheeled vehicles into Texas;
and he was the first European to scout out that portion of the Chihuahua Road from San Felipe Springs up Devil's River and across to the
Pecos Valley — a segment of about 150 miles.

Almost a hundred years passed, then, before Spaniards made another probe into Texas with any real bearing on this story. Juan Domínguez de Mendoza was in a small party sent into northwest Texas in 1654 to scout out the rumor of pearls in the land of the Tejas. They found a few mussel-shell pearls, but no kingdom of the Tejas. Mendoza had to wait a long time for his own day in the sun as leader of an expedition.

He had to wait through the days of the great uprising of Pueblo Indians in New Mexico, which wiped out the Spanish settlements there as survivors fled south to settle on the river below El Paso del Norte. He had to wait until the Jumano Indians around La Junta undertook to reopen relations with the Spanish upriver. These long and tenuous negotiations brought on scene the first Jumano to emerge into history as a distinct personality: Juan Sabeata, chief of a sub-tribe that had people not only at La Junta but also on the buffalo plains far to the east, near the River of Shells, the Concho.[14] Sabeata told his famous story of a cross appearing to him in the sky, with the divine message that he should ask the church for missionaries to convert not only his own people but also those of the Gran Quivira, the "great kingdom of the Tejas [or Texas]" as well. Much later he confessed the story was his own fabrication, designed to stimulate the Spaniards into action. It had the intended effect.

Without waiting for the viceroy's consent, Governor Cruzate allowed Fray Nicholas López, energetic superintendent of all the mission work in that area, to take missionaries with him and move down to La Junta. Soon they had churches and dwellings for the missionaries under way among seven villages in the vicinity of La Junta. But the mission was much larger than that; it had to be extended eastward on the plains, to the Gran Quivira and the always tantalizing land of the pearls. Cruzate chose Capt. Juan Domínguez de Mendoza, at long last, to head the military phase of the expedition. After joining Father López at La Junta, his assignment was

> to examine carefully the Nueces River [not the river now known by that name; one branch of the Concho was then known by that name because of the abundance of pecans in its bottoms], bring back samples of pearls and other products, and learn everything possible about the Indians . . . The venture had a commercial phase, and the instructions provided for the regulation of trade with the Indians.[15]

Fifty-three years of age when his expedition began in early 1684, Mendoza was a perceptive observer, steady and patient even with the visionary Sabeata. He carried through his assignment in a fashion that made it a model for Spanish exploration. And he was the kind of traveler historians love, for he faithfully kept a daily journal, signed each day by himself and witnessed by his officers. Fray López, also, filed a "memorial" concerning his search for the kingdom of the Tejas — which proved hopeless. [16]

Mendoza moved up the Alamito Valley and passed in the vicinity of present-day Alpine, camping at the water known later and successively as Charco de Alsate, Burgess Spring, and Kokernot Spring. [17] From there he ranged too far northward to encounter Comanche Springs or to come directly to the Horsehead Crossing of the Pecos River. [18] Along there, on the east side, his scouts discovered a great "saline" or salt pond: Juan Cardona Lake in Crane County. It had been the age-old source of salt for Indian traders coming up the Alamito from La Junta, and it continued to be the goal for Mexicans from the west and Anglo settlers from the east through most of the nineteenth century. [19]

Mendoza finally found the hard-bottomed ford which came to be known as Horsehead Crossing. The old Indian trail, later the Comanche War Trail, led from there up through Castle Gap and on across the rolling plains of west-central Texas to the branches of the Concho. Mendoza and López spent two months on those rivers, duly collecting samples of pearls and pearly shells, but seeming to marvel more at the abundance of pecans, "wild hens" (turkeys), and the great variety of other game in the river bottoms. They arrived March 14 at a river they called the "Glorious San Clemente," which could only have been the Texas Colorado near where the Concho joins it. They stayed there until the second day of May, drawing great visitations of Indians from twenty or more tribes, but none they could identify as the long-sought Tejas. [20]

While encamped at San Clemente, Mendoza and Fray López built a temporary mission, which served also as a bastion in case of Apache Indian attacks. The Spanish party and the Indian delegations camped with them killed more than 4,000 buffalo from the enormous surrounding herds during their stay.

When he had finally ousted Juan Sabeata for perfidy, realizing that Sabeata's stories of the Gran Quivira sprang from the man's own imagination, Mendoza withdrew, ranging on this return trip much farther to the south. The record of his itinerary through this segment is confusing, but West Texas historians have concluded that in a circuitous route he touched the "Llano River, the Devil's River, and crossed the Pecos River at a point near where Live Oak Creek empties into the Pecos" and from there to Comanche Springs.[21]

From somewhere near Alpine, then, Mendoza followed the Alamito Creek back to La Junta, where he used the occasion, on June 13, 1684, to take possession of the north bank of the Rio Grande as a part of New Mexico, delivering "rods of justice" to four Jumano chiefs. Leaving two priests at La Junta to continue missionary work,[22] Mendoza and Fray López returned to El Paso del Norte. Historian Eugene Bolton says that they went "by way of the Conchos and the Sacramento, because the Sumas were in revolt and the Rio Grande high."[23] Chihuahua City now lies between the Conchos and its tributary the Sacramento; therefore, if Bolton is correct, Capt. Juan Domínguez de Mendoza must be credited with having traveled and recorded an alternate branch of the Chihuahua Road, all the way from the Pecos past Comanche Springs to La Junta and up the Conchos to the site of Ciudad Chihuahua. The Conchos portion had, of course, been frequently traveled, but Mendoza was the first to record the 200-mile route between La Junta and the Pecos.

The complex machinations of the Spanish in extending from Coahuila and the lower reaches of the Rio Grande into southern and central Texas, in the late seventeenth and early eighteenth centuries, brought about the blazing of yet another 200-mile segment of the Chihuahua Road. Evangelization of the Caddo and the elusive Tejas tribes and the determination to counter incursions of the French (i.e., La Salle in 1684 and St. Denis in the first decade after 1700) provided the impetus for this push.

The news in 1685 of La Salle's landing the previous year at Matagorda Bay and his construction of a fort had brought consternation to the Spanish Crown and to all of colonial Mexico. Intensive searches were launched by sea along the Texas coast and by land from across the Rio Grande. The eventual discovery that La Salle and most of his men had perished, and that his fort had fallen in ruins, allowed this massive military effort to be dismantled. The experience had left the Spanish hypersensitive, however, to any suggestion of French intrusion into the Spanish borderland of Mexico.[24]

The French Crown did get its foothold established on the Gulf Coast in 1699, when Pierre Le Moyne de Iberville founded his colony near the mouth of the Mississippi River. Undermanned though the tiny enterprise was, it was not long before the energetic French traders extended themselves across the Sabine to make contact with the Caddo nations.

The Spanish in Coahuila had little real facts about these activities, but they suspected much. Furthermore, missionary zeal still prompted the church to reach and evangelize the illusory Tejas. Father Damian Massanet had been with Gen. Alonso de León when he discovered the ruins of La Salle's fort on the Garcitas Creek in 1689. They were told then of the Tejas or Caddo Indian nations to the north, and Massanet made up his mind to reach them. Next year the viceroy ordered Fray Massanet to the Caddo country with a sizeable body of troops, supplies, and trading goods. They made contact with a branch of the Caddos, the Nabedaches, on the upper Trinity River in mid-May of 1690, establishing there the church of San Francisco de las Tejas. De León and Massanet left a small party of clergy and soldiers and returned to Monclova, certain that a flourishing base for evangelization — and a foil against the French — had been established.

The following year was a different story. Growing resentment against the demands of the Spanish soldiers and the callous clumsiness of the priest left in charge developed into open hostility when Governor Domingo Terán of Coahuila brought Massanet back. By 1693, conditions had so worsened that the soldiers and Massanet concurred in abandoning San Francisco de las Tejas and the entire missionary project.

During that same period, the missions at La Junta, far up the Rio Grande, had also been abandoned when the harried Jumanos finally gave up resistance against the Apaches and joined forces with their old enemy. The Jumanos were thus absorbed, and they disappeared from history, while all effective Spanish mission work into Texas was suspended.

One stubborn, dedicated priest never gave up: Fray Francisco Hidalgo. As one of the staff missionaries at the Caddo outpost, he had opposed closing the mission, and from the moment he got back across the Rio Grande into Mexico, he worked for restoration of the evangelistic program. Nevertheless, twelve years were to pass before the Spanish reached the Caddo stations again.

Fray Hidalgo did get as far as the Rio Grande near present-day Piedras Negras in 1700, after several stagings along the way, and with the escort of a seasoned frontier soldier, Capt. Diego Ramón. A cluster settlement grew at that

strategic point on the Rio Grande: Presidio San Juan Bautista, its small supporting settlement, two missions, and Indian settlements at each mission. It proved such a useful listening post that the viceroy accepted the *faits accomplis*. Father Hidalgo and his confreres [with Captain Ramón commanding the new presidio] took care to supply the viceroy with rumors of French activities in the Tejas country, and for another decade prayed and planned for return to their forsaken mission.

In that same year, the French governor Bienville had

led a reconnaissance group up the Red River as far as the Natchitoches settlements. His party included the exceptionally able young officer Louis Juchereau de St. Denis, whose destiny was to be linked with the Caddos for more than forty years. . . . His trade relationship with the Natchitoches was continuous from 1701, and he won their complete confidence.[25]

The Spanish were lethargic in responding to the new French competition. True, from 1707 through 1709, Fray Hidalgo had been able to send out small survey parties as far as the San Marcos River, under leadership of a younger but equally zealous missionary, Fray San Antonio de San Buenaventura y Olivares. In 1709 Fray Olivares, escorted by Capt. Pedro de Aguirre, scouted out the headwaters of the San Antonio River and found the San Pedro Springs, which Governor Terán had admired in passing twenty years before. Olivares became convinced that this fertile valley, watered by many springs at the foot of the limestone hills, would be the ideal spot for the new mission to which he aspired. But he still had to wait and continue his prayers.

When St. Denis appeared at the gates of San Juan Bautista on July 19, 1714, after crossing all of Texas from Louisiana and the Caddo nations on the border, the shocked Spanish authorities were sure that he was spying out the land as a precursor to conquest. To assuage them, St. Denis politely proffered a very official letter from French officialdom praying that he be allowed to seek out the mission of Fray Francisco Hidalgo, in order to buy horses and cattle for the Louisiana colony. The document asserted that Hidalgo had written the French inviting such a visit.[26] The Frenchman blandly professed that since he had learned that Hidalgo had come back to the Mexican border — twenty years before — he was simply following up on his orders. The Spanish suspicions were not at once allayed; St. Denis was passed under guard all the way to Mexico City for interrogation. But the Frenchman so charmed them, and at the same time so alarmed them with the implications of French expansionism, that the Spanish at the end of two years organized a huge party to escort their guest, or hostage, back to his base. The escort was to be launched from San Juan Bautista, and St. Denis was to be used as emissary in establishing Spanish bases against the French frontiers in eastern Texas. It was at last the fruition of Fray Hidalgo's dream.

St. Denis had improved his opportunities in Mexico during these two years, to the extent that he had wooed and won the granddaughter of Captain Ramón at San Juan Bautista. Now his wife's father and uncle, commanding the expedition, were escorting him back to Louisiana.

And this grand new entry to the land of the Caddoes provided the realization of Fray Olivares's plans as well, for he was authorized to move a lagging Mexican mission and reestablish it at the San Pedro Springs of the San Antonio River. The Spanish authorities had realized that an important sub-station would be needed along the Camino Real in order to maintain communications with the distant outposts. On May 1, 1718, Mission San Antonio de Valero had its formal beginning at San Pedro Springs under Fray Olivares, while Coahuilan Governor Martín de Alarcón came along to do the honors in establishing the presidio of San Antonio de Bexar nearby only four days later.[27]

Another result of Spanish concern over French expansionism was the establishment in 1721–22 of Presidio La Bahía del Espíritu Santo de Zuniga on Garcitas Creek, the exact spot where La Salle had built his fort.[28]

The significance to this story of the fort of La Bahía and its adjoining missions is that in locating and serving its original site, by sea from Matagorda Bay and by land from San Antonio de Valero, the Spanish blazed a new trail. The fort and missions were moved twice, first in 1726 to the Guadalupe River some seven miles above today's Victoria, and finally in 1749 to their permanent location on the San Antonio River, where the village of Goliad grew up beside them.[29] Settlers from the Canary Islands reached San Antonio in 1731, establishing the villa of San Fernando de Bexar, the first organized civil government in Texas.

Several of these Canary Islanders pushed on down the road toward La Bahía, founding *ranchos* along the San Antonio River all the way to its junction with the Cibolo Creek.[30] Soldiers from the presidio in San Antonio moved constantly between their base and Presidio La Bahía, protecting the new chain of *ranchos* along the way. Thereby, on foot and horseback, then with pack animals and finally with trains of *carre-*

tas, the soldiers and priests and ambitious settlers of Imperial Spain
had beaten out the road from the Texas coast to the interior of Mexico,
two centuries after Cabeza de Vaca first probed his way persistently toward the same objective. The 130-mile stretch from Matagorda Bay to
San Antonio became the southernmost segment of the Chihuahua
Road, and that portion of the Camino Real from San Antonio west to
the Leona River eventually added another eighty miles. From the
Leona the Camino Real veered off southwesterly from the Chihuahua
Road toward the Rio Grande at San Juan Bautista. This left only the
segment from the Leona to San Felipe Springs not known to have been
scouted out by the Spanish — about seventy miles.

Henry E. Meadows, a retired petrochemical engineer at Midland,
has for years researched the history of the Trans-Pecos country. In the
early 1960s, Meadows developed a paper called "The Chihuahua
Trail," in which he cites various segments of the road discovered and
opened by the Spanish. In summary he says:

> Credit for finding, traveling and recording the way for the Chihu-
> ahua Trail belongs entirely to the early Spanish explorers with but a
> few additions or modifications contributed by the later Texians.[31]

That independent observer is correct in recognizing the achievements of the Spanish explorers. A tragic aspect of Anglo-American
takeover in the early nineteenth century is that they made an almost
total break with the past, ignoring for near half a century the wealth of
records the Spanish had left, much of it right under their noses in the
Bexar Archives in San Antonio. As a consequence, the Texians had to
start all over, from the Nueces and Llano rivers westward, in feeling
their way at great loss in time and lives toward El Paso del Norte, La
Junta, and the rich resources of Chihuahua.

[2]

First Road:
Santa Fe to Chihuahua

On a corner of the Plaza Mayor in Santa Fe, across the little park
from the Governor's Palace, stands a stark granite slab. Its inscription
seems as anachronistic to historical perspective as does that cold gray
granite to all the muted tones of adobe, sand, and weathered timber in
that warm plaza:

> *This stone marks*
> *The End of the Santa Fe Trail*
> *1822–1879*
> *Erected by the Daughters of*
> *the American Revolution and*
> *the Territory of New Mexico*
> *1910*[1]

That text is enclosed within graven outlines of the state — or territory
— of New Mexico, with the adjacent states of Texas, Colorado, Oklahoma, and Kansas duly labeled, and only a void to the south as if Mexico never existed. One branch of the trail is shown starting in Kansas,
another in Colorado; they join inside the New Mexico line and loop
westward to this town of the Holy Faith — *Santa Fe* — of St. Francis.
And there the depicted trail does indeed stop short.

16

No hint is given that Santa Fe, a town of some three to four thousand souls during the half century bracketed on the monument, was, as already observed, only an *entrepôt*. It served as a point of exchange where some of the American goods freighted down from the States met the wealth of Mexico's mines — silver, gold, and copper — as it found its outlet up from the south.[2]

That section of the commercial artery which ran down from the Missouri River landings in Kansas was properly called the Santa Fe Trail, because many Yankee traders did stop there. But from Santa Fe down the long valley of the Rio Grande to El Paso del Norte, and across the deserts to fabled Ciudad Chihuahua, ran its earlier and essential link: the first of our roads to Chihuahua.

A few astute historians with broader perspective than that of the Daughters of the American Revolution did recognize the real significance of the roads that met at Santa Fe. Max L. Moorhead wrote in the preface to his *New Mexico's Royal Road,*

> This book is the outgrowth of a suggestion made many years ago by Professor Herbert E. Bolton at the University of California. The famous "Santa Fe trade" of the Nineteenth Century was, he postulated, not so much the interchange of goods between Missouri and New Mexico as it was a very extensive commerce which was merely channeled through the ports-of-entry of those two frontier states but which involved a large part of both the American and Mexican nations . . .[3]

No means of financing the Santa Fe trade would have existed had not Chihuahua specie and bullion offered the medium of exchange. Actually, as the scribe of the Santa Fe traders, Josiah Gregg, was careful to set out in his data tables, during the years 1833 through 1843, almost exactly half of the total goods brought down the Santa Fe Trail from Missouri and Kansas went on through Santa Fe to Chihuahua.[4] Something of the same proportion continued during the life of the wagon freight era. Yet one is astonished to find that many of the popular books on the well-worked theme of the old Santa Fe Trail either completely ignore the existence of Chihuahua or mention it only in passing.[5]

Santa Fe is older, to be sure, by almost half a century than Ciudad Chihuahua. Settlement of Santa Fe grew out of reaction to the brutal expedition of Don Juan de Oñate in 1598 as he explored, "pacified," and exploited the upper reaches of the Rio Grande from his base at Parral, in the southern part of what is now the state of Chihuahua. In his probe northward from there he paused, perhaps to establish a staging point in the valley of Chihuahua, where the city now stands. At El Paso del Norte, already recognized as the northern border point of Nueva Viscaya, he took possession of all the lands beyond in the name of King Phillip II.[6] Oñate continued far up the Rio Grande, stopping at last at a place called San Juan de los Caballeros. That was not precisely Santa Fe, but historian H. H. Bancroft says that name emerged, identifying the final settlement of the Villa San Francisco de Santa Fe, between 1609 and 1617. The new governor, Pedro de Peralta, formally established it at the order of the Crown, in 1610, to embody the scattered colonists' "hopes for stable, dignified lives at last, after a dozen years of uncertainty and hardship in expropriated pueblos." [7] The settlement prospered, it was destroyed in the terrible Indian uprising of 1680, and it was reoccupied, permanently, by Diego de Vargas, December 30, 1693. From then on, Santa Fe was the key city of New Mexico.[8]

The silver lode at Aquiles Serdán, long known as Santa Eulalia, fueled the growth of Ciudad Chihuahua and provided the wealth that made the Santa Fe-Chihuahua trade possible. The city itself soared to a population of 70,000 in the heyday of the mines, but had dwindled to about 10,000 in the middle part of the nineteenth century.[9]

During all this period, Santa Fe stood "like a sentinel on the very rim of European civilization." [10] Spain's northern colonies were badgered on every side by France, by Russia, by the United States, and by the pervasive Indian.

> Santa Fe now became the hub of long exploratory spikes sent out to connect the new outposts with the old. [It was] more than ever a strategic outpost, but now chiefly against the Indians . . . .[11]

What of the new Americans, the *norteamericanos?* Spain had discreetly given aid to the rebellious British colonies in their revolution. That war was scarcely over when the Yankees resumed their relentless push westward. Spain watched with fearful fascination as the Anglo-Americans moved down the Ohio Valley toward St. Louis on the Mississippi. This trading post had been established in 1762 by the Choteau brothers, Auguste and Pierre, under sponsorship of New Orleans merchants with license from the governor of Louisiana.

That same year France ceded these western lands to Spain, but Spain did not assert her authority there until 1770, when a Spanish lieutenant governor was established at St. Louis for Upper Louisiana. St. Louis thereby became an amalgam of French traders and Spanish officials and soldiers. So strategic was its location as the apparent Gateway to the West that it was clear to the Spanish king's men within their narrowing compass of the Southwest that whoever controlled St. Louis would command the West. Yet there never had been direct communication, cross-country, between Santa Fe, or any part of New Mexico, with that vital trading post far up the Mississippi.[12] Furthermore, a new element had entered into Spain's long-range strategy for maintaining peace with the Indians in the *provincias internas*. King Carlos III, "the last of the able Bourbon monarchs," was nearing the end of his three-decade reign, but he still sought the key to stabilization on those distant frontiers of empire.[13] A brilliant and informed soldier, Bernardo de Gálvez, had just succeeded his father as viceroy of Mexico. He found that, for once, Spain had a team of competent administrators governing the frontier provinces.

Gen. Jacobo Ugarte was governor-general of all the *provincias internas;* Juan Bautista de Anza was governor of New Mexico at Santa Fe; and for Texas, Domingo Cabello occupied the new but unpretentious Governor's Palace in San Antonio. Under the new concept passed down to these administrators, the key to peace lay with the Comanche nations. Governor de Anza had started tentative peace feelers with the Comanches some years earlier, but there had been no organized response. Cabello had peaceable relations in northern Texas with the Taovayas, one of the Caddo tribes, and he thought they might serve as emissaries to the Comanche nations.[14] With Ugarte's backing, the design fell into place for trading routes across the provinces so that these new relations could be developed. The first demand was for a route from Texas to Santa Fe.

Cabello in San Antonio had the man for the job: Pedro Vial, born in Lyons, France, about the middle of the century, but known as an itinerant gunsmith and trader among the Caddo nations on the French-Texas frontier as early as 1779. Cabello had used Vial on increasingly important missions until he was sure the obscure wanderer had the qualities he wanted as trailblazer and negotiator. Then he recommended Vial to the governor-general. Ugarte responded promptly in enthusiastic approval.

October of 1786 had come before Vial got under way, with expanded orders to make a long detour northeastward for visits with the Taovayas and Tawakoni and then to aim for Santa Fe. He and his aide,

Cristobal de los Santos, traveled with horses and small supplies of tobacco and goods for gifts.

The journey started badly. On the second day out, Vial lost most
of his provisions in crossing the Guadalupe River, and a few days later
he fell seriously ill. Santos devotedly nursed the sometimes delirious
leader as they wandered northeastward for weeks searching for a Tawakoni village. When they finally did establish contact, Vial had to conduct delicate negotiations to mend old relationships before he could
even ask treatment for his illness. The Tawakoni finally took care of
him, skillfully, and probably saved his life.

It was December before Vial could resume his journey, this time
to the Red River bases of the Wichitas and Taovayas. Here again he
had to harangue vigorously in council in order to reestablish amicable
terms and to gain Taovaya support in making peace with the Plains
comanchería. By mid-January, Vial and Santos were with the Comanches, who were impressed that he had come to open a road from San
Antonio to Santa Fe so that Comanches could travel in peace from one
part of the country to another.

They helped him along the way, but the two travelers eventually had to hole up in a winter camp until March. As they pressed
westward, then, other Comanche tribes hosted them and helped
them, until at last, on May 26, 1787, the trailblazers rode trium-
phantly into Santa Fe. The journey had taken seven months, but in
the light of the tribulations of later explorers, it was a stupendous
achievement. Not only had Vial forged strong links in a new accord
with *comanchería,* but, despite his long detour to the northeast, he
had also opened for the first time in history a feasible link between
Texas and New Mexico.[15]

Under a more generous dispensation from de Anza than Cabello had been able to give him, Pedro Vial settled down in Santa
Fe. The grand alliance conceived by the two governors, which
Pedro Vial had helped put together, did work for a while.[16] According to Elizabeth John,

> Both Spaniards and Comanches enjoyed greater safety in their homes
> and profited by the trade that flourished in both Texas and New
> Mexico. These benefits were shared by all Spain's Indian allies: Nor-
> teños and mission Indians in Texas, and Pueblos, Utes, Jicarillos,
> and Navajos in New Mexico.[17]

It was but a temporary respite. After the death of Charles III and his succession by an inept son, and the transfer and retirement of de Anza and Cabello, with lesser men following them, all within a year or two, the good relations those men had put together fell bit by bit into disarray. Within a quarter century the Plains Comanches were once more joined in deadly warfare against the entire Mexican frontier.

Vial still had time, however, for more contributions to the knowledge of the land. José Mares and two other Spaniards, escorted first by a party of Comanche chiefs and their women, and finally by the sons of a Comanche chief, made a winter passage from San Antonio, arriving in Santa Fe on April 27, 1788. They had traveled a shorter route, shown them by the Comanches.

Two months later Vial set out on his longest journey, outfitted by the new governor, Fernando de la Concha, with four companions including an official journal-keeper. They traveled with ten horses, two mules, and adequate supplies for the trip. It was to be a stupendous probe: back across the Llano Estacado to again visit the Taovayas on the Red River; then along the river's course to Natchitoches, to link up with the Spanish occupying officials in Louisiana; south and west along the Camino Real through Nacogdoches to San Antonio de Bejar; and once more northwest across the lower plains of Texas, between the Colorado and the Brazos, homing again upon Santa Fe. That leisurely and much-interrupted circuit took the rest of 1788 and almost all of 1789.[18]

For three years Don Pedro Vial, as he was being called by then, befitting his advancing years, pursued his own affairs on the Southwestern frontier. The new Spanish viceroy, Juan Vicente Guemes, Count of Revillagigedo, then called him back to work in 1792 for the most significant mission of his career: to blaze out a trail from Santa Fe northeastward to St. Louis. This was before any Anglo-American, with the exception of James Mackey, had ventured into the lands west of the Mississippi.

Pedro Vial with three companions struck out eastward across the seemingly illimitable Llano Estacado, then from what is now the top of the Texas Panhandle and across the Oklahoma Panhandle, northward across Kansas almost to Iowa, and finally turning eastward across Missouri to the trading post at St. Louis.

The passage was marred by a horrifying encounter with a party of Kansas Indians, who attacked, stripped, and almost beat the travelers to death. The odyssey took Vial from May to October of 1792. Vial presented his credentials to Zenon Trudeau, commandant at St. Louis, on October 6. Trudeau did not record what the sturdy polyglot traders at St. Louis thought of this elderly apparition out of the Southwest. He wintered there with them and returned by a more northern route, to treat with the Pawnee nations in the spring of 1793, arriving in Santa Fe on November 15.[19] The Mississippi River basin was now connected with the great Southwest, though the man who had linked them was virtually forgotten for a century and a half.

Pedro Vial's demonstration that a road could be opened from Santa Fe was further validated fifteen years later. By this time Spain had lost the Louisiana Territory, including St. Louis, to France, and Napoleon had forthwith sold it to Thomas Jefferson. With the United States already claiming that the territory extended all the way to the Rio Grande, Spain was feeling the pressure from both the north and east. Certainly, as Noel Loomis observed, "in 1808 it was still as desirable as it had been in 1789 to have a road between Santa Fe and San Antonio."[20]

The man who sparked Mexico's later, alarmed attempts to open up communications between New Mexico and Texas was the best known of all the early visitors, Lt. Zebulon Montgomery Pike. Described by Robert Luther Duffus as a "courageous, patriotic, almost boyishly ingenuous figure," Pike was only twenty-seven when he started his own great adventure in the West. His exploration was part of the general push by Thomas Jefferson's administration to examine what had been bought from Buonoparte for $15 million, and to justify the expense.

Much has been made of the fact that Zebulon Pike was actually put on the march by Gen. James Wilkinson, that sinister figure who was a known co-conspirator with Aaron Burr on vast designs for the Far West. Regardless, however, of the extent to which Pike may or may not have been a tool of Wilkinson, his far-ranging exploration can stand on its own merits as one of the great monuments of western development. Certainly it stirred up international feelings to such an extent as to assure that trade along the roads from St. Louis to Chihuahua and from San Antonio to Chihuahua would soon become a reality.

Pike started from St. Louis in July of 1806, about two months before Lewis and Clark returned from their epochal trek to the shores of the Pacific. His orders were to explore the Arkansas River to its source and return to the Mississippi by way of the Red River. Many believe that his secret orders bade him find opportunity to divert into New Mexico to scout out Santa Fe as well.[21]

With two lieutenants, a surgeon, and sixteen privates, Pike followed the Arkansas as ordered into the deepest fastnesses of the Rockies, sighting the peak which bears his name. He sent half his party home then, and with the remainder continued westward until cold weather caught them, bogging them down in heavy snows. They spent most of the winter there, starving and freezing. Leaving in bivouac those of the party too weak to travel, Pike struck toward the southeast, ostensibly seeking the Red River, but came actually to the headwaters of the Rio Grande. Holed up in a makeshift fort on the banks of that river, he was found in February by Spanish outriders, who escorted him to Santa Fe. The Spanish troopers generously sent a detail back into the mountains to rescue those left behind.

Governor Joaquín del Real Alencaster received Lieutenant Pike with punctilious courtesy in the provincial capital. He heard with straightface Pike's story that he thought he was on the Red River (U.S. territory) when he found he was on the Rio Bravo (Spanish land). The governor confiscated all of Pike's papers after a bit of sleight-of-hand by the lieutenant in trying to conceal them, then gave his Anglo visitor a beautiful shirt to replace the rag he was wearing and held a dinner in his honor.

These were troubled times between Spain and the United States as each parried the other's claims as to the rightful boundaries of the Louisiana Purchase. Neither Alencaster nor Pike, at dinner in the splendid isolation of Santa Fe, could be sure that his country was not already at war.[22]

Alencaster next day started Pike and his men down the long road to Chihuahua, nominally under guard, though the trek became all but a royal progress, as the Yankee adventurers were feted in one village after another. The romantic young officer was witness to the most bucolic aspects of the Chihuahua Trail in its halcyon days, before its ever having been assailed by the iron-tired wagons and the even rougher ways of the Yankee trader.

In the more serious atmosphere of Ciudad Chihuahua, Pike encountered a governor-general whose opening sally was severe:

> "You have caused yourself and us a great deal of trouble."
> Pike fired back with spirit, "Involuntary on our part, sir, and by your own choice on yours!"[23]

Don Nemesio Salcedo gradually thawed, though he declined, politely but with authority, to return the explorer's papers. These remained undisturbed for three generations, until a twentieth-century historian found the faded packet labeled "El Viajero Piake." [24]

On April 28, 1807, Salcedo started the American toward San Antonio and to the United States border, beyond in Louisiana. Pike's journal documents that Salcedo sent him by way of Presidio Rio Grande, San Juan Bautista. He and his escort, upon leaving Chihuahua, traveled southeast, skirting to the south of the dread Bolsón de Mapini, passing through Jimenez and Monclova, and reaching the Presidio Rio Grande late in May of 1807. They crossed the Rio Grande some thirty miles below present-day Eagle Pass and followed the Camino Real to San Antonio de Bejar, where they were entertained for a week by Governor Cordero. Then Pike left San Antonio on June 14, continuing on the Camino Real across Texas to Nacogdoches and finally to Natchitoches, where he saw the Stars and Stripes flying on July 1 — after fifteen days less than a year on the trail through the great Southwest. [25] The governors of New Mexico, Chihuahua, and Texas had been studiously correct and hospitable to Pike as they passed him through their territories. But as soon as he was out of the way, letters sped up the line to their superiors.

The colonial government was shocked that one young officer and a squad of men could have broached the rigid isolation of Mexico. One of the reactions was to order a renewed and more massive reconnaissance of the territory between Santa Fe and New Mexico. Commandant-General Nemesio Salcedo y Salceda directed Governor Cordero of Texas to set the expedition in motion. Cordero selected for the task Capt. Francisco Amangual, commandant at La Bahía, in South Texas.

A native of Majorca, Amangual had been a soldier of Spain on the vast Texas frontier for thirty years: a lieutenant in San Antonio in 1779, still a captain in 1808 at age sixty-nine. [26] This tough old *hombre del campo* was eminently suited, he proved, for the job assigned him. He took 200 soldiers with him, a formidable party for those austere days in Spanish America, and he lost not a man in the wilderness. On his way out to Santa Fe he followed much the same route that Pedro Vial had taken on his last trip, ranging between the headwaters of the Colorado and the Brazos.

On his return to San Antonio, however, he blazed out a road that was an eerie forerunner to those that the Anglo-Saxons struggled so desperately to establish forty years later. Amangual traveled down the Chihuahua Trail to El Paso del Norte; then, staying on the Texas side of the Rio Grande for near thirty miles, he arrived at the presidio then known as San Elzeario (Elizario).[27] The Indians, and the soldiers stationed there, knew of the ancient trail eastward past the valued salt lakes[28] and on over the foothill hump of the Guadalupe Mountains to the Pecos River. That is the way Amangual went. When Maj. Robert S. Neighbors in 1849 sought a practicable way east, an old retired Spanish soldier at San Elizario guided him by that route, calling it the "Military Road." [29] It became the "Immigrant Road" for the Forty-Niners in 1849–50, and the "Butterfield Stage Road" a few years later.

Amangual directed his 200 soldiers and 800 mules and horses to the Pecos and turned down it. He may have turned eastward at Horsehead Crossing, long used by the Plains Indians, for that was the only feasible ford along a great reach of the river. Heading east, then, through Castle Gap, he sought the headwaters of the San Saba, where he must have known that the San Saba Mission had been established in 1757 but was long since destroyed and abandoned. He did find the San Saba River, but he moved south before reaching its confluence with the Colorado and came on across the Llano through the hill country, fording the Pedernales, the Blanco, and the Guadalupe, camping finally on familiar ground at the Cibolo Creek. On December 23, 1808, he entered San Antonio.

Encumbered with 200 men, his huge train of animals, and most significant of all, wheeled vehicles, he had come down from El Paso in thirty-seven days of travel, 684 miles by his route (18.8 miles a day), and he lost no man and only twenty-seven animals out of his 800. That would have been an enviable record for any of the Anglo-American expeditions of the 1850s.

Loomis summed up this spate of exploration:

> . . . within eighteen years, there were four westward crossings of the Llano Estacado — all relatively unknown by historians: two by Pedro Vial, one by Jose Mares, and one — the tough one — by Francisco Amangual . . . The roads had been opened to Santa Fe — but it would not be the Spaniards who profited from them. Those who would use them would be the restless Anglo-Americans. They were already coming overland, and within a very few years they would start pouring down the Santa Fe Trail that Vial had blazed in 1792.[30]

Zebulon Pike had received no immediate acclaim from officialdom for his exploit into New Mexico; he was in fact something of an embarrassment to Washington. However, in 1810 he published in Philadelphia his journal, and it has gone through many editions since then.[31] Jack Rittenhouse calls the journal "the first report in English that described a possible route to Santa Fe, and there are indications that it was soon read by some Missourians."

Indeed it must have been, for the tide of adventurers lusting for trade soon began to run, southwest from St. Louis and then from the river landings on the Missouri much farther west at Independence and Westport, where the twin Kansas Cities were to be built.

Since the main thrust of this book is to celebrate the lesser-known Chihuahua Road across Texas, and since at least twenty-five competent books have been written on the Santa Fe Trail portion of that far western road, no attempt to detail the traffic which bloomed there between 1824 and 1868 will be made here. Several of those books have already been mentioned, while Jack Rittenhouse's bibliography masterfully summarizes the range of other notable works.[32]

One look must be permitted at the more leisurely paced life that existed along the road from Ciudad Chihuahua to Santa Fe before the *yanquis* came. The economy of northern Mexico moved to the slow pulse of seasonal markets, with an annual fair at San Bartolomé in the southern part of the state of Chihuahua in December, and the capital's own fair in January.

Ciudad Chihuahua was not, certainly, the end of the line in either direction; it did not exist independent of the rest of the country. Its silver was coveted by the national capital, Mexico City, the *distrito federal*, as well as by the new nation to the north, and it could be acquired only by trade.

Caravans made up of as many as 200 mules, each laden with as much as 300 pounds of goods, plodded up from the interior. Heavier goods moved in *carretas*, the primitive, solid-wheeled carts drawn by oxen. Luxuries which had left Europe perhaps a year before were thereby carried up to Nueva Viscaya: jewels, fine fabrics, sophisticated firearms, the exotic foodstuffs and liqueurs that meant civilized existence to the effete colonial hierarchy, along with furniture, crafted silverware, and pottery from the south.

Florence and Robert Lister, in their *Chihuahua, Storehouse of Storms*, captured the atmosphere of the marketplace and annual fair at the desert capital as it was in the early years of the nineteenth century.[33]

The market was fueled from the north as well as from the south, of course, and Chihuahua had to send out its silver largesse to tempt the trade goods down:

Once a year the caravans traveled up to Santa Fe on the Camino Real, two ruts worn deep over malpais and adobe, around sand dunes, through arroyos, up mesas, connecting the sleeping civilization of New Mexico to the vigor of the capital [Mexico City], a distance of 1800 miles and as far removed in advancement . . .

On the return trip to Chihuahua, wagons and mules carried the booty of New Mexico in the form of hides and beaver pelts, Chimayo and Navajo blankets and rugs, piñon nuts, and turquoise. Sheep were driven south for sale in Chihuahua. At El Paso del Norte, more *arrieros* joined the party with strings of mules packed with fresh and dried fruits grown along the warm bottomlands of the Rio Grande. Grape products, particularly raisins, *aguardiente,* and wine, were highly prized in the southern markets. They timed their arrival in Chihuahua to coincide with the annual fair.[34]

The caravans hardly ever moved as placidly as this picture would suggest, however. They were constantly in fear of the raiding Apache bands, and their apprehensions were realized more often than not. By the 1820s, the several strains of the Apache nations in these northern reaches of Chihuahua, and the Plains Comanches crossing the Rio Bravo into southern Chihuahua and Coahuila, held Mexican commerce and the landed gentry in the grip of terror, systematically despoiling them of cattle, horses, harvest, and slaves.

A Yankee merchant of unimpeachable integrity who was engaged in the trade at Chihuahua for many years was Edward James Glasgow. Born at Belleville, Illinois, in 1820, he grew up at St. Louis among the adventurers and traders. At only twenty years of age, with his father's backing, the boy sailed from New York to open a business on the west coast of Mexico. He stayed for two and a half years at Mazatlán, disposing profitably of the cargo of three successive vessels sent out from New York. He filled these ships for their return voyage with precious dye-woods and mother-of-pearl gleaned from the Gulf of California.

After a brief visit to New York on the last of his ships, he returned to Vera Cruz and then proceeded on horseback through the interior of Mexico to Chihuahua, where he formed a partnership with Dr. Henry Connelley, one of northern Mexico's most notable Anglo merchants. He continued then in the overland trade with Independence for five years, until interrupted by the Mexican War.[35]

When Josiah Gregg first reached Chihuahua in October 1839, three years before Glasgow, he found a "city" much reduced from its earlier glories under the Spanish rule, which had ended in 1824. Nevertheless, it was larger by far than any town to the north and west

of the Mississippi. In Texas, San Antonio had no more than 3,000 population at the time; no other town in that Republic had more than
1,500 persons. St. Louis, Missouri, may have been able to count as
many as 25,000; Santa Fe, 4,000; Presidio del Norte perhaps 2,500.
There was no other settlement as large as those in all the West. Gregg
wrote:

> When compared with Santa Fe and all the towns of the North, Chi-
> huahua might indeed be pronounced a magnificent place. The
> ground plan is much more regular than that of Santa Fe, while a
> much greater degree of elegance and classic taste has been exhibited
> in the style and architecture of many buildings, for though the bod-
> ies be of adobe, all the best houses are cornered with hewn stone, and
> the doors and windows are framed with the same . . .

Gregg was impressed, as have been all visitors, by the splendid
cathedral, although he found it much delapidated within. He found
also "a rough mint in Chihuahua . . . yet most of its silver and gold
have been coined in the cities further south." He called the people
"Chihuahueños," an appellation which is often used to this day.[36]

Though he made only four complete round trips from Independence, including the one to Chihuahua and beyond, during his nine
years in the business, Gregg became so familiar with the personalities
of both the American traders and the people they dealt with in New
Mexico and Chihuahua that his memoir gives an unequaled insight to
the scene during the 1830s.

One of the men who went down the Chihuahua Trail in the very
early years was James Kirker. Santa Fe and northern Mexico would
have done better without him, but unfortunately the pages of southwestern history from 1822 through 1847 are stained by the misdeeds
of Jim Kirker, the prototype mercenary scalp hunter.

Though it would be simpler to ignore entirely the man's tawdry
career, his crimes had such a profound and lasting impact upon Anglo-
American relations with the Indian tribes, particularly the Apache and
Comanche tribes, and extending even down into the Big Bend of the
Rio Grande River, that he must be mentioned in the context of the
Chihuahua Trail's earliest years.

Kirker's origins, the setting in which he operated on the New
Mexico frontier, and his exploits there are set out in detail and are well
documented by William Cochran McGaw in his *Savage Scene: the Life
and Times of James Kirker, Frontier King*. The problem with McGaw's
book is that, while recording in gory detail the havoc wrought indis-

criminately by Kirker, for pay, against Indian men, women and children, the author nowhere acknowledges clearly that the seeds of hate sown by Kirker reaped a harvest of violence against the white man throughout the Southwest far greater than the value, if any, of short-term deterrents that might be claimed for him. The reliable Josiah Gregg documents that the bounty traffic backfired.[37]

In the long range it was a major factor that slowed the opening of roads, helped pin down the United States Army for forty years, and wrought a dreadful toll in lives on both sides of the conflict.

During the Mexican War of 1846–48, Alexander Doniphan made his dazzling expeditionary thrust across the heartland of Chihuahua. Because Texas was at the center of the controversy which brought on the war, later chapters of this book devoted to that commonwealth give some attention to how the conflict between the United States and Mexico was precipitated. Doniphan's expedition, given short shrift by twentieth-century historians, demands at least some attention here.

The grand strategy of the war-planners in Washington in 1846 called for a pincers movement upon northern Mexico, with Gen. John Wool bringing the Army of the Centre across Texas, into Coahuila, and then north to Chihuahua, while Col. Stephen W. Kearney (soon to be brigadier general) would move his Army of the West down the Santa Fe Trail past Bent's Fort into New Mexico. After taking Santa Fe, Kearney would then leave an occupation force under Sterling Price in New Mexico and send Doniphan on south to conquer as he went and meet General Wool in Chihuahua. Kearney, meanwhile, would move west across the Arizona deserts to execute the land half of another pincers movement upon California, meeting a U.S. Navy landing force in the south of that Mexican province. Remarkably enough, all of this took place, with the exception of John Wool's move across Coahuila to Chihuahua. He was held in central Mexico to help Gen. Zachary Taylor deal with Antonio López de Santa Anna at Buena Vista.

As it turned out, Alexander Doniphan did not need General Wool's help. With his 924 effective militiamen from Missouri, plus some 350 wagon drovers and their wagons, which he picked up on the way south from Santa Fe, he took El Paso del Norte and moved south toward Ciudad Chihuahua. The Mexican army sought to interdict Doniphan's column eighteen miles north of the capital, near a crossing of the smallish Sacramento River. The Mexicans had more than 4,000 men, including 1,200 cavalry, 2,000 infantrymen, artillery, and perhaps a thousand poorly armed militia. All were in ambush behind stone fortifications, in trenches, or on bluffs squarely above the road Doniphan would have to take to reach the Sacramento crossing.

History has never paid enough attention to the stunning victory which Alexander Doniphan and his 1,200 men, after marching all the way from Missouri, achieved that afternoon of February 28, 1847, against those overwhelming odds. By a brilliant maneuver, circling out over impossible terrain, he was able to throw his entire force — pell-mell cavalrymen and yelling Missouri foot soldiers, backed by 250 ponderous white-bonneted freight wagons and a unit of field cannon — in direct frontal assault upon the astounded Mexicans. With better artillery than the enemy could bring into action, and through the ferocious hand-to-hand attack of the infantry by frontier lads far from home, who knew their lives depended upon success, Doniphan broke the Mexican ranks. In less than two hours the Mexicans were in utter rout, fleeing afoot for Chihuahua City and beyond.

Doniphan lost only one man on the field, another died later, and from seven to eleven were wounded. At least 300 of the Mexican force lay dead on the field and an equal number were wounded. Two days later, Doniphan with his jubilant troops entered and occupied the capital city without resistance.

Later in the spring they marched another 450 miles across central Mexico to report to Generals Wool and Taylor. They had to walk the rest of the way, travel-worn and ragged, to Matamoros to take ship to New Orleans and eventually to Missouri.

Why has their astounding victory never been given the full recognition it deserves? One is forced to conclude reluctantly that the professional soldiers up the command line were embarrassed to see Alexander Doniphan, a civilian lawyer and militiaman, with not one regular army man in his command, win his victory against such overwhelming odds, and by such a margin of success, bringing all of northern Mexico under United States control.[38]

The entire route of Kearney's forces to Santa Fe, and Doniphan's on to Ciudad Chihuahua, was on the Chihuahua Trail. None of their successes could have been achieved had not that road been opened and made travel-worthy by persistent traders moving their wares from source to market.

What of the traders, wagoneers, and scouts left stranded when Alexander Doniphan vacated the capital and marched south? About thirty or forty of them left the city within a week after the army's departure, but they went north up the Camino Real toward El Paso del Norte and Santa Fe. In this group were Josiah Webb, Solomon Houck, Cornelius Davy, and Ebenezer W. Pomeroy.

Then there was the handful of adventurers who some months later drifted down the Conchos Valley, or down the Rio Grande, to Presidio del Norte at La Junta. How many of them were actually involved in Doniphan's expedition is not of record, but several were known to have been engaged variously in New Mexico and the state of Chihuahua up until the time of the war.

Ben Leaton was with John James Johnson in the perfidious ambush of the Apache Chief Juan José in 1837.[39] Sometime in the 1840s, Leaton had married a Chihuahueña named Juana Pedraza. This tempestuous girl, at the age of twenty-one in 1833, had bought or somehow secured dubious title to an enormous tract of land across the Rio Grande from Presidio del Norte. Leaton took her with him to Presidio in 1848, esconcing her in the great adobe pile, across the river and a few miles below, now known as Fort Leaton or *El Fortín.*[40]

Of equally exotic origins is Milton Faver, who became the *don* of great landholdings, also across the river in Texas. Accounts have been contradictory concerning Faver's background, but the best-authenticated is that told by Mrs. Hart Greenwood, who lived until recently in the fortress *La Ciénega* built by "Don Militon." According to Amy Greenwood, Faver came from Independence, Missouri, having fled that part of the country before the Mexican War because of a shooting in which he believed he had caused the death of his opponent. A neighbor of Faver's in Missouri, John Adam Pool, Amy's grandfather, migrated to the Chinati Mountain country east of Presidio, bordering on Faver's holdings, in the early 1880s. Only when Pool encountered the recluse there did Faver learn that the man he shot many years before in Missouri actually had survived the shooting, that there was no need for Faver to have been on the run.[41]

After fleeing Missouri, Faver had shown up in Meoqui, some miles south of Ciudad Chihuahua, where he worked in a flour mill for Don Francisco León. While there he married a girl, reputedly a great beauty, named Francisca Ramirez, a sister-in-law of Richard C. Daly, who was also a pioneer settler in the Big Bend.[42] James W. Spencer and Leaton were so closely associated with John D. Burgess and Richard Daly, when they all showed up in Presidio del Norte in 1848, that a reasonable assumption may be made that they had worked together

during the Mexican War. They, along with Milton Faver, William
Russell, Larkin Landrum, and John W. Davis, formed the nucleus of
the Anglo-American settlement in and across the river from Presidio
del Norte after the Treaty of Guadalupe Hidalgo settled the boundary.
All of them, from their bases in that locality, strongly affected the development of the third road to Chihuahua, the one from Indianola and
San Antonio.

There was another key figure among the Doniphan stragglers.
When dismissed as a captain in Doniphan's Traders' Battalion, the
huge train of wagons that backed up the expeditionary force, Henry
Skillman joined those traders and wagonmasters who went north up
the Camino Real toward Santa Fe. He showed up later that year scouting for Gen. Sterling Price in the El Paso area. As Skillman, heading
an advance party, entered El Paso about November 1, he had the pleasure of capturing former New Mexico Governor Manuel Armijo, who
had ventured back into the borders of the state he had ignobly abandoned in the face of Kearney's invasion. Skillman turned the fat *don*
over to military authorities, who put him under parole, which he
promptly skipped.[43]

Whatever the extent of Skillman's work under Sterling Price may
have been, it led to his eventually settling down for a while at Concor-
dia, just above El Paso.[44] And that made him most fortuitously available to Lt. William H. C. Whiting for a key assignment: when that
fine young officer made his way up through the trackless wastes of the
Big Bend to El Paso early in 1849, opening the roads west from the
Texas Gulf Coast.

[3]

Second Road:
Connelley's Trail

T. U. Taylor, dean of the University of Texas college of engineering for many years, was an East Texas pioneer freighter in his own right. Reared on his father's freight wagon, he had followed and taken part in the building of these roads since right after the Civil War. Writing for *Frontier Times* in 1938 a rambling discourse on half a dozen of the brave new nineteenth-century roads that opened up Texas, Dean Taylor observed: "As a matter of fact in the United States there were at least three Chihuahua Trails."

So far as the record shows, this is the first public recognition of the idea that three major roads served the silver and merchandise traffic with Chihuahua. Taylor identified one of these as the Santa Fe Trail into Chihuahua and another as the Chihuahua Road from Indianola through San Antonio, which occupies the principal attention of the latter part of this book. As to the other, Dean Taylor noted:

> In 1839 Dr. H. Connelly [*sic*] with a great train of bullion made the Comanche Springs [Fort Stockton, Texas] a resting place between Chihuahua City and Arkansas on the initial trip which opened up the great Chihuahua Trail. This Trail extended from Chihuahua City to old Fort Towson in the Indian Territory.[1]

33

Henry Connelley was one of several practicing physicians who turned from medicine in the nineteenth century to become adventurers and trailblazers in the Great West.[2] He came honestly by his proclivities for exploration and trading: his ancestors had emigrated from Ireland's County Armagh in 1689 to the neighborhood of Charleston, South Carolina. After the American Revolution, members of the family began to move westward, and they established new and very prolific families wherever they settled. In 1789 twin brothers John and Sanford Connelley, with their wives, two half brothers, and half sister moved from Virginia to Nelson (now Spencer) County, Kentucky. There Henry Connelley was born to John Donaldson Connelley and Frances Brent in the year 1800. He began his academic education not far from home under the tutelage of the great frontier scholar, James I. Dozier.

Henry, his younger brother James, and a friend and classmate, Ware May, all journeyed from Dozier's classroom to the medical school at Transylvania College, Lexington, Kentucky, and were among the first graduates of that department in 1828. Brother James stayed in Kentucky to practice medicine, but Henry and young Dr. Ware May set out for the western frontier soon after graduation. Henry hung out his shingle at Liberty, in Clay County, Missouri, barely across the county line from Independence and the beckoning river landings on the Missouri.[3]

Ware May remained in Missouri and the West to rise to the top of the medical profession, but adventure sang its siren song to the twenty-eight-year-old Henry Connelley. After a few months of medical practice he closed his office and, before the year 1828 was over, had joined a "man named Stephenson" on a wagon train to Chihuahua.[4] The journey south was punctuated by "many adventures with the Indians and much suffering from hunger and thirst."[5] Henry Connelley liked what he found in Chihuahua, however, for he made it his home for twenty years.

His first job was as a clerk in the store of a Mr. Powell, where he so well mastered the business that he soon bought out the store from Powell. This became the foundation for his extensive trading and merchandising enterprises, to which he eventually drew into partnership the estimable Edward J. Glasgow, as already related.

Some years before that development, however, Connelley was dividing his time between Chihuahua City and the mining town of Jesus María, where he had opened a branch trading post. While there he married a Spanish woman, and they were still domiciled at Jesus María when his first son Joseph was born in August of 1838.

Henry Connelley had now spent ten years in northern Mexico. He was accepted as a Mexican businessman of acumen and good repute. As with many others of the Chihuahua trade, both Mexicans and North Americans, Connelley chafed under the prevailing system that brought goods down from the United States only through Missouri and Santa Fe — a long circuitous route which exposed the incoming merchandise and the outgoing silver bullion to custom levies both in New Mexico and in Chihuahua. So obvious were these inefficiencies that both Henry Connelley and his friend Josiah Gregg conceived at about the same time, but not in communication with each other, the idea of moving freight more directly from the Arkansas frontier.

In the spring of 1839, Gregg had brought a wagonload of goods to Van Buren, Arkansas, and was poised to head west with it across what is now Oklahoma and the northern part of the Texas Panhandle to Santa Fe. That would at least eliminate many miles in the transit from the Mississippi to the New Mexico capital.[6]

Connelley's plan was more direct: from Ciudad Chihuahua he would follow the ancient trail of the Jumanos, the *conquistadores,* and the priests down the Conchos River Valley to Presidio del Norte at La Junta. From there he would strike northeastward across the undeveloped western part of the Texas Republic to Fort Towson beyond the Red River.

The United States Army had established Fort Towson, in the extreme southeast corner of today's Oklahoma, in 1824 to control the depredations of outlaws and Indians along the Red River, which was then the boundary between the United States and Mexico. The fort was also to serve as a base for the protection — and control — of the Choctaw and Chickasaw Indians. Abandoned once, it was reestablished in 1831 by Maj. Stephen Watts Kearney of the Third United States Infantry, about six miles north of the Red River and a little south of Gates Creek. The present village of Fort Towson is nearby.[7] The fort itself was insignificant; more important were the towns just beyond. At Van Buren, Arkansas, and Shreveport, Louisiana, steamboat traffic on the Red River could offer the same freight facilities furnished by Independence, Missouri — but at a savings of hundreds of miles in distance.

Henry Connelley's concept was shared by a number of Mexican merchants in Chihuahua, several of whom joined him organizing the expedition. Posterity is indebted to Josiah Gregg for a lengthy footnote in *Commerce of the Prairies,* on these merchants' probe across North Texas. Gregg said he received directly from Henry Connelley "a very interesting sketch of the adventures of this pioneer party, which I regret that my plan will not permit me to present in detail." [8]

Gregg learned from Connelley that the caravan included about a half dozen proprietors, fifty dragoons furnished by the governor as a military escort, and enough cart drivers, herdsmen, foragers, and servants to round out over a hundred men altogether. They had on the outgoing trip only seven "wagons" — possibly Mexican *carretas* — but about 700 mules to provide teams for the much larger number of vehicles coming back. And the six or seven traders had raised almost $300,000 in specie and bullion for the purposes of their venture, stowing it in cowhide bags within the carts. [9]

A major advantage offered the traders was that Governor José María Irogoyen de la O (yes, that was his name), [10] besides providing the escort of dragoons, had agreed to extend the courtesies of his office at the customs station in Presidio del Norte, assuring the traders that only a nominal duty would be imposed on the goods they proposed to bring into Mexico. [11]

So far as is known, this was the first international trade endeavor of consequence across the Trans-Pecos area of Texas. The road down the Conchos watershed to the Rio Grande had been used for Indian commerce since before the dawn of history. Pack trains had ventured beyond to garner a harvest in salt from encrusted lakebeds on the far side of the Pecos River. Walter Fulcher, listening to the stories of *viejos* in the Terlingua country of the Big Bend more than half a century ago, retrieved some accounts of legendary traders living along Terlingua Creek around 1800, who would purchase trade goods in Chihuahua or Meoqui and peddle them by *carreta* among the *rancherías* along the Rio Grande or even out on the far plains. [12] These were all localized efforts among indigenous peoples.

Connelley and his fellow merchants from the capital now struck out to forge a link directly with the Yankee commerce beyond the Mississippi, apparently ignoring the Republic of Texas and its possible claims against their passage. They left the capital April 3, 1839, moving out with their huge treasure and their mules through the bandit-haunted pass to Bachimba and turning northeastward, then, past the fountains of Julimes. Fourteen years were to pass before Julius Froebel, the wide-eyed young German wanderer, [13] would record in detail the hardships and the mystique of a desert passage from Julimes through Chupadero and La Mula to Presidio, but the seasoned Chihuahua traders apparently took it in stride, for Connelley left no record of significant problems.

Presidio del Norte, where the desert road met the Conchos at its mouth on the Rio Grande — La Junta de los Rios — was probably much the same in 1839 as it was when Jack Hays found it in 1848 and as W. H. C. Whiting did in 1849. It was a straggling, sun-baked village of less than 2,000 souls, stagnating on the farthest fringes of the new Mexican Republic's frontier, but blessed with just one bounty of nature: the dependable river-bottom harvest of squashes, melons, and corn that assured the settlement's long life, even until today.

For historians, La Junta also had in that decade another treasure: an enlisted soldier who kept a gossipy journal throughout his long tenure at the presidio. Francisco Colomo usually filled his pages with the trivia of village life and post routine — perhaps that was all that usually went on there — but on April 20, 1839, he served history well by recording: "The general started his journey to the United States, having with him one hundred men as guards." [14]

The date was seventeen days after Connelley's departure from Chihuahua, 175 miles away — about right for a train that traveled fourteen miles a day and would have lain over then at Presidio for a few days. And the "general" — did Colomo upgrade him even as he exaggerated the number of soldiers? — could only have been the officer-in-charge of the Mexican dragoons riding escort on the treasure. However queasy the statistics, Colomo preserved the only firsthand record of the expedition's passage into Texas.

With seven wagons or *carretas* the expedition must have gone up Alamito Creek, which debouches upon the Rio Grande about six miles below Presidio, for that was the only feasible way to the east for wheeled traffic. They would have left the Alamito after seventy-five miles in its valley, climbed out onto the grassy steppes to Antelope Springs, and continued on over Paisano Pass to present-day Alpine. Antonio de Espejo may have been the first European to quaff those cool waters, if Cabeza de Vaca missed them in 1534, but Henry Connelley was almost certainly the first Anglo-American to visit the spring, which about that time was becoming known to Indians as *Charco de Alsate*. [15]

To find enough water and forage for their *caballada,* the party must have then moved past the Leoncita Spring, next the Leon Water

Holes, and finally to the huge Comanche Springs where Fort Stockton was later built. These last two were points on the Comanche War Trail, which was marked by the bones of thousands of animals, and so would have been easy to follow.

Still following the Comanche War Trail, the Chihuahua party made a dry passage from Comanche Springs northeastward to Horsehead Crossing on the Pecos. From there they must have continued to range generally northeastward without benefit of trail or useful map. Gregg says only:

> They took the Presidio del Norte in their route, and then proceeding northwesterly [*sic*: He clearly meant northeasterly] finally arrived at Fort Towson after a protracted journey of three months; but without meeting any hostile savages, or encountering any serious casualty, except getting bewildered, after crossing Red River, which they mistook for the Brazos. This caused them to shape their course nearly north, in search of the former stream, until they reached the Canadian River.[16]

From the Red River to the Canadian, which runs parallel, is something like a hundred miles; therefore, by the time they realized their error, they were well north of their target. But on the Canadian they fortunately met some Delaware Indians, who piloted them safely to Fort Towson.[17] With a little luck, they might have purchased their trade goods, loaded new wagons, and made the return trip that fall, as had been their intention. Without specifying the troubles, however, Connelley told Gregg that weather and other delays caused them to postpone leaving until the spring.

Little has been written in the past concerning how Connelley and his associates changed their "two or three hundred thousand dollars" in silver for enough merchandise to fill the "sixty or seventy wagons" which Gregg tells us made up the return train. Fortunately, Thomas Maitland Marshall, early in his career as a student of the northern frontier of Texas, in 1917 published evidence that the goods were obtained at Shreveport. Marshall reported, apparently in partial error, that

> In May of that year [1839] a company of Mexican traders arrived at Shreveport, Louisiana. They had been forty days in making the journey from Chihuahua to Fort Towson, a distance of six hundred miles . . .[18]

The wandering route the Connelley party had followed was nearer 800 miles; they seldom made over fourteen miles in a day. If they had reached Shreveport in May they would certainly have been able to start back that fall. Gregg quotes Connelley specifically as saying that "they finally arrived at Fort Towson after a protracted journey of three months," which would place them there in July and still a considerable distance from Shreveport.

In his findings and conclusions, Marshall also erred in identifying Presidio del Norte. Clearly not having seen Gregg's extensive footnote on Connelley's journey, nor being very familiar with the geography on the Rio Grande, Marshall quoted a published letter from one of the traders, adding his own conclusion that "from Chihuahua they traveled to 'Fort del Norte,' no doubt meaning El Paso."[19] But Presidio del Norte, or "Fort of the North," has always been the presidio in the heart of the Big Bend at La Junta, as distinguished from Presidio del Rio Grande, at San Juan Bautísta Mission, near present-day Eagle Pass, on the lower reaches of the river. The name of a presidio has never figured in identifying El Paso del Norte.

The important fact developed by Thomas Maitland Marshall in this and other evidence he cites is that the Chihuahua traders did go from Fort Towson to Shreveport to do their trading. Since they both lie on the Red River, the likelihood is that Connelley and some of his traders journeyed down the river, either by boat or along the banks, to make their purchases at Shreveport, which even then was a busy inland port near the head of steamboat traffic.

Sometime in 1841, the Shreveport *Intelligencer* published the letter from one of the traders and commented enthusiastically upon the possibilities of the trade, pointing out that "the route was the best for commerce between the United States and Mexico, other trails being much longer." [20]

Political considerations would have dictated that Connelley leave his Mexican dragoons encamped in the no-man's-land near Fort Towson, rather than take them into Arkansas and Louisiana of the United States. No doubt he and his associates bought the sixty or more wagons needed, recruited additional teamsters, loaded the wagons, and took them back out to Fort Towson.

In this fourth year of the Republic of Texas, the Red River frontier was completely isolated from the settlements in southeastern and south-central Texas, which constituted the whole of the body politic. Otherwise, the presence of fifty Mexican dragoons under a commissioned officer, moving back and forth on that frontier, should most certainly have created grave concern among the truculent Texians in

the government of that precarious commonwealth. In 1840 President
Mirabeau Lamar did send Col. William H. Hunt, engineer, to scout
out a "Military Road from Red River to Austin." [21] Perhaps this undertaking, and the "National Road of the Republic" which added to
it, from Dallas through Paris to Fort Towson, served in some degree as
a response to belated information reaching Austin about the Chihuahua traders' casual breaching of the international frontier. In the early
spring of 1840, however, Connelley moved imperturbably about his
affairs. He told Gregg:

> I have never been more hospitably treated, or had more efficient
> assistance, than was given us by the citizens of Red River. All
> seemed to vie with each other in rendering us every aid in their
> power; and our Mexican friends, notwithstanding the hostile at-
> titude in which the two countries stood toward each other, were
> treated with a kindness which they still recollect with the warm-
> est feelings of gratitude. [22]

Of course, the spending of a quarter of a million dollars in hard
silver among those money-starved communities could have been a lu-
bricating factor in such amicable experiences. Nevertheless, as J. W.
Williams observed in his brief article on the expedition, Connelley
himself "doubtless was chiefly responsible for maintaining cordial relations between the Mexicans of his party and the settlers of North
Texas." [23]

Gregg said that upon "learning that the Texans were friendly disposed to them, they now turned their course through the midst of the
northern settlements of that republic . . . he [Connelley] passed the
Texan border early in April." [24] This would have been over the Red
River south of Fort Towson and just east of Clarksville, Texas, for testimony exists in court records of 1894 that "the Chihuahua Traders
came from Fort Towson by the mouth of the Kiamichi River and by
Pinhook." [25] From Pinhook they ranged southwesterly past the present-day site of Paris. Williams traces their course from Paris through
Bonham, Whitesboro, and present-day Saint Jo, and along a prairie
ridge between the future towns of Montague and Nacona before plunging into the Cross Timbers. [26]

As the Texas-Santa Fe expedition found out the next year, the
Cross Timbers was a dreadful expanse of territory to transit on an unimproved trail with wheeled vehicles. The plow and the bulldozer have
largely erased it today, but in the consciousness of nineteenth-century

Texians, the Cross Timbers was as distinct a geographic entity as the Big Thicket, the Edwards Plateau, or the Llano Estacado.[27] The ground was hummocky, much of it encumbered with dense thickets, and in the early spring of 1840 the heavy rains had left water standing in the soaked hollows between the hummocks. The caravan, with its sixty to seventy laden wagons, the men now increased to 225, and their hundreds of mules, floundered across both the Upper and Lower Cross Timbers for days on end, seeking to intersect their track of the previous year somewhere beyond the timber's edge. However, they unknowingly crossed the faint trail and soon became lost. In a few days they turned south and found the route at a branch of the Colorado.[28]

Their route has been reconstructed as passing near the points now known as Seymour, Benjamin, Aspermont, Snyder, Colorado City, and Stiles, the latter being some seventy miles west of today's San Angelo.[29] They may have found the Comanches' standby watering places of Mustang and Wild China ponds, which would then have led them directly along the Comanche War Trail again, through Castle Gap and down to the Horsehead Crossing of the Pecos. Or, as some believe, they may have reached the Pecos farther south, at Pontoon Crossing.[30]

Of the Pecos crossing Gregg related that though it was very narrow, it was too deep to be forded. Not a stick of any kind was to be found to make a raft, so the traders resorted to "an experiment characteristic of the Prairies." Using one wagon body, they bound empty water kegs beneath it so that it served as a ferryboat for their goods. From the Pecos they continued on their old trail, in reverse, all the way to Presidio, without incident. But a stunning disappointment awaited them at the Rio Grande.

Their benevolent friend Governor Irogoyen de la O, forced out of office by ill health, had just died on May 24, the reins of office passing to a hostile administration under Francisco García Conde.[31] The contract upon which Connelley and his fellows had relied for a diminution of their duties was abrogated or forgotten. They now faced a charge of full tariff which, with the expenses of their protracted journey, would have broken them.

For forty-five days the train tarried on the east bank of the river while the owners pleaded, cajoled, negotiated. At last a compromise was reached, not so onerous as the full rate, but still high enough to trim off all their profit. They paid and entered Mexico; on August 27, 1840, they were in Chihuahua City with their goods, having been in the field for 508 days.[32]

Of Connelley's venture, Gregg summarized: "The delays and accumulated expenses of this expedition caused it to result so disastrously to the interests of all who were engaged in it, that no other enterprise of the kind has since been undertaken.[33]

President Lincoln appointed Henry Connelley as territorial governor of New Mexico in 1861. His distant relative and chronicler, William Elsey Connelley, rendered this tribute:

> Governor Connelley was a pioneer, the descendant of pioneers . . . a gentleman of refinement and intelligence, honorable and upright in all the relations of life . . . He went out into the world to profit by the advantages offered a man of integrity and enterprise in a new country. He was to this commercial new world what Kit Carson, Fremont, and others were to their spheres. Commerce, not the invader, after all is the conqueror.[34]

[4]

Third Road:
Austin's Dream

Few observations have been made by historians about the earliest origins of this road.[1] Only Eugene Barker gives attention to the fact that in the year before the Texas Revolution burst into full bloom, the Father of Texas, Stephen F. Austin, was already advancing a lively argument that the prosperity of both Texas and Coahuila, still joined as one political entity, depended upon the opening of a road from the Texas coast into the rich mining areas of northern Mexico.

Austin had left Texas in late May 1833, reaching Mexico City on July 18. He was sequestered there, much of the time under arrest, for a full two years. Eugene Barker says of this period, in his biography of Austin:

> He now had opportunity to work . . . at a plan that had been in his mind for years for diverting to Texas ports the important trade that had grown up between St. Louis, Missouri, and Northern Mexico through the gateway of Santa Fe. He had written in 1829 that "the whole trade of Chihuahua and Sonora and New Mexico must ultimately enter in one of the ports of Texas, either Galveston or Matagorda." (Austin to Henry Austin, Aug. 27, 1829) and he reverted to the subject now in his Explanation to the Public.

His plan for accomplishing this was a road through Texas from the Gulf to Chihuahua.[2]

This "explanation" or *exposición* was a lengthy brochure, printed only in Spanish, which Austin distributed from his quarters in the capital city.[3] To his friend Samuel May Williams of Galveston he wrote, on February 14, 1835:

> I think I shall be able to leave here in about 15 days. [He did not get away until July.] . . . I have some idea of employing this interval in tring to get some aid of the Gen'l Gov't toward opening a road from Texas to the Paso del Norte, or in a direct line (or as nearly as the country will permit) to Chihuahua. I speak of this enterprise in my exposición copies of which I have sent to Monclova & by this mail I send you one . . . It has been very well received here, and has satisfied every reasonable man . . . The Chihuahua road is a great hobby with me — I intend to persevere until it is completed.[4]

Though Austin's printed monograph as a whole was a review of and an apology for his and his colonies' relations with the parent country, the long section proposing expanded trade between Texas and northern Mexico builds a compelling argument for the Chihuahua Road, conceived thirteen years before any expedition ever headed in that direction:

> Everyone who has any knowledge in regard to the commerce of Texas must know that the Mexican markets are the best in the world for the products of Texas. [Austin then proceeded to show that ginned cotton and corn commanded prices four to six times as high in Mexico as in Texas markets] . . . and the same proportion holds true with reference to all the products of Texas . . . It is worthy of note that every year about two million *pesos* worth of merchandize enters New Mexico and Chihuahua from Missouri across more than 400 leagues of desert. This commerce with Mexico is entirely outside the course which the geographical situation of the country and nature itself has marked out; the ports of Texas were evidently designed for it. There is no difficulty in opening highways from Texas to the state of Chihuahua and to New Mexico, whose length would not be over half the actual distance over which merchandize is now transported . . . The work of opening these roads is certainly of the greatest importance, since it would change the course of the commerce that now comes from Missouri from that foreign country to the Mexican ports of Texas, and consequently all the advantages from the payments for freight and transportation would pass from the freighters of Missouri to Mexican citizens.[5]

While these are only excerpts from an exposition that was wider-ranging among other subjects, even from today's perspective a better argument for the Chihuahua Road could hardly have been marshaled.

The astute Stephen F. Austin did not live, however, to see his prescient dream realized. Antonio López de Santa Anna, who had ascended to the presidency of Mexico in 1833, turned out not to be one of those "friends in the Gov't" of whom Austin so confidently spoke. Santa Anna had a deep-seated distrust of the Anglo-American colonizers in Texas. The Texians, on the other hand, stood on the basic issue that they had established their colonies under the clear terms of a valid contract with the Mexican government that was founded on the Constitution of 1824, and Mexico still professed to recognize that constitution. Administrations that had come to power in the past six years, however, and most notoriously that of Santa Anna, had ignored or abrogated numerous terms of the contract for colonization; Austin had spent the better part of his time in Mexico pleading for recognition of the colonies' status as guaranteed by the Constitution of 1824.

Before Austin could complete his long journey back to the colonies, the government had instituted further repressive measures that inflamed the already exacerbated passions of the settlers — not only among the former Yankees and Europeans, but also in a number of solid Mexican landholders. Hostilities broke out at Gonzales, and a Texian army that had enlisted Austin's reluctant leadership moved to surround San Antonio de Bejar.

From San Antonio, Austin wrote to the consultation of citizens in emergency session at San Felipe, urging that "a declaration be made in favor of the Federal Constitution of 1824" and that the developing civil war be waged "in defense of the Constitution and the Federal System." On November 6, 1835, the consultation did agree to organize a provisional government "upon the principles of the Constitution of 1824." [6]

The revolution then proceeded through the tragedies of the Alamo and Goliad to ultimate victory at San Jacinto and independence for Texas — only fifteen months after Austin had published his fervent plans for continued profitable coexistence.

His health broken, Austin survived only eight months after the Battle of San Jacinto and the founding of the Texas Republic; his dream for a great flow of commerce between Texas and northern Mexico lay dormant for half a dozen years.

As already related, Texas had been traversed repeatedly by Span-

ish exploring parties since the days of Cabeza de Vaca. El Camino Real
lay well beaten across the land from San Juan Bautista, near present-
day Eagle Pass, through San Antonio de Bejar to the piney woods of
East Texas, with settlements and missions along and branching out
from it. Nevertheless, when the Anglo-Americans took over the province in 1836, most of the lore accumulated in three centuries of exploration and development was lost to them.

South of El Camino Real the terrain was well scouted, known,
and mapped; virtually all of the settlements, both Spanish-Mexican
and Anglo-American, lay within that area. North of that road and
west of the Colorado stretched huge expanses, larger than the state
of New York, all the way to the Canadian River and to New Mexico,
which Stephen F. Austin did well in his monograph to call "deserts"
in the sense of their being devoid of habitation, the domain only of
"barbarous tribes . . . wanderers and the enemies of civilized settlements." [7]

Walter Prescott Webb, in his history of the Texas Rangers,
clearly indicated that no Ranger, and certainly no other Texian known
to the body politic, had had any experience whatsoever in the country
beyond the Pecos River before 1848.[8] The Rangers, in pursuit of Indians, did make scattered penetrations into those river valleys opening
out of the Edwards Plateau along the Balcones Fault — the Medina,
Sabinal, Frio, and Nueces rivers, even as far as Las Moras Creek. Furthermore, the San Saba country north of the Llano and west of the Colorado had been known to a few Anglo adventurers since earlier days because of the ruined mission there and the legends of the Lost Mine,
which drew such treasure-seekers as Rezin and James Bowie before the
revolution.[9] But north and west of these points was the unchallenged
domain of the Comanches and the Apaches, illumined only by vague
rumors of the tumbled mountain fastnesses along the Rio Grande and
of the Great Staked Plain, or Llano Estacado.

Into the latter, that abyss of mystery, ignorance, and misinformation, plunged the ill-fated Texan-Santa Fe expedition in 1841.
Total failure that it was, in terms of stated objectives, it must be considered as one major step toward opening communication with northern Mexico.[10]

Two years after Austin died, the Third Congress of the struggling
republic had adopted, on January 26, 1839, a joint resolution, providing that the president be authorized to give every encouragement and
support, consistent with the nation's safety, to trade between the west-

ern settlements of Texas and those of Mexico on and beyond the Rio Grande.[11]

Within a few months this first stirring of interest was further stimulated, though in a counter-reactive mood, by Henry Connelley's efforts from Chihuahua to establish that second road, which would connect with the Red River in Arkansas and Louisiana, and then to the east. The adventure would become known in Texas in 1839, as Thomas Maitland Marshall related:

> This border trade attracted the attention of the press, speculators, legislators, and officials of Texas. A report of the first caravan [to the Red River country] appeared in the Houston *Telegraph and Texas Register* on July 17, 1839. On April 8, 1840, an article was published in the same paper, the substance of which had already appeared in the *Sentinel* of Austin . . . The account stated that the author had been frequently asked concerning the feasibility of opening a direct communication between Austin and Santa Fe. He estimated the distance was four hundred and fifty miles and that the road would traverse a rich, rolling, and well-watered country.[12]

Such arrant misinformation as this about the geography on the way to New Mexico was in part responsible for the inadequate logistics of the expedition that evolved the next year.

Throughout 1840 and the first half of 1841, the Republic of Texas see-sawed in its policy, from an eager desire and intention to develop peaceful trade with Mexico, to a demand for an actual declaration of war against that country, and back to plans for an expedition to open up relations with New Mexico. President Lamar, unable to get the Congress to authorize funds for his expedition, let the governmental body dissolve and go home. Then he "transcended his Constitutional powers," as Marshall has put it, and ordered the army to proceed with the plan and the treasury to finance it.[13]

The flamboyant chief of state of the Republic did not rest on his official launching of preparations for the expedition. For the first time he drew San Antonio, the logical hinge for any road westward, into the machinations for his great project.

Men of substance on the San Antonio scene, such as Samuel A. Maverick, Juan Seguin, John Twohig, and José Antonio Navarro, were the target of Lamar's promotional tour, but Maverick's wife Mary was the one who recorded the president's visit to old San Antonio de Bejar:

> President Lamar with a very considerable suite visited San Antonio in June. A grand ball was given him in Mrs. Yturri's long room . . .

General Lamar and Mrs. Juan N. Seguin, wife of the Mayor, opened
the ball with a waltz . . . The general was a poet, a polite and brave
man and first rate conversationalist — but he did not dance well.[14]

In her memoirs many years later, Mary Maverick wrote that President Lamar's visit "was to sanction and encourage an expedition to
Santa Fe, New Mexico. The object was . . . to open a line of commerce
between the two sections and get a share of the lucrative trade between
Santa Fe and Lexington, Mo." [15]

President Lamar had commissioned Col. Hugh McLeod, a patriot
with a long record of service to Texas, to be military commander of the
venture. As "commissioners" to represent civil interests in the foray,
Lamar chose three men from widely scattered areas of the Republic:
Col. William C. Cooke, who had just completed the survey for a military road from the Brazos to the Red River; Dr. R. F. Brenham, who
was later to join the Mier expedition and die in the rebellion against
the Mexican guard at Salado in 1843; and Don José Antonio Navarro,
the doughty Texian patriot born in San Antonio in 1795 while it was
still a part of Coahuila. Navarro knew that he should not accept the appointment, for not only was his health doubtful, but also he was born
a citizen of the state of Coahuila and was a marked man in Mexico as
one of the original planners of the Texas Revolution. Reluctantly,
though, he went along.

Since the Texan-Santa Fe expedition, as it came to be called, did
not aim for Mexico proper — though that is where it haplessly ended
— and since it did not serve directly in opening up a viable trade route,
this study will not dwell upon the misadventures of the project. H.
Bailey Carroll's synthesis of the principal narratives surviving from the
expedition is recommended for the reader who would fix the exact
point-to-point course.[16]

The party's marshaling point was on Walnut Creek, just north of
Austin, and the final point of departure on June 19, 1841, was from
Brushy, a few miles away.[17] One of three principal sources, an Englishman accompanying the foray, noted that

It had been proposed that the route to be taken should be from the
San Saba, or in the course of the Colorado to the Puerco [Pecos] and
along the line of this river to San Miguel. It was, however, determined to proceed, if practicable, to the Red River, and after crossing
it, to get upon the Missouri Trail to Santa Fe.[18]

This was a tragic mistake, as it turned out, compounded by the fact that not a man in the company had ever seen a mile of the westward part of the journey that lay before them, and no reliable map existed. They set out bravely enough, 321 men in all, a colorful caravan in new blue uniforms, pinned with the high hopes of the Texas government, of hundreds of families, and of their own various dreams.[19]

The first "real topographic hazard" they encountered was a few miles beyond the present location of Fort Worth, when the long, straggling column of wagons and mounted men entered the celebrated Cross Timbers which had so encumbered Dr. Connelley only a year before, as he returned to Chihuahua from Fort Towson. And indeed, after some eight days of laboring in the rough hummocks, boggy bottoms, and stubborn brush in present-day Montague County, when the Texans emerged upon the great open prairie — barely twenty miles from the Red River, which they never reached — they came directly upon Connelley's trace.[20]

This slash of wagon tracks left in the mud and grass of the plains was Connelley's return trail made in the summer of 1840. Here the paths of Texas adventurers for the first time crossed that of earlier traders from the West.

Two months later, exactly, the expedition began to break up, after incredible misadventures. They had been lost for weeks and were stalled at the base of the looming Caprock, which forms the border of the dreaded Staked Plain. And after still another month, on October 5, when one segment after another had straggled into New Mexico only to be captured by Governor Manuel Armijo's soldiers, Hugh McLeod and the last of his tattered, exhausted command laid down their arms to a body of Mexicans at Laguna Colorado.[21]

If they had had any inkling of the tender mercies in store for them at the hands of the devious governor who ordered them seized, they might have chosen a more desperate course. But it was too late; the dispersed and shattered party, in the charge of Capt. Damasio Salazar, was put afoot on the road to Mexico. It was a dismal pilgrimage, harassed by the brute Salazar, who cut off the ears of those who died from exhaustion, or who were shot, and sent them back on a leather thong to his commanding officer to provide an accounting. The "invaders," as Mexican history still calls them, never even glimpsed Santa Fe, but trudged from San Miguel through the Rio Grande Valley and El Paso del Norte, through Chihuahua City, and eventually to the capital itself and beyond to the noisome prisons of Acordado, Puebla, and Perote.[22]

Fortunately for the later course of trade with the Mexican people,

the remnant of adventurers who dribbled back to Texas over the next
three years reported honestly the distinction between the generally
compassionate attitudes of the people themselves and the arrogant
cruelties of Santa Anna's minions, who still smarted under the memory
of San Jacinto.

Mirabeau Lamar's remaining months as president were darkened
by mystery as to the fate of those hundreds of men who had marched so
bravely from Brushy toward Santa Fe. No sure word came until after
the presidential election had been held. Lamar's fierce devotion to the
cause of Texas independence and his early espousal of public education
were largely forgotten as the citizens faced the spectre of a bankrupt
treasury. They turned again to the old hero, Sam Houston, giving him
an overwhelming vote into the presidency. It was not until four weeks
after his taking office on December 13, 1841, that Houston — and the
nation — learned of the Texans' capture and of the brutal conditions
under which the prisoners were being marched down the long road to
Mexico City.

In reaction the Texas Congress, ignoring the huge public debt,
adopted a resolution to annex virtually all of northern Mexico, plus
both the Californias, and New Mexico, and to wage war with Mexico.
In high scorn, President Houston vetoed the measure. The Congress
tried to override the veto, but failed, and adjourned.[23]

In the few remaining years of the Texas Republic, other abortive,
ill-conceived armed incursions from and into Mexico were undertaken:
Rafael Vasquez's raid and two-day occupation of San Antonio in 1842,
setting off a panic flight which was dubbed "The Runaway of '42," as
a parallel to the Runaway Scrape of 1836; Gen. Adrian Woll's seizure
of San Antonio's merchants and lawyers in September of the same year,
marching them down to Perote Prison; William S. Fisher's "Mier expedition" into Mexico, reaching its nadir in the notorious drawing of
the black beans at Salado. As with McLeod in New Mexico, Maverick
dealing from his housetop with Adrian Woll, and Fisher confronted by
Pedro Ampudia in Mier, all experienced the duplicity of Santa Anna's
subordinates: humiliation, physical abuse, and starvation. However, it
must be repeated that these were not the acts of typical Mexican citizens. They were carried out under the policies and direct orders of an
opportunistic tyrant who was exploiting his own people as unmerci-
fully as he was avenging himself upon the Yankee colonists who had
humiliated him at San Jacinto.[24]

Only one factor justifies recital of these dreary marches into Mexico: their rosters were studded with the names of men whose experiences later helped to open the channels of peaceful trade exemplified by the Chihuahua Road — Samuel A. Maverick, Bigfoot Wallace, George T. Howard, Thomas S. Torrey, José Antonio Navarro. Many others as well, more obscure, trudged barefoot along the stony trails of Coahuila to languish in dark prisons, but returned to Mexico another day driving the big freight wagons of commerce. They were all men schooled to keep their eyes open; they saw much along the way that was to profit them in the later years of more amicable dealings with their neighbor country.

If the Texans as members of a republic could not impose their will upon Mexico, the United States with Texas a member could and did, as the years 1844–48 demonstrated.

Dr. Anson Jones, close to Sam Houston, was elected to succeed the old warrior, who was constitutionally prevented from standing again for reelection. Jones took office in December 1844, in an atmosphere charged with excitement over the issue of annexation to the United States — a question already occupying the attention of the United States Congress. President John Tyler's last achievement, in March 1845, was to sign the joint resolution passed by Congress which would bring Texas into the Union upon her acceptance of this action, or by treaty, at the option of the president of the United States.

This was the year that the phrase "manifest destiny" became common coin in barroom and pulpit, on the street and in the cloakrooms of the Capitol in Washington. In specific reference to the pending annexation of Texas, editor John L. O'Sullivan of the monthly *Democratic Review* in New York had decried the nation's lack of a channel westward as

> limiting our greatness and checking the fulfillment of our *manifest destiny* [italics added] to overspread the continent allotted by Providence for the free development of our yearly multiplying millions.[25]

The new president, James K. Polk, was the handpicked protégé of ailing, sinking Andrew Jackson, who had been eight years out of office. Polk's primary mission was to carry out his old chief's dream of a continent-spanning nation, epitomized baldly in the campaign slogan, "Texas and Oregon!" Almost a year had lapsed, however, before he could see Texas garnered safely into the Union fold. On February 16, 1846, in front of the rude capitol in Austin, Anson Jones delivered his valedictory and struck the tri-colors of the Republic. The Stars and Stripes ran smartly up the halyards to fly for the first time over the Lone Star State.

Santa Anna had been deposed from the presidency of Mexico. His exile had started just two days before Anson Jones had become president of Texas in December 1844. Throughout almost all of Jones's tenure as the last president of Texas, the intrigue and counter-intrigue carried on by Texas, Great Britain, and the United States focused upon an intelligent but vacillating interim president of Mexico, José Joaquín Herrera.[26]

From Washington, President Polk pursued with Herrera his rather crass proposals to buy the United States's way through to the West Coast. Had the Mexican leadership been so inclined, they might have negotiated a sale, probably at a handsome price, of New Mexico, which then included Arizona, and Southern California. According to historian K. Jack Bauer, in his comprehensive review of the Mexican War, "it was in their inability to recognize that Mexican public opinion considered acceptance of the loss of Texas a shattering of national honor and dignity that the American leaders made their greatest mistake." [27]

Certainly Mexico's bankrupt government was teetering on the brink of collapse; her army was at the point of mutiny. Bauer depicted President Herrera as

> one of the few Mexican leaders to recognize the stupidity of fighting the United States over Texas . . . but he could do little to deflect the tidal run toward suicidal war promoted by his opponents. So great were these pressures that he had to make public motions in support of war measures . . .[28]

Therefore, beginning June 4, 1845, he restated Mexico's old claim to Texas, forsworn by Santa Anna in 1836, and he vowed that he would support that claim by armed force as needed. He followed this up by calling up to active service all state and federal armed services, and before June was out had brought the Congress to the capital in special session to take such action as might be appropriate toward Texas.

President Polk deemed that Mexico's sabre-rattling required that he make preliminary moves for protecting the new state's boundaries as soon as annexation became a fact. He directed Gen. Zachary Taylor in Louisiana to be prepared, instant upon Texas's acceptance of annexation, to move troops by sea and across the coastal plain toward Matamoros, particularly to display United States presence between the Nueces River and the Rio Grande. This forbidden land had been the area of sharpest dispute between Texas and Mexico ever since 1836.

General Taylor did not wait upon formalization of Texas's entry into the States; he started moving troops by sea from New Orleans on July 24, and cavalry along the coastal plain, to reach the shores of Corpus Christi Bay at the mouth of the Nueces River. There "Colonel" Henry L. Kinney had a ranch and fledgling settlement. By the end of the month, Taylor had his force there and within a few days established outposts across the Nueces River to provide *de facto* United States presence in the disputed strip. In March and April of 1846, Taylor moved his forces on down the coast to the Rio Grande opposite Matamoros.

Herrera's government had fallen; he was supplanted in a coup d' etat by Maj. Gen. Mariano Paredes y Arrillaga, who drew his strength from aristocratic elements in the army, the church, and aspiring monarchists. In his bellicose inaugural address, Paredes vowed "to support the integrity of Mexican territory as far as the Sabine River, the eastern boundary of Texas." He then sent troops toward Matamoros to make a show of force against Zachary Taylor's incursion.[29]

Mexico had lost forever its chance to negotiate a profitable settlement of the northern colossus' aspirations toward the Pacific.[30] But one officer's remarkable march up from Matagorda Bay through San Antonio and into Mexico profoundly influenced the opening of Stephen F. Austin's envisioned road to Chihuahua.

The full impact of the war with Mexico descended upon the Texas coast's Matagorda Bay on August 1, 1846. All day long, army transports from New Orleans had filed in through Paso Cavallo and anchored offshore. A spare, slightly graying sixty-two-year-old general, bursting with nervous energy, came ashore in a captain's gig to make arrangements for landing. He was John Ellis Wool, the third highest ranking officer in the United States Army.[31]

Between the War of 1812 and the new war with Mexico, Wool had served for a full quarter-century as inspector-general, and he knew his army inside out. Only two weeks after the declaration of war on May 13, 1846, Wool received orders to muster all the volunteers in Ohio, Illinois, Kentucky, Tennessee, and Mississippi. On July 11 his orders were expanded: to take charge of the command and march it from San Antonio across Mexico to capture the city of Chihuahua. By early July, despite the limitations of communication and transport on

the frontier, Wool had organized fourteen and a half regiments and had
them on the way to the front. He sent 10,000 of these troops down the
coast to Gen. Zachary Taylor and took more than 2,000 along with
him to Matagorda Bay. On his way through New Orleans, ever alert,
he helped himself to some of the wagon transportation allotted to General Taylor. After all, Zachary Taylor had been junior to him for years;
Wool had no reverence for a political promotion that had catapulted
Taylor ahead of him.[32]

The tight schedule General Wool was following had not permitted his making any advance arrangements in Matagorda Bay for disembarking his troops and materiel. He simply made a quick reconnaissance of available facilities, noted the squalid, unhealthful conditions
surrounding the German immigrants' camp at Indianola, and settled
upon the village of Lavaca, now known as Port Lavaca.

Within a few hours he had lighters from the ships afloat with
wagons and mules, harness and teamsters. Other lighters were bringing to the docks contingents of foot soldiers, who marched smartly
through the village, to the delectation of the townspeople, and set up
a temporary camp on the hard-shell banks just inshore.

John Wool, who had a long record of inspecting other officers'
camps, now had his first chance since the War of 1812 to mount a full-
fledged combat operation. He was making the most of it. Like a worried old wasp, he was everywhere, needling his officers, hurrahing the
men, rasping at civilians who had been employed to help assemble the
wagon trains.

As fast as harness could be unpacked and the restless mules run in
under it, they were hitched up, and the teamsters drove the wagons
out to the docks to take on their loads. Likewise, as soon as a group of
laden wagons could be assembled, Wool started it off, accompanied by
platoons of soldiers, up the track to Victoria on the 140-mile march to
San Antonio.

Their primitive road across these bottomless shoreline bogs and
up from Victoria through Goliad was at first muddy after heavy rains,
then sandy, and finally deep in dust.[33] The road was altogether unpre-
pared for heavy military traffic, and no building materials were available for repairs. Marching under the August sun between the groups of
wagons, the foot soldiers were tormented by thirst.[34] But, from the
moment the first lighters came ashore at Lavaca until the vanguard of
wagons rumbled into San Antonio, only twelve days had elapsed. A
century later Col. M. L. Crimmins, writing his analysis of the move-

ment, said that General Wool "set the example of hard and consistent work and he overcame difficulties rather than letting difficulties overcome him." [35]

Wool and his troops poured into San Antonio from the Goliad Road, then up Alamo Street to Commerce, where the only bridge across the San Antonio River led them to Main and Military plazas. There they joined up with and absorbed the command of Col. William S. Harney. At San Antonio, with never-flagging zeal, Wool whipped together in six weeks the "Army of the Centre" from many diverse elements. The foot soldiers had a brief rest before drill commenced to enjoy the exotic delights of San Antonio: the melons and fresh figs, the highly seasoned foods served *al fresco* on the Plaza, and the fandangos. No doubt they formed an enthusiastic gallery at the bridge over the river to watch the barely clad maidens tumble gaily in the crystal waters. The teamsters, however, with their 500 wagons, were turned directly around and started back to Lavaca to load up and bring along the remainder of the supplies and gear.

By the last week in September, General Wool had 1,112 wagon loads of supplies and at least 2,400 men in San Antonio, doubling the population of the little city and putting a sharp strain on all its resources. [36]

The route which Wool was to follow southwestward into Mexico lay along the same road the Mexican general Adrian Woll had made infamous four years before when he drove his San Antonio prisoners down to the Rio Grande and through Guerrero on the humiliating trail to Perote Prison. That difference of only one letter in the two generals' surnames, with each man using and bringing fame or notoriety to the same road, has caused considerable confusion to the casual reader in later years. Texians, naturally, settled upon the term "The Wool Road" for the route that led westward to the Leona Creek and then turned down, toward what became Eagle Pass on the Texas side of the river, to the ancient fords of Las Islas. This was also the Camino Real of Spanish colonial history. And it must not be forgotten that the Wool Road, as far west from San Antonio as the Leona Creek near the later location of Uvalde, became also the Chihuahua Road.

A longtime friend and protégé of John Wool, Capt. Robert E. Lee, had joined the command in San Antonio on September 21, 1846, to share duty with Capt. William E. Fraser as Wool's senior engineer officers. It was the future Confederate general's first visit to Texas and, much more important to him, his first combat assignment after twenty years of service in the United States Army.[37]

Within three days Lee and Fraser had gathered together such tools for road-making and bridge-building as were available in San Antonio. On September 23, Wool ordered Lee forward along the road to reconnoiter "for wood, water, forage, and camp-sites and to make such repairs of the road as were necessary." [38]

Three days later, Wool pushed out 1,400 men as the first contingent of the Army of the Centre, backed up with 175 wagons and provisions for two months. His advance guard was commanded by the fiery Colonel Harney. General Wool and his staff followed September 29; Colonel Hardin and his First Illinois Regiment moved out October 2; while the inspector-general, Col. Sylvester Churchill, made up the rear guard a few days behind. Such spacing out of the units was necessary because there was not enough water or forage along the way for the whole force at one time, and the road had to be repaired after each group of wagons labored over it.

Four boats for pontoons had been loaded on the first wagons. Captain Lee was waiting for those wagons when the marching army reached the Rio Grande. He had selected a crossing somewhat above the old Spanish crossing of Las Islas, from among a number of known fords in that stretch of the river. Lee's choice lay at a point between the uppermost crossing, "Pagcuache," and the next named one downstream: "Paso de Nopal." [39]

Lee put the pontoons out with timbers over them to form a "flying bridge." It could float 200 soldiers over at a time. Battle-ready soldiers started crossing into Mexico on October 10, two months and one week after the first untrained men reached shore at Lavaca, 330 miles away. Some of the last wagons loaded at that port had pushed on through San Antonio and down to the river without a day's layover. The crossing of the Rio Grande into alien territory was accomplished in two days, as of October 12.[40]

To Wool's vast relief, he at last received orders in late November canceling the unpopular mission of taking Chihuahua, diverting him instead to Parras and eventually to Saltillo.[41] After marching almost 900 miles from Lavaca across a wild and poorly provisioned land, he joined up with another 2,000 men from Zachary Taylor's forces, and the combined armies of about 4,600 soldiers confronted more than 15,000 of Santa Anna's troops at Buena Vista.

It was the crisis, the turning point of the war. But the Army of the Centre, alongside Taylor's troops, met that crisis on February 23, 1847. Losses on both sides were dreadful; Santa Anna tacitly admitted defeat by withdrawing his armies from the field and returning toward Mexico City. Assessing the performance of Wool's Centre, Colonel Crimmins said, "For sheer audacity and rigid discipline, its march to Saltillo ranks with the heroic march of Xenophon, and its celerity and efficiency made the victory at Buena Vista possible." [42]

In a literally mundane way, also, General Wool's march from La-vaca as far as the Leona Creek was of vital importance to the future Chihuahua Road: his 500 wagons, laboring back and forth under heavy military supplies, left an imperishable trace across the prairie turf, marking that section of the road for the forty years of traffic ahead.

For early descriptions of the road between Matagorda Bay and San Antonio, turn back to late August of 1846. As General Wool's division, on its way to Mexico, had struggled up to San Antonio without needed advance reconnaissance, Maj. George T. Hughes, chief of the topographical staff, Centre Division, ordered two of his officers to make a more thorough survey of the two known routes from the bay to San Antonio. Their reports, submitted in September 1846, give the first professional description of the alternate courses from the coastal plain. [43]

Bvt. Lt. W. B. Franklin, topographical engineer, began with an unqualified statement that

> there are two roads leading from LaVaca, Texas, to San Antonio de Bejar. One of these, the shorter of them, diverges from the other at Victoria, Texas, thirty miles from LaVaca. This passes through Goliad, and is the same which was used by General Wool for the transportation of his supplies. The other [which Franklin surveyed] passes through Gonzales and Seguin. [44]

Lieutenant Franklin then explained the sketchiness of his notes: that he had had only a pocket compass, rather than regular surveyor's instruments, and further, that they had had to travel at night. "During the day the flies are so numerous that the horses are set nearly frantic, and humanity as well as his own comfort will dictate to the traveller that he must lie by during the day and travel by night."

It was accepted practice among explorers and the military in the nineteenth century to identify one bank of a river from the other by designating them "left" or "right" as one faced downstream, no matter which way he might be traveling. Therefore, Franklin related that the road he followed went up the "left" bank of the Guadalupe, in this case the eastward side, all the way to Seguin. He mentions only Gonzales and Seguin as settlements encountered on this route, after leaving Victoria. He found Gonzales to be

> a small place of but little interest, containing about three hundred inhabitants . . . situated near the junction of the St. Mark's [San Marcos] and Guadalupe Rivers. The former is crossed by a ferry, the road still continuing along the left bank of the Guadalupe.

Seguin also was a small place but

> little larger than Gonzales. Here, as well as along the whole route, the houses are built of logs. They are divided into three parts. The centre is merely a shed, the roof of the house being all that protects it from the weather. The other two parts are on each side of the centre shed and are the kitchen, bedrooms etc. of the establishment. They are rude but very comfortable dwellings, particularly for so new a country.

Franklin had evidently not heard the universal term, "dog-run," as applied to that kind of construction.

He found that the road finally crossed the Guadalupe about two miles beyond Seguin, and on a wooden bridge. Franklin noted the Cibolo, between Seguin and San Antonio, as "a fine clear stream, about thirty feet in width, very shallow but with a fine gravelley bottom," and related that after riding interminably through the mesquite over rolling parallel ridges, expecting any moment to see San Antonio, the traveler despairs "until the gray walls of the Alamo, immediately in front of him, give the pleasing assurance that his journey is ended."

Captain Sitgreaves carried *his* account of the route Wool had followed all the way from the coast. He started August 31: "from LaVaca, eight miles, to the Placedores [now known as Placedo Creek] a small rivulet, course nearly west across level prairie." And here Sitgreaves set the tone struck by most travelers who followed him: "a very muddy prairie — very muddy from recent rains." He found that the road continued about west-northwest over the same type of terrain until it reached a belt of timber two miles from Victoria, which was thirty miles out of Lavaca.

> At Victoria cross the Guadalupe, some two hundred feet wide, by a ferry,[45] thence about two miles, through a thickly timbered bottom, to an open rolling prairie, dry and hard . . . twelve miles to the Coleto, a small clear stream with hard sand and rock bottom. Thence,

thirteen miles to the Manahuila, the crossing of which was muddy and difficult.

A ford "with hard bottom" might be found in only one or two places along a hundred miles of a stream. In western history this accounts for many a strange diversion in a route, to reach a known feasible ford on a river.

Sitgreaves did not remark — because he may not have known — that between Coleto and the Manahuila he passed within a mile of the Fannin battleground. There, ten years before, Col. James William Fannin and his 350 Texian volunteers, surrounded without water on the open prairie by a superior force of Mexicans, had surrendered on what they believed to be honorable terms, only to be massacred on Santa Anna's orders.

It was but six miles from the Manahuila into old Goliad, then a small settlement which had not yet recovered from the shattering chaos of the revolution. Beyond, in what became Karnes County, Sitgreaves made no note of any settlement in the area of the little crossroads community of Alamita. It began to grow about that time, on a tiny creek called the Alamita, where in 1852 Thomas Ruckman founded his trading post which became bustling Helena.[46] Twelve miles away the surveyor did find a crossing of the Cibolo, "a considerable stream with a hard stony bottom" and on the right branch a *rancho*. This was the Carvajal Crossing of the Cibolo, at the place where in 1758 Don Andrés Hernandez had established his large ranch.[47]

Six miles beyond the crossing, Sitgreaves passed over "a small stream," which was the Marcelina, and then veered west through the present-day site of Floresville, skirting along the left (eastern) banks of the San Antonio River, which he found then to be "some one hundred feet wide, with very high, steep banks." He sighted another ranch there. This was ancient Los Choyopines, built as an agricultural outpost of San Antonio's Mission San Juan Capistrano, and later called Rancho Florena for the Canary Island family of Flores which occupied it.[48]

From there, the Old Goliad Road was clearly marked, as it is today, on into San Antonio. Sitgreaves noted Calaveras Creek "at Canteen's rancho, on a fine stream, with steep banks at its crossing"; then twelve miles to the Salado, and another nine miles to San Antonio, which they reached on September 6.

These alternate ways up from the coast constituted the options open, depending upon seasonal variations, for traffic on the Chihuahua Road, still five years in the future.

[5]

Colonel Hays
Enters the Trans-Pecos

As the Mexican War progressed and its outcome was apparent, farsighted Texans began to realize how much more strengthened their position would be. No longer would they be under the ever-present shadow of Mexican occupation; no longer would they have to base their own economy upon the doubtful fabric of their own fledgling republic, a poorly capitalized, experimental government. Now they would be undergirded by the political and economic structure which most of them had once scorned or chafed beneath, but which had now proven itself through two wars and a half-century of development.

Perhaps most important of all, the United States would not continue to tolerate a lawless and chaotic western frontier, whether the trouble started with their own freebooters, or the Mexican fringe elements, or the increasingly hostile Indians.

Among those who saw their opportunities in this newly dawning era was Samuel A. Maverick, who had comfortably established his family in an eight-room house on the peninsula of Matagorda Bay, shortly after his release from Perote Prison.

In her memoirs, wife Mary A. Maverick wrote:

But after all, the Peninsula was not home to us in the full sense of the word. Mr. Maverick was constantly returning to San Antonio on business, and on each visit he was making new investments and knitting his interest and his sentiments more and more with the life of San Antonio and the surrounding country . . . On the 15th day of October, 1847, with bag and baggage, we left the Point and set off for San Antonio . . . Sunday, October 24th, at 3 P.M. we reached San Antonio and stopped at Aunt Ann Bradley's . . . everything was covered in dust and the heat dreadful. The town seemed much changed since 1842; many strangers had settled here and immigrants were arriving daily . . . We learned that many people were sick with colds and diarrhea, and almost every day somebody died, which left us quite doleful. I recalled our first residence in San Antonio, and it seemed in those days there was scarcely any sickness. Now, all of our children suffered from some illness. [1]

San Antonio was indeed changing, beginning to inherit the complexities of a growing frontier metropolis. As a Spanish Colonial settlement, the population had reached around 3,000 by 1800. The warring factions of the revolutionary period in Mexico had laid a heavy hand on the outpost of San Antonio de Valero, while the battles of Texas's own revolution had again divided and scourged the city, so that at the end of 1836 the widely scattered collection of adobe and stone structures, pleasingly grouped on the plain between San Pedro Creek and the San Antonio River, was occupied by no more than 2,000 people. With the return of some of the Mexicans, the determined digging in of many Texans of United States origin, and the new influx of German immigrants arriving through the Matagorda Bay ports, by 1850 San Antonio had rebounded to a census count of 3,488 persons.

After the signing of the Treaty of Hidalgo in February 1848, Sam Maverick felt free to extend his holdings westward. He remembered the splendid valley of Las Moras, which he had sighted on the way to prison at Perote, and of which the young Ranger Jack Hays told him even more. Mrs. Maverick recorded that

on April 4, 1848, Mr. Maverick left with Mr. Tivy, deputy surveyor, and a considerable surveying party, to have a pet location on Las Moras creek surveyed. He located our headright certificate on the head spring, and Fort Clark is on that tract — he also located much land below that survey. [2]

This tract was only thirty-five miles from the Rio Grande. As the future site of Fort Clark, it was a vital point on the Chihuahua Road and the farthest point west in Texas yet claimed and surveyed by an

American citizen.[3] The closest competitior was Ben Leaton's El Fortín at Presidio del Norte, which he purchased August 18, 1848, an establishment which figures significantly in the later opening of the road into Mexico.

Sam Maverick paid a dear price for his enterprise. While he labored with his surveying crew more than a hundred miles away on Las Moras, his beloved seven-year-old daughter was struck down by a dread "billious fever." She was attended day and night by her agonized mother and by Dr. George Cupples, but despite all their ministrations Agatha sank rapidly.[4] Mary Maverick's memoirs, although written thirty-two years later, still reflect the despair of a pioneer woman left alone with a family subject to the hazards of that day: "Her father was still out on his surveying expedition on Las Moras, and we had no means of communicating with him."

The child died May 9, ten days after the onset of the fever, but Sam Maverick did not learn of his loss until May 26, when he was told by an acquaintance whom he met on the road to San Antonio. Mary wrote:

> He went to the grave and threw himself upon it and remained there until it was dark. No one but God could tell the depth of his anguish . . . He said we should humble ourselves in sackcloth and ashes — and he never removed that sackcloth in spirit whilst he lived — was ever after a sad, changed man.[5]

But the spirit of restless outreach had not seized Sam Maverick alone. Other associates in San Antonio, on Matagorda Bay, in Corpus Christi, and in Gonzales were dreaming once more of a passage to Santa Fe, El Paso del Norte, Ciudad Chihuahua. In this period, also, the United States Army had experienced the frustration during two and a half years of having no practicable communications between its forces in New Mexico and those in San Antonio and the lower reaches of the Rio Grande, below Eagle Pass.

Working in the 1920s and 1930s, a small group of scholars pulled together the threads of activity that had resulted in the veritable opening up of the Southwest in the twelve years between the end of the Mexican War and the beginning of the Civil War. These researchers included Thomas Maitland Marshall of Washington University at St. Louis; H. Bailey Carroll, University of Texas at Austin, whose studies of the Texan-Santa Fe expedition have already been noted; Mabelle Eppard Martin, author of "California Emigrant Roads Through Texas," published in the *Southwestern Historical Quarterly* in 1925; Averam B. Bender, a student of Thomas Maitland Marshall at Washington University, whose "Opening Routes Across West Texas, 1848–1858," appearing in the *Quarterly* in 1933, broadened Ms. Martin's original thesis; and Ralph P. Bieber, also from Washington University's history department, who collaborated with Bender in editing the remarkable journals of Phillip St. George Cooke, William Henry Chase Whiting, and Francois Xavier Aubrey, for the volume *Exploring Southwestern Trails, 1846–1854*, which appeared in 1938. These works, with the documentation from original sources provided by the author-editors, established bases for understanding why and how the sudden burst of activity following the Treaty of Guadalupe Hidalgo finally accomplished what had so painfully been sought for many years.

Bender summarized the push:

> In the twelve years following the close of the Mexican War, the United States inaugurated and conducted an extensive program of exploration in the State of Texas. This was a phase of general policy carried on by the federal government in the entire trans-Mississippi country in the interest of the immigrant, the settler, the soldier, and the merchant. The annexation of Texas, the Mexican cession, and the California gold discovery created new Indian and immigrant problems. The immigrant wave which followed the acquisition of the Mexican cession necessitated the adoption of a definite governmental policy in the Far West.
>
> The federal government acted promptly. Its elaborate program involved: (1) the opening of the Far West to trade and settlement; (2) the survey of routes for Pacific railroads; (3) frontier defense; (4) survey of the southwestern boundary . . .[6]

But while, as Bender says, "the federal government acted promptly," the group of San Antonio entrepreneurs and other South Texas associates acted even more promptly.

After distinguished service at Monterrey and Mexico City in command of the First Regiment, Texas Mounted Volunteers (Rangers who had been incorporated into the United States Army), Col. Jack Hays at war's end had returned to Texas by steamboat from Vera Cruz, debarking at Powderhorn, on Lavaca Bay.[7] After he and his fellow Rangers had been given a welcoming ball, he proceeded on a sort of triumphal tour up through South Texas that ended in San Antonio with as grand a reception as the city could muster. It was inevitable that the San Antonio businessmen, at this propitious moment, should turn to Jack

Hays. They asked him to lead their expedition to seek out and at last establish a practicable road to El Paso del Norte — and to the treasures of Chihuahua.

John Coffee Hays was still only thirty-one after eleven years of violent action on the frontier and was certainly the most renowned and popular officer in Texas.[8] There had been time, between campaigns, for him to pursue his profession of surveying, and he was employed on occasion by the Republic of Texas to make surveys on the frontier. Meanwhile, his brilliant exploits as a Ranger and his qualities of leadership brought him a commission as captain from President Lamar in 1840. Though not always successful in his campaigns — often because of the poverty of support provided by the Republic[9] — his courage, élan, and audacity were unfailing. Walter Prescott Webb said that during this time and "under his leadership, the best tradition of the Texas Rangers was established." [10]

When the San Antonians approached Hays in June 1848, asking him to direct their explorations westward, the idea appealed to him, for he had made up his mind to resign his commission in the United States Army. He could already see that the Rangers faced an uncertain future now that Texas was a state in the Union. Therefore, he would be at liberty for a new venture, even though he had scarcely settled down again with his young wife in the home he had built for her, just before the war, on the corner of Nueva and South Presa streets.

Hays recognized that Texas was no longer a free agent in opening up her frontiers; this should be a part of the larger enterprise which the United States would direct. He suggested that since he wanted to go to Washington to settle up his fiscal accounts as commandant of a volunteer regiment, and muster out, perhaps he could get approval while there for this new enterprise.

The San Antonians agreed with alacrity, and Hays made the long round trip to Washington in June and July. He consulted authorities, presumably the War Department, about opening up the San Antonio-El Paso Road, and "not only did they authorize his proposed exploration of the area, but they also approved his use of Rangers from an outpost." [11]

Immediately upon his return, Hays wrote to Col. Peter Hansborough Bell, new commandant of the Rangers and soon to become governor of the state, asking him to provide military support for this venture into *terra incognito*. Bell responded promptly, saying that he had ordered Capt. Sam Highsmith, with a detachment of thirty-five men on the Llano River, to be ready to join Hays and his men there on August 22.

Highsmith was a bit older than most of his contemporaries in the Ranger service. He was born in Boone County, Kentucky, in 1804; his family moved to Missouri when he was eight. During the 1820s he migrated with his older brother Abijah to Texas; later fought in the Battle of San Jacinto; and thereafter enlisted in the Texas Rangers. During the Mexican War he had served as a captain in Hays's Texas Mounted Volunteers. Of all the men in this new expedition, it might be least expected that he should be the one to succumb to its privations.

The informal party recruited in San Antonio grew to about thirty-five men also. Samuel A. Maverick had given his support to the project; he was one of those who had chosen Jack Hays to lead it, for they were friends of long standing and Maverick had served as a Minuteman under Hays in the early days of the Republic. But Sam Maverick at forty-five was a shattered man since the death of his daughter Agatha. Mary Maverick wrote:

> Col. Hays asked me to persuade Mr. Maverick to go with the expedition. I answered, "Oh, no, he is not well enough for such a hard trip." Then Hays replied, "Don't you see Mr. Maverick is dying by inches? Everyone remarks how gray he has grown, how bent and feeble he looks, and this will be the very thing for him — he always thrives on hardship, and his mind must be distracted from his grief." I recognized the truth and force of this reasoning and that Hays loved him dearly and I set to work to persuade him to go. My husband was quite reasonable, and quickly saw that the trip had become a necessity for him. [12]

Through this the party gained the additional lustre of Sam Maverick's presence, while history benefited by Maverick's terse journal, with his professional surveyor's notes. It is the only surviving day-to-day account of the journey.

Jack Hays recruited several civilian scouts, most notably Richard Austin Howard, who had failed to graduate from the United States Military Academy because he flunked a course in philosophy in his last term. Now twenty-four, he had been improving himself in the frontier's school of hard knocks.

The Hays project was organized as the Chihuahua-El Paso expedition. The understanding was that the entire round trip to El Paso should not be more than 700 miles, and that it should be accomplished in seventy days. This poor intelligence accounts for the deficient logistics — an old, old story. The outfit for the party "included provisions and all necessary supplies . . . As the use of wagons on such an expedition was impracticable, everything was carried on pack mules . . . one to each mess of four men on which to carry equipage and rations for 40 days." [13] They would have been shocked at any idea that these leathery beasts of burden would themselves become part of the rations before any man saw San Antonio again.

The year of 1848 was one of hard times in Texas. Little cash was in circulation, but the San Antonio people had raised some $800 to finance the expedition. Whether this included the supplies, which were "contributed by public subscription," cannot be discerned from the record. On August 27, amid much laudatory publicity in Texas newspapers, the party set out horse- and mule-back for rendezvous with Highsmith's company on the Llano River.[14] Their original intention was to take a northern route up the San Saba and Concho rivers; then westerly across to the Pecos, or Puerco, River.[15] They knew only that Presidio del Norte lay somewhere above the Great Bend of the Rio Bravo — somewhere west of the Pecos, which none had seen.

Maj. John Caperton, lifelong comrade-in-arms with Hays, in furnishing biographical notes on Hays years later, commented about the expedition:

> Up to this time, there was no knowledge of the country lying west of San Antonio de Bejar beyond a distance of 200 miles. Col. Hays had gone as far in his expeditions over this country as any white man had gone, but had never got much beyond the Las Moras River, on which stream he had had fights at various times with the Indians.[16]

In four days the San Antonio contingent reached the village of Fredericksburg. In another day they made it to Highsmith's camp across the Llano from the tiny new German settlement of Castell, the most remote outpost on the frontier and their last touch with civilization until October 18.

In council with Sam Highsmith, the officers reached what, in retrospect, appears a ludicrous conclusion. In his later report to Colonel Bell, Hays explained: "It was deemed inadvisable to go [north] by way of the San Saba at that season [because] of a scarcity of water, and we consequently changed our direction by way of the Las Moras, a river heading about west from this place." [17]

In those days reports frequently used the term "this place," which referred to the place where the report was later being written, rather than the point where the described action had been taken. Las Moras was indeed due west from San Antonio, where Hays completed his report in December. But it was full *southwest* of their camp on the Llano at the end of their fourth day out. Therefore, after having traveled and depleted their rations for seventeen more days, when they finally camped at the springs of Las Moras they were no farther from San Antonio, nor any closer to Presidio, than when they left the Llano.

Aside from the possible shortage of water on the northern route, the only apparent reason for this expensive detour is that when Hays and Highsmith got together and realized how utterly alien to them all was the land northwest of the Llano and the San Saba, especially at that time of the year, they decided they had better cut back at whatever cost to a starting place — the valley of Las Moras — which was at least familiar.

To reach that place, they ascended the south fork of the Llano to its headwaters in the lovely hills above the present site of Rock Springs. Maverick records that this was at a "Paint Rock," half a mile above a spring.[18] They then crossed the rugged divide to the beginnings of the Nueces and moved south down the Nueces Valley.

Jack Hays's biographer, James K. Greer, dwells at length on the story of a buffalo hunt drawn from John Caperton's reminiscences of the leader. This account portrays Hays as performing an astonishing feat of endurance and skill, beyond the capacities of his Indian scouts, in chasing down, on foot, a herd of buffalo and killing several.[19] Greer chooses to place the incident out on the Pecos, when the party was desperately in need of meat. Surely Greer had never seen those magnificently desolate and rocky ravines bordering the Pecos near its mouth: buffalo did not frequent that area in recent centuries, and if any had stumbled down there they would have been as anxious to get out as was Hays. Samuel A. Maverick's laconic journal makes its only mention of buffalo on September 13, the third day of their journeying down the relatively luxuriant valley of the Nueces River. His entire entry reads: "down the Nueces. We killed two or more of the six buffalos — 3."[20] Maverick's last figure, "3," represents miles traveled that day, which jibes with Caperton's account; therefore, evidence supports placing Greer and Caperton's bit of hero worship on the Nueces, September 13.

Now replenished with meat, but "already getting out of bread," as Maverick noted, they struck west two days later, probably in the vicinity of the old Laguna Crossing of the Nueces. This led across rolling

open country toward Las Moras Creek, and while still many miles away
they were gladdened to see lifting above the horizon the twin sugar-
loaf mounds also called Las Moras, which landmark the area. The party
reached the springs on September 17, after spending twenty-one days
on the road and logging 285 miles, though both Hays and Maverick
knew these springs are no more than 130 miles from San Antonio by
the usual route.

After a day's rest, they moved on west, crossing the lands Maverick had surveyed that spring and a creek named after him.

Hays tells of coming next day to the "San Phillips," calling it "a
river as large as the San Antonio." [21] This was the San Felipe springs
and creek, the first mention, so far as known, in Anglo-American re-
portage, though well known to early Spanish explorers. Within a year
the campground at those fine springs was the southwestern hinge of
the burgeoning Chihuahua Road.

From this point the party of seventy men launched out into what
John Caperton in his sketch of Hays called, whether in drollery or in-
nocence, the "terror incognito." They went fourteen miles beyond the
San Felipe, down into the canyon of a stream "almost as large as the
Colorado [of Texas]" and near its mouth upon the Rio Bravo. Though
later travelers almost universally described with enthusiasm the exotic
beauty of that canyon, with its clear, strong flood racing down along
the limestone channels of its bed, Jack Hays's company was too much
oppressed with finding how they could get out of the canyon to linger
upon its charms.

Maverick logged the crossing at "a remarkable ford in the hills,
with beaver," where they climbed up on the high harsh ground of the
divide, traveled fifteen miles along the ridge to a dry camp, and next
day had to descend again "5 miles in horrid ravine down to Devil's
River for water."

Spaniards had marked this river on their old maps as the "San
Pedro," although Hays says that on his maps the surveyors had mis-
taken it for the Puerco. Perhaps it was the next morning after that
painful descent through the horrid ravine, as they now waded and led
their horses for three miles up the channeled limestone and gravel rapids, with convoluted pink cliffs towering on each side, that Jack Hays
exclaimed to his companions: "San Pedro! Men, we shouldn't hang
anything like this on poor old St. Peter. I say, let's call it the Devil's
River."

That was the basis for Maverick's use of the name, the first on record, and as it has been called to this day, although the Lake of Friendship, *Amistad,* now fills the canyon to its brim.

The group found a way out, after those three miles of wading, which was certainly far below Pecan Springs, the source of the river. They climbed up to and across the Pecos divide for what Maverick called twenty-five miles, making another camp without water.

Something of a mystery appears at this point. Richard Howard, the civilian scout attached to the party, is officially credited with having discovered — or rediscovered from the old Spanish days — on this expedition the spring or "well" that bears his name in the wild lands between the dry upper Devil's River Canyon and the Pecos.[22] But Howard's Well lies more than forty miles northwest of the last running water of the river, while Sam Maverick records that the next day, after that dry camp on the divide, they descended fifteen miles to the Pecos River itself, and he underlines: "in great thirst." Clearly, then, they did not find "Howard's Well" on the outbound leg of their journey, and there is equal difficulty in fitting the discovery into their return trip. So important, however, was this well in making feasible a wagon route from Devil's River westward that this narrative must later examine how it came into use.

Return now to Jack Hays, Sam Highsmith, Maverick, Howard, and the rest of the seventy, with horses and pack mules, in the canyon of the Pecos River, somewhere in the northwest of today's Val Verde County. In his report to Bell, Hays said of this period only that "we came to the Puerco, or properly calling it, Pecos. This is a bold, rapid stream, but perhaps not as large as the Devil's river. Its waters are muddy and brackish, and from its mouth for near one hundred miles the face of the country is if possible more rugged and impassable than the last-mentioned river."

But Maverick tells how from the Pecos they struggled, "Out among the hills and ravines, zig-zag — going not more than 5 miles," and then were forced, "after travelling nine hours hard over rocks again to the Pecos." On the fourth day in the environs of the Pecos, Maverick penned his vignette of their crossing the river to "go up crawling like flies, on side of mountain, gaining not over 200 yards." [23]

September 30, after thirty-three days on the trail and yet barely more than 200 miles from San Antonio, Hays had come to realize that the guide Lorenzo was not familiar with the country and was leading them into further trouble. Therefore, having made up his mind to follow his own instinct, Jack Hays plunged desperately across some of the most formidable barrens in all the West. After a three-day forced march of about thirty-one miles in and around rocky ravines, during which for the first time they were reduced to eating one of their pack animals, they reached the Rio Grande on October 2.

The only area where the Pecos and the Rio Grande lie even roughly thirty miles apart is just west of Langtry. Beyond that point, the Pecos comes from the north while the Rio Grande continues for quite a long way right out of the west, and they bear rapidly farther and farther apart. The conclusion is clear, then, that Jack Hays brought his party down to the Rio Grande on that awesome stretch of canyon where the river, running due east, crosses the border between Terrell and Val Verde counties. The expedition was launched by now upon an incredible trek, always within one or two days' agonized march of the Rio Grande (in order to sustain life with its muddy waters), all the way around the Big Bend of the river and up to Presidio del Norte.

On October 3, the day after first reaching the Rio Grande, Hays undertook to get out on higher country, but Maverick recorded that they "intersect[ed] a big trail and followed to the Rio Grande again at a great Indian crossing." This may well have been the mouth of Sanderson Canyon, a huge wash which cuts deeply into the walls of the Rio Grande Canyon.

Two days later, Maverick said they "camped at water hole in rock. Watering with pans . . ." This scanty description fits Indian Well, a strange *tinaja* or natural cistern which lies in Candilla Canyon directly on the Terrell-Brewster county line about six miles from the river. Bev Greenwood, who came through that area with John L. Bullis in 1879, said Indian Well had such a small surface opening that when they found it, it was covered with a slab of rock apparently slid there by Indians to protect or to hide it.[24] Maverick's phrase "watering with pans" sustains this identity, suggesting they had to dip down into the opening to get water for their animals.

At the time they had first reached the banks of the Rio Grande, they had killed and eaten a panther. A week later, Maverick noted, "we begin to eat bear grass." What the early Texans called "bear grass" or "mezcal" is the sotol plant (*Dasylirion leiophyllium*), with a great spread of narrow, spiny blades growing out of a heart, just at the surface of the ground. This moist chunk of immature blades, when stripped bare like a pineapple, was more commonly roasted in a pit in the ground by the Indians and the border Mexicans, while in later years it has been the recourse of many a rancher in surviving a drought, by simply turning the plant over with a grubbing hoe, to expose that head to the livestock. [25]

In this case, Sam Maverick and Jack Hays, bred gently on the plantations of South Carolina and Tennessee, looked with a wary eye upon resourceful Dick Howard as he brewed a soup from the sotol heart. Nevertheless they ate, while gazing wistfully at the next mule. [26]

On October 10, Maverick recorded a more varied diet for the seventy men:

> Kill mule and eat our breakfast . . . Found abundance of fine tunas [the fruit of the prickly pear cactus, the delicacy that had sustained Cabeza de Vaca in the wilderness 300 years before]. Camp at head of Mezcal Canon — sick of tunas. Our mule meat very poor and tough. R. A. Howard's bear grass soup.

Mrs. Maverick, in her comments on the journey afterwards, asserts that she had learned from Hays that her husband "had cheerfully eaten roots, berries, mule meat and polecats, and had chewed leather from the tops of his boots, to keep his mouth moist." [27]

Hays was trying to take his party on a shortcut across the tip of the Big Bend, a venture he had to abandon. In the effort, the party must have found and passed through the notch known as Bullis Gap, named for the great army scout and Indian fighter who used it thirty years later. From there they had to go around the head of Reagan's Canyon, which may have been the basis for Maverick's entry on October 7: "Going W. N. W. Camp on edge of impassable ravine."

Next day, traveling "in worst hills," according to Sam Maverick, they met three Mescalero Apache Indians whom they passed without incident and, following their back trail, came out into the dry bed of a great canyon they called Mezcal Creek. Maverick says they traveled up that canyon for more than two days, or, according to his log, at least thirty miles. Only Maravillas Canyon in that whole area could have offered the party such a lengthy course. A riddle is posed, however, in that Maverick says of the second day's journey up his Mezcal Canyon: "Pictures on walls. Splendid high walls. 16 [miles covered that day]."

Maravillas Canyon certainly rises to "splendid high walls" in its course toward the Rio Grande, but old-timers who have spent their lives in that part of the Big Bend say that no paintings decorate those walls at any point along the Maravillas — any at least that could possibly be seen by a party journeying up the floor of the canyon. But on one of the tributaries, Bear Creek, which with others forms a confluence just above Stillwell Mountain to join and give Maravillas Creek its full strength, such a canyon wall does stand today bearing a highly visible collection of Indian pictographs.[28]

The only possible conclusion, then, is that Hays and party lost the main bed of the Maravillas, strayed three or four miles up Bear Creek, and saw those pictographs. A confusing web of small creek bottoms comes together here in a kind of delta. Trying to continue westward, the wanderers picked a valley heading upstream in that direction — and it led them squarely up against the bluff ridge of the Santiago Mountains where they become the Sierra del Carmen.

In those days the main thoroughfare of the great Comanche Trail crossed that ridge at Persimmon Gap, just as the highway into the Big Bend National Park does today. Local people believe, however, that Hays struck this ridge a few miles south of Persimmon Gap, where a remarkable chasm called Dog Canyon cuts clean through the barrier.[29] Thus Maverick says, on October 10: "Here we are at highest mountains, with horizontal strip of limestone."

Then, without mentioning the canyon passage as such, he says of the next morning that they traveled *up* one and a half miles, while from then on, everything was downhill, when they came "to big trail going S. of W." and camped on a creek running west-southwest, and next day continued "down same creek and over broad plain for ten miles." That description puts them unmistakably down Nine Point Draw and onto the alkali flats of Tornillo Creek, west of the Santiago Range. They must have looked longingly across those shimmering white flats at the rising dark fastnesses of the Chisos Mountains, knowing there must be ample water there — but they were out of reach. Instead they had to head down once more toward the Rio Grande, in great distress.

At the very crest of the party's passage, on October 11, two Indians riding horses and accompanied by a dog had cut off eight horses and mules from Hays's *remuda,* escaping with them. Pushing on south, the strain and privation finally caught up with the expedition's only medic. Maverick noted tersely on the night of October 13: "Dr. Wahm crazy." Continuing desperately, they made thirty miles next day, "breaking down 10 or 15 horses trying to reach water," but had to "camp late at night on stony hill without water." That same dismal night "Dr. Wahm rode off in a fury. Suppose he is lost." At midday on October 14, the advance elements finally reached some water, no doubt a pool in the bed of Tornillo Creek, and sent one party back for the lamed stragglers, with another party searching for Dr. Wahm. On the morning of October 15 they moved a short way to the ford on the Rio Grande where the Comanche Trail — a skein of some twenty parallel pathways — crossed into Mexico.

Both the lame and the searchers stumbled into camp. Somehow in that harsh wilderness, they had found Dr. Wahm, but since they did not tie him, Maverick says they "finally lost the unhappy crazy man in the black ravines." He was given up for dead.

Several accounts aver, however, that friendly Indians found the distraught doctor wandering senselessly, nursed him back to health, and that about a year later he made his way back to civilization.[30]

Somewhere along the Comanche Trail yet another band of Mescalero Apaches had advised Hays that if his party should cross into Mexico, they could follow a road upriver to the ancient village of San Carlos. Seeking that town, they waded the river and followed the big raiding trail eighteen miles into Mexico toward Durango, making camp without food at a spring. Next morning they left the Comanche Road and turned northwestward toward San Carlos. That night, in celebration of the prospect of relief, they killed and ate their fourth pack mule. On the morning of the eighteenth, after only six miles more on the trail, they encountered the welcome sight of an irrigation ditch, or "irrigable creek." This they followed up four miles and found the very old village of crumbling adobes on the opposite bank.

The San Carlos villagers turned out to see these gaunt scarecrows from another world. Colonel Hays, with Caperton and Mike Chevaille, rode over and paid their respects to the *alcalde,* making careful apology for having invaded Mexican territory, but pleading the compulsion of "hunger, the strongest necessity that men could urge." [31] The Mexican official waived the trespass generously and, despite something of a famine in the country, the good people of the *rancheria* plied the starving men that evening and the next day with tortillas and goat milk.

Strengthened and heartened, with a good road pointed out to them up the river toward Presidio del Norte, the Chihuahua-El Paso expedition started out on the morning of October 20, making fifteen miles a day for two days. Three days later, obviously alerted to the presence of Ben Leaton's fort a little below Presidio, they recrossed the river into Texas, making camp "about one mile E. of Fort Leaton." This point must surely have been near the mouth of Alamito Creek, probably at the old village of Loma Pelona, since Maverick records that they stayed there "9 days in old adobe house."

He noted October 23 as their fifty-seventh day on the road, reckoning that they had traveled 747 miles: "418 to where we left the Pecos, and 329 to P. [Presidio] del Norte." As the crow flies, it is only about 210 miles from their jumping-off place on the Pecos to Presidio; this gives some idea of how they meandered to keep in touch with water.

Of Fort Leaton and Ben Leaton himself, more will be told later, but for this encounter from the eastward, let the words of Jack Hays, Sam Maverick, and John Caperton suffice. Hays reported to Bell:

> Six miles below Presidio del Norte on the American side, a gentleman named Leaton has established himself and is engaged in erecting a large fort to protect himself from the Indians. We remained with this gentleman for ten days to recruit our horses, and were furnished by him with supplies to return.

Maverick, more the businessman, added wryly about those supplies: "8 cents per lb. for meal; $16 [per pound] for powder; horseshoe nails $4 per lb." John Caperton embellished the picture somewhat, saying that Leaton

> was a remarkable man who had been all his life in the mountains, knew nothing of government or law, was a law to himself. He had his family there, and his servants. His fort was a considerable enclosure, and he had a small howitzer mounted there. They made him an American flag and presented it to him, and he hoisted it with great pride over his fort, and fired off his cannon, and had a great celebration.

While Quartermaster Ralston was purchasing supplies during the layover, Hays and some of his party visited Presidio del Norte, the old town, which at that time counted some 1,200 residents on the high banks across the river. Once more Colonel Hays tendered his apologies to officialdom for his unauthorized passage up the west bank of the Rio Bravo. Jack Hays was aware that his name, as commander of the Texas Mounted Volunteers in the war just closed, was not popular in Mexico; he prudently made every effort to present the nature of the expedition in its true light.

While in the Presidio-Fort Leaton area, the colonel questioned everyone available about the feasibility of a road on up the Rio Grande to El Paso. No doubt he was told how the Indians, the priests, and the Jumano traders had journeyed up and down that valley for centuries, but he may have neglected to query whether they had used wagons on such journeys. He would have found that they did not — nor could they.[32]

Hays could not have known, while isolated at Presidio in October 1848, that the gold which had been discovered that spring in California would make a through road to the West Coast doubly urgent. So far as the merchants of San Antonio and South Texas were concerned when he left, the ultimate goal of the exploration, as indicated by the name of their expedition, was to open up a feasible road to the silver mines and markets of Chihuahua City. It is curious, then, that there was not a mention in Hays's report nor in Maverick's diary that a reasonably good wagon road did already exist directly from Presidio del Norte up the Conchos River Valley to Ciudad Chihuahua. Since Ben Leaton had a sharp eye for trade, one might have expected him to urge that road upon Hays. But the record is silent.[33]

Hays had great difficulty in "recruiting" [34] the horses, mules, and provisions to meet the barest essentials, and he felt that his men were too worn to undertake the additional hundreds of miles up to El Paso del Norte, especially since that would mean a return trip across the open plains in the dead of winter. Therefore, he concluded that he must return to San Antonio from Presidio, but would scout out an alternate route home that would avoid the horrors of the lower Big Bend.

They set out on October 31. Two possible routes out of Presidio to the grassy highland plains of the present-day Marfa area were available. One went up the Cibolo Creek past where the Shafter silver mines stand today, but the upper reaches of that trail had no water. The other was up the long watercourse of Alamito Creek, the ancient lower Salt Road of the Indians, to the very base of the mountains at Paisano Pass. One could not determine from Hays's report which way he chose, but a definite conclusion may be drawn from Maverick's notation at the end of the second day, when they were twenty-eight miles out, that they were camping "at the foot of a knob which from Leaton's bears N. 55° E." Plotting that on a large-scale map puts the party unmistakably in the Alamito Valley, at the foot of San Jacinto Peak, always a noted milestone on the Chihuahua Road and visible from high ground in the vicinity of Fort Leaton.

This is important, for it does establish that Hays was the first Anglo-American, in scouting out the Alamito Creek route, to use it as a link in the ultimately feasible road to the Gulf Coast. He no doubt got careful advice on this passage from Ben Leaton, for Leaton and his wife Juana Pedraza entrusted to Hays's watch-care their six-year-old son, whom they were sending to school in South Texas.[35]

The records do not show whether the party, coming up out of the headwaters of Alamito Creek, found their way precisely through Paisano Pass, though in that vicinity they did journey within sight of "a very sharp peak," which fits the description of Mitre Peak, a landmark to the north as one emerges from the pass. Then, in the blast of the season's first norther, they were out on the plains. After traveling "two days and nights and four hours" without water, they reached "a spring on the prairie," either León Spring, nine miles west of the present town of Fort Stockton, or the great Comanche Spring, where Fort Stockton itself was established later. It appears that they must have borne far to the northeast from that camp, for when they reached the Pecos on November 10, they were able to recognize they had hit it too far upstream,[36] and Hays said they had to descend the river seventy miles, which required five days, to reach a resting-up camp at Live Oak Creek.

From that pleasant encampment, with its rippling stream of clear, sweet water, ample firewood, and good grazing — soon to be the site of Fort Lancaster — Hays turned the party southeastward, intending to reach the Concho and San Saba rivers. Plotting their course from Maverick's log for the next four days shows that they came up out of the Live Oak and Pecos canyons and passed slightly north of the present site of Ozona, then bore a little south of east to the area just north of the present Sonora. The water holes Maverick noted at their camp on the night of November 24 may have been at those dry-lake depressions which still show in that neighborhood.

The party of seventy, with their horses and mules, had had the frequent experience of reaching a water hole after a long, dry march, only to find that the little pond could not supply that many thirsty consumers. Therefore, huddled in council around their mesquite-root campfire that night in Thanksgiving week, when the temperature at Sonora often falls well below freezing, Hays and Highsmith decided that they should divide forces the rest of the way home. Highsmith and his Rangers would cross northward to the headwaters of the Concho, only thirty miles away, and by that route get to their permanent camp on the Llano. Hays, with his civilians and the little Leaton boy, was to strike southward to the head of the Nueces, then via Las Moras into San Antonio.

So there, reported Hays, "we separated from Captain Highsmith and his men. We regretted to leave them in a somewhat destitute condition, with very little provisions, and horses nearly all exhausted."

Hays tells nothing of the particulars of his journey from that point; Maverick records that, traveling southeast and south-southeast for four and a half days, they reached a pond at the head of the west branch of the Nueces. Scanning that circuitous route, which Maverick has pretty well traced in his log, it appears certain that the party at no time came within twenty-five miles of Howard's Well, and that they were determined to avoid the Devil's River country to which that famous spring leads. Certainly it is possible, though not likely, that Hays might have deployed Howard out on a far-reaching reconnaissance. Only upon that conjecture could be pinned the historicity of Richard Howard's discovering his well during the El Paso-Chihuahua expedition. Far more likely is it that he made the important find the following year with W. H.C. Whiting.

The day the Hays party reached the Nueces, they had an encounter on the trail with two Comanches herding fourteen stolen animals and a captive lad named Phillip. They rescued the boy, recovered the stolen animals, and took one of the Comanches as their own captive. From there they bore down the Nueces but found too much Indian traffic in that valley, so once more pulled out and cut over to Las Moras Springs, not so very far out of their way.

The way home was clear now, and Sam Maverick's spirits were picking up. On December 3 he noted, somewhere just west of Uvalde: "Camp at hole in creek running SE in prime Elm and mesquite lands. [The camp is] 1 mile west of fine running creek, running S, and *first rate* location, timber and land."

But if Maverick and Hays were not worried, San Antonio and South Texas were. No San Antonio newspaper issues from November and early December of that year are available, but other contemporary papers copied the anxious speculation being printed in San Antonio about the Hays expedition.

The natural concern for a popular hero and his friends had by now become infused, also, with an impatient, almost obsessive lust to find that road west. The gold strike on Sutter's Creek in California that year had started a tide rolling which was mild at first, but which by November had become frantic.

The emigrant road from Independence, Missouri, to California was closed by winter storms. Some goldseekers were already embarking on ships to round Cape Horn, a passage that was both expensive and time-consuming. Others landed at the Isthmus of Panama to make a dash through the jungles across Darien and embark once more on coasting ships to the Golden Gate. But many were already seeing, too, that a practicable, all-seasons route ought to be available from the Gulf of Mexico across Texas to El Paso, and then across New Mexico to the gold fields on the wagon road that Colonel Cooke and General Kearney had begun to open up during the Mexican War. But by what route across Texas?

Houston and Austin interests were certain that it should lead through those cities on to the San Saba and across the plains to El Paso. In Corpus Christi, merchants were already impatient of waiting longer to be assured of a road through San Antonio; they were encouraging Gen. William Cazneau in his organizing a wagon train that would go through Eagle Pass to Monterrey and from there — no one knew.[37]

San Antonians were scanning the horizon for their own Jack Hays and whatever word he might bring. He had planned to be back in seventy days, but that time had passed in early November and by the first week in December rumors were flying as to what might have happened.[38]

Finally, Hays did reach San Antonio on the late evening of December 9. The *Corpus Christi Star,* gleaning items from San Antonio newspapers, on December 23 trumpeted:

> We are truly pleased to be enabled to announce to our readers the return to San Antonio of Col. J. C. Hays, who left that place some time in August last for Chihuahua. After encountering innumerable hardships he has reached the place from which he set out. We refer the reader to the following extract of a letter dated San Antonio, 10th instant, and published in the *Victoria Advocate:*
>
> "Col. Hays got in at 9 o'clock last night. He reports verbally that he succeeded in finding the route for a good road to Chihuahua. The Priest of Chihuahua made him a present of a fine mule and sent him word that his people were highly in favor of establishing the road and had lots of cash to buy goods, &c. The party of Col. Hays suffered considerably from hunger, having to eat some of their mules. One man died from hunger, refusing to eat the mule meat. Col. Hays looks in fine health itself."
>
> Before entertaining the belief that "a route for a good road to Chihuahua" has been found by Col. Hays, unless he struck the

Rio Grande near Presidio, we must await a report from the Colonel himself.

That desired account, the text of Hays's report to Colonel Bell, did not reach the *Star* until late in January 1849. The editor printed it in full.[39]

The citizens of San Antonio had turned out joyously to welcome Hays and his coterie with a traditional grand ball and reception. Mrs. Maverick found that the "three and a half months of hardship had done wonders for Mr. Maverick, just as Colonel Hays had thought." But the spirits of all were dashed a few days later with sad news from the Llano concerning Sam Highsmith.

The late Clayton Williams, Sr., of Fort Stockton, historian of the West Texas scene, who recognized Samuel Highsmith as one of the true heroes of frontier Texas, described the final desperate days of the Rangers' trek home, and its tragic aftermath:

> Highsmith's straggling party, astride worn-out horses, moved toward the southern tributaries of the Concho River. An exhausted portion of the party, miles behind those in advance, lay down on their pallets in a thicket for a night's rest. Indians stole their horses, a few saddles, and other equipment. With almost super-human effort, those Rangers on foot overtook their associates. The reunited party reached the Concho. Here their night sentinels fell asleep, and the Indians got away with 13 more horses. Half of the Rangers then were on foot.
>
> Taking turns riding, the Rangers left the Concho and crossed over the divide to the head of Brady Creek, where they were hit by a snowstorm. Their summer clothes in rags, and short of food, the majority of the Rangers shivered in crude shelters, as Samuel Highsmith with a few men braved the storm to get to the Ranger camp on the Llano. Relief was sent to the desperate men on Brady Creek. They got in safely, just 47 days after they left Fort Leaton . . .
>
> Samuel Highsmith, the lion-hearted champion of the cause of Texas settlers, handed his report of the expedition to Col. Bell on December 15. The valiant Ranger contracted influenza, was defeated, and reported to his maker.[40]

In the conclusion of his own report to Colonel Bell, Hays said:

> I had felt the utmost confidence when leaving San Antonio that if we were ever successful in finding a road to Chihuahua it would be by the Las Moras. But at present I am satisfied that the way by the San Saba is preferable . . . There will be nothing to detain a wagon on

this route, except in crossing the Pecos, which is a narrow stream and can be forded except when high. Although I have not examined the whole way to the Paso del Norte, I am satisfied from authority on which I fully rely, that the road can be constructed without obstruction to that place, by ascending the Pecos fifty miles and crossing over to the valley of the Rio Grande . . . A party leaving at this season of the year would necessarily suffer from the cold north winds and would not find as good grass as would be had at any other time. But even now I feel confident the trip might be made. The distance from Matagorda Bay to Paso del Norte cannot exceed 650 miles, the way the road will run, and I am fully satisfied it must be the road to California at all seasons of the year, having every advantage over the Missouri route either as it regards distance, climate, or country.

Although this portion of Hays's written report stated Chihuahua as the objective of his expedition, no further word in the text referred to that Mexican city. The whole emphasis was upon a way to El Paso — a way-station to California. Nevertheless, in interviews which one of his companions gave shortly after his return, that unidentified person did speak in more specific and informed terms about the road to Chihuahua. The Houston newspaper printed on January 12, 1849:

> *Route to Chihuahua* — We have conversed with a gentleman who accompanied Colonel Hays on his late expedition to the Rio Grande to discover a new route to Chihuahua, and we are gratified to find that he positively asserts that the route from Houston to Chihuahua is far superior to any that can be opened from any point on the coast west of the Brazos. He is so fully satisfied of this fact that he intends to return in a few weeks with a quantity of goods to Chihuahua. He will proceed to the head of the San Saba, thence in a direct line to the point of the Pecos River where the Chihuahua Expedition crossed it in 1840; and thence by the route followed by Colonel Hays to the Presidio del Norte. From the latter town to Chihuahua there is a good wagon road leading by San Pablo — the distance from the Presidio to Chihuahua is only 180 miles, by a road practicable at all times for wagons. There is another road which can be traversed only by horses and mules which is only 150 miles.[41]

This information on the two roads from Presidio to the capital of Chihuahua is surprisingly accurate. Why did this unnamed member of the expedition have this information while Hays did not mention it in his report?

Jack Hays was sensing the pressure from gold-seekers — and from the merchants who wanted the "argonauts" to pass by their doorways

— for a workable way to get out to the California gold fields. Indeed, within a few months the doughty colonel would himself be on the way. That same issue of the *Corpus Christi Star* which ran Hays's report in full placed directly beneath it this little gem of nineteenth-century journalism, which reflects well enough the feverish mania that had seized the country:

> The *New York Sun* is particularly eloquent on the subject of the California gold mines. The following is sufficient to give almost anyone the *yellow* fever:
>
> "A million of persons employed on the vast mines would leave space for a million more, and thousands of millions of dollars still leave the soil an inexhaustible fountain of gold. It is not a crevice in the rock, not a vein deep in the earth, but a track, broader than the state of New York, a very empire of gold, glittering from the earth's surface down into its dark bowels. The mire of the river is precious; the rocks are steeped with it to their lips, and far and wide, for three hundred miles in length to sixty in width, wherever the spade is struck, gold, gold, only gold springs forth in perennial abundance.
>
> "It is not the wash of the mountains; not the pebbly plumes of the isolated veins, but a solid earth of gold, reeking yellow, to every man's hand."[42]

[6]

Whiting
Blazes the Way

Viewed in retrospect, Jack Hays's reports on his expedition were not on a par with his otherwise exemplary achievements during a long and useful public career. Both his report to Bell and a shorter one to Secretary of War William S. Marcy,[1] as well as his statements to the press, suggest that he gained reliable knowledge in the course of the expedition that there was a feasible wagon route up the Rio Grande Valley from Presidio to El Paso. This, in fact, was only speculation, and arduous follow-up exploration proved his conclusion incorrect. Nor was his assessment borne out that the "upper road," via San Saba to Comanche Springs, was the best route from San Antonio to that point.

Nevertheless, the party's ordeal and Colonel Hays's unflagging courage in leading it offer another stirring example of the survival of brave men under great privation. The experience provided the needed public glow of achievement to maintain enthusiasm for the great road west.

Maj. Jefferson Van Horne of the Third Infantry, stationed at San Antonio at the time of Hays's return, accepted his recommendations at face value when the colonel gave him a courtesy copy of his report to Bell. Van Horne wrote the adjutant general of the army to that effect

82

on December 18, 1848, enclosing the copy of the Hays report; the major may have been the channel, as well, for the report to Marcy.[2]

Pressure to improve the nation's military stance along the border had, however, already stimulated action in Washington. Secretary of War Marcy on December 10, the day after Hays's return to San Antonio, had signed orders in Washington for Maj. Gen. William J. Worth to proceed to Texas and undertake exploration of the country along the United States side of the Rio Grande to find whether there was a feasible route "for troops, munitions of war, etc." between San Antonio and Santa Fe.[3] General Worth, when established in San Antonio as commander of the Eighth and Ninth military departments, and having studied the Hays and Highsmith reports, on February 9, 1849, detached Lt. William H. C. Whiting of the engineers and Lt. William F. Smith, topographical engineer, to accomplish the directive of the secretary of war.

Their charge was to scout out the trail that Hays had followed to Presidio del Norte, to determine if a military route could be found between El Paso and the Gulf of Mexico that also passed near Austin or San Antonio de Bejar. The orders were clear that if Whiting, as officer in charge, were to find the passage from Presidio to El Paso not feasible, he should return by a more direct route via the Pecos and San Saba rivers.[4]

Though small in number — only fourteen — the escort assigned to Whiting was as compact and carefully chosen for experience as any similar party on record in that era. The nine army enlisted men were "well-versed in frontier life and experienced as woodsmen and hunters." Of two Mexican drovers and foragers, one, a twenty-one-year-old named José Policarpo Rodriguez,[5] known familiarly to the party and thereafter as "Poli" or "Polly," came to win Whiting's admiration as an excellent hunter, surveyor, and tracker.

Whiting's selection of Richard Howard as chief scout was perhaps the most fortunate of all, for he brought with him all the lore of the Hays expedition, its mistakes and its accomplishments, as well as Dick Howard's own formidable talents as a scout. The manner of Whiting's getting together with Howard and Policarpo illuminates the personalities of all three men.

Whiting had received orders to Texas while on engineering duty in Florida. On the long voyage by ship to Texas, young Whiting had plenty of time to cogitate on how he, at the age of twenty-four and totally new to the western frontier, might find men with savvy necessary to offset his own lack of experience. Billy Whiting did not lack self-confidence; it was that very quality of being able to recognize his needs that gave strength to his makeup.

His ship arrived early in January at Corpus Christi, a village of 600 souls. Whiting strolled through the town to get a feel for the new land where he had just set foot. As fate would have it, Dick Howard, who never lay over to rest, had taken a surveying assignment on the coast immediately upon his return to San Antonio with Hays. He brought along Policarpo, and they thrashed around the swamps of Copano Bay through the Christmas season. When they got low on rations, early in January, they went into Corpus Christi and were buying provisions in one of the few stores the town boasted, when a familiar voice spoke in Howard's ear: "Dick! What are you doing here?"

Howard turned to recognize his former West Point classmate, the shining light of the Class of '45, natty now in his traveling uniform, with first lieutenant's bars on his shoulder. Policarpo, many years later, recorded the conversation which followed. Well aware of his mud-soaked boots and three-week growth of beard, Howard grinned and said,

"Hello, Billy! I'm surveying. What are *you* doing here?"

"I'm going on a long trip, Dick. Reporting to San Antonio to get ready; then I'm going through to Paso del Norte to see if a road can be opened up through that country."

No doubt Howard, in amazement at the coincidence, told Whiting of his own recent experience with Jack Hays. Whiting, who in school had liked this practical, stubborn Mississippian who couldn't cope with the cerebral intricacies of philosophy, saw he had found his man.

"Come and go with me, Dick! I'll pay you well."

"Why, I'm surveying here, making money."

"Well, come along with me; I'll give you good wages and you can see the country and locate land, if you want to. It's a wide-open country, out there at El Paso."

"What'll you give me?"

"Three dollars a day and found."

"If I go, I'll want to take this boy, too," nodding at Polly, who stood near, drinking in the conversation. Whiting turned to take in the sturdy figure, the open countenace, and flashing black eyes of Policarpo Rodriguez.

"What can he do?"

"Why, he can do more than I can. He can hunt, and he can find

water. He can do most anything in the woods. He'd be mighty useful on your kind of trip."

"I'll take him."

"What'll you pay him?"

"Two dollars a day."

"Will you go, Polly?"

"I'll go if you go, Dick."

"We're going, son." [6]

Throughout W. H. C. Whiting's subsequent reports he com-
mended Howard's performance.[7] Whiting's second in command,
William Farrar Smith, a native of Vermont, was graduated from the
military academy also in 1845, entering the topographical engineer
service as brevet second lieutenant. He reached Texas in early 1848
to engage in mapping and exploration along the southern Rio
Grande, and so had had some brief service of that nature before the
venture with Whiting.[8]

Blessed indeed was William Henry Chase Whiting to have this
able team to back him up on a venture parallel to that which had almost destroyed the intrepid Colonel Hays and party only a few months
earlier — for he himself had never even been west of the Mississippi
until a few weeks before. Yet "Little Billy," as his Confederate troops
later called him in affection, decorates the often ill-starred annals of
southwestern exploration as one of the most engaging, discerning, and
successful personalities of the frontier era.

Born in Biloxi, Mississippi, to army parents from Massachusetts,
young William received his secondary education at the English High
School in Boston, entered Georgetown College in the District of Co-
lumbia at the age of fourteen, and graduated in 1840 first in his class.
Appointed to the United States Military Academy in 1841 at the age
of seventeen, he led his class upon graduation July 1, 1845, with a
higher average than attained by any previous student at West Point.[9]
Now, after three years' service with the Corps of Engineers in Florida,
Whiting was transferred to the military department at San Antonio.[10]

None of this background, save perhaps the reputation of Boston's
English High School, would lead one to expect the literary flavor that
embues the journal he kept of his expedition across the totally new —
to American eyes — wilderness of the Davis Mountains and the Rio
Grande above Presidio. He perceived and recorded through the eyes of
excited, impressionable youth, yet in a style controlled by soldierly
discipline.

In one passage, the reader knowing of young Whiting's subsequent history feels a stab of pathos in his wistful comment: "Northward appeared the symmetrical heights of Sierra Blanca, and far away to the northeast, valleys and mountains which we had never seen but promised ourselves one day to explore." [11]

For Whiting never returned to the Big Bend, though he continued for some years with the Corps of Engineers, conducting useful reconnaissance in other parts of Texas and in opening wagon roads through New Mexico to California. He cast his lot with the Confederacy in February 1861, winning recognition as one of the most able engineers in the Southern service. Wounded during a Federal fleet's bombardment of Fort Fisher, North Carolina, in January 1865, near the end of that melancholy conflict, Brig. Gen. W. H. C. Whiting was taken as prisoner to Governor's Island, New York City, where he died of his injuries March 10, 1865, at the age of forty-one. [12]

On the late afternoon of February 21, 1849, though, when Whiting jogged out of Captain Eastman's camp at Fredericksburg with fifteen men now, besides himself, it was a launching of high adventure for the young man who had so recently arrived on the frontier. He knew that no white man's dwelling lay between them and Presidio del Norte. [13]

He wrote that through the good graces of Captain Eastman, he employed "another man, William Howard; he had been out with Hays. We now number sixteen, including Lieutenant Smith, Dick Howard, the two Mexicans, my servant, and myself." [14]

As they passed beyond the Llano River country and up Comanche Creek, three days later, Whiting recruited the same Delaware Indian scout who had served with Hays the year before: Jack Hunter. They ascended Comanche Creek to a high divide between it and the San Saba, crossed and came down into that valley where, on Bowie Creek, a tributary, they camped near the gloomy ruins of the old San Saba Mission. Their route from there lay all the way up the San Saba Valley, beyond the head springs, to a series of ponds, about where Fort McKavett was later located. There they climbed out of the valley onto the high plains, leaving, as it turned out, the last water they were to find for three days. Highsmith had come home that way just the past December, and Whiting counted on finding water at ponds reported by that Ranger. Howard homed the party directly to the location of the ponds — but they were dried up.

Soon they reached Hays's trail, and again Dick Howard and the Delaware, Jack Hunter, expected to find water at ponds they had used only three and a half months before — but they, too, were dry.

On the night of March 4, at the end of their second day without water, Whiting wrote: "We . . . camped in the dry bed of a creek or arroyo. Our animals began to show signs of suffering. Few of them grazed much, and we ourselves felt far from comfortable."

His entries for March 5 deserve a place here, as an articulate man's account of what it was like to struggle ahead into the unknown, on the very brink of collapse from thirst:

> We moved breakfastless, at daylight. Our march, now become painful and almost insupportable, was continued until twelve, each place where those who had been with Hays expected water, having none . . . at half-past five again halted in the bed of a dry creek, where some fresh wild rye promised a little help to the train, now nearly broken down.
> . . . The road has been fine, but has the curse of thirst upon it. At twenty minutes past seven we were again en route. Judging that we could not be far from the Pecos or its tributaries and knowing that another night without water would set us afoot, it was thought best to push on. How weary were the miles of that last march. Silent, unmurmuring, each man rode on, his weary mule unable to make more than a mile and a half an hour. We took an old trail and traveling through a canyon, or ravine, about S. 60° W., at half-past twelve the grateful sound of rippling water reached our ears.[15]

Policarpo relates of that moment:

> there was a high bank, but the mules and men ran right over it and plunged into the water. The lieutenant called to us that we were in as much danger, now that we had found water, as we were before, if we drank too much. I drank about a quart and stopped; later I drank more. We were so tired and broken down that we turned the mules loose, and we all lay down to sleep.[16]

Whiting noted that they were "encamped on the west bank of Live Oak Creek, a little tributary of the Pecos. Our day's march has been over 42 miles, extraordinary ride, considering our animals." Dick Howard had given Whiting the compass reading that would home them in on the campground the Hays party had so much enjoyed the previous December, and Polly said, "He held us on the course."[17]

Whiting set a leisurely pace for the next several days, to let the horses and pack animals recover somewhat from their ordeal. Two miles above the mouth of Live Oak Creek on the Pecos, he constructed a temporary footbridge from logs carried out of the oak groves on the creek. The bridge was situated at a point where the narrow rushing stream divided into three little islands. They proceeded, then, three days up the Pecos.

It was along here that the party found and Polly captured a fine mare which Dick Howard and Jack Hunter identified as that of Dr. Wahm, who had wandered away from the Hays party almost six months before, unbelievably at a point more than 125 miles away, as the crow flies.

The second day, also, they encountered a family of Lipans, headed by the old chief Capote, who approached cautiously, conferred awhile, and then took off up the river, proposing to bring his great chief back for a conference. But Whiting continued on Capote's trail, and on March 12, the fourth day out from Live Oak Creek, struck the Comanche War Trail where it crosses the Pecos and heads southwest. Whiting found it much the same in appearance as Hays had, more than a hundred miles to the southwest: "Close together, twenty-five deep-worn and much-used trails made a great road, which told us that this was a highway by which each year the Comanche of the North desolate Durango and Chihuahua." They followed it that evening until they came to and camped at Escondido Spring — the one west of the Pecos, not to be confused with one sometimes found, hidden, as its name implies, between Howard's Well and Live Oak Creek.[18] The one Whiting mentions, beyond the Pecos, was more frequently called by later parties "Tunas Spring," at the head of Tunas Creek.

Next day they camped early at what Whiting called Awache Spring, later corrupted to Comanche Spring, where Fort Stockton was founded. Today the springs are dry, depleted by heavy irrigation from deep wells through all that country, but those early wayfarers marveled at the "clear gush of water which bursts from the plain, unperceived until the traveler is immediately upon it, and soon swells in a clear running brook abounding in fish and soft-shell turtles." Evidence was at every hand, in firesites and scattered bones, that the Comanche used it as a frequent camping place on their trail.

One day later they found traces of Connelley's wagon trail to Presidio, following it westward until it pointed them, nine miles out, to León Spring, much like the Awache.

Whiting chose from here to continue somewhat west of north toward a looming purple mass of mountains before them, rather than turn southwestward along the trail by which Connelley and Hays had come up from Paisano Pass. No doubt he was drawn by the likelihood of water in the mountains. The result was a very useful probe, for the first time by Anglo-Americans, into what was named later the Davis Mountains. It also brought them into a fearfully dangerous confrontation with an overwhelming horde of Apache warriors.

On the afternoon of March 17, as they entered the foothills of those mountains, the party met, on trail, an Apache family. Whiting says only,

> We gave them a little tobacco, and they went on their way well pleased, but not before the old Indian had set the grass afire. This looked ominous {it indicated he had set a signal} and we proceeded cautiously, Smith, Howard, and the Delaware scouting in advance. [19]

That was all Whiting told of the encounter. Policarpo put it in a different perspective:

> We came suddenly upon an old gray Indian with four or five squaws and a boy . . . the boy ran off into the bushes and stood looking as wild as a scared buck. The squaws stood still, with their mouths open as if struck dumb and paralyzed. The old Indian commenced muttering and turning around as if making some incantations. He lifted an old blanket on two ramrods and waved it back and forth, all the time muttering. He then stooped down and gathered handsfuls of dust and rubbed them on his breast . . . He bellowed like a bull . . . {Apparently this was his death chant in the face of expected massacre by the whites.}
>
> I thought I would speak to him in Spanish and I called, "Don't be afraid; we will not hurt you."
>
> He quickly replied in good Spanish, "I do not know and never knew that fear is. What do you want here? This is our country; what are you after?"
>
> One of our party, Brady, said in English, "Let's kill the old fool and the squaws and go on."
>
> "No," said the lieutenant, "we will not harm them. The old man is making no attempt to hurt us, and we will let them alone. My orders are not to fire first on any Indian."
>
> "Orders? What are orders here in these wilds? I say let's kill them."
>
> "Brady, I obey orders everywhere. These Indians shall not be hurt."
>
> The old Indian, suspecting that his end was near, said in Spanish, "You can kill us, but you will soon be ground to dust."

"And who will do it?" said we.

Gathering up a handful of dust and pointing to the mountains he said, "These mountains are as full of Indians as my hand of dust, and they'll make powder and dust of you."

[Policarpo sparred along with the old man in conciliatory manner. Finally] . . . he seemed convinced and came a little nearer. His next question was, "Have you got any tobacco?"

"Yes, come and get it." He came up, a tall grizzly old Indian, and we gave him tobacco. The squaws came up also and got tobacco. But one of them had set the prairie on fire. I said, "What does that mean?"

"It is to call the Indians here, and then you'll tell what you are after." [20]

After that last thrust, the two parties went their separate courses, Brady cursing because the Indians were not shot. Perhaps Whiting mentioned the encounter so briefly in his report because he was unwilling to put on record the murderous intent of his man Brady.

Within the hour, catastrophic developments crowded so close and fast upon the little party that W. H. C. Whiting's own words are best, for only this literate observer could tell it so well. [21]

. . . our scouts came galloping in from the front, closely pursued by a larger band of Apache, and simultaneously we were enveloped front, rear, and left flank by five different parties. Issuing from every gorge hard by, the painted devils came crowding up at full speed, and looking about us, we could see them on every hill . . . On our right was a little recess between two spurs of the boundary ridge of the valley. Wishing to avoid, if possible, a collision, yet if obliged to fight to do it to the utmost, I remained alone among them, while Smith and Howard and the party moved gradually to this point, extricating themselves coolly from their hostile neighbors. They pushed close on me and on the party. To gain a little time for the men to tie their mules together and make their few preparations, I called out to the chiefs to stop and parley. They came out, one an old and portly man, his hair in long plaits, his countenance the only one among the painted ugliness that had anything pleasing in it. He appeared influential; he was not so fierce in his demeanor. Another, Gomez by name, the terror of Chihuahua and a byword in Mexico, [22] a well-made fellow, apparently about thirty or thirty-five years old, dressed something like a Mexican and speaking excellent Spanish, was hostile and insulting and evidently desirous to fight us.

They sternly demanded who we were and whether we came to the Apache country for peace or war. I answered Americans, en route for Presidio. We came peaceable; if we remained so, depended on them.

In the meantime, the mules had been tied up, their heads together; and in front of them appeared the Texans, squatted to the ground, their mouths filled with bullets, and their faces showing every variety of determined expression . . . Howard, more fluent in Spanish than I, came down to interpret . . .

Gomez insisted we should go to their camp, adding if we didn't move, he'd make us; he called out: You are afraid. But the defiant reply of our intrepid young guide and interpreter, and the significant cocking of pistols and rifles which accompanied it, changed the tone of the . . . crowd . . . the chiefs, to Gomez' great dissatisfaction, agreed to my demand that before conference they must call off their people and come up unarmed. They did so. It was agreed [then] that they should precede us to the springs hard by, where they were encamped; we would follow, take our position, and decide our future relations by a council.

Cautiously and with apprehension on the part of my men of treachery from the savages, we followed the yelling bands . . . Two hundred Apache, superbly mounted, set off by their many-colored dresses, their painted shields, and hideous faces . . . We came shortly upon a spring of cool, clear water issuing from a hillside.[23] Here was the *caballada* of the Indians and their large drove of cattle, all, of course, with Mexican brands.

We took our posts in a little rocky gully which seemed, in a treeless valley, to offer the best chance [for escape]. Each man, unsaddling his mule with one hand while the other held his rifle, placed his packs together; and closed we sat down, our movements curiously watched by the Indians. Gomez, riding up, insultingly demanded why we made no fires, why we didn't scatter and collect firewood (here very scarce), and go to cooking. But observing his band still mounted, their bows still strung, he was answered that we held enough wood in our hands; and we all remained together, gloomy and almost despondent of escape.

At dusk the five chiefs came down for powwow. They wanted a statement of United States intentions toward them, and Whiting, seeing that two hundred warriors against thirteen armed men pretty well held the cards, made his interpretations as mild and innocuous as possible.

The portly old chief, Cigarito, accepted this earnest of peaceable intentions, saying at the conclusion of an oration, "I live in these mountains; my relations and my tribe are here. We wish to be undisturbed and to be at peace with your people. I and my band are friends of yours." The others were of the same mind, save Gomez, who remained truculent throughout. The chiefs, concluding the council, repaired to their lodges and their *caballada,* while that small probe of the United States government, hundreds of miles from any support, settled in their places among the rocks, in the darkness, supperless, their arms in their hands as they lay tense and sleepless.

On the morrow, the soldiers learned from a Mexican captive they engaged in conversation that all the chiefs had held a war talk after the council, and that only the solid opposition of Chiefs Cigarito and Chino Guero[24] prevented Gomez from attacking the army group as they lay in darkness at their camp. Whiting knew it was high time to move on. After a hasty and meager breakfast, they saddled up, supplied with part of a beef from the Indians. Gomez demanded their ammunition, saying that if they were friends of the Apache, they would not need it. He got no ammunition from the Texans.

Cigarito offered to guide them as far as his town, and said one of his men would be provided to show them the way out of the mountains. Whiting accepted gratefully.

The chief and his warriors led the party far up into the mountains, to his own town of some twenty-five lodges, with a great *caballada* grazing on the nearby slopes. They made camp there. That afternoon Whiting and Howard visited the town and entered Cigarito's lodge, the most imposing of the group. There they had further talks with the old chief. Cigarito was anxious to be disassociated from Gomez and his warlike intentions. At his request Whiting gave Cigarito a note addressed to General Worth which attested to the chief's helpfulness.

They prevailed upon a distrustful young brave on a magnificent horse to lead them to a trail which would take them out of the mountains southward — but they accomplished this only by paying him with two blankets that he coveted. He took them far up the creek they called Perdido, showed them a towering peak, and said that their road would pass at its foot, with plenty of water. The young brave then turned his horse and raced back down the valley to join his fellow Apaches.

By nightfall Whiting was entering a "splendid defile," with water everywhere, and there they camped. Daylight showed them a lovely little stream flowing through the gorge among trees and mountain meadows. Anxious as they were about the troubling likelihood of ambush by Gomez, Whiting and his companions took time to marvel at a luxuriant growth of "wild roses," the first the young Easterner had seen in Texas. These were actually the indigenous "Apache Plume," not a true rose.[25] But the explorers promptly dubbed the gorge "Wild Rose Pass" and Policarpo offered the Spanish name "Limpia" for the limpid stream. These names were adopted by following parties over the years and are preserved for posterity by bronze plaques on the highway which cuts across Wild Rose Pass.

More serious matters than roses were pressing on that March morning in 1849. On the horizon behind the explorers, alarm smokes and signal smokes were rising, and they were being answered ahead from the south. Whiting was sure that Gomez expected him to take the trail out of the canyon to the south and there intersect the "Presidio trail" through Paisano Pass to the Alamito Valley. The lieutenant was determined to steal a march on his foe.

In the afternoon, after coming out into high, broad uplands where the Limpia Canyon turned sharply right and rose into the mountains, they made camp at a lagoon in a great grove of cottonwoods (on the northern outskirts of present-day Fort Davis). They barely took time to note that Comanches, not Apaches, had inscribed many crude painted figures on smoothed portions of the tree trunks.

Whiting ordered his men to go about their chores, staking out horses with all appearances of preparing for the night. As darkness gathered, they built campfires, but the men had carefully put their packs in order and eaten a quick bit of supper as they worked.

After dark, with the fires still burning brightly, the party withdrew into the shadows, then mounted and stole off out of the canyon. "No man spoke," Whiting wrote.

> I may live a long time yet, but I shall never forget the still and oppressive hours of that somber march. The night was clear in its cold starlight. The wind swept by over the bleak plain in fitful and furious gusts from the west; to the eastward above the hills of the pass rose the lurid glare of the gathering fires of the Apache. Anxious and with senses keenly alive to every sound, we moved in close order over the plain, listening each moment for the Indian whistle and the rushing of his horses' hoofs. We had left the trail as an additional precaution and were steering a west course. [To intersect the head of Cibolo Canyon rather than southerly to Paisano Pass.]
>
> About eleven, on our left, a brilliant fire suddenly flashed into light from the summit of a lofty peak. The whispered words "a signal," "a signal," ran through our party. We knew that our movement was discovered. The lurking spies about our camp had found

we had gone and had made all speed to their signal hill. How intense
the excitement of the next two hours! That fire flashing on our left;
while every little space the dark figures distinctly visible, would pass
between us and the light, heaping on the brush and feeding the
flame. Answering back in the east were the mountains, lit up with a
long red line of fire. I moved upon the dark outline of a hill before
us, which promised some shelter from the wind (now blowing a chill
gale) and perhaps defense and rest. At half past one we reached it and
found the rocks at its base a fine natural work. Here, without water,
weary and desperate, we lay down upon our arms. No fires were lit
and the tired sentinels kept up their watch undisturbed.

They had escaped. Four days later, having traversed the Cibolo Creek
through its length, they were at Fort Leaton.

This earliest encounter in the Davis Mountains has been presented in detail, for it was one pregnant with the fate of the Chihuahua
Road. One false move, one inflammatory ill-chosen word, and young
Whiting with his dozen armed men almost surely would have been
snuffed out. The shock and mystery of their loss would have been a severe hindrance to the opening of the Trans-Pecos. But Whiting's common sense, his reliance on the cool and informed authority of Dick
Howard, and the whole group's sauciness in extricating themselves,
make their passage stand as one of the brighter moments in western exploration.

If the party had followed Brady's impulse to kill the old man they
first met, who turned out to be the father of one of the chiefs, there is
no doubt that when the murder had been discovered, Whiting's entire
party would have been killed without mercy. Indeed, the record shows
that in the entire length of their round-trip journey, through many
precarious brushes with Indians, Whiting's command fired not one
shot against the Indians. If more men like William H. C. Whiting
had been on the frontier in those early days, its history during the next
thirty years might not have been so sordid and bloody.

The expedition's reception at Fort Leaton was on much the same
order as that enjoyed by the Hays party six months before: overwhelming hospitality, every evidence of total cooperation in resupplying its
provisions and train — but enormous prices for everything they had to
buy. Whiting did not think this unreasonable for, as he wrote, "Mr.
Leaton has to supply himself totally from Chihuahua. The neighboring
village [Presidio, across the river in Mexico] is a poor, stricken town,
and the journey into Chihuahua is one of no common peril."

After a visit to the commandant of the presidio itself in that Indian-ravaged old town, Whiting as the first regular army man to study the area concluded in his report:

> Fort Leaton will become an important site to the United States in view of the treaty stipulation and the Indian aggressions. It will make a convenient post, or depot, and refuge for the roving camps of dragoons which must be placed upon the great warpath. Presidio is at the western part of that large bend of the Rio Grande where most of the passes into Mexico exist. It is in convenient striking distance, also, of the upper passes of the Apache. With a proper and efficient system of mounted troops, heavy blows will at one time [or] another be struck from this post. It will also become the customhouse for the Chihuahua trade, destined to pass, henceforth, if I mistake not, not by Santa Fe, but from New Orleans and the Southern states. It appears to me one of the most important places on the Rio Grande.[26]

Although Leaton cautioned against the extreme danger of likely encounters with the numerous tribes of Apaches wintering in the valley north of Presidio, Whiting pressed on with his plan to complete that leg of his assignment, up to El Paso del Norte. After only five days of rest and rehabilitation, and that largely consumed with refurbishing their tack, outfitting the new animals to replace those that had to be surveyed, and recruiting as an additional guide John W. Spencer, one of the three or four original Anglo pioneers of the area, they moved four miles up the river on the east bank for a starting point. Leaton spent the last night with them, and Whiting was moved once more by Leaton's hospitality and goodwill when the latter sent along his favorite man as added protection.[27]

Whiting's progress up the Rio Grande through the next twelve days, with diligent reconnaissance, brought him to the conclusion that a wagon road from Presidio up the river to El Paso was not economically feasible because of high canyon walls often pressing upon the stream with impassable rocky ravines and hills back from the river. This finding was integral to eventual decisions on the route to El Paso and beyond. And it lent more urgency on the need to develop a road from Presidio to Ciudad Chihuahua.

Proceeding with great caution along the river, the explorers were fortunate, on the fifth day, to find the great winter quarters of the Apache vacated. Whiting, in some awe, noted that the hundreds of deserted lodges, the evidence of large droves of cattle and horses, "showed how extensive a band dwelt here — enough to have rubbed

out our little party. This is a winter town. This nomadic tribe, subsisting almost entirely on the spoils of the unhappy race which they regard
as slaves, move into the lofty recesses of the mountains during the
spring and summer months." [28]

A few days later Whiting and party emerged from the narrow,
torturous defiles of the river passage into the broad farming valleys
where lay the old Spanish-Indian towns of San Elizario, Socorro, and
Ysleta, the latter named for the river island on which it was situated.
They refreshed themselves there with the produce of that area: eggs,
milk, and excellent small loaves of wheaten bread. And at last, on the
evening of April 12, "the party was encamped near the Santa Fe road,
opposite the town of El Paso at a place known as Ponce's Ranch." [29]
They had concluded the first planned, successful probe from the south
by Anglo-Americans to establish contact with the great artery from the
north, the Santa Fe Trail.

Safely bedded down at Ponce's Ranch, Whiting reviewed soberly
and with thankful heart his situation at this

> terminus of our outward march. For fourteen days we had toiled
> among the wild mountains of the Apache. Many of our animals, one
> by one, had given out. Few will ever know, none may realize, that
> march of this little party, regarded by those behind us as moving to
> certain destruction . . . The numerous [Apache] towns we passed
> upon the river justified the forebodings of the people at Presidio,
> taught by sad experience the nature of those who dwell in them. We
> owed it to their fortunate absence that we now rejoiced in the sight
> of houses, pleasant vineyards, and green wheat fields. [30]

If this book were to serve no more than to help upset gallant Billy
Whiting's modest prediction as to the impact of his argosy, it would
be worthwhile. No part of the frontier was easily won, and these men
deserve a secure place in the annals of its winning.

Whiting soon found that it was impossible to resupply his train
from the meager resources at hand. He learned, however, that Lt.
Delos B. Sackett of the First Dragoons was stationed at Doña Ana,
forty miles upriver. By happy chance, also, he found in the El Paso area
the noted adventurer Capt. Henry Skillman, who had fought with
Alexander Doniphan at Sacramento, and who appears later in this story
as stageline operator and driver. Whiting now employed Skillman to
make an express ride to Doña Ana to apprise Sackett of his presence
and to plead assistance in getting provisions for their return journey.
Skillman got back in three days with Sackett's letter assuring help as

soon as his supply train arrived at Doña Ana from Missouri. That might well have been a matter of weeks or months, but by good chance Sackett arrived only two days later with the needed supplies.

Sackett was from the same Class of '45 at the academy that had graduated Smith and Whiting, which gave the latter occasion to note in his journal that Sackett "received from Smith, Howard, and myself that delighted welcome which officers meeting far from their homes always extend to each other, especially when, as now, all four had been companions and classmates at West Point." [31] Whiting thereby gracefully sidestepped mention of Dick Howard's status, including him in the circle as if, indeed, he wore the class ring.

After much inner debate and no doubt counsel from these trusted associates, Whiting had decided that his inability to endorse the route from Presidio to El Paso mandated that he should scout out a more direct road back to the Pecos. He had, however, left valuable papers, baggage, and several fine animals at Presidio for safekeeping. Henry Skillman volunteered to strike off downriver, accompanied as far as Presidio by William Spencer and two other men, recover the goods left there, and cut across country to rejoin Whiting on the Pecos.

Whiting, on Howard's advice, would move down the Rio Grande only so far as the neighborhood of the Apache towns. Here, on their trip upriver, they had cut the trail of their old enemy, Gomez, as he left winter quarters for the Davis Mountains, where they had confronted him. They planned now to follow Gomez's trail through totally unknown country to the Limpia Canyon, and from there head back to the Pecos and down to Las Moras.

They found that Gomez had turned away from the Rio Grande farther downriver than they expected, leaving towering Eagle Mountain on their left. He had not gone up Glenn Greek, which might have seemed an obvious choice, but chose an outlet twenty miles below there. (A little farther down and across the river are the remains of the old village of Porvenir, dominated today by the Misión Iglesia Bautista, sponsored by Texas Baptists.)

The creek Gomez had followed — to be followed also by Whiting — is unnamed on any local map, but a rocky ranch road now climbs up its course, over a ridge, and into the wide valley of Van Horn Creek. Quite certainly this was the route that Whiting followed, for he describes near that ridge a "singular rock coming up sharp to a point and apparently a column of basalt," which he called "the Needle," as it is still called. After crossing the winding ridge of the valley and reaching its summit, he wrote, "to our great joy, the Sierra Diablo unexpectedly broke on our view, distant about thirty miles from us with a level prairie extending to its base." [32] This was Lobo Valley immediately beneath him.

Whiting had found an upper road from the plains to the river, perhaps not the best, but one that might be followed all the way to El Paso del Norte. He even, at this point of discovery, had some prescience of the eventual route of the wagon and stage lines, the railroad that followed, and the teeming highways of today, for, speaking of the grassy plain before him, he noted "this prairie is part of a very extensive valley lying between the Rio Grande range and the Sierras, and extending from the Cibolo below to a high range of mountains to the northward, probably the Guadalupe. Its appearance in that direction confirms the idea of a pass toward the Sierra Blanca." He was precisely right.

They struck off across that plain to the very heart of the Davis Mountains, floundered for a couple of days in the formidable defiles of their western ramparts, but eventually found their way once more to the head of Limpia Canyon and their former campground among the cottonwoods. Here they saw that Gomez and his tribe had camped at the remains of Whiting's own fires, upon discovering the white men's escape, and had added Apache decorations to the surrounding tree trunks — scurrilous graffiti relative to the army's failure to stand and fight. The men called this "Painted Camp," and that name or its variant, "Painted Pass," stuck for a long while.

In early October 1854, when the army decided that more forts were needed to protect the growing tide of commerce and immigration, Col. Washington Seawall stopped at Painted Camp and was followed by Gen. Persifor Smith, commanding, Department of Texas. Seawell felt that he had found a suitable site for a post. General Smith, on October 23, 1854, issued Order No. 129 to Colonel Seawell, from "Painted Camp on the Limpia," directing him to establish the camp as Fort Davis. The site picked was actually a mile or so away. [33]

Whiting chose, on his return trip, to exit the mountains by Limpia Canyon. They were subjected to a fearful hail storm, an experience which was repeated two days later as they reached Comanche Springs.

Leaving Escondido Spring the next day, they had a bristly encounter with a party of thirty Lipans, who were at first disposed to fight, but backed down under Howard's stern reception.

They reached the Pecos on May 6 and turned down its valley,

Whiting at this time becoming anxious about the fortunes of Captain Skillman, detailed to come up from Presidio and meet him. The valley was in the full dress of spring, but the mosquitos and gnats were intolerable. When the party reached their old camp near the mouth of Live Oak Creek, they found that their little footbridge had been washed away by a rise in the river, but otherwise there was no change and no indication that anyone had been there since March. This was the point established for rendezvous with Skillman. Whiting decided that he must leave a note there at the appointed spot and push on, but with much concern about the plainsman's fate.

Finding well-established trails down the west bank of the Pecos, Whiting chose to follow these for a while on a southerly heading. The first day's march was easy enough, but there the valley played out, the canyon pinched together between walls, and further progress along the river was not practicable.[34]

As the men rigged lines across the river to transport their gear to the east bank, they were relieved to see the brave Skillman and his party arrive with the horses, baggage, and provisions.

Skillman had met with Gomez and learned that

> the wily chief, outwitted by the events of the nineteenth and twentieth of March, had, after our escape, moved down to the vicinity of Presidio. Well knowing that he deserved but little at the hands of Americans, and fearing our approach with stronger forces, he made a treaty with Skillman to pass through his whole tribe unmolested. He manifested great anxiety on the part of his people to be friendly with the United States, and begged to be recommended to General Worth's consideration. He will be![35]

The treaty did not last, however, for Gomez raided wagons and settlements from his eyrie in the Davis Mountains for years to come.

The combined party, strengthened with fresh provisions, now struck southeastward, from their point eighteen miles below Live Oak Creek, up a toilsome canyon. They came out upon the elevated table lands, where there was good grass, but they nooned without finding water. Since they were now somewhat within the vicinity of Howard's Well, one should pay particular attention to Whiting's notes. Of that afternoon's travel, he said,

> We find the country to consist of a vast table elevation cut up by some convulsion of old time into numerous ravines or canyons. The great difficulty here is the passage from the ravine to the table, for by either, so long as they can be followed, the travelling is good. The

valleys are rendered pretty by groves of live oak and cedar, with occasional groups of trees whose names I do not know . . . We were rejoiced to find abundance of water for ourselves and animals in the holes of the limestone rocks. *We encamped upon quite a pool, exceedingly thankful for the good fortune which seems our constant companion.* [It had been a rainy spring.] [36]

Whiting neglected that day, May 11, to record his mileage, but assuming it was on the order of twenty miles, that would place him thirty-eight miles out of Live Oak Creek, by a winding route. It seems almost certain that on this day's march, most likely at the pool mentioned above, Howard's Well was discovered. Lt. Col. J. E. Johnston, whose march from San Antonio later that same year will be reviewed, was the first traveler on record to mention "Howard's springs," and his scribe, Capt. S. G. French, noted that "From thence to Live Oak creek, the next reliable water, is a journey of thirty-two miles, though after rains water may be found in pools in the rocky bottoms of ravines near the road." [37]

Whatever may have been the precise circumstances of its discovery, this well named for the estimable Richard Howard was the essential key to the passage between the Devil's River and the Pecos in dryer seasons; and Howard's reconnaissance under Lieutenant Whiting had now filled all the gaps.

Next day, continuing southeast, they topped the divide between the Pecos and the Devil's River in a region of fine grass often remarked on by travelers who followed. Again there was plenty of water in the creek beds — a phenomenon of that particular season — and they entered a broad valley leading toward Devil's River Canyon. On the basis of where it led them, that must have been Cedar Canyon — sometimes called Cedar Bluff Canyon — for just below the wide mouth, in the dry wash of the river bed, they came upon "a still and beautiful lagoon of clear, blue water" with "a frowning background formed by the huge gray cliffs of limestone half hidden by a dense grove of lofty pecans." This could only be Beaver Lake, renowned stopping place in later years, but today only a sometime pond in a raw bed of gravel, for the canyon has been ravaged repeatedly by huge floods, most recently in 1954 — floods which are the fruits of overgrazing in the hills above. Close about, Whiting found the frames of many Comanche lodges, with trails converging there from the headwaters of other Texas rivers. Beaver Lake was in truth a gathering place for the tribes as they assembled for their forays into Mexico.

Another day's travel over very rough ground above the dry canyon brought them to a magnificent stand of giant pecan trees enclosing bright blue water: Pecan Springs, the actual head of the running stream of Devil's River, today located within Hudspeth River Ranch. From there, cutting across great sweeping bends where they could, they passed the later favorite Second Crossing — or Baker's Crossing — and the future site of Fort Hudson, established only a few years afterward.

A little later Dick Howard pointed out traces of Hays's trail, which departed the river canyon and struck out into the hell of the lower Pecos Canyon.[38]

Whiting this day detached Lieutenant Smith, Howard, and Skillman to press on ahead into San Antonio with word of the party's safety.

After two full days of marching below Pecan Springs, while Whiting and his men were on the high ground west of the Devil's River, the humblest member of the party came forward to solve one of the project's most difficult dilemmas: finding a reasonable passage across the lower Devil's River Canyon. It was "Old Francisco, the muleteer," who recognized a small size canyon.

> as a famous Comanche Pass, to which he had been a long time ago, in pursuit of some Indians out of San Fernando. He added that if we would examine the larger caves on our right hand, we would find their walls covered with Comanche paintings. It was as he said. In a vaulted chamber upon the rock, the Indians had drawn in colors rude pictures of adventures in Mexico. Here we halted to dine, and I gave to this pass the name "Painted."[39]

For more than thirty years countless wagons, and later the first route of the Southern Pacific railroad, marked this Painted Cave as a notable landmark on the way. Its canyon provided, as Whiting noted, "an easy descent to the San Pedro [Devil's River], here a beautiful stream. The crossing we found to be exceedingly good, and the ascent on the other side equally so." This crossing had eluded Jack Hays and Howard on their outward passage, thereby aggravating their overall problem in finding a reasonable way westward.

For Whiting, Smith, and their handful of weary men, the remainder of the road was almost routine: across country to the San Felipe Springs, to the mountain and creek of Las Moras, and by way of the springs at the foot of the Balcones Fault, into San Antonio.

But near the Leóna, they met a scout who directed them to the camp of Captain Eastman, the same hospitable officer who had bade them Godspeed far to the north beyond Fredericksburg a hundred days before. Eastman had shocking news: cholera and other epidemics had raged in San Antonio for the past six weeks, taking the lives of scores. Dick Howard's brother Russell was down with smallpox, incurred while nursing a friend. Dozens of small children had died of cholera, and one finds that Mary Maverick in her memoirs commenced her account of that April 23-24 with the simple, woeful lament, "O world of griefs!" for she and Sam Maverick had to watch their second daughter Augusta succumb to that dread disease.[40] And the same plague, no respecter of persons, on May 7, 1849, took Whiting's commander, Maj. Gen. William Jenkins Worth, the officer who had written his orders.[41]

The expedition he had activated was long since given up for lost or dead. But William Henry Chase Whiting, on a jaded mule, at the head of a dozen men, jogged into San Antonio de Bejar on May 25, after 104 days in the wilds. They had lost not a man; they had executed their orders in all respects; and they had a road.[42]

During the middle months of 1849 a veritable explosion of traffic occurred across the western half of Texas, with unofficial parties, stimulated by the lure of California's gold, taking off like erratic rockets, sometimes along unproved trails. Fearful hardships were endured by many, and there were casualties from Indians as well as by privation, but in the light of hazards encountered by even the most seasoned explorers, the known losses that year were surprisingly light.

Meanwhile the army continued methodically to sponsor and conduct its thorough reconnaissance of the principal potential roads.

The competition and jealousy existing between the more developed eastern part of the state, represented by Houston, Galveston, and Austin, and the southwestern area, primarily Corpus Christi and San Antonio, became even more intense concerning which area should be the springboard for the plunge to the markets and the gold fields of the Far West.

Before he became a casualty of the cholera epidemic, General Worth maintained an open mind on the subject, having but recently arrived in Texas. During the few months of his tenure in San Antonio he tried objectively to make a fair assessment of the merits in the situation.

Even while Lieutenants Whiting and Smith were assembling the party for their memorable probe, General Worth had heard the case of the Austin group. On February 26, five days after Whiting and Smith started out, Worth authorized Robert S. Neighbors and John S. (Rip) Ford to scout out the possibilities of a more northerly route to El Paso.[43] The objectives of this group seemed to center primarily in behalf of the commercial interests of Austin and Houston, on opening a road for the clamoring flood of emigrant goldseekers who were disembarking from every ship docking at Texas ports. Hundreds of Texas residents, also — those who were ready to pull up stakes once more in search of that elusive talisman — were joining the tide. But Averam Bender, in his valuable study published more than fifty years ago, cautioned that "the notion that the Neighbors-Ford expedition was purely a commercial venture on the part of the citizens of Austin is not borne out by the evidence. This expedition was a part of the federal government's exploration policy in Texas." And he cited Neighbors's report to Gen. W. S. Harney, June 4, 1849, to support the thesis of the expedition's official nature.

Neighbors and Ford did scout out a northern route that was feasible. Since this probe did not bear directly on the eventual Chihuahua Road, all of it lying far to the north, it does not justify an accounting here. But eliminating their adventures deprives this narrative of some marvelous anecdotes, for Rip Ford was one of the more colorful Texians of his era, and he wrote a full account of the journey.

Upon beginning the return trip from El Paso, Neighbors had found an old retired Spanish soldier from San Elizario, "Señor Zambrano," who guided him on an ancient colonial road from "San Elceario" eastward through the foothills of the Guadalupe Mountains and on to the Pecos River. More than a century later, historian Kenneth F. Neighbors found in the Archivo General de la Nación, Palacio Nacionál, Ciudad Mexico, a muster list showing that Alvino Zambrano was a sergeant stationed at San Elceario in 1816. Therefore, in 1849 these new *norteamericano* adventurers had at last established a tenuous connection through Zambrano with the early nineteenth-century Spanish explorers.[44]

In addition to the narratives of Ford and Neighbors, Mabelle Eppard Martin, in the *Southwestern Historical Quarterly*, 1925, detailed a host of other parties that either reached Texas by ship or were organized within the state, which found their way to the Golden West.

The great Gold Rush was on for fair, and Texas was getting its share of the traffic, a fact which has been little noticed in the annals of the winning of the West. That part of the route which Neighbors had scouted out, from the newly rediscovered Horsehead Crossing up to the Guadalupe Mountains and across to El Paso, became the Southern Emigrant Road over which passed hundreds of trains from North Texas, Arkansas, Tennessee, and Kentucky in ensuing years.

Neighbors brought his party back, down from the Llano to San Antonio, reaching there June 2, to report directly to General Harney, who had succeeded to command of the new Eighth Military District upon the death of General Worth.

With the reports of Whiting and Neighbors, filed in San Antonio almost simultaneously, around June 1, 1849, the army had hard information with which to compare the merits of the upper road and the lower road. On the face of it, the upper road seemed barely to have the edge in the argument, according to contemporary observers, but in that first week of June, Harney plumped for the lower.

Encamped on the Salado Creek just north of San Antonio was a large military train under the command of Lt. Col. Joseph E. Johnston, of later Civil War fame, and Bvt. Maj. Jefferson Van Horne, impatiently waiting for orders to proceed by one or the other routes to El Paso. They had 275 wagons and 2,500 animals, with the stores and property of the Third Infantry Battalion, to be established at El Paso and other key points around the hinge of the Texas-New Mexico border.

Harney ordered Johnston, as chief topographical engineer of the army, to form two topographical parties for service between San Antonio and El Paso. Johnston himself was to be attached to one of these, to "direct the march of the 3rd Infantry via the Smith-Whiting or Southern Route," while Lt. Francis T. Bryan of the topographical engineers was to examine the upper road as reported by Neighbors. Van Horne was in charge of the train itself, on the southern route.

On June 3 the unwieldy train, encumbered with wild mules and men not yet experienced on undeveloped trail, moved in foul weather out toward Las Moras. Johnston, fortunately, had taken on Lt. Wm. F. Smith, just returned from his trek with Whiting. Beyond a doubt Smith and Whiting had stoutly recommended both Dick Howard and Policarpo Rodriguez, for both of them showed up as civilian scouts on Colonel Johnston's roster. This became, then, Richard Austin Howard's third arduous sortie across the Trans-Pecos in fifteen months. A remarkable man, he is still too little known in proportion to the large contribution he made as the principal scout for the three definitive reconnaissances of the hitherto unknown way to Presidio and El Paso.

Among notable emigrants who attached themselves to this train

was Col. John Coffee Hays himself, along with his close friends Maj.
John Caperton and Maj. Mike Chevaille. They were answering the lure
of the gold fields; their Texas careers were concluded; and although
they found no gold as such, Jack Hays built a new and illustrious career in the San Francisco area as peace officer and land promoter. He
came to own and later develop most of the land on which the city of
Oakland was built.[45]

Whiting stayed behind with Harney's command to make prepa-
rations for another far-ranging probe of the frontier a few months later.
His orders, written October 1, came from the new commander of the
Eighth Military Department, directing him to make a military recon-
naissance from Eagle Pass on the lower Rio Grande northeastward to
Coffee's Bend near the mouth of the False Wichita on the Red River.
Thus W. H. C. Whiting departed to establish his proper place in a
broader history of the Southwest.

Johnston, leaving the main body of the great train under Major
Van Horne, pulled out ahead at the Frio River. He was accompanied
by his topographical engineer Smith, his scouts, and some twenty civilian "engineers," that euphemistic label for the poor devils who,
with pick, shovel, crowbar, and a little blasting powder, while sweat-
ing in the blistering sun and exposed to the slings and arrows of the
enemy, have throughout history hewed out the road for the heroes who
followed them.[46] As it was with Johnston, so it had been with Hanni-
bal and Washington, and so it was to be again when the Seabees and
engineers carved out ports and airstrips on a hundred forgotten islands
of the Pacific in World War II.

Johnston brought along with him "a small train of Wagons," to
see how they would fare. Bear in mind the portent of that action: These
were the first wheeled vehicles driven by Anglo-Americans to make an
organized assault upon the upper reaches of the Chihuahua Road. The
record does indicate that in the preceding two months perhaps a half
dozen wagons had miraculously crashed and careened down the Alamito Creek to Presidio del Norte from the beginning trace of the upper
road, but they were a sport of bravado, and their fate was dubious.[47]
Johnston methodically prodded his army wagons behind his engineers
to El Paso in 100 days, reaching there September 8.

The route they followed was a distillation of the experience
gained by Hays, Whiting, Smith, and Howard: Las Moras, Painted
Cave on the Devil's River, a cutoff just short of Beaver Lake to Howard's Well, Live Oak Creek, a point up the Pecos that became Pontoon

Crossing, then Comanche and León Springs, Wild Rose Pass and Limpia Canyon in the Davis Mountains, a new transit up Lobo Valley to
the Rio Grande above Eagle Mountain, and then up the river to El
Paso.

Capt. S. G. French, acting quartermaster under Johnston, was
detailed to be the reporter of this trip. Since some mystery remains surrounding the actual rediscovery of Howard's Well by Anglo-Americans, French's description, the earliest in English of this essential way-
station, is useful. As Dick Howard brought Johnston's party to the
well, this is how Captain French saw it:

> The nearest water after leaving the San Pedro is found at Howard's
> springs, forty-one and a quarter miles distant. The road is good and
> the grass in the valleys very fine, consisting of gramma and fine mez-
> quite [grass]. The springs, from the large basin they form, afford a
> small stream of running water, which, after flowing a short distance,
> sinks into the ground. Wood, in sufficient quantities for fuel, is
> found near the springs. It is a place much resorted to by the Indians.
> From thence to Live Oak creek, the next reliable water, is a journey
> of 32 miles.[48]

After Johnston's arrival at Coons's store, opposite El Paso del
Norte, the main body of the train under Major Van Horne labored in,
much of it spaced in separate units so as not to put too much strain on
water and grass supplies at the way-stations. In the ensuing weeks various units of the Third Infantry were dispersed up and down the river,
while others remained at Coons's on the newly leased government land
to form what eventually became Fort Bliss.

While Johnston lay over to supervise these operations, he dispatched Lieutenant Smith with a small party to make a twenty-day exploration of the Organ and Sacramento mountains in New Mexico, to
find a wagon route westward through what had been a troublesome
barrier. Smith succeeded, thereby linking the roads through Texas
with the route Col. Philip St. George Cooke had scouted out in 1846-
47 through Arizona and Southern California to San Diego. Passage was
now feasible all the way from the Gulf of Mexico, or overland from the
southern states, through El Paso to the West Coast.

And the emigrants took quick advantage. A current report estimated that as early as July 1849, as many as 1,200 wagons and 4,000
emigrants were encamped at Coons's and up the river as far as Doña
Ana, in great distress, waiting direction and encouragement to undertake the road on west. They now began to filter on out.

While Johnston and Van Horne were testing the practicality of the southern route, Harney had directed Lieutenant Bryan to do the same thing for the northern route. He left San Antonio with thirty men on June 14, moving via Fredericksburg up the San Saba and Concho rivers and through Castle Gap to Horsehead Crossing. They floated their baggage across the Pecos on rafts lashed together of empty water casks and spare wagon tongues. From there they surveyed out the route opened by Neighbors and the emigrants, around the base of the Guadalupe Mountains and by the Hueco Tanks, arriving in El Paso July 29.

When Bryan reported to Colonel Johnston, and while Smith was off exploring the New Mexico mountains, Johnston took advantage of having another topographical engineer at hand. He pressed Bryan into service, took Dick Howard and his shadow, Policarpo, and made an engineering survey of the Rio Grande Valley from below Ysleta up to Doña Ana.

Johnston left few people idle. On the day W. F. Smith returned from his twenty-day scout through New Mexico, Johnston set out with Smith, Dick Howard, Polly, two Delaware guides, and twenty-five men for the return journey to San Antonio along the northern route. They were trailed by a train of twenty-five wagons. Johnston had intended to examine the country around the heads of the Brazos and Colorado rivers, but the weather on the plains had become so severe that when they reached the Pecos they turned south and followed a variant of the lower road back to San Antonio, arriving November 23.

It had been a crowded year; the frontier world was transformed. When Jack Hays had returned to San Antonio with his exhausted, tattered squad on December 9, 1848, the Trans-Pecos was still a vast, unsolved mystery. Eleven months later, thousands of tenderfoot emigrants had swarmed across it and the army had mapped much of it. The army was the instrument, but gold, the great energizer, had wrought the miracle.

[7]

As Wagons
Rolled

Commercial enterprises were quick to take advantage of the newly opened way from Gulf Coast deepwater on Matagorda Bay to the burgeoning markets of the West. Major Van Horne was scarcely more than bivouacked in his new post near Coons's store and Magoffinsville — soon to become El Paso — when Benjamin Franklin Coons himself started a wagon train toward Matagorda Bay in the early fall of 1849. Upon departure he had some twelve or more wagons and 275 mules and was carrying along corn to supply a unit of the Third Infantry, at that time encamped on the Pecos.[1]

In the Guadalupe Mountains he was attacked by a party of seventy or eighty Apaches and having only fifteen men with him had to retreat to the Salt Lakes west of the Guadalupes "to find favorable ground for defense." First reports, published in the *Houston Telegraph and Register,* January 3, 1850, were that two men were killed, Clement Howard wounded in the arm, and Ben Coons's valuable mule shot from under him, leaving Ben's $500 saddle to the Apaches. Two companies from the Third Infantry came out of El Paso to their relief. Upon arrival, the soldiers escorted Coons's train on to a point well beyond and east of the Guadalupes.

A later dispatch from the Houston paper's unnamed correspondent in San Antonio brought the good news that Coons had arrived in San Antonio in early January, that Clem Howard was only slightly wounded, and that the two men believed killed in the Guadalupes had trailed safe and sound into San Antonio after Coons's arrival.[2]

This same San Antonio dispatch of January 13 also recorded that "Mr. Aubrey, the celebrated 'Santa Fe trader,' has just arrived by the Government route, having left Santa Fe on the 1st day of December." This was, of course, Francois Xavier Aubrey, who was renowned throughout the West for his remarkable speed runs, both by horseback and with wagons. Aubrey had with him "Mr. Stone, a large merchant of Independence, Mo., who leaves tomorrow for New Orleans and will return this way in thirty days."

The immediately awakened interest of these traders in the shorter route to deep water at Indianola reflects the impact which the news of this opening was having on the Santa Fe-Chihuahua trade. Aubrey told the San Antonio correspondent that the new road was generally excellent, that traders who used it could get goods into New Mexico at lower prices than those who came out of St. Louis. He believed it was the best route for the Santa Fe mail and for the Chihuahua trade. Glowing with civic pride, the San Antonio writer effused: "The whole Santa Fe trade must come this way. It cannot be helped. These two large traders are but forerunners of what is to come." [3]

Aubrey was reported by this dispatch to be traveling with 250 mules, and by an accompanying news story in the same edition of the *Register* to have twenty wagons. When they passed through Victoria on their way to Indianola, the *Victoria Advocate* recorded that they had eighteen wagons. The *Advocate* also noted that Coons's train followed soon after.[4]

Coons must be credited with having been the first far-western trader to *start* a trading expedition toward the coast, but since Aubrey apparently got ahead of Coons at San Antonio, Aubrey must, by the *Advocate's* account, be recognized as the first to *reach* a deepwater port on the gulf.

This hard-driving jehu had created an international sensation only two years before by riding alone 780 miles from Santa Fe to Independence, Missouri, in five days and sixteen hours. Now, on the return leg of his trip to Indianola, he announced as he passed through San Antonio that he was taking his eighteen wagonloads of merchandise to the Chihuahua market.[5]

Only scanty mileposts of this journey are on record, and it has

been impossible to document with finality the route by which he went
to Chihuahua City. The following evidence suggests that he took the
route by Comanche Springs down to Presidio del Norte and then to
Chihuahua. He left Victoria February 15 and San Antonio February
27. While passing Turkey Creek, near Las Moras, his train was attacked by Indians and one man was mortally injured.[6] He encountered
a heavy snowstorm beyond the Pecos, losing forty mules by freezing in
one night. Since heavy snow rarely falls in that area after mid-March,
this suggests it was no later than about March 20 when he was near
where the El Paso and Chihuahua roads forked at León Springs. Yet it
is of record that he was arriving in El Paso on April 27.[7]

  With F. X. Aubrey's penchant for pushing hard on the trail, it
would be altogether out of character for him to consume five weeks in
traveling the 200-odd miles direct from León Springs to El Paso. On
the other hand, Aubrey might well have been able to take his train
down the Alamito Creek and through Presidio up to Chihuahua City,
dispose of his stock quickly, and then drive on up the Santa Fe Trail to
El Paso by April 27. Therefore, the probability is strong that Aubrey
was the first freighter to move a train of trade goods all the way out the
Chihuahua Road from Indianola to Ciudad Chihuahua, by way of Presidio del Norte.

  Along with Aubrey and Coons, the traders arriving in Victoria,
Lavaca, and Indianola to outfit and supply their return trains included
one of San Antonio's largest merchant firms of the decade, Lewis and
Groesbeck. This establishment took its name from Nathaniel Lewis,
then forty-five, and John D. Groesbeck, thirty-five, who not only sold
merchandise from their store at the northeast corner of Military Plaza,
but also for a time in 1850 owned the city's only newspaper, the *Western Texian*.[8] There was a connection, then, when the issue of February
8 included in its advertising columns a notice saying:

> The subscribers will engage Forty or Fifty Wagons to convey Freight
> from Indianola to El Paso, and for which a liberal price will be
> paid.   Lewis and Groesbeck.

and in the editorial columns:

> We learn that Brevet Major J. T. Sprague (8th Infantry) has been de-
> tailed to command the expedition to El Paso del Norte which is to
> leave here about the last of April. A large amount of supplies go
> through for troops stationed in New Mexico. It is supposed there
> will be upwards of four hundred Mexican carts in the train, to be

supported by two companies of mounted troops . . . Merchants from
that quarter (E. P.) have passed through our city on their way to
New Orleans and New York to purchase goods, intending to have
them here in time to take advantage of the protection afforded by
U. S. troops . . . Those of our fellow citizens desirous of going to
New Mexico or California should improve this opportunity.[9]

The evidence is plain, then, that at this early date commerce was
already having to depend upon the army to see goods safely conducted
across the western deserts.

That durable entrepreneur, George T. Howard, was also steadily
expanding his freighting operations, in partnership with Charles
Ogden. Though his carts are not specifically named as having been in
Indianola to take on supplies in that bustling spring of 1850, it seems
likely they were there, for he had extensive contracts with the army to
supply their camps and new posts on the frontier. As he passed
through Houston on his way to Washington in January 1850, he told
the *Telegraph* that he had recently been out as far as the Pecos and returned with a government train to San Antonio by way of the head of
the Nueces River.[10] The major put in a plug for this route, claiming
that it was "entirely practicable for wagons at all seasons." Howard and
Ogden continued to expand their operations until they were reputed to
have 800 teams on the road.[11] In March, one Charles Wiggins of St.
Louis was in Port Lavaca, loading out a wagon train for Santa Fe.[12]

All this development impinging upon the villages around Matagorda Bay created an unprecedented stir of activity. The *Victoria Advocate* spoke successively during these months of ships arriving in March
and April with goods and wagons to outfit a large wagon train headed
for Chihuahua;[13] of J. O. Wheeler of Victoria being authorized to
purchase 140 yoke of oxen and hire an additional 125 teamsters;[14] of
how "the preparation for the great El Paso train creates much stir here.
Only think of 550 to 600 wagons fitting out at a single town at one
time!"[15]

The local roads up from the coast, however, were posing a real
problem. Between the landings on Matagorda Bay and the inland
higher ground lay sloughs, swamps, and sandy barrows or dunes that
gave perpetual harassment to all wheeled vehicles. A Galveston paper,
not altogether objective, referred to the way between the port towns
and Victoria as "the worst in that part of the State." The *Advocate* itself, which touted the Indianola route to the extent honestly possible,
foresaw that

Messrs. Lewis, Groesbeck, and Coons's El Paso train will have a hard
time getting up from the Bay with their loads. Some fifty wagons
have already loaded and are on the way up. The train will consist of
one hundred fifty wagons and two hundred fifty Mexican carts. Each
wagon will be drawn by six mules and [or?] six to eight oxen, and
each Mexican cart by at least four oxen.

Sure enough, the *Advocate* soon reported that the train, which left Indianola in April, was having all sorts of trouble, having to order fifty
new wagon tongues from Victoria merchants. [16]

What was the visual aspect of these coastal roads? No detailed description from the early 1850s exists, but seven years later, when Frederick Law Olmstead, the distinguished architect and acidulous observer of the western scene, traveled in 1857 from Victoria to Lavaca
and Indianola, he noted:

The road was a mere collection of straggling wagon ruts, extending
for more than a quarter of a mile in width from outside to outside, it
being desirable, in this part of the country, rather to avoid a road
than to follow it. We had heard, the day before, at Victoria, that two
people who wished to meet, had passed one another unnoticed, and
it seemed quite credible; one had taken the right of the road the
other the left. [17]

Despite all the difficulties, those early trains did get through the
swamps and up the somewhat better roads toward Goliad, or alternately through Yorktown and Sulphur Springs[18] and so into San Antonio. Beyond there, Coons's train, which pulled out of San Antonio in
June, faced misadventures that made broken wagon tongues seem insignificant. [19]

During these same months, the notorious confidence man, Capt.
Parker H. French, cut his sorry swath across Texas from Matagorda
Bay through San Antonio to El Paso. Having pulled together in New
York City upwards of 200 victims, gullible young men from all over
the Northeast who succumbed to his blandishments — promises of
luxurious passage, at cut rates, from New York down the coast by
steamer to Lavaca, and then by ambulance to the gold fields — he kept
his game going on fraudulent paper and the passengers' cash.

It all began to fall apart, however, in the western reaches of
Texas. The men he had gulled and exploited finally rebelled in El
Paso. They ran him and a handful of henchmen off into Mexico, then
tried to retrieve something from their folly by auctioning off their ram-

shackle vehicles and stock. Most of the unfortunates actually made their way on foot or with pack mules to the West Coast.

As for French, with astounding resiliency he turned his talents into one high-flown scam after another, culminating in an incredible adventure with William L. Walker, the filibuster who took over Nicaragua, briefly, in a jingoistic extension of America's "manifest destiny." Walker was finally stood up against the adobe wall and *fusilado,* while Capt. Parker H. French trailed off down the inexorable road of the flimflam artist.[20]

And what of Ben Coons, whom Parker H. French had left in the summer of 1850 with his wagon trains stretched out along the Pecos River? The forward section of the train struggled into El Paso September 19, Coons sending a report in advance to Major Van Horne that he had been harassed throughout the trip by his own ruffianly gang of teamsters, about 120 in this section, "a lawless and desperate set of men, over whom they could exercise no control."[21] These drivers had wasted and destroyed much of his property, let 250 of his oxen go astray, and had driven off Coons's agent, Smith. The best Coons could offer Van Horne was to have the gang disarmed before they reached El Paso.

The second section of the train, under a wagon master, Fred Percy, whom Major Henry had met laboring through mud along the Pecos on September 1, had by late September traveled as far as a pond of fresh water then called "Salt Lake," later known as "Crow Spring," westward between the Guadalupe Mountains and the Cornudos del Alamo.[22] There, handicapped by loss of animals and by broken-down wagons, they halted, knowing they could not pull their huge store of government goods on across the desert with only the water they could carry. They camped forlorn on that desolate pond for two months. Boundary Commissioner John R. Bartlett, himself out of supplies and numbed by a snowstorm, found them there November 10, stayed with them two days, and went on. When he reported the train's plight to Van Horne, that soldier sent out a relief party to help the wagons at last into El Paso. They had been more than a year on the round trip to Indianola.[23]

The first bloom of promise in the easy road to Indianola had been rubbed off by the harsh reality of undeveloped roadbed and the ferocious attitude of the Indians. F. X. Aubrey tried one more trip from Santa Fe to Texas in the fall of 1850. In the course of that trip, he completely reversed his earlier opinion.[24] In San Antonio on November 23, 1850, he wrote the *Daily Missourian Republican:*

> Indians often come within a few miles of this place, to remind the citizens they are still in the wild country . . . It is likely that the subsistence stores for the posts at El Paso, Doña Ana, and those south of the Jornado del Muerto will be brought from Missouri. The freight would cost the Government at least fifty per cent less. With the Government it is a question of dollars and cents, and there is no doubt that the Quartermaster General will discover that the Missouri route is the best, safest, and cheapest.[25]

Aubrey never returned to Texas. Perhaps it is just as well; he might not have been welcome. As early as September 19, 1850, the *Western Texian* referred sourly to "an extract from a St. Louis paper quoting F. X. Aubrey in a derogatory statement about the state of the roads between El Paso and San Antonio." The San Antonio editor used a recent report from Lieutenants Smith and Bryan of the topographical engineers to refute Aubrey's allegations, then summarized:

> This great jornado is thus proved to exist only in the imagination of Mr. Aubrey or of the authors . . . The good people of Missouri are not inactive in puffing their route for the Chihuahua trade nor backward in decrying every other. We choose rather to let the facts speak for themselves . . . The Chihuahua trade will soon be to St. Louis and Independence among the things that have been. We are glad to see our merchants preparing with largely increased stocks . . . to furnish the many trains that will be repairing hence.[26]

The fulminations of civic pride, however, were not enough to make the Indians go away. For instance, that same edition of the *Western Texian* carried the report of Maj. W. S. Henry's arrival from El Paso on the trip in which he encountered Captain French's argonauts as well as Coons's long-suffering train. In addition to relating these encounters, the paper went on to tell of another more ominous confrontation. Near the Concho, on September 6, Henry had met two parties of Lipan warriors, a hundred or more, with three well-known chiefs: Castro, Capote, and Chiketo. The Lipans, in friendly mood, told him all the Comanches were now hostile to the whites. While they parleyed, a band of thirteen Kiowas appeared on the scene. They showed fight against the eighteen whites, but the Lipans gathered about and said that if the Kiowa were determined to attack, they should have to fight the Lipan tribe as well. As the powwow dispersed, Chief Chiketo volunteered to pilot Major Henry's little train to Lipan Creek and put him on the road to San Saba — a courtesy that Henry gladly accepted.[27]

Against the fact that Maj. Robert S. Neighbors only a year before had been able to traffic peaceably with the Comanches and even hire them as guides, their hardened attitudes as reported by the friendly Lipan becomes significant. The change is understandable. Both Neighbors, meeting with the Comanche chief on Brady Creek, and almost simultaneously W. H. C. Whiting, in his precarious negotiations with the Apache chiefs in the heart of the Davis Mountains, had dissembled as to the intentions of the United States. They tried desperately, in order to get through the country and complete their missions, to allay the suspicions of these two great tribes. But the worst fears of the red man had been realized almost at once, with the sudden relentless tide of development in West Texas and New Mexico.

Retribution was not long in coming. The Apaches launched their attacks first, with fierce depredations against the defenseless immigrant outfits. The Comanches were slower in focusing their attentions upon the *norteamericanos*, for they were still in the heyday of their profitable incursions against northern Mexico, which yielded rich booty in cattle, mules, and more tractable prisoners.

As early as August 1849, Gen. George M. Brooke, who had succeeded to the post of army commandant at San Antonio, had requested Governor George T. Wood to establish three Ranger companies to be based at Corpus Christi, ranging across South Texas to assist the army in suppressing the Indian depredations. By the end of 1850, Brooke had called for an expansion to five companies of seventy-nine Rangers each.[28] Except for the first one, under Rip Ford, little is known about how well these companies got organized and into the field, but the total effort clearly did not meet public demand.[29]

In March of 1850 the *Houston Telegraph* announced that

> General Brooke has at length become alarmed at the threatening attitude of the savages on our frontier, and has written to the department in Washington calling for more troops along the line of the Rio Grande and between the Trinity and the Nueces. He has ascertained that the prairie tribes of Texas have been so hostile that the communication with El Paso is almost entirely cut off and small parties of emigrants and traders are compelled to travel the long and tedious route by the west bank of the Rio Grande . . .
>
> The whole Indian country is on fire and a general war seems about to burst forth . . .[30]

In the Trans-Pecos country, no issue reacted more cruelly against the *norteamericanos,* especially in the country around Presidio del Norte, than the revolting traffic in Indian scalps, revived and fostered by the government of Chihuahua State and exploited in particular by two San Antonians, John Joel Glanton and Mike Chevaille.[31]

To understand how this bloody chapter came to disgrace the annals of border life, it is first necessary to recall the role of Ben Leaton at his *fortín* on the Rio Grande just below Presidio. Jack Hays and Lt. W. H. C. Whiting, during their visits to Leaton's establishment in 1848 and 1849, respectively, had looked askance at their host's dubious role in trading with the Indians and playing the Comanche tribe off against the Apaches. But they may have felt, as the German traveler Julius Froebel frankly noted three years later, that this interplay pragmatically preserved a delicate balance in the area for the white man.

Nevertheless, this balance was thrown awry when the government of Chihuahua State, harassed by Indian depredations against the *haciendas* of the interior, offered a bounty of *dos onzas* — $32 — for each Apache scalp brought to Chihuahua City. This blood money was later raised to $200 for a warrior's scalp, $150 for a woman's or child's, and $150 for a live prisoner. Into this sordid milieu in 1849 rode John Glanton of San Antonio.

Glanton was a young brute of the worst caliber. After a record of undue violence in the Mexican War, he went to San Antonio and somehow married a girl of excellent family. His alcoholic binges having gotten him into trouble with the law, he listened to stories coming out of Chihuahua about the gold to be made at scalp hunting among the Indians. With a handful of other men looking for easy money, they left San Antonio by night, horseback, in the early spring of 1849 and found their way to Ben Leaton's *hacienda* on the Rio Grande.

After embarrassing Leaton with forays against the local Apache villages, they moved on to Ciudad Chihuahua and struck a deal with the authorities to bring in Apache scalps at the going price. The band made two successful sweeps into the hinterlands, bringing back an impressive harvest of carefully dressed scalp-locks, until they saw that their bloody game was catching up with them: they had been getting their dreadful trophies in innocent Mexican settlements as well as from strikes at the Apaches. Grisly stories were beginning to reach the capital.

Glanton and confederates fled on westward through the Sierra Madres in a series of rowdy, violent escapades. They then brutally preempted the ferry on the Colorado at Yuma Crossing from a group of Yuma Indians who were peaceably operating it. The enterprise was lucrative because of the many gold-seeking argonauts using the new road west. But one night when the pre-emptors were all sleeping off a wild, drunken orgy, the Yumas moved back in on them. And that was the end of John Glanton and his band of scalp hunters.[32]

Meanwhile, Governor Angel Trias of Chihuahua, insensitive to the fact that he had opened Pandora's box by offering bounty for any and all Apache scalps brought in, wrote on October 10, 1849, to Emilio Langberg, military inspector at El Paso del Norte, for attention of Major Van Horne across the Rio Grande in the new El Paso. In his letter he complained about the activities of Ben Leaton at El Fortín near Presidio del Norte,[33] and he charged the trader with supplying arms and ammunition to Indians in exchange for booty they had stolen in Mexico.

Leaton happened to drop in on Van Horne at his headquarters in El Paso about the time the Trias complaint reached Van Horne. In high dudgeon Ben pointed out that Trias's own government had hired Glanton and his like to kill Apaches indiscriminately, with the result that the Apaches, assuming that any *norteamericano* was of Glanton's kind, killed and robbed any white on sight between El Paso and San Antonio. Leaton especially took credit for having maintained friendships with such Apaches as Cigarito and Gomez — a claim that appeared to have validity in the light of Henry Skillman's safe conduct through Gomez's territory earlier in the year. But, said Leaton, Glanton had attacked these very tribes, then run for cover in Leaton's own *fortín*, to the trader's considerable discomfiture.

Major Van Horne passed the Mexican governor's letter on to Gen. George Brooke, commanding the Eighth Department, at San Antonio, and Brooke bucked it on to Adj. Gen. R. Jones in Washington. Jones eventually instructed Major Van Horne to tell Governor Trias that the United States had its own basis for serious complaints in the explosive results from the Chihuahuensans' having hired Glanton and other mercenaries to take Apache scalps.[34]

That was Ben Leaton's last appearance in history. He died, probably in the vicinity of San Antonio, sometime in 1850 or 1851; no stone survives to mark his grave.[35] He was succeeded at El Fortín, and as Juana Pedraza's husband, by a Scotsman, Edward Hall, customshouse officer and interpreter, who in turn was eliminated by John D. Burgess. Leaton and Burgess were original Chihuahua traders, along with John Spencer; they had drifted down to La Junta de los Rios only two short years before, at the end of the Mexican War.[36] They expected traffic to build up on this obvious route from the Texas coast to Chihuahua; they had found that traffic a little slow in developing, but still in sight.

In one of his letters to General Brooke, November 8, 1849, Major Van Horne revealed, perhaps, why he was reluctant to denounce Ben Leaton: "it is highly probable that the Presidio del Norte will be an important point on the great route of trade from San Antonio, Lavaca, Corpus Christi, etc., to Chihuahua, Durango, etc., which is an additional reason why troops should be stationed there." [37] Lieutenant Whiting, five months before, had more specifically pointed out the role of Fort Leaton itself, predicting that it would make a convenient post for dragoons seeking safe haven on the warpaths. General Brooke, at his headquarters in San Antonio, agreeing with these conclusions, sent in a request that Washington authorize such a post.[38] Fort Leaton, however, remained in private hands as a trading post, hospitality house for passing travelers, and occasional refuge for soldiers and freighters when the Indians pressed close upon them. It became important to the army after Fort Davis was established in 1854, with troops from that base using El Fortín as a command post while they engaged in reconnaissances up and down the border.[39]

The aggravations caused by Anglo-American scalp hunters in Mexico were not solved, however, by the exchange of stiff notes between the U.S. Army and the governor of Chihuahua, nor by Glanton's sordid death at the hands of the Yuma Indians. Another San Antonian, one who would scarcely be expected to engage in this ugly business, showed up hard on the heels of John Glanton. This was Maj. Mike Chevaille, one of that trio at the ball for President Lamar in 1841 whose boyish antics Mrs. Maverick had found so amusing. At twenty-four, he already had years of border warfare behind him as a member of his close friend Jack Hays's ranging company. Walter Prescott Webb named him among such stalwarts as Ben McCulloch, Sam Walker, Bigfoot Wallace, Rip Ford, and Arch Gibson as men who had distinguished themselves before 1845 in the Ranger service; who, in the Mexican War "entered the national service and their fame spread over the nation of which Texas had become a part." [40]

In that war, Major Chevaille served as third in command of the First Regiment of Texas, Mounted Troops, under Colonel Hays and Lt. Col. Samuel Walker, and in a variety of other assignments, always with valor, at the center of action. Nevertheless, indications of unbridled temper and needless violence do appear.[41] He returned after the war with Jack Hays to San Antonio, taking part quietly in the ordeal of the expedition to Presidio del Norte in 1848.

As already noted, Hays and Caperton pulled up stakes in June of 1848, traveling with Major Van Horne to El Paso, and eventually, after long delays, on to California. Mike Chevaille, footloose, a professional soldier without a war, went westward with that train. He parted company somewhere along that border trail and sometime after June of 1849 rode south to Chihuahua City.[42] He quickly found employment in that capital, judging by a chauvinistic article that appeared in the Houston paper September 13, 1850:

> . . . The State Congress of Chihuahua passed the Indian appropriation bill to defray the expenses of an Indian war to be waged by foreign chivalry under contract with the State Government. Major Chevallie [*sic*], of renowned fame in Texas, with some twenty-five well-armed and equipped Americans, was the first to enter the field in the subjugation of the troublesome foe. [The terms were listed:] . . . $200 each for scalps of warriors; $150 each for those of women and children, and $200 each for prisoners — all captured animals to be retained by the Major and his command.

The story pridefully reported that "in his first engagement the Major secured nine scalps, four prisoners, and would enter upon another campaign in a few days." [43]

Just how long Mike Chevaille's raids against the Apaches continued is not known, nor can his activities be sorted out from, or coordinated with, those of Glanton and perhaps other bands of "foreign chivalry" operating at that time. In some contemporary reports, Glanton's and Chevaille's names were linked in a common complaint.[44]

Dr. Eugene Bolton has recorded a formal documentation of Chevaille's status with the Mexicans in his guide to the Archives of Mexico. He cites this entry, found in the regular files of the *Archivo de la Secretaria de Gobierno,* Chihuahua: "Legajo 175:1849 — No. 19, concerning the campaign against the Indians undertaken by the American M. Chevaille. Proposal, contract, report of plunder taken, etc."[45]

Altogether, says John Upton Terrell in his *Apache Chronicle,* "the bounty system had created an intolerable situation . . . it had intensified and spread warfare between all Indians and all white men to such an extent that all of northern Mexico was a gigantic field of slaughter . . . It had united the red people to a degree that had never before existed." [46] Terrell's comment was applied to the situation prevailing seven or eight years earlier when James Kirker was rampant as a bounty killer, but it would be all the more applicable in 1849–50 under the revived era of blood money.

The waves from this sea of havoc lapped down and overwhelmed at least one respected trader operating near La Junta. David and John Torrey owned the trading post near the future site of Waco, from where Robert Neighbors and Rip Ford had started their journey in early 1849. Within a few months after that, the Torreys had wearied with the quiet life along the Brazos in Central Texas, determining to seek broader opportunities in the beckoning West. When they arrived at El Paso sometime in 1849, John Torrey engaged in freighting work into New Mexico. David Torrey, along with one or more associates, moved down the Rio Grande River, trading as he went, and soon established a post of sorts across the river from the Presidio del Norte, between John W. Spencer's *rancho* and Leaton's El Fortín. He undoubtedly dabbled in illegal horse and mule trading with the Indians, as well as in more legitimate goods. [47] He might have gotten away with this in Mexico had it not been for the repercussions from the wanton aggression by bounty hunters such as Glanton and Chevaille.

David Torrey was well known and liked in the more settled parts of Texas; therefore, when word seeped back to his shocked friends that he had lost his life, they pursued inquiry as to how this had occurred.

On February 17, 1850, an unnamed correspondent in San Antonio wrote land developer Jacob de Cordoba, Esq., in Houston, relating that, as requested, he had talked to Captain Skillman and learned the details of David Torrey's murder. Skillman told him that Torrey, in company with other Americans and Mexicans, had made several trips into Mexico to the camp of about seven to eight hundred Apache Indians — the last time developing an excellent trade with them. On this last trip, Torrey was two days on the homeward leg of his journey from the encampment when a party of Apaches and Comanches returned to their home camps from a marauding expedition into Durango. They were in foul spirits, for a gang of *norteamericanos* had set upon them, killing a number of their people. When the returning warriors learned that a party of Americans had just been at the encampment, they immediately set out upon the trail and overtook Torrey's group. The Indians slaughtered the whole party but one, a Mexican who had escaped and from whom Captain Skillman learned the particulars. [48]

John Joel Glanton was totally insensitive to such far-reaching effects of his deeds; he was born a brute, lived and died one. But Mike Chevaille must surely have found himself out of his element in this grisly business. Seeing himself dishonored, he took his life.

Maj. Horace Bell related a fanciful story of how Mike Chevaille came out of Mexico into the brawling life of Southern California, living as a swashbuckling gunman, until he met his match. His adversary forced Chevaille, as the tale went, to sheathe his guns and leave Los Angeles forever. Bill asserts that

> Mike saddled his horse and left the [city of] slumbering angels before day, returned to Monterey gloomily, fixed up his earthly affairs, willed his revolver and bowie to Bill, and committed suicide by taking two ounces of laudanum. Alas, poor Mike! For the first time in his wild career, he mistook his man.[49]

Major Bell's dramatic story about Mike Chevaille does not ring true for a man who rode with Jack Hays and Bigfoot Wallace. There is only one other script to consider, a brief item that appeared in the *Houston Telegraph:* "A report has been in circulation at the west to the effect that Major Chevallie [*sic*] has committed suicide by blowing out his brains . . . We do not credit that report." [50] The editor said he could not accept the veracity of the story because he thought Mike was too smart a man to do such a thing.

Beyond these two reports, the record is silent; Mike Chevaille disappeared from history at that time. There is no reason to doubt that by one means or another he did end his own life — a gallant soldier of the frontier, corroded by too many years of bloodshed. He was still on the 1850 census roll in San Antonio; a census-taker's notation says he was "absent but resident," age thirty-three, in the year he died.[51]

[8]

Ports at the
End of the Road

The ocean terminus of the road — Indianola and associated little port towns on Matagorda Bay — had come into being originally in the 1840s not with the long-range objective of serving commerce with Mexico but with the much more immediate purpose of debarking the sudden flow of German immigration.

Political unrest and economic chaos in some of the German states had led a number of philanthropic noblemen in that unhappy part of Europe to see in Texas, whose founding as an independent republic had drawn worldwide attention, an opportunity for settling their dislocated people. Notable among these activists was Prince Carl zu Solms-Braunfels.

In 1842 Prince Carl and a dozen other noblemen joined in forming a society for the purchase and colonization of lands in Texas — the "Meinzer Verein: A Society for the Protection of German Immigrants in Texas." Known also as "Adelsverein," its goal was to establish in the southwestern part of the Republic townsites that might serve and draw upon the only established city in the interior, San Antonio.[1] New Braunfels, Seguin, Fredericksburg, and Comfort were the principal nuclei that grew out of this endeavor, along with a great influx of German folk into San Antonio itself.

The prince was not of a practical nature, and he indulged in many eccentricities, but his thinking was clear on one aspect of his great project: he must have a landing place on the Gulf of Mexico as close as possible to its ultimate destination, for the rigors of cross-country travel in Texas with wheeled vehicles had already become well known. A look at any Texas map would show that of all the navigable inlets on the Texas coast, the headwaters of Matagorda Bay lay closest to San Antonio and its environs — only 125 to 130 miles as the crow flies.

The teeming waters and white shell beaches of Matagorda Bay and its subsidiary, Lavaca Bay, had lain dormant and largely unoccupied since the seventeenth century, when La Salle's 1685 incursion had caused its spate of Spanish pursuit, exploration, and ineffectual development.

However, only thirty miles inland from the bay, Don Martín de León in 1824 had founded the town of Guadalupe Victoria on the east bank of the Guadalupe River, at the old crossing on the trail leading up from the Spanish presidio and missions on Garcitas Creek. He had received a royal grant to settle forty-one families that same year, the last year of the Spanish colonial government in Texas and the year that the famous "people's constitution" was ratified.[2] With an expanded grant from the new Mexican government in 1829 for 150 families, Martín de León, with his son Fernando as commissioner of the colony, and their many relatives, made Victoria a proud and flourishing little settlement and a center for Spanish culture in the next decade.

Commissioner de León and many of his fellow Victorians threw their lot vigorously on the side of Texans in the revolution against the Mexican government in 1836. After the battles of the Alamo and Goliad, and the climax at San Jacinto, however, emotional reaction against anyone bearing a Spanish surname brought about a persecution of the Victoria colonists that is one of the darker pages of Anglo-Texan history. The de León family lost much of their land, cattle, and personal possessions from Anglo-Texan ravages, while many of the family, including Don Fernando himself and his mother, the widow of Don Martín, had to flee to Louisiana for their own personal safety.[3]

Though some of them returned later and eventually recovered a portion of their lands, the close culture of the de León family, with its well-springs flowing from ancient Burgos in the north of Spain, was broken up. Victoria, one of the first three towns to be granted a charter of incorporation by the new Republic of Texas in 1836, absorbed an overwhelming Anglo-Texan infusion. Rough and raw then, perhaps, but it was imbued with the bounce and enterprise that has developed one of the wealthiest small cities in the nation.

Among the earliest of the settlers from across the North Atlantic was John Joseph Linn, arriving in Victoria only five years after the town was founded. Born in Antrim County, Ireland, he was thirty-three years old when he reached Victoria in 1829, making himself at home among the patrician de Leóns. They dubbed him "Juan Linn" and installed him as *alcalde* of the city — the last *alcalde,* it turned out, under the Spanish regime. A better choice for pioneering the fusion of the two cultures could scarcely have been found.

After the revolution, in which he took an active part, Linn became the city's first elected mayor, in 1839. These civic obligations, however, did not interfere with his development of a thriving mercantile enterprise — and that takes the story back to Matagorda Bay.[4]

To provide an economical port of entry for the stocks of merchandise and trade goods he was bringing by the shipload from New Orleans, Juan Linn established in the late 1830s the little port town of Linnville. He built it on the closest point of relatively deep water available on Lavaca Bay, about twenty-eight miles across the boggy coastal flats from Victoria. He constructed a rudimentary wooden wharf and soon more than twenty houses, along with a substantial general store and warehouse, clustered about these landing facilities.[5]

The catastrophe which fell upon Linnville on August 8, 1840, was sparked by the Council House tragedy on Main Plaza in San Antonio a few months earlier.[6] Consumed by a raging thirst for vengeance, the Comanche nation organized the greatest striking force in its history; 600 or more warriors, alleged to have been led by Buffalo Hump, came raging down the Guadalupe Valley in an unchecked swath of destruction. They struck Victoria, a yelling horde swirling through the town, burning whatever would take the torch and looting elsewhere. Some families forted up in the more substantial structures.[7]

When the raiders had plundered or burned all that was readily at hand in Victoria, killing some thirteen citizens, the Comanche force regathered and struck off southeasterly toward the sea — and Linnville. Perhaps a part of their objective was to show that the Comanches had mastery all the way to the coast, but perhaps also those fierce riders of the far plains simply wanted to see the great shining water.

The people of Linnville had no word that the raiders were coming, until someone saw them riding full speed, fanned out in crescent formation, to envelop the town. The citizens knew that resistance was futile in their flimsy box houses — but a lighter, anchored just off-shore, offered refuge. When the 600 Comanche warriors, after killing a lone wagon freighter whom they had encountered along the way, swooped in from the tidewater flats, they found Linnville all theirs, uncontested and almost abandoned. They caught and killed the collector of customs, Maj. H. O. Watts, and five other people, and captured Mrs. Watts, who had been married only twenty days, a Mrs. Crosby, and three others.[8]

The rest of the population of Linnville was clustered in the lighter and a schooner, both of which swung on their hawsers, barely out of musket and bow shot, while all the small boats were tied alongside them or drifting out into Matagorda Bay on the ebb tide. Frustrated, the Comanches turned their attention to the clutch of poor dwellings and John Linn's store and wharf. After dumping all the goods into the street, they put the torch to every structure, one by one, as agonized owners watched from the bay. Strewing plunder everywhere as they broke open trunks, boxes, and bales, the raiders donned brightly colored clothes, men's or women's, frontward, backward, or awry, as they found them, and raced wildly up and down the beach before the vessels. As the warriors disappeared toward the interior in a cloud of dust, the desolate but saved people on the vessels saw flying in the wind from the last pony's tail thirty feet of bright red hair ribbon. It marked, ironically, the end of Linnville.[9]

This was also the last time the Comanche warriors penetrated to the coast. After careening unchecked all the way to the coast and turning back, the band was trailed doggedly by a growing force of Rangers, Minutemen, and volunteers, eventually joining under command of Gen. Felix Huston of the militia. The converging units brought the Indians to a halt at Plum Creek near the present town of Lockhart on August 12, 1840.

The marching Indians were encumbered with unwieldy plunder and a huge herd of captured horses and cattle, 2,000 or more. When Huston finally ordered the charge, upon the impatient urging of Ranger Capt. Matthew Caldwell, the Comanche *caballado* stampeded, the Indians broke ranks, and the rout was on. From sixty to eighty Comanches were killed on the battlefield, and the pursuing Texians harried the remainder on up the San Marcos River valley to the old San Antonio Road.

After the battle was over, Mrs. Watts, wife of the slain customs collector at Linnville, was discovered lying in the brush with an arrow in her breast. Her whalebone corsets had slowed the stone point's entry. Rev. Z. N. Morrell and a Dr. Brown of Gonzales cut the arrow out and she recovered. Three other captives lay nearby, slain.[10]

The spirit of the Comanche, the ferocity of his warfare, was not dampened by this catastrophe, but as Walter Prescott Webb has observed,

> never again did they send a large body into or below the settlements, never again did they attempt to wipe out a town. Henceforth they came in small bodies, stealing horses, killing women and children, and fighting the larger bodies of citizens and soldiers only when they had to.[11]

On Matagorda Bay, a replacement was needed for Linnville. Two or three miles to the south, landing facilities of a sort had existed for several years at a spot called Port Lavaca. Local historian Paul Freier in recent years retrieved customs records for the landings and ports on Matagorda Bay which show that, beginning in 1837, the "Port Lavaca" landing accommodated numerous small groups of passengers from ships calling there, as well as very considerable consignments of goods destined for the bay area and for San Antonio. José Antonio Navarro, W. B. Jaques, Samuel Maverick, José Antonio Menchaca, and a Mr. Zembrano were among San Antonio businessmen who had goods waiting there in 1837 and 1838 with customs duties due. After the death of Linnville, an actual settlement got under way at the Port Lavaca landing, but as late as 1844 it still boasted only seven small log houses.[12]

On a reconnoitering visit to Texas, Prince Carl zu Solms-Braunfels arrived at Matagorda Bay on November 22, 1844. After looking at Port Lavaca, he bought land at Indian Point, some six miles southward down the coast, designating it as the landing point for his colonists.[13]

A persistent point in favor of this and other lower locations was that they were simply that much closer to deep water — to the narrow, precarious Paso Cavallo, whose five- to eight-foot soundings provided the only navigable inlet through the offshore islands into Matagorda Bay.[14] Shipping interests in later years complained often that the upper reaches of the bay, especially in rounding Gallinipper Point between Indian Point and Lavaca, were made hazardous by shifting shoals and bars.

Though Solms had specified Indian Point as his landing place, when the first hundred German families arrived from Galveston in three ships in December of 1844, they were disembarked at what was then called Miller's Point, about three miles farther down the coast.

Debouched forlornly on this rude alien shore and moved up to Indian Point, the settlers spent a cheerless Christmas trying to erect some kind of shelters to shield them from the rigors of the coldest winter in many a year along the Texas coast. Prince Carl had named their little tent city "Carlshafen," because he, Count Castell, and Prince Lieningen of the Society all had the given name Carl. There the immigrants stuck it out for two months while the dashing prince (some said he wore an ostrich plume in his velvet hat) scouted out horseback the interior to fix upon a destination for the colonists.

The Meinzer Verein, or Adelsverein, had been fleeced in two earlier purchases of large tracts far to the north in the Llano-San Saba watersheds, which turned out to be impracticable because of their isolation and vulnerability to Indian attacks. Solms next made a fortunate choice when he brought from the Veramendi family of San Antonio the site beside the junction of the Comal and Guadalupe rivers, nestled at the base of the Balcones Fault on the old Camino Real from San Antonio de Bejar to the East Texas missions. Known as "Las Fontanas," for the huge Comal Springs, it was intended as a temporary staging point, but it eventually turned out to be the most stable and prosperous German settlement in the Southwest: New Braunfels.[15]

At this early stage in the great settlement adventure, however, when the prince returned to Carlshafen early in March 1845, he found only tragedy. Weakened by the cold and by poor food, the colonists had been ravaged by dysentery and pneumonia. Many had died and were hardly half-buried in shallow trenches. The survivors, shivering in their huts at night, listened as the wolves fought over their kinfolks' bodies.[16]

They barely had strength to creep about when Solms returned, but he knew he must get them on the road if the colony were to survive at all; besides, each family had contracted to go all the way to the point of ultimate settlement. So with such small store of goods as remained, loaded on the carts that could be mustered, a contingent moved out, painfully, up the Guadalupe River valley: the first train to leave what became Indianola. On March 21 they crossed the Guadalupe River to the site of their new home.[17]

The settlement at New Braunfels did survive, and after the first few years of stark privation it prospered. Dr. Ferdinand Roemer, a contemporary German paleontologist studying the natural history of Texas, made notes on the progress of German immigration and reported extensively about the settlements when he returned. He had seen the beginnings of New Braunfels in 1845, then passed through on his way back to Germany in 1847. By then he could report that "much had been built and the whole place looked much more like a city." [18]

Nevertheless, once their obligation had been absolved, a number of New Braunfels settlers, dissatisfied that the Meinzer Verein had not given them the full promised amount of farm land, filtered back to the shores of Matagorda Bay between Indian Point and the Powderhorn, where additional masses of German immigrants were arriving. [19]

The managers of the Meinzer Verein were inexplicably shipping hundreds and then thousands of new settlers into Galveston and on into Matagorda Bay without providing for their sustenance upon arrival. [20] By early 1845 the German-based management of the Society had made up its collective mind that Prince Carl, however generous and high-minded he might be, was not suited to administration. They sent word by one of the many ships plying from the continent to New Orleans that he should return to Germany as soon as his successor arrived.

The Society could not have made a wiser choice than the man who accepted their nomination as that successor. Born Ottfried Hans Freiherr von Meusebach in Dillenburg, he was the son of Baron Carl Hartwig Gregor von Meusebach, who was judge of the Superior Court in Berlin. Young Ottfried was well established in a career of administration in the complex government of Germany when he became attracted to the cause of the Society. Though he was already affianced to a handsome gentlewoman, Agnes Elizabeth von Hardenburg, he yielded to the call when Count Carl Castell of the Adelsverein asked him, on February 24, 1845, to take the post as commissioner. When Agnes Elizabeth agreed to wait until the young baron could become established in America, he made the final decision to leave Germany and cast his fortunes in Texas. He arrived in New Orleans April 10 of that year, and in Texas early in May. When he stepped ashore on Matagorda Bay he renounced all his titles forever, becoming plain John O. Meusebach — one of the steadiest and most respected of early Texas leaders. [21]

John Meusebach reached Carlshafen at twilight on May 8. The local agent for the Society, Ludwig Willke, met him there and filled in for the new commissioner a dismal picture of the situation. Early next day they left for New Braunfels, where, upon their arrival, Meusebach was the more confounded to learn that Solms was already on his way to Galveston to take ship for Germany. Meusebach rode hard to catch the prince and intercepted him in Galveston. No account exists of the nature of their meeting, but the new commissioner did learn that the Society owed $20,000 in Texas and was in a most precarious state.[22]

Meusebach doggedly went ahead with arrangements to transport the flood of incoming colonists on down to Matagorda Bay, where they disembarked at Indian Point. In the fall of 1845, the new commissioner made an expedition into the hill country to locate more land. North of the Pedernales River, about eighty miles from New Braunfels, he acquired for the Verein a tract of several thousand acres. Here, eventually, the second village, Fredericksburg, was established.

After an unsuccessful trip to New Orleans in February 1846 to raise money, Meusebach went back to Houston, where he persuaded the Torrey brothers, largest operators of teamsters in Texas at the time, to accept $10,000 in drafts of the Society in Europe as payment for bringing sufficient wagons to Carlshafen to transport his immigrants to the interior. Meanwhile, as Roemer recorded,

> the spring of 1846 arrived and with it the heat of a semi-tropical climate. About three thousand of the poor immigrants lay crowded on the sandy coast, without an adequate water supply and fuel, living in sod houses or tents which afforded no protection against the rain nor against the hot rays of the sun . . . Malaria, bilious fever, and dysentery soon became general, and the mortality increased with alarming rapidity. A general cry of distress arose to leave this dreadful place.[23]

But now, after all the stress from heated passions aroused by the annexation of Texas, the United States declared war upon Mexico.

The first Torrey wagons had barely arrived on the Matagorda beaches and loaded up one contingent of frantic settlers when the United States government requisitioned all of the Torrey brothers' rolling stock to move Gen. Zachary Taylor's army, which had been stationed since the year before some seventy-five miles farther south at Corpus Christi. Those first few wagons did move out to New Braunfels, but Meusebach's remaining throngs were left still stranded on the beach, and no orderly supply of wagons was available through the remainder of the war.[24]

Some of the immigrants in despair gave up their plans for settlement and decided to join the army and fight the Mexicans. From the host of disconsolate pilgrims huddled on the shore emerged a talented leader, Augustus C. Buchel, who began organizing a company of his fellow immigrants. With the rank of captain, he took his sixty-three men into the First Texas Rifle Volunteers. Other young Germans stranded at the Point enlisted in other units of Taylor's army, and altogether it has been estimated that as many as 500 immigrants took that course to get off the beach.[25]

Meanwhile, under dreadful conditions, the main body of surviving immigrants straggled out on their way toward New Braunfels, along the new trail beat out through Victoria, Yorktown, and the embryo settlement at Seguin. Some of them dropped out before they reached their destination, finding a toehold in those communities. Many others struck directly out across the mud flats to intercept the old Spanish cart road through Victoria, Goliad, and on to San Antonio. They settled in the San Antonio area before and during the months in 1846 when General Wool employed that route to move his army to Mexico. Thereby was reborn the old road of the Spanish soldiers and *padres* who had blazed out the way through Bejar to Matagorda Bay in their reaction against La Salle's ill-fated landing.

Roemer said of that heart-breaking period for the Germans: "It is certain that in the few summer months of 1846 more than one thousand of four thousand German immigrants who had come to Texas in the fall of 1845 . . . died, and not more than one thousand two hundred actually settled upon the land secured by the Verein." [26]

Among those families who did survive that harrowing period, one in particular must be mentioned. This family produced the greatest wagon freighter of them all, the man who traveled more miles and carried more freight along the Chihuahua Road and other border roads than any other: August Santleben. He was three and a half months old in June of 1845 when his parents, Christian Santleben and Sophie Haas Santleben emigrated from Hanover. Their ship, the *Karl Wilhelm*, left Bremen with a full crew and 130 passengers on board. They made landfall off Galveston about the middle of July. Some of those passengers who lined the rail to gaze with joyous anticipation at the promised land never set foot on that land, however. The ship ran aground while passing through the channel into Galveston Bay, only a half mile from port. It broke up there, and most of the passengers were rescued by lifeboats which put out from shore.[27]

The Santleben family, including five-month-old August, were among those who survived, but all their possessions were lost: wagons for transport, farm implements for starting anew, everything but the clothes on their backs and a few dollars in their pockets. But Christian Santleben managed to arrange passage on to Port Lavaca for himself and family, and there to contract with one Plasedo Olivarri to transport them by wagon upwards of 200 miles to the Medina River above the new settlement of Castroville. They made there, at Castro's Corner, the most austere of beginnings, camping out "under the canopy of heaven, exposed to all kinds of weather, until a suitable shelter could be erected." [28] From that rude and inauspicious advent emerged, a generation later, the sturdy personality of August Santleben, who, more than any other among the thousands who participated, became the prototype and articulate spokesman for the wagon freighters of the Chihuahua Road.

Meanwhile, in 1847 Meusebach negotiated with the Indians to arrange the Meusebach-Comanche Treaty. This almost unique compact opened to roads and settlement the vast area between the Colorado and Llano rivers: the Fisher-Miller Grant.

The flood and ebb of German immigration on the shell beaches of Matagorda Bay did not pass without leaving its monument. Several enterprising tradesmen became convinced that a permanent port city could be developed near Indian Point. Dr. Levi Jones had surveyed and laid out a townsite near the Powderhorn inlet, and settlement began to gravitate there. The Indian Point area became known as "Old Town," and today the small pond lying behind it from the coast is still known as Old Town Lake.

Among the first business houses in the new town were those of the Runge brothers, known popularly as "the long Runge" and "the short Runge"; Henry Huck; Augustus Fromme; William Dove; and Jacob Haas. As early as 1845, the Runges established inside a tent a banking operation that would maintain continuity over the years to become known as the oldest unincorporated bank in Texas. [29]

Not until early 1849 did the citizens get together and petition that the town officially be called "Indianola," a name that had been devised by Mrs. John Henry Brown, wife of one of the earliest journalists located there. On February 7, 1853, the state legislature approved an act to incorporate the city of Indianola. [30] The entire west shore of Matagorda Bay had originally been a part of Victoria County; but as shipping and settlement developed on the bay, the new state of Texas on April 4, 1846, created Calhoun County out of portions of Victoria, Matagorda, and Jackson counties, to include all the new communities along the bay and on Matagorda Island, with Port Lavaca as county seat.

Port Lavaca itself had prospered during the German immigration. Other ambitious townsites made their bids for eminence during the boom of the Mexican War: La Salle, known today as Port O'Connor, lay six miles down the coast across Powderhorn Lake; on the gulfside conglomerate of sandy islets called Matagorda Island blossomed Saluria. Early settlers there included James Power, Alexander Somervell, who had led the expedition known by his name; John W. Rose; and two governors, Henry Smith and Edmund J. Davis.[31] Saluria prospered until the Civil War, when it was burned to deny it to Union troops. Despite valiant promotional efforts by Hugh W. Hawes, the town was never rebuilt.[32] The site was swept clean in the hurricane of 1875.

During these efforts by other towns to gain ascendancy, Indianola continued to gain strength. In an election held August 2, 1852, the people of Calhoun County voted to move the county seat from Port Lavaca to Indianola. On September 29 the first called session of the court was held in that town.[33] Five more years passed, however, before the community assembled enough resources to erect a permanent courthouse. The two-story structure, built with concrete blocks composed of beach sand, shell, lime, and cement, was completed in 1857. It was the only major structure to escape serious damage in the storms of 1875 and 1886. All the people who took refuge there were saved.[34]

Indianola, then, became the southern anchor and gulf terminal of the Chihuahua Road. In Brownson Malsch's book, *Indianola, The Mother of Western Texas*,[35] the author postulates that Indianola was born at the right time and right place to make possible the Chihuahua Road and its traffic. In that sense it was, as the subtitle says, "The Mother of Western Texas."

[9]

Observant Strangers
on a New Frontier

When the United States and Mexican representatives wound up
the War of 1846–47 by affixing their signatures to the Treaty of
Guadalupe Hidalgo on February 2, 1848, neither they nor the people of their countries had any reason to view the terms as any more
one-sided than might have been expected. This was, after all, still
the first half of the nineteenth century, the period in which Napoleon Bonaparte had imposed his will on most of the European nations; in which bloody revolutions raged up and down the American
continents, with dramatic settlements that toppled the Spanish empire. Justified or not, the United States had won this war on the
field of battle; it was now ready to settle for about one-third of the
territory comprising the Republic of Mexico — the third which
Mexico had been least able to develop. The victors furthermore had
been willing to pay $15 million for that vast, unproved desert of
California, Arizona, and New Mexico.[1]

It was an irony of the fate which dogged Mexico in that century
that a month before the treaty was signed, gold in incredible quantities
had turned up in a California creek, below a mill erected by a Swiss
named Sutter. But it took many weeks for word of that strike to per-

colate out to the rest of the world, and more months before the significance of the find was realized.

Meanwhile, both nations set about soberly to consummate one of the obvious obligations of the new treaty: to survey out a boundary at last between Mexico and the United States, along a thousand miles of the storied Rio Grande and almost another thousand miles of an abstract line westering across the desert to the Pacific. It was not only an obvious need, but also one specifically spelled out in the treaty, requiring that each nation appoint a boundary commissioner and a surveyor, and further stipulating that their joint findings be considered as part of the treaty, as fully enforceable as though they had been terms of the original document.[2]

This large task, fraught with scientific demands and political challenge, set off in the United States a chain of speculation and jockeying for advantage in finding the man who could take on the responsibilities of the commissioner. One of the first persons considered was the young army officer, Lt. William H. Emory, who had served with distinction under Kearney in the Mexican War and then executed a difficult assignment as a topographical engineer on the Northeastern Boundary Commission. But Emory was a soldier, plain and simple, and the politicians felt, when the import of the gold discovery at Sutter's Mill sank in, that a man of delicate political sensitivity would be required. This recognition was heightened, insofar as southern politicians were concerned, when they learned that one of the major possibilities for a railroad route to the West Coast lay uncomfortably close along the new southern boundary line. Determination of whether the route would lie within the United States or partly within Mexico carried enormous implications to the economy of the southern states.

So Lieutenant Emory was passed over for the top job, though he was attached to the survey commission as an engineer, and along with Lt. Amiel W. Whipple soon began actual survey operations, starting east from a point a few miles south of the port of San Diego.[3]

After three abortive selections, Congress came round to choosing for its fourth commissioner a scholarly scientist of the mid-nineteenth century *genre:* writer, artist, and generalist in many fields of the natural sciences. This was John Russell Bartlett, who in a gentlemanly way operated a bookstore in downtown New York and moved in the best circles of dilettante scientific studies.[4]

Bartlett turned out to be a miserably poor administrator, squandering much of his appropriated funds on magnificent leisurely progressions through parts of the Southwest far from the purported boundary, in pursuit of his scientific interests. Nevertheless, to those wide-ranging studies the nation remains indebted for some of the best of early ethnological and geographic records in Arizona, New Mexico, western Texas, and the Mexican states bordering on the Rio Grande.[5]

The new commissioner and the people he had selected in the East for his party gathered at Indianola on August 31, 1850. Since that little town was at that moment launching into the prominence it would occupy for three brief decades, commissioner Bartlett's impressions are useful here:

> From the several examinations which have been made of Matagorda Bay, it appears that the harbors on its western shores, the chief of which are La Salle and Indianola, possess advantages above any of those ports on the Gulf of Mexico, between the mouth of the Mississippi and Vera Cruz, with the exception of Galveston . . .
>
> In the contest for superiority, Indianola seems to have carried away the palm; for while the highly applauded site for the city of La Salle is almost unoccupied, the former has grown into a large and thriving town, second only to Galveston among all the ports in Texas. Indianola is now the port for the extensive commerce with Western Texas, Chihuahua, and portions of New Mexico; a railroad has already been commenced to connect it with San Antonio, the chief city of the State, and two lines of steamers plying between it and New Orleans will continue to add to its prosperity. Should one of the contemplated railroads to the Pacific be extended from San Antonio, with its terminus here, Indianola will rank second only to New Orleans among the cities of the Gulf in commerce and population.[6]

Such a booster as that deserves to be lionized, and he was. A September 5, 1850, article from the Victoria *Texian Advocate* tells of 150 persons at a banquet given by the people of Indianola for the commissioner and his officers. The news article quoted verbatim a total of fifty rounds of toasts which were drunk in the course of the evening, Bartlett of course being the first honoree.[7]

After that, the mundane matter of shoeing 150 wild Mexican mules might have seemed anticlimactic, though it included the necessity of adapting to their relatively dainty hooves the oversized ironware which New York manufacturers had hammered out for what they thought to be a much heavier breed. But it was time-consuming for, if we are to believe Bartlett, each terror-stricken animal in turn had to be manhandled into a two-by-six-foot stall, lifted off the ground and spread-eagled, lashed there by each hoof, and worked on by four far-riers at a time. The operation took two weeks.[8]

Eventually the caravan of some forty ambulances and wagons did get under way, with 140 persons including a military escort headed by Col. Lewis S. Craig, a half dozen draftsmen and artists, and an extraor-dinary quantity of astronomical and surveying instrumentation, which led the expedition to be called "the most extensive geodetic work ever projected by any nation." [9]

The military escorts wore red flannel shirts and white hats; the engineers sported blue flannel shirts and white hats. The pace was set by Commissioner Bartlett himself, there on the boggy Texas coastal plain just as in Arizona's rocky canyons 1,500 miles and two years later. His large "carriage" as he called it, drawn by four mules, with roll-down waterproof curtains and a collapsible bed, was also a travel-ing arsenal. Shotguns, rifles, Colt revolvers, and derringers provided a total capability of firing 37 rounds without reloading. These weapons were hung, stowed, and lashed at every possible point within the car-riage to provide ready access in case of an attack.[10] They did serve that collective purpose one time, in Mexico, when Bartlett's party was sub-jected to a classic running encirclement of howling Comanches.

Bartlett's descriptions of landmarks along the Chihuahua Road demonstrate that he was one of a small handful who were articulate enough to report upon major portions of that road. His route was a combination of several: the standard Indianola-Victoria-Goliad road (before Helena established its identity) to San Antonio, then via Fred-ericksburg to the Emigrants Road, Castle Gap, Horsehead Crossing, and the uppermost road, through the Guadalupe foothills to Hueco Tanks and El Paso del Norte.

One very important project was undertaken from the start, partly as an afterthought to keep his surveyors busy, Bartlett confessed:

> I caused a party to be organized to make a chain and compass sur-vey, and carry a line of levels to determine a profile from this point [Indianola] to El Paso del Norte. The eyes of the South had long been directed this way; for whether there might be a more practicable route or not further north, it was a question of great importance to the Southern section of the Union, that all infor-mation possible should be obtained with reference to the part of the country we were about to traverse, and its practicability for the purpose of a railroad.[11]

This undertaking was the first systematic line-and-profile survey from the gulf across the state to its farthest corner, most of it on the Chihuahua and El Paso Road. In a summary of his labors, compiled at the end of his tenure, Bartlett added that "from El Paso the survey was continued to the Initial Point of the southern boundary of New Mexico on the Rio Grande, making altogether a distance of between nine hundred and a thousand miles surveyed." [12] The party arrived at Major Van Horne's military post alongside Coons's Ranch, across the Rio Bravo from El Paso del Notre, on November 13, 1850, thirty-three days out of San Antonio, having endured the same privations of water and rations experienced by those who came before them.

No work whatever had been accomplished along the actual border since Lieutenants Whipple and Emory had been pulled off the job in California in mid-1849. The two had been separately ordered to report in to Washington. Whipple made his fresh start from there with Bartlett, while Emory was ignored and left to cool his heels in the capital.

Not without reason had the classmates of William Helmsley Emory dubbed him "Bold Emory" in their West Point yearbook. Single-minded, sober, sometimes truculent over the lack of progress on the boundary survey, Emory continued to pursue his own ends in Washington to get back onto the commission.

It was not Bartlett's frittering away of appropriated funds on irrelevant enterprises but a much more damaging political mistake that became the commissioner's eventual undoing. This had to do with determining the point on the Rio Grande from which the boundary would proceed west. Working from the most reputable map of the day, Disturnell's "Map of the United Mexican States," dated 1847, the treaty makers had accepted the latitude of 32°15' N. They also agreed that the point of departure westward from the Rio Grande, as the southern boundary of New Mexico, should be as shown on the map, presumably only about eight miles north of El Paso. [13]

But as soon as Commissioner Bartlett got together with his Mexican counterpart, Gen. Francisco García Conde, [14] and their surveyors made valid astronomical observations, they found that El Paso del Norte was actually a full thirty miles south of the indicated latitude. Furthermore, the Rio Grande and the town of El Paso were almost two degrees of longitude east of where they were shown on Disturnell's projection — about a hundred miles.

After months of argument and staff work in the field, Bartlett finally agreed to setting the westward departure point at the *true* 32°22'N, almost thirty-eight miles upriver from El Paso. He seemed unaware of the significance that he was thereby signing away a strip of land some 35 miles wide and 175 miles in length: the very terrain through which much of any feasible wagon road, and later any railroad, should have to proceed, a matter of immense importance to the South. It was an honest capitulation, but reached in precisely the kind of political naïveté the Congress had feared from military men.[15]

The storm broke and raged, both among Bartlett's own subordinates on his staff and in the public forums back East. The controversy was not finally settled until long after Bartlett's departure, but it was certainly one of the major factors in his removal. The ultimate settlement, of course, was the "Gadsden Purchase," which not only established a more southerly line, at 31°47'N, but also reconciled urgent problems in the Mesilla area, northwest of El Paso, which Bartlett's first line had caused.[16]

When the first line was announced many settlers, mostly old New Mexicans, had moved back south to establish themselves as Mexican citizens in the very desirable Mesilla Valley area, across the river from Doña Ana. Aside from these legitimate homesteaders, there were also speculators and promoters who were sure the eventual railroad would pass through there, and they wanted to establish a prior claim on the land that would be needed. All these considerations had to be settled.

To bring this about, the new Democratic administration in 1853 sent James Gadsden, a railroad financier and former army officer on the early Florida frontier, to Mexico City as minister, with powers of negotiation. He reached agreement, ratified on April 24, 1854, to buy the disputed land, covering all claims of the Mesilla settlers, and also to indemnify Mexico for Indian depredations occurring from United States territory. This was an obligation spelled out in the Treaty of Guadalupe Hidalgo, but the new treaty terminated this obligation as of its effective date. The total settlement was $10 million, and its resolution of the controversy, greeted with enthusiasm by the *norteamericanos,* became known as the Gadsden Purchase in the United States, but has been called the Mesilla Treaty by the Mexicans.[17]

It was distinctly relevant to the Chihuahua roads, because for thirty years it enabled wagons and stage traffic to continue westward to California from Indianola and San Antonio, while in the long range it cleared the way for the Sunset Route, the Southern Pacific Railroad, which spelled the ultimate doom of the wagon freighters.

Bartlett had run through two principal engineering officers, Col. A. B. Gray and Col. J. B. Graham, both of them competent surveyors but of a temperament which simply could not put up with Bartlett's dilettante approach to the mission. The army at length fixed upon William H. Emory, the real veteran of boundary surveys, who had been dourly awaiting action in Washington. He was promoted to brevet major and posted out to El Paso to take over the engineering work, combining the titles of chief surveyor and astronomer. When Emory reached the little military post at Coons's Ranch, he learned that Bartlett was making the grand tour in California, at one time more than 600 miles from the boundary line he was commissioned to fix.

Bartlett, eventually hearing of Emory's reporting to the new job, decided it was time they might get together — and took from April 14 to August 18, 1852, to journey from San Francisco to El Paso. [18]

The new chief surveyor and astronomer had simmered awhile in El Paso, watched unpaid and unpayable bills drift in from all over the Southwest, and finally, being a man of action, organized parties to work on various sections of the Texas Rio Grande, moving his own headquarters downriver to be more closely among his men. Therefore, when Bartlett did arrive at the Pass of the North, his new number-two man was gone. Bartlett was alone to face the music of the unpaid men, the exhausted appropriations, the political storm over what was being called the Bartlett-García Conde Line, the feuding among his own closest assistants.

The forty-eight-year-old scholar had lost a little daughter from illness at his home in New England; he had suffered a broken shoulder in the desert when a mule threw and then kicked him; he had seen his closest military aide, Col. Lewis S. Craig, brought in from the desert a corpse riddled with arrows from an Indian ambush; and he had had to write one of his strongest supporters in Washington, a senator, that his young son, a member of Bartlett's crew, had been killed in a barroom brawl. The sensitive scientist and artist was exhausted and dispirited. Whether or not he realized that his tenure as commissioner was drawing to a close, he decided he must go to Washington to vindicate himself.

Somehow he exchanged letters with Emory, who had established a camp for astronomical observations a hundred miles down the river, near where Fort Quitman was later built,[19] and was already preparing to move his base to Fort Duncan, 400 miles farther down the river. They agreed to meet at Ringgold Barracks, below Rio Grande City, in December.

The normal route for Bartlett, in the fall of 1852, would have been to take the lower road from El Paso through the Davis Mountains, Live Oak Creek, Howard's Well, the Devil's River, Las Moras, to Fort Inge at Uvalde, and on down to Ringgold. But Commissioner Bartlett, once again the wide-eyed, eager traveler, listened readily to news that Indian depredations along that road were especially fierce at this season. He seized on a suggestion that they might proceed through Mexico via Chihuahua City, Durango, and Monterrey. And so he did, adding another long and adventurous progression to his eventual personal narrative.[20]

Chief Surveyor Emory, with his assistants Lieutenants Nathaniel Michler, M. T. W. Chandler, and others, had carved out epochal new bodies of knowledge about the canyons of the Rio Grande, traversing hundreds of miles of utter wilderness and eerie gorges never before seen by European men. This was indeed the boundary between the United States and Mexico, as it is today, and those hardy souls were not out there sightseeing.

Many gaps were still to be covered, however, both along the river and in the western deserts. The meeting between Emory and Bartlett at Ringgold Barracks on December 21, 1852, was stiff; the commissioner saw that Bold Emory would be as hard to get along with as had been Gray and Graham, while the soldierly Emory had little respect or patience for the gentleman scholar. But the cold fact was that the expedition was broke; it could not pay its bills; and the thorny matter of the Bartlett-Conde Line had to be settled. So they did agree they must all pack up and go to Washington before any further legitimate progress could be made.

By wagon and horseback the top officials of the commission traveled across the prairies to Corpus Christi. Bartlett marveled at the teeming game, the immense herds of wild mustangs, streaming literally for miles, the luxuriant waist-high grasses upon which they fed, in the areas that are today the tangled brush of the *brasada* and the grain fields of the Coastal Bend, crisscrossed by drainage ditches.

At Corpus Christi, while others chose to ride overland, Bartlett was determined to take passage by boat up the Laguna Madre to Indianola, where shipboard passage might be engaged to New Orleans.

His conveyance was but a tiny shallow-draft boat, but Mr. Bartlett had traveled 5,000 miles in his outlandish carriage and on the backs of horses and mules, and at this point anything looked better than more of that. The little sailing scow bucketed back and forth across Corpus Christi Bay and through the tortuous channels of the laguna leading finally into Matagorda Bay, requiring four days for the passage.

They debarked at Decrow's Point and stopped at an inn there, upon learning that a steamer from Indianola, bound for New Orleans, would put in the following day on its way out through Paso Cavallo.

Next morning, January 8, 1853, the steamer *Louisiana* did arrive off Decrow's Point, with Major Emory, Dr. Webb, and those members of the party who had preferred to travel overland already aboard.[21] And so, there where the Chihuahua Road begins, at the entrance to Matagorda Bay, this narrative must bid goodbye to John Russell Bartlett, turning him over to the politicians, who made short work of him in Washington, and to posterity, who will continue to enjoy and profit by his observations, written and graphic, however little they may have had to do with the boundary between the United States and Mexico.[22]

It was some months after the party's arrival in Washington before Bartlett was officially separated from his post, but Emory apparently almost at once was given authority, as chief astronomer and surveyor, to resume the work. He dispatched orders, dated 4, 1853, to Lieutenants Michler and Chandler, back in Texas, charging them with "the responsible duty of completing the unfinished portion of the survey of the Rio Grande, which forms the boundary between the United States and Mexico, between Fort Vincente [*sic*] and the mouth of the Rio Pecos."[23]

These indefatigible engineers proceeded to contract for prefabricated boats in San Antonio, took them by wagon train up the Chihuahua Road to a point on the Pecos above the site of Fort Lancaster then called "Pecos Springs," and then struck off across the Big Bend wilderness with their wagons, toward San Vicente, the old Comanche Trail crossing of the Rio Grande. They labored through totally untracked wilderness before finally reaching the river near the "Lipan Crossing," in what is now the Big Bend National Park. There they placed their frail boats of unseasoned wood in the torrent, commencing an almost incredible voyage through the great lower canyons that occupy so much attention today from adventurers in vastly more sophisticated equipment.

Michler's account, buried and almost forgotten in Emory's report, could stand alongside the later writings of professional journalists. It is an epic of the first water-borne journey through these canyons by any humans, European or aboriginal.[24] Their efforts in simple survival through successive roaring rapids were complicated by the demands of their assignment to devise, by what means they could, a serviceable tracing of the river's meanders — the international boundary, which they had been called upon to survey. The party did complete the transit of those canyons, emerging in more tranquil waters at last below the mouth of the Pecos River. They reached Fort Duncan, at Eagle Pass, in the late summer.[25]

More than a year earlier, even before his trip east with Commissioner Bartlett, William H. Emory had recorded his impressions of La Junta de los Rios, that key spot on the Chihuahua Road:

> We arrived in front of the Presidio del Norte July 8, 1852, and found watermelons ripe and corn in the tassel. [Here those melons show up again, as they have appeared all the way back to Cabeza de Vaca's time.] The town, isolated and very remote from any other settlement, had been suffering from famine. The Indians had run off most of the cattle, and the drought for the three preceding years had caused a failure in the corn . . .
>
> The relations between the Indians of this region and several of the Mexican towns, particularly San Carlos, a small town twenty miles below [more accurately, nearly 45 miles] are peculiar and well worth the attention of both the United States and Mexican governments. The Apaches are usually at war with the people of both countries, but have friendly league with certain towns, where they trade and receive supplies of arms, ammunition, etc., for stolen goods. This is undoubtedly the case with the people of San Carlos, who also have amicable relations with the Comanches, who make San Carlos a depot of arms in their annual excursions into Mexico.[26]

Major Emory made one important direct contribution to the opening of the Chihuahua Road — that part of it which leads from Presidio up Alamito Creek to Paisano Pass. It had long been traversed, of course, by the Indians, the Spaniards, by Henry Connelley, and four years before by Col. Jack Hays on his return trip from Fort Leaton. But now Emory sent his engineers up the trail to clear obstacles and make it more readily passable to wagons. He recorded,

> . . . The road which I opened from the Presidio del Norte to the Leon Spring . . . was opened for the double purpose of communicat-

ing with my parties on the lower Rio Grande, and of shortening the distance from San Antonio to Chihuahua. The route followed by the merchant trains is by way of El Paso, a distance greater by 300 miles. It is possible a shorter way may be found, but our explorations led us to believe this was the shortest one where a permanent supply of water could be obtained . . . Fort Davis has been established since our survey. There is now a constantly traveled road connecting Fort Davis and Chihuahua, via Presidio del Norte.[27]

Emory did not receive his formal appointment as commissioner until August 4, 1854, though he had continued to direct the work as chief surveyor and astronomer. It still took him two years after that to complete his mission. Paul Horgan, in his all-encompassing work on *The Great River,* summed up Bold Emory's work:

He was an able and orderly soldier, calm, dignified, and firm with all the versatility of so many officers in the mid-nineteenth century army; . . . The longer he worked the more he seemed interested in the harsh country that slowly yielded itself up to his knowledge . . . the Mexican officers on the Boundary Commission who worked with him were intelligent, courteous, and cooperative . . . In the journals of the joint commission, the daily entries were signed alternately in first place by the Mexican and United States Commissioners, to balance the precedence of the two nations in their common effort. The survey was harmoniously concluded, to the satisfaction of both governments.[28]

In early May of 1853, while Lieutenants Michler and Chandler were preparing their assault upon the lower canyons of the Rio Grande, another remarkable and most agreeable young man was loading his gear upon a "waggon" at the western end of the Chihuahua Road. In the ensuing three months, he was to document in detail for the first time a full west-to-east passage of this newly opened thoroughfare, all the way to Indianola.

The man was Herr Julius Froebel, under thirty years of age, wealthy, enterprising, and another scientist of the mid-nineteenth-century generalists. He was, at this time, already in the seventh year of a leisurely, genteel peregrination he would memorialize in a book when he returned home to Germany.

Froebel had just spent the winter and early spring months of 1852 socializing with new friends in the town of Chihuahua; he took the opportunity, as well, to make exploratory side trips in the mountainous countryside, to visit the great silver mines, and to observe the

natural history of the area. It was pleasant there, in that cosmopolitan
society, but inevitably he must move on. Young Froebel's account of
the circumstances that provided him with an opportunity to get
through to Texas gives posterity a valuable sidelight on the economics
of the new Chihuahua Road:

> The trade in the interior of North Mexico is in such a primitive
> condition that remittances for goods are almost always made in coin.
> The time, therefore, arrived when my friends had to send some cart-
> loads of Mexican dollars to the United States; the consignment was
> to go to Texas, and I determined to take this opportunity of return-
> ing to the East. Our caravan was headed by Don Guillermo . . . It
> consisted of seven waggons and about 100 mules, with a proportion-
> ate body of men; Don Guillermo considered it advantageous to have
> a surplus of Mexican servants with the mules, who, on their return
> to Chihuahua, would become drivers, as it was intended to bring
> back a fresh transport of goods.
> The preparations were soon made. The money was sewed into
> wet bullock hides in parcels containing 3,000 pesos [dollars], and
> packed into two of the waggons; the other five were loaded with
> maize for the mules, and provisions for ourselves, and on the evening
> of the 12th of May our caravan took the road to the Presidio del
> Norte, by the ascent of the Cerro Grande. We were accompanied by
> friends from the town, till night compelled them to return.[30]

Here is evidence that in barely three years since the first military opening of the El Paso Road, with its branch down to Presidio, the merchants of Chihuahua had already established a pattern of trade on their
end which was bringing substantial hard cash into and through Texas.
If two of the "waggons" (*carretas*), were loaded with rawhide bags of
coins, each containing 3,000 dollars, there must have been $100,000
or more in that one shipment.

The train moved out of Ciudad Chihuahua in festive spirits, accompanied by their well-wishing friends as they made the ascent of the
Big Hill. It is illuminating to find documentation that they continued
by the trail used four years earlier by Henry Connelley that leads down
the east side of the Rio Conchos. Some traffic, not with wheeled vehicles, moved down the west side of the river, through the towns of Aldama and Coyame, all the way into Presidio. Professor Francisco Almada, historian of Chihuahua, asserts that there was also one route
which started on the west side through Aldama but near Coyama cut
across the river, above the chasm of La Barranca Pegues, to complete
the journey down the east side.[31]

Froebel, however, meticulously details his exciting journey with Don Guillermo through "the Cañon del Ojito, a pass between the plain of Mapula and that of Machimba" and down to the Hacienda de Bachimba.

> Between Bachimba and the warm baths of Julima, we passed over a plain covered with yuccas in full bloom, the most enchanting sight which Mexican scenery can display; their gigantic pannicles, covered with the richest profusion of large white bells, rising from a circle of stiff, radiant leaves, on a stem of ten to twelve feet in height.
>
> The village Julima is a bathing place of great repute in northern Mexico, and we found here a numerous assemblage of our friends from Chihuahua . . . There are seven different springs, varying in temperature from 31° to 35° of Reaumur.[32]

At the same time that Emory's crews were subsisting on hard rations as they battered their way down the canyons of the Rio Grande a scant 150 miles away, and Bigfoot Wallace was hoorawing Henry Skillman's stage full of exhausted passengers across the dusty arroyos toward El Paso, it is instructive to consider this effete scene which Froebel recreates at the spa of Julima just across the river:

> The Rio Conchos, near where Julima is situated, is a clear stream, in which soft-shelled turtles are found. One measuring $1^1/_2$ foot in diameter was caught by one of our servants. It happened that a French gentleman living in this part of Mexico, the Marquis de V———, was then in our camp and he offered to make us some turtle soup of superior quality. We possessed the ingredients he required, namely, Bordeaux, Madeira, vinegar and spices, and, as the Marquis was a skilled gastronome, we had a dish, literally, fit for a king, and which was not the less enjoyed from being eaten out of tin plates, and lying on the ground.[33]

But they were soon back to the harsh reality of the desert:

> Beyond Julimas, we had to make two forced marches, both of about ninety English miles, without water. [A somewhat exaggerated estimate. They measure out more like sixty miles each.] The intervening watering place, called El Chupadero, was a well, which we were obliged first to clean out, before we could reach the water with a bucket. In order to water our cattle, we dug a hole, trod the ground down hard, lined it with stones, and then filled it by buckets from the well. It required more than half a day's work before the animals could have a drop of water . . .

Coming directly out of several years' travel in South and Central America and Mexico, Froebel spoke flatly of one strong impression gained at the border with the United States:

> The people here are savage, and their habits as rude as the nature around them. The Norteños — as the inhabitants of the Presidio del Norte are called in Mexico — are the allies, spies, powder purveyors, the receivers and buyers of stolen goods, of the Texan Comanches. Necessity may have driven them to this, for, isolated and exposed as they are, they could scarcely otherwise have held their ground between the Comanches and the Apaches. Their alliance with the Comanches is in so far advantageous to their Mexican countrymen, as by it they assist in the extermination of the Apaches. This friendly intercourse is maintained by some of these tribes by written correspondence, which the Comanche chiefs carry on by means of their Mexican prisoners. The system of special treaties between individual villages and ranchos and the Indians is universal in Mexico, and neither patriotism nor morality can say much against this fulfillment of the law of self defense.[34]

Froebel's assessment of the function of the Presidio community, with respect to the warring factions surrounding it, is not inconsistent with that made by William H. Emory a year earlier. Emory, however, as a responsible officer in a delicate bi-national enterprise, may have spoken with more restraint than required of this casual but more independent visitor from Germany.

Froebel was able simply to step out of that unhappy milieu:

> We took our loaded waggons over the Rio Grande on a ferry; the empty ones were drawn through the stream by oxen. We encamped on the other side — in Texas. Our camp was not far from a large building surrounded by a mud wall, called by the North Americans Leaton's Fort, and by the Mexicans only El Fortín. A North American, not then living, had fixed himself on this spot in defiance of the Indians, in order to oppose their depredations.

This oblique reference is perhaps the first printed record of Ben Leaton's passing, which had apparently occurred sometime in 1850 or 1851, according to conclusions to be drawn from probate records filed in the county clerk's office, Bexar County, San Antonio.[35]

Don Guillermo, Froebel, and their party had spent June 20 and 21 in the vicinity of Presidio del Norte. On June 22 they were again in motion. According to Froebel, the road they took was "known as Connelly's Trail, after a Dr. Connelly [*sic*], who a few years hence made the first carriage track through the wilderness. This road, at the watering place called Agua Delgado [León Springs], joins the more frequented one which connects El Paso with San Antonio in Texas." [36] This road up Alamito Creek, besides being Connelley's Trail, was of course also the Old Salt Trail of the Indians; Espejo's road back home from the plains; the track which Jack Hays had followed on his return from Presidio; the one Henry Skillman had used in catching up with Billy Whiting in 1849; and that which Major Emory had further engineered only the year before. Froebel's contribution was to give the first clear and detailed description of many of the major points along that segment of the road, as he did all the way from Comanche Springs to Indianola.

Those points between Fort Leaton and Comanche Springs include, from the Rio Grande, Los Alamos on the tributary creek of that name; then Punta del Agua, which must have been near the later settlement of Casa Piedra; and next, a landmark Froebel called *Cerro de Jacinto,* San Jacinto Peak, on the later Rawls Ranch. On down to where the road departed Alamito Creek Canyon was *El Saucillo* (the Willow Bush), a spring at the lower end of San Esteban Lake; followed by the passage up the Painted Caves terrace of rhyalite or tuff at the upper end of San Esteban Lake, which Froebel called *Cuesta de San Estevan.* [37]

There where the road climbed up sharply over raw tuff and through jagged little passes, the actual trace of the heavy iron tires as they pounded ruts into the soft stone for forty years may be seen more clearly today than at any other place on the entire route. [38] There also, just after reaching the crest of the terrace, the old wagon road is now intersected by the Kansas City, Mexico and Orient Railroad, which was constructed from Paisano Pass to Presidio in the early 1930s. The railroad comes down off the high plains into Alamito Creek Canyon by a long descent cut into the almost perpendicular wall of the valley, while the wagon road, on its course eastward, turned a little southward across the prairies to reach the landmark Froebel recorded. This he called *Ojo del Berrendo,* or Antelope Spring:

> . . . a very suitable name, for we saw numerous herds of antelope all around. This watering place had a good spring, but it was insufficient for all our animals. Quite near there was an abundance of standing water, of a coffee-brown color, in pits in the ground, among which separate bunches of rushes grew. This water was so saturated with soda that it tasted like lye, and it made the skin slip-

pery. Notwithstanding this our animals drank it. The plateau, smooth and sterile, with the rushes and water-pits in the foreground, and the rocky peak of the Picacho de la Cienaga de Valles in the background, formed a most characteristic desert scene.[39]

The "picacho" he alludes to must have been Cathedral Mountain, to the northeast. The scene at Antelope Spring, now on the Ritchie Reynolds ranch, originally the Frank Mitchell ranch, is still remarkably the same, with water pits still full of coffee-brown alkaline water.

They then climbed through Paisano Pass, which he admired, as do all travelers, and reached the valley where the town of Alpine and Sul Ross University now stand. He described with enthusiasm the spring which soon began to be called Burgess Spring and later Kokernot Spring.

When Froebel reached León Springs, he called it *Agua Delgada* (narrow or slender water), an apt enough description of the little valley in which it runs. It is all underground today, trapped by pumps which worked night and day to feed nearby irrigation systems — to feed them, that is, until even that deep entrapment failed, and the irrigable fields stood fallow once more.

Even as Whiting noted in 1849, when at this place he saw Connelley's wheeltracks turning down toward Presidio, Froebel also said, "The road from Presidio joins that from El Paso here." [40]

Froebel called the great waters at the site of Fort Stockton "the spring of Ahuancha, an Indian name corrupted into Comanche spring." Clayton Williams, Fort Stockton historian, believed that the term had originally been two words, *Agua Ancha,* meaning broad water, and that the appellation "Comanche Springs" was of separate derivation.[41]

The traveler took note, after that, of "the Ojo Escondido, or Hidden Well, a clear but brackish spring." This was often, in later years, also called Tunas Spring; the little stream which ran off to disappear into the desert bore the same name. This road led to the Pecos River at the spot later known as Pontoon Crossing. It is an area now generally barren in appearance, studded with oil well locations, sump pits, and glittering storage tanks, leading to Iraan, the oilfield boom town of the 1930s. But hear Froebel:

Hitherto we had found but little fresh grass on our road, and our animals had only the dry haulm of the previous year; low moist places, and the bottoms immediately around the springs, had been the only exceptions. But now, as we approached the valley of the Pecos, an entire change took place in the scene. On the 31st of May we arrived at a plain covered with grass and flowers, and surrounded by regularly-formed table-mountains. The grass and flowers were so thick and high that our horses had difficulty in making their way through, and the sweetest perfume, principally of the superb american centaurea [star thistle] filled the atmosphere. This transition to a more advanced season was not caused by any difference in the level above sea, but was the result of heavy rains, which had not fallen more to the west. From hence eastward to Texas [*sic?*] the steppe was in its most gorgeous beauty.[42]

His impressions of the Pecos River paralleled those of all the early travelers.

Along this stretch of the Pecos, above what Froebel's British translator rendered as "Life Oak Creek," an incident occurred which must be enshrined here, as introduction to the stagecoaches which also frequented this road:

The mail from El Paso passed us here. Two carriages, each with four mules, coachmen, guard, and passengers all fully armed. One of the passengers was a little girl of three or four years old, who — entrusted to the coachman, and with no other companion — was sent the 700 miles from El Paso to San Antonio. The other passengers, however, joined in taking care of her; and it was touching to see how these rough, bearded men, with their pistols and daggers, supplied the place of a mother's care to the tender little creature. It was a true picture of wild American life, where the highest qualities in human nature are often found united with the roughest externals.[43]

This was Henry Skillman's stage line. Beyond a doubt one of those "rough bearded men" was the fabled Bigfoot Wallace, for he and a team he had recruited were providing guard service for Skillman's coaches at the time.

[10]

Old Helena and
the Cart War

With freight traffic booming on the old cart road from Matagorda
Bay to San Antonio in the early 1850s, opportunity beckoned for a
commercial way-station between Goliad and San Antonio. This need
was recognized by an astute young schoolteacher, Thomas Ruckman,
who arrived on the Texas frontier late in 1850. Born of Dutch descent
in Northumberland County, Pennsylvania, Ruckman had graduated
from the College of New Jersey, now Princeton University, in 1848,
taught school in South Carolina for a year, and then responded to the
call of the West.

Reaching San Antonio on Christmas morning, 1850, he began at
once casting around for a place to make his beginning. Perhaps on the
way up from the coast he had noticed the tiny Mexican settlement in a
clump of giant cottonwood trees on Alamita Creek.[1] He would have
recognized that it served not only the Matagorda Bay-San Antonio road
but also the old Spanish road from East Texas. The latter ran through
the Alamita settlement to the Alamita crossing of the San Antonio
River and on west, forking some miles beyond — one way to Oakville
and eventually Matamoros, and the other to Eagle Pass.

By whatever means he may have found the location, Thomas
Ruckman moved there in 1851 to open a trading post. Business flour-

150

ished at once. Within a year Dr. Lewis S. Owings had joined Ruckman; as partners they opened the Owings and Ruckman General Store, which became the nucleus of a thriving town. In 1852 Charles A. Russell, Goliad County surveyor, laid out the new townsite, which the entrepreneurs named "Helena" for Owings's wife Helen.

Ruckman built a grist mill and then a saw mill, and finally, on the clay banks of the San Antonio River, a brick kiln from which he built his own mansion. With these resources available, other businesses and settlers followed quickly; by 1853, Ruckman and Owings were petitioning for establishment of a new county. On February 4, 1854, the Texas legislature created the county of Karnes, named after the late Texas patriot, Henry Wax Karnes, with Helena designated as the county seat. In that same year, Dr. Owings began operation of a regular stage line from San Antonio through Helena to Goliad.[2]

The only town of consequence in the new county was Ruckman's creation, Helena, and it wasted no time in proceeding toward organization of the county structure. Three weeks after the legislature's action, election of the first county officials was held February 27, 1854, on the gallery of the Owings and Ruckman store. The new county soon built a frame and clapboard courthouse across the main road from the store, where the town plat had designated the courthouse square. A separate building was put up for the county clerk, while a small wooden structure on the square constituted the first jail. If there was any indication a prisoner might undertake to break jail, he was fitted with shackles at the blacksmith shop and chained to a heavy beam in the jail.[3]

Lyman Russell, son of surveyor Charles Russell, recalled fifty years later that among the early enterprises building up around the original Owings and Ruckman store were shops owned by John Glynn and John Mahon; an ox-freighting business operated by L. S. Lawhon; Louis Adler's blacksmith shop; medical practices conducted by Drs. E. H. Walker and Sam Dailey; and a hotel, "The Traveller's Home," kept by William Odell. John Ruckman himself became the first postmaster at Helena.[4]

Farm families began to settle in the fertile San Antonio River valley, finding a market for cotton, corn, hay, cane syrup, and vegetables in the town, especially with freight trains passing through. The east-west road leading to the Alamita Crossing was planted with trees, helping to establish a more graceful air to the raw little community.

Late in the same year that Karnes County became an entity, a pio-

neering movement entirely different in nature from that of Helena
began to materialize less than ten miles away, in the wedge-shaped
tract of land formed by the confluence of the Cibolo Creek and the San
Antonio River. This was Panna Maria, the first Polish settlement in
the United States. Its establishment was conceived and stimulated by
Father Leopold Moczygemba, a Silesian Polish priest from the Regency
of Opole in the southeastern tip of Prussia. Father Moczygemba had
served as pastor of the German church in New Braunfels, and then for
three years in the struggling new Alsatian community at Castroville,
the first settlement west of San Antonio on the Chihuahua Road. He
harked back, however, to his own people, isolated in Silesia, which in
the mid-1850s "was a region of great poverty, rising food costs, rampant cholera and typhus epidemics, and an oppressed Polish peas-
antry." [5]

Writing from Castroville, Father Moczygemba urged his family
and friends to come to Texas, pledging that he would have a place to
settle and farm when they arrived. In April 1853 he had bought
twenty-seven acres just south of New Braunfels, apparently as a start
toward settling those who came. However, he changed his plans and in
1854 began to explore with John Twohig, the San Antonio merchant
and land developer, a fellow Catholic, the possibility of moving his
colony to the area south of San Antonio. [6]

Twohig had large holdings, undeveloped, on the Andrés Hernandez Spanish grant at the confluence of the San Antonio and the
Cibolo. A second-generation chronicler says that "in the early part
of 1854, Father Leopold and John Twohig spent several days riding
over the land and looking at it from various angles." [7] And a latter-
day historian adds: "there are . . . reasons to believe that unforeseen
circumstances prompted the Polish missionary from New Braunfels
to turn to Twohig." [8] Whatever those circumstances, Father Moczygemba did buy, or committed for the settlers' purchase, enough
land for his colony.

Setting out in the fall of 1854, about a hundred families from
Moczygemba's home village of Pluznica and from nearby villages,
among them four Moczygemba brothers, left their homeland forever.
Having sold their farms, packed such bedding, clothes, and farm
equipment as they could transport, and traveled by train to the German seaport of Bremen, they sailed on the *Weser*. Nine weeks' sailing
brought them to Galveston. Here they trans-shipped to Indianola,
where they rented Mexican carts to transport their belongings. [9] They

trudged beside these carts up the long road to San Antonio, while people in the small Anglo-American towns of Victoria, Goliad, and Helena gawked at the strangers in their middle-European country clothes. So taken were the cowboys at seeing the girls' sturdy ankles flashing beneath embroidered skirts that one of the Polish fathers, writing back to a relative preparing to follow, advised him to have the young ladies lengthen their skirts before they reached America.[10]

The emigrants unknowingly passed their future home on the Cibolo, and went on into San Antonio. But Father Leopold, hearing they were on their way, hastened from Castroville and met them as they arrived, to lead them back to their settlement area. Tradition has it they reached the site overlooking the junction of the San Antonio and the Cibolo on Christmas Eve, 1854. Beneath a large oak which still stands, they offered their first midnight Mass, naming the place Panna Maria (Virgin Mary), after the beautiful St. Mary's Church (Kosciol Mariacki) in Cracow, the capital of the Polish kings.[11]

After severe hardships in adjusting themselves to the new land without adequate capital, these hardy Polish settlers and the groups which followed from Silesia in 1855, 1856, and 1857 did establish a thrifty, productive community at Panna Maria. They put up a modest church in 1856. When it was destroyed by lightning in 1877, the parish undertook a new and larger stone building in 1877-78, further remodeled and expanded in 1937. Today the handsome Church of the Immaculate Conception, with its soaring steeple dominating the countryside, is the oldest Polish church in America and the seat of the oldest Polish parochial school in the country.[12] This and subsequent Polish settlements at Hobson, and at Kosciusko and Czestochowa in adjoining Wilson County, added significantly to the development of a stable economy along the general line of the great road and its alternates leading into San Antonio.

Not all the newcomers in the 1850s were of the sturdy, thrifty inclination reflected by the Polish colonists. Texas as a whole in the nineteenth century had also been subject to the influx of rootless or uprooted folk from the older states in the Union — those who made "G. T. T.," Gone to Texas, a mocking byword throughout the country. Old Goliad and the thriving new Helena seemed to get more than their share, attracted no doubt by the money and goods flowing by oxcarts and mule-drawn wagons up and down the Chihuahua Road. Robert Thonhoff concluded that

not all . . . was peaceful, sober living in Helena. Helena was rough
and raw, too. Many outlaws who fled from other states congregated
at Helena, and there were many shooting scrapes and gambling dens
— and saloons. Horse-stealing became a regular business with many
outlaws, since they found a ready market just across the border. [13]

These elements of the population, along with many new entrants
into the freighting business who were working under the weight of
newly purchased manufactured equipment and less-experienced crews,
unreconciled to low wages, were posed against the Mexican carters.
The latter — patient, dogged folk, with generations of experience
feeding their skills, and operating with the huge *carretas* hand-built
from native woods and rawhide — formed the very backbone of Texas's
freighting industry in the ante-bellum days. August Santleben, who
became the dean of wagon freighters after the war, got his first introduction to freighting on the Chihuahua Road at the age of eleven,
about 1856, when he helped drive his father's ox-cart on several trips
between Port Lavaca and San Antonio. From the perspective of half a
century, Santleben said in his memoirs in 1910: "The Mexican trains
. . . were managed more successfully because of the strictness with
which they conducted the business." [14]

Frederick Law Olmstead, the sharp-eyed architect-traveler, visiting San Antonio in 1856–57, observed that

> the transportation of [the merchants'] goods forms the principal sup-
> port of the Mexican population . . . All goods are brought in from
> Matagorda Bay, a distance of 150 miles by ox-teams, moving with
> prodigious slowness and irregularity . . . In a favorable season the
> freight price is one-and-a-quarter cents per pound from Lavacca [*sic*].
> Prices are extremely high and subject to great variations, depending
> on the actual supply and the state of the roads. [15]

One might question Olmstead's conclusion as to the predomi-
nance of the freighting business at that stage, were it not for the testimony of the United States Census, first conducted in San Antonio in
1850. The official total population of all Bexar County as found in that
census is quoted at 3,488, while the original handwritten manuscript
record, "Free Inhabitants in San Antonio in the County of Bexar,"
enumerated as of September 27, 1850, concludes with the line: "Total
no. of families 716, inhabitants 3,168 in San Antonio." [16]

It is startling to find that among those 716 families in the town
itself, the overwhelmingly largest number of gainfully employed, 343
in all, listed themselves in the freighting business. There were fewer

"laborers" even than "cartmen." Those 45 additionally listed as independent "wagoner," including a handful named "wagonmaster," were with only a very few exceptions *not* Spanish surnamed. On the other hand, those identifying themselves as "cartmen" were, without exception, Spanish surnamed: 170 of them. And then, shown as wagonmasters and wagoners employed by the Army Quartermaster Department, were 128 men of whom not more than four or five were Spanish surnamed. Not counting the army enlisted men at the post, the nearest competitors to those in the freighting business were the common laborers, 152, followed by 44 carpenters, and a slightly lesser number each from the ranks of stonemasons, gunsmiths, barkeepers, and clerks.[17]

Those statistics were made in 1850, when the army forts to the west of San Antonio were just beginning to be built. By 1857, at the time of Olmstead's observations, construction and supply of the forts was in full swing, while much more considerable immigration of settlers and trade with Chihuahua was under way. Therefore, probably an even larger number engaged in freighting, out of a fast-growing population which reached over 8,000 by 1860.

The preponderance of Mexican cartmen, or *carreterras,* among those manning the freight trains set the stage, inevitably, for the shameful "Mexican Cart War" precipitated in 1857 by chauvinistic elements along the road in the Helena-Goliad area. To gain a perspective on this outburst, one needs to look once more all the way up the road to Presidio and to El Paso.

Traffic on the Chihuahua Road direct from Indianola and San Antonio, through Presidio del Norte, had become an ordered, if hazardous, way of life. As early as June 1853, Mayer & Co., which until then had operated out of Independence, Missouri, through Santa Fe to Chihuahua, sent a large train from Chihuahua on the new route. It arrived in San Antonio about June 20, taking thirty-seven days, "seven of which," noted the San Antonio paper, "must be deducted for delays along the route." The newspaper stated specifically that "Mayer & Co. passed through Presidio and not El Paso, saving . . . some two hundred-fifty miles. This course would make the distance from Matagorda to Chihuahua about 900 miles."[18]

Mayer & Co. apparently not only found the new route profitable, but also chose a few months later to start with new equipment from Indianola, for the *Ledger* reported on January 12, 1854, that

H. Mayer & Co.'s train for Chihuahua passed through our city today. It is composed of twenty-six large wagons, all new, with ten mules each. The train is worth over $20,000 and the freight is estimated at $130,000, most of which is indentured goods. This train is said to be the best fitted-out that ever left this city . . . [19]

The early establishment of Fort Bliss, followed in September 1854 by that of Fort Davis, with others opening during that same period, created an immediate demand for transportation facilities to handle supplies for the army. The army maintained some wagon trains itself, but in mid-1855 the War Department made a policy decision to deemphasize its own trains and contract with private operators for a large part of its hauling. [20]

This provided an immediate opportunity for entrepreneurs to gain a more stable basis for their freight operations. As already noted, one of the more successful of these in the whole decade of the 1850s was the astute Maj. George T. Howard. Others active in government hauling included George H. Giddings, the stagecoach operator; J. R. Jefferson; and San Antonio Mayor J. R. Sweet. Ed Hall of Presidio del Norte, who had succeeded Ben Leaton upon his death, as possessor not only of El Fortín but also of Leaton's widow, claimed his share of the government trade. [21]

Maj. James Belger, longtime quartermaster for the Texas Department, housed in the partially rebuilt Alamo buildings in San Antonio, was contracting officer for these operations. When Col. William Grigsby Freeman, assistant adjutant general of the army, made the first formal inspection of the Texas (Eighth) Military Department in 1853, he had given some of his warmest words of commendation to the work of Major Belger in handling shipments from Indianola and disbursements to the frontier from this point:

> To do this, requires a large amount of transportation. Independent of the post teams proper and hired means occasionally resorted to, fifty-two wagons driven by citizen teamsters are constantly employed in transporting public supplies from the coast to San Antonio, while seventy-two wagons, also belonging to the depot, driven by soldiers detailed from the regiment supplies, are occupied in distributing the stores to the posts where they are required . . . The operations of this depot are on the most extensive scale, and too much praise cannot be given Bvt. Major Belger for the order of judicious economy introduced into every department. [22]

Colonel Freeman's visit to the Alamo depot was in early June, 1853, before Fort Davis was open. He found that "the cost of hired transportation from Indianola to San Antonio had averaged during the year $1.15 per hundred pounds; by the public trains [government owned] the cost ranges from $1.05 to $1.10." [23]

By 1855 the cost of "hired transportation" had risen slightly. The standard rate awarded freighters then was $1.25 per 100 pounds from Indianola to San Antonio; from San Antonio to Fort Inge, Fort Duncan, and Fort Clark, a flat rate of $1.10 per 100 pounds, though the distance varied considerably; and beyond that, to Fort Davis, Fort Bliss, and to Fort Fillmore in New Mexico, $1.70 per 100 pounds *per 100 miles*.[24] A major factor in that extra surcharge in the far western areas was no doubt the danger from Indians as well as the hardship upon teams and crews from poor forage and scarce water.

When Col. J. F. K. Mansfield made the next official inspection of the Department of Texas, in 1856, Col. Albert Sidney Johnston had taken over command from Gen. Persifor Smith in April of that year. Shortly thereafter, Capt. E. E. McLean relieved the diligent Major Belger as quartermaster. By that time the policy had progressed to the point that Colonel Mansfield found most supplies to be transported by contract. Nevertheless, he learned that despite progress, the San Antonio depot still had in its employ "65 teamsters at $20 per month; 1 guide at $45, 2 cart drivers at $18 . . . 195 wagons, 2 carts, 44 horses, 691 mules, 4 ambulances." The rates paid the contracting haulers were the same as reported the year before: $1.25 per 100 pounds from Indianola to San Antonio.[25]

These earlier freight rates are introduced here to give perspective to what happened in 1857, when the notorious Cart War broke out along the road through Helena and Goliad.

All the evidence indicates that Major Howard, George Giddings, and other large government contractors still relied heavily, though not exclusively, upon sub-contracting to Mexican drovers with their slow and old-fashioned but economical *carretas*, while newer hopefuls trying to break into the trade had invested in factory-built American wagons. All the elements for incendiary friction were present.

The first major incident occurred on July 18, 1857. It was reported in the San Antonio paper as "a gross outrage . . . committed on a party of Mexican cartmen near Goliad." According to the paper, the cartmen, bringing up government freight from the coast, had gone into camp for the night,

when they were attacked by a party of fifteen or sixteen Americans who fired into them, wounding three and driving off the balance. The ruffians then cut down the carts [i.e., broke up the wheels, dropping the laden axles onto the ground] and decamped without molesting the freight . . . the only cause of this high-handed, outrageous conduct was the fact that the Mexican cartmen hauled for less than American wagoners could afford to . . .[26]

Five of the Mexican cartmen attested to this incident in an affidavit given to C. E. Jefferson in San Antonio, July 27, 1857.[27] The affidavit, signed by Gavinio Brito, Antonio Flores, Francisco Martinez, Francisco Morales, and Juan Flores, supported the earlier press report in all major respects, except as to the attackers not molesting the freight. The deposition purported that "the said fifteen or twenty men took, stole, and carried away four sacks of corn from the *carretas* . . . and that the corn the train . . . was thus conveying was for the Government agents." A "sack of corn" as handled in the frontier freight traffic was usually a heavy fiber bag containing well over a hundred pounds of shelled corn, though how men mounted on horses could have handled that is conjectural. This affidavit was sent to Governor Elisha M. Pease as an enclosure to one of the appeals which were peppering in upon the governor from disturbed San Antonio authorities.

Anglo-Americans, if accompanying Mexican cartmen, were not immune from attack. A second affidavit was from C. G. Edwards,[28] who said that "on the last of July" about seven miles up the road from Goliad on "the Caviza," he was sleeping under his cart when, at midnight, armed men attacked the train. In the act of getting up, Edwards said, he was shot in the breast and fell senseless. When he regained consciousness an hour later, he found the attackers gone, the goods from the wagons all strewn about, and two of his Mexican carters wounded. As for himself, one bullet had passed entirely through his chest, while each knee had also been perforated by gunfire.[29]

Enough alarums had been sounded by August 4 that John A. Wilcox, a San Antonio businessman commanding the newly organized militia company, the Alamo Rifles, was moved to write the governor:

> In view of the alarming and repeated depredations committed by the citizens of Goliad County upon the cartmen and teamsters generally of this city and vicinity, I conceive it my duty as a good citizen and as commanding officer of the Alamo Rifles to tender to your excellency, if you deem it expedient, the services of my company.[30]

The attitudes of San Antonio-based enterprise, as reflected in this and other letters and in the newspapers of that city, might understandably be somewhat different from those of interests in the Goliad and Helena communities. Indeed they were. Echoes of mid-nineteenth-century chauvinism still linger in this passage from a history of Karnes County written more than a hundred years later:

> The merchants of San Antonio got tired of paying $3.00 per 100 pounds for freight from Indianola and had hundreds of Mexican carts imported from Mexico! This brought many more Mexican people swarming back to the trail before the bitter enmity of the Texas War for Independence and the Mexican War had subsided. Soon it was war time in Southwest Texas again. The Mexicans were accused of helping the Negro slaves to escape from their owners across the Rio Grande into Mexico, and even of instigating a Negro uprising against the American white people. Brazos County promptly barred all Mexicans from within its bounds. Goliad County held a meeting and issued similar orders. But the Mexican drivers disregarded the orders and called forth the wrath of Goliad to such an extent that we may say what is known as the Cart War really began there.[31]

Though gentle in nature and usually generous in his observations, the founder of Helena, Thomas Ruckman, had this to say in his memoirs:

> Mexicans could never have traveled the highways of Mexico so undisturbed, yet with characteristic lack of gratitude, they failed to appreciate their privileges here and to respect the country they traveled through. They were early accustomed to stealing and butchering the cattle along the road. This won for them the hostility of the American freighter, for with their free meat and stolen provisions, the Mexicans need very little money and haul more cheaply than can the Americans. Thus the ranchmen and the white freighters made common cause and determined to drive the Mexicans from the road.[32]

The resentment against Mexican drovers was certainly more broadly based than upon the issue of their freight rates alone. The problem of runaway slaves making their escape into Mexico, allegedly at times through the connivance of carters plying the roads, constituted a real drain upon East Texas planters' most valuable assets. Hostility centered upon Mexican folk: as early as 1853, twenty families had been driven out of Austin on allegations they were horse thieves; a couple of years later all Mexican residents were expelled from Seguin. Emotion reached its highest pitch in 1856 at Columbus, between Houston and Victoria, when a purported slave conspiracy for rebellion

against their masters was "uncovered," with rumors that local Mexican
people were co-conspirators. Nearby Matagorda County simply ordered all Spanish surnamed people to get outside the county borders.
In Uvalde County, west of San Antonio on the Eagle Pass road, citizens
passed a resolution that after August 1, 1857, no Mexican should pass
through the county without a "passport." Since no one defined what
kind of passport was required, and since there was no one to issue any
kind of passport, this order seemed an effort to halt all Mexican
traffic.[33]

Those first outright attacks upon Mexican cart trains, in July,
were followed shortly by others of increasing violence. Mayor J. R.
Sweet, Colonel Wilcox, Judge I. A. Paschal, and other substantial
men of San Antonio organized a horseback party to scout out the Goliad road and try to get a sounding of the people's temper in the warring counties. They were baffled by the hostility and by the solid front
of indifference to law and order they encountered.[34]

Scarcely had they returned early in August when one of the fierc-
est and most brutal of the entire sorry train of events occurred. On September 12 a group of some seventeen carts, traveling in advance of a
large train under W. G. Tobin to which it was attached, encamped not
far north of Helena.[35] In the dead of night a body of about thirty men,
all disguised as Indians or with their faces blackened, attacked the
camp. In this case the cartmen resisted, returning the fire and wounding several of the attackers. But two or three of the Mexican cartmen
were wounded and the elderly captain in charge of the train, Antonio
Delgado, a well-known and respected citizen of San Antonio, was not
only killed but also "brutally mangled." [36]

Sentiment erupted in San Antonio. Judge I. A. Paschal fired off
a letter to the governor, written in such heat and so hastily that the
words fairly tumble, almost illegibly, across the pages. Dated September 13, the letter refers to "an express informing us that an attack was
made last night upon a train of Mexicans . . . about 55 miles below
this place" (an indication that the people of San Antonio had a pretty
good courier service). After describing the attack and the murder of
Delgado, Judge Paschal continued:

> I believe the civil authorities of Karnes County to be wholly in-
> adequate to the protection [against] this kind of depredations . . .
> There exists as great a necessity for placing protection on this road as
> there was on any part of our frontier.

Any man to make an affidavit against these guilty parties
would sacrifice his life.

A large party will go down tomorrow under the escort of the
sheriff but they are justified in going no further than the line . . . I
believe this matter will not be easily quelled. For God's sake give us
authority to raise a company for the protection of the people on this
road . . .[37]

Colonel Wilcox was on the next horseback scouting party from
San Antonio, to which Paschal referred. Wilcox wrote Governor
Pease on September 17, relating that he had just returned from the
second scouting expedition to Karnes County, "and am satisfied
that without prompt executive interposition consequences of the
most serious nature may be apprehended." After referring to the
Delgado murder, he went on:

The sentiment is unanimous in favor of your calling out a company.
For God's sake do it and prevent the awful consequences that await
delay. The Mexicans are already speaking of retaliation. Great God,
what will be the consequences? — there will not be one left from
here to the Rio Grande . . . There are men of wealth in this town
who have taken sides with the murderers of Karnes and Goliad, and
they, the people of K. and Goliad boast of it . . . I have spent 17
days from my office in trying to arrest this difficulty . . . I am done
. . . What about the arms for the Alamo Rifles? I have heard nothing from you . . .[38]

San Antonio people must have been putting the same kind of
pressure upon Brig. Gen. David E. Twiggs, commander of the Department of Texas, based in the Alamo City. General Twiggs had
every reason to feel that he was more than fully committed in
spreading his troops out across the western frontiers in some nineteen forts and camps, to resist the constant depredations of Indians,
as the citizens equally demanded. Nevertheless, as at least a temporary measure, on September 19, just two days after Wilcox had
again implored the governor to raise troops, the United States Army
commander issued his Special Order No. 122, in which, "with great
regret," he recognized "the necessity for having an escort with the
Contractor's train transporting stores for the troops from Indianola
to this city." He continued:

A detail will therefore be made: one subaltern, two sergeants, 20
privates, to be in readiness and 22nd instant, to escort the train to
Powderhorn and back . . . to be responsible to protect the stores and

persons in charge from all attacks . . . offer no resistance to any civil processes issued by any magistrate . . .[39]

Judge Paschal and his associates still thought the state as well as the United States Army should act in this civil affair. One day after Twiggs's order was issued, Paschal wrote Pease again, in the same vein as in his first letter. To that missive Samuel A. Maverick appended an endorsement in his own handwriting, which read in part:

Unless you can place a force on the road to discourage these lawless persons I feel that within a few days we will be thrown into a serious civil strife. We ask for a force to prevent bloodshed and uphold the law. In Karnes County the issue is a political one, and emanates from Know Nothingism.[40]

Elisha M. Pease was finally stirred to action. He went to San Antonio himself September 23 to sound out what was going on. He held conferences with a number of people in Bexar and surrounding counties, but very carefully did not venture into those counties where the actual disturbances were occurring. When convinced of the seriousness of the situation, he issued a proclamation on the spot. It offered "a reward of $500 for the arrest and delivery to the sheriff of Karnes County" of those who had committed the offenses.[41]

The *San Antonio Herald,* whose sympathies had by now settled warmly with the Mexican carters and San Antonio business interests, had said editorially on September 19:

We understand that another train of Mexican carts is shortly to leave San Antonio for the port . . . The Mexican carters say that it is now a question of life or death, that if driven from the pursuit of their legitimate calling, their families must starve or go to another country, and they are determined to resist to the utmost any attempt to force them from the road.[42]

Twiggs's detail of an armed escort for a train to leave on September 22 may have specifically averted the crisis. On September 26 the newspaper took note that "the murder of Antonio Delgada [*sic*] and the wounding of his companions, near Helena, in Karnes County, would seem at last to have arroused the citizens of San Antonio into active interference."[43]

Twiggs named Lt. George Bell, of the First Artillery, to command the army escort that took the train down to the coast on September 22. They apparently ran the gauntlet of Helena and Goliad safely, for no sensational reports on that passage wafted back home. As Bell was preparing to leave the coast with the laden army train, however, a disturbing piece of intelligence was communicated to him by the highly respected John J. Linn of Victoria. Under date of October 9, 1857, Bell sent a dispatch to his commanding officer in San Antonio:

> I have just learned from a Mr. Linn of this place that the citizen train accompanying us will undoubtedly be attacked between Goliad and the Cibolo. He says his authority is unquestionable, he is an old and responsible citizen and the report has been corroborated by other respectable citizens. It is possible, I also learn, that the Mexicans in charge of our train will be attacked.
>
> A body of at least 60 men are organized for that purpose. Winian, a young man living on the Mainmer, was wounded in the attack on Delgado's party. He was in Lavaca watching the movements of the other train during all the time of loading. It is said that several of the attacking party in the aforesaid affair were wounded, it is this which has exasperated them . . . Several meetings have been called in Karnes County to make preparations for our return.[44]

Being forewarned, Bell seems to have been able to avoid a conflict on the return trip, despite the hostile surveillance by young Winian — the sole publicly identified participant in all the attacks upon the cartmen.

Word of the disorders soon reached all the way to the eastern states. The editor of the *San Antonio Herald* wrote in September that he had seen "a late issue of the *New York Times* which inveighed against the matter." He quoted a passage saying that "even at San Antonio, where the Mexicans form a majority of the population, an attempt was made to raise a posse for the Sheriff to drive them from their homes, and the scheme was only frustrated by the refusal of the Germans to take part in it." [45] No evidence has been found in contemporary records that such an attempt was made.

Meanwhile, Governor Pease had yielded to the importunities of the San Antonio people to call up an armed company to protect the Mexican carters. With good common sense, he steered clear of authorizing a San Antonio-based company of militia to take the responsibility, for such a local unit could well have been labeled as representing the financial interests in that center of trade. Instead, he called up a special company, to be recruited elsewhere in the state but to be commanded by Capt. G. H. Nelson, who was chief marshal for the city of San Antonio. Nelson had been first lieutenant in Captain Gillespie's company of Rangers in the storming of Monterrey; he took command of the company when Gillespie was killed there.

Historian Walter Prescott Webb deemed the new company to have been a temporary Ranger force and remarked that it was the first time Texas Rangers were called upon to quell a civil disturbance, setting a precedent for their frequent use thereafter in that capacity.[46] The validity of this conclusion is doubtful, since none of the official actions and correspondence involved in this matter makes any use of the term "Ranger." Writing to General Twiggs on about October 1, Pease said that he had called out "a company of mounted volunteers to suppress certain outrages against the public peace." In his message to the Senate on November 11, he called it a "company of militia," and again in his November message only the term "militia" was used.[47]

In his letter to General Twiggs, Governor Pease negotiated with the United States Army for issuance of 75 rifles and 150 horsemen's pistols, noting that the Texas government had no arms whatever upon which to draw. After certain niceties of red tape were unraveled, and still noting that it was in direct violation of orders from the War Department under which he operated, Twiggs gave orders to his quartermaster at the Alamo to issue the needed arms to Captain Nelson.[48]

Governor Pease's evident desire to avoid the controversial elements in San Antonio is seen again in the fact that Captain Nelson was sent to San Marcos, Lockhart, and New Braunfels to raise the volunteers for his company. Writing to the governor from New Braunfels on October 14, after recruiting in the other two towns, Nelson reported:

> I have found more difficulty in raising the company than I had anticipated. [Every] sort of rumor and opposition has been thrown in my way to intimidate and disuade men from joining the agents, or those feeling a sympathy for the people engaged in this affair have been very active.

Nevertheless, Nelson expected that after visiting San Antonio to pick up his arms and other equipage, he would be on the road to the troubled area by the following week.[49]

While Nelson was putting his company into shape, and while Lieutenant Bell was actually on the road protecting his train of Mexican carters, the whole matter blossomed into international proportions. From the Mexican Legation in Washington on October 14 and again from New York on October 19, the minister to the United States from Mexico, Eduardo Robles y Penzuela, addressed letters to the secretary of state, Lewis Cass, giving a dramatic and somewhat hyperbolic account of the train of incidents which had occurred. He included the punitive resolution in Uvalde and one apparently groundless charge that many Mexican citizens had been driven out of San Antonio. There was a specific reference to Antonio Delgado as among "upwards of 75 victims." [50] Though bitter and reproachful in tone, the letter was studiously courteous in expressing full confidence that the United States would take effective steps. [51]

Passing these letters to Governor Pease on October 24, Secretary Cass expressed his own full confidence that the governor would correct any irregularities and send him a full account, enabling the secretary "to be fully informed upon a subject which is likely to be productive of unpleasant consequences." [52]

Captain Nelson took his company of nearly seventy-five men down the Chihuahua Road toward Karnes County on October 26 and was not heard from for more than three weeks. Finally, from Lavaca on November 8, he dispatched a long letter to Governor Pease, saying his report had been delayed by his own illness. Nelson related that he and his company had camped on the Cibolo, no doubt at Carvajal Crossing, for a full week, awaiting a delayed train from San Antonio. Nelson had used the interval to ride down and visit "Helina [*sic*] when court was in session, which gave me a good opportunity of ascertaining the sentiments and opposition of the people." In one long, breathless passage Nelson portrays his shock at what he witnessed:

> . . . and I assure you that I was never more surprised in my life than I was to find so much prejudice and disregard for law and order no one appeared to think the law had anything to do with the matter of stopping carts from traveling the road, the only matter in question was the practicability of the thing can we stop them or not, and the more wild and absurd the tale told to the crowd, the more eager it was listened to, but I was enabled to ascertain beyond a doubt that all that has been said about the cartmen acting in a disorderly manner when passing through Helina and Goliad was false. Citizens of each place told me that no train could pass more orderly or quietly than they did, in Helina considerable pains was taken to convince me that Karnes County had no hand in it, but thought that Goliad was to blame for it, but my own observation convinces me that the head and front of the whole difficulty lies in and about the town of Helina . . . [53]

When the delayed train did arrive at the Cibolo, Nelson's company moved forward with it. As they came into Helena, people who had gathered along the wooden sidewalks threw jeers and taunts at the militiamen, while the frightened Mexican carters hunched upon the lumbering *carretas.*

As the armed militiamen pulled up to the head of the train, "one of a crowd of drunken rowdies congregated at a grocery store ran out and drew a pistol on one of the cartmen." Fortunately, a Mr. Storm, presumably a citizen of Helena, was near enough to hasten out and prevent the man's firing, at the same time calling out to Captain Nelson to wheel the company back alongside. This Nelson did, letting the mounted militiamen remain halted, occupying the streets of the straggling town, until the entire train had passed.

"I have no doubt," said Nelson, "from the demonstration made that if the train had been without an escort, some of the cartmen would have been killed. There is no doubt in my mind that the men who killed Delgado were there congregated in town and drunk enough to have done anything." From Helena on to the coast the train met no demonstrations of hostility, and Nelson did not believe "that any serious difficulty [would] occur so long as the trains are properly escorted, but there is no security for Mexican cartmen except something stronger than the civil authority as the law is administered in this part of Texas." [54]

Nelson's return trip was not so successful. He started back to San Antonio about November 17, apparently without a train to escort. In Karnes County, just north of Helena, the company met a southbound train composed of Mexican carts owned by or under contract to G. L. Pyron of San Antonio and commanded by William Pyron, his brother. Captain Nelson reported later to the governor that Pyron did not ask for his escort, so Nelson did not force an escort upon him.

On the morning of November 20, after camping near Helena, Pyron's cartmen went out from camp to round up their grazing oxen. They were ambushed; two were killed and two others fled on foot back toward San Antonio. Pyron and his remaining men loaded the dead drovers on a cart, turned the train around, and left the county to go to their Cibolo crossing. He buried the murdered men there and about that time made contact with Lt. S. A. Jackson of the militia company, who was stationed in the neighborhood. They turned around once more, with Lieutenant Jackson escorting them safely through to the coast. [55]

When word of the fatal attack upon the Pyron train got around,

Nelson came under some criticism. Governor Pease felt constrained to absolve Nelson of any blame, on the ground that Pyron had not asked for escort.[56]

In his November 11 message to the Senate, Governor Pease had taken a forthright stand on the obligation of the state to protect the Mexican residents:

> We have a large population of Mexican origin in our Western counties, many of whom are highly educated and have rendered important services to the country in our days of trial. Doubtless there are some bad men to be found in this class of citizen, but the large mass of them are as orderly and lawabiding as any in the State . . . and are entitled to the protection of the laws in any lawful employment they may choose to pursue . . .

Pease concluded that the only remedy was to punish those responsible. He reminded the Senate that the "company of militia" he had called up were enrolled for only sixty days and their term would expire about the first of December.[57] Addressing the Senate once more on November 30, Pease suggested that

> it becomes a matter for your consideration whether the citizens of a county that permits such acts to be done with impunity should not be compelled to pay a heavy pecuniary penalty, this would arouse them no doubt to the necessity of preserving the public peace. It is now evident that there is no security for the lives of citizens of Mexican origin engaged in the business of transportation along the road from San Antonio to the Gulf unless escorted by military force . . . The militia now employed will expire on the 8th day of December. Unless some action is received from the Legislature to continue their services, I shall find it my duty to discharge them on that day. It will require an appropriation of about $14,500 to pay the services of the company and for their subsistence and forage.[58]

The temper of the legislature then in session, already preoccupied and inflamed with the issue of slavery, may be judged by the fact that they took no move to continue the special militia in force, nor any other action toward controlling the disturbances along the Cart Road.

Belligerent resolutions were adopted when Karnes County citizens gathered at a public meeting in Helena on December 4 to consider the situation anent the Cart War. According to one local historian, speakers expressed indignation that Governor Pease had gone to San Antonio to get information about the trouble in Karnes County, suggesting that he had been unduly influenced there by parties sympathetic to the Mexican carters. The gathering adopted eight resolutions, the sixth of which, according to the writer, "showed directly that the people of Karnes County were far from sympathetic to the Mexican cart drivers."[59] This resolution held that

> the citizens of Karnes County regard the continuance of Peon Mexican Teamsters on this route as an intolerable nuisance; and we therefore request the citizens of San Antonio to withdraw them as early as practicable, and substitute others, or provide some means to prevent them from committing depredations upon our property, when it is impossible for us to guard and watch it.[60]

Violence did abate for a time, to a large extent simply because most of the carters were deterred by fear from undertaking to cross Karnes and Goliad counties. That shortage of freight bottoms created precisely the situation San Antonio business interests had feared from the beginning: the price of hauling between Indianola and San Antonio soared from the established $1.25 to $3.00 per 100 pounds — and the ones who profited were the newcomers to the business.[61]

The Texas legislature let pass the December 8 deadline for giving the special militia company a new lease on life; therefore, it was dismantled as quickly as practicable. So ended the armed escorts on the southern end of the Chihuahua Road, and the first venture by the state in subduing a civil disturbance.[62]

Responding to the Mexican minister's protests, as transmitted by the U.S. secretary of state, Governor Pease had written Secretary Cass on December 10. He enclosed a copy of his special message of November 11 to the Senate, which he said would give the full background of events and the measures he had undertaken. He felt confident that "laws will doubtless be passed by the Legislature of this State now in session which will prevent such offenses for the future." [63] The governor's letter was more optimistic than the situation deserved. The legislature enacted no measures aimed at cooling down the Cart War.

Most commentators covering that unpleasant episode have assumed, from the dissolution of Nelson's militia company, that the disorders were over. Considerable evidence exists, however, that hostility, fear, and violence continued to stalk the Goliad Road well into 1858. A February item in a San Antonio paper asserts that the carters were making attempts to start a bypass road which would avoid Helena and Goliad altogether.

The proposed new road would proceed on a more southerly course from San Antonio to St. Mary's on the inland waterways in Refugio

County, where reports said docking facilities existed only 102 miles from San Antonio. The road never materialized, but its very suggestion alone might have helped chill the ardor of merchants in Helena and Goliad.[64]

In its February 20 issue, the San Antonio paper observed that "during the week a number of carts arrived from the coast, and breadstuffs and other necessaries are consequently becoming cheaper. Flour is down to $13 a barrel." [65]

As late as March 12, however, terrorists killed two more Mexican carters near Goliad. Some beginnings of a shift in attitude appeared in a letter to a San Antonio paper:

> A citizen of Goliad writing to the *Herald* of this city says: "The feelings and sentiments of good citizens are quite changed from what they were last summer, and I can assure you and the citizens of your town that there will be nothing left undone to ferret out the perpetrators of this bold highway murder." [66]

These good intentions, sad to report, produced no perpetrators.

The scarcity of Mexican carters on the road, a situation which the ruffians themselves had produced, finally led the masked marauders to make the mistake of turning their looting activities upon whatever else was available — which turned out to be Anglo-American wagon freighters. Only then was effective righteous indignation raised against such lawless depredations. Local vigilante groups organized to "wreak terrible vengeance," and offenders were readily caught. It was then, in August 1858, that the hanging tree which still spreads its massive limbs over the Goliad courthouse yard came into its widest use. As many as five offenders at one time were said to be swinging from those sturdy branches.[67]

An economic indicator suggests that the impact of the Cart War peaked in February 1858: A San Antonio newspaper on March 27, 1858, reported that "the price of hauling has fallen to $1.25 per hundred from the Bay, a mighty change from the middle of February, when the price was five dollars.[68]

The irresponsible free-booters, probably used as pawns by selfish interests staying in the background, found that public opinion up and down the road had withdrawn its protection. They began to let the carters pass. At last, the Cart War was over. Only the more subtle warfare of technology gradually phased out the picturesque *carreta* as *norteamericanos* and Mexicans alike acquired efficiency in operating the larger modern wagons drawn sometimes by oxen but increasingly by mules.

[11]

Halcyon Days
Before the War

Close upon Colonel Johnston's opening of a clear wagon road from San Antonio in 1849 — with upper and lower alternative routes, in fact — pressure developed for mail connections and passenger facilities.[1] The Gold Rush to California, though peaked in late 1849, would continue as an immigrant tide for years. Strong demand came from the East and the South for means of communication with the thousands who had moved to the West Coast, while entrepreneurs envisioned a constant flow of passengers not wishing to be burdened with providing their own means of transportation.

Henry Skillman's first overland transit from El Paso del Norte down to San Antonio, as a scout in Lieutenant Whiting's employ in 1849, fired the ambition of that resourceful plainsman; he began to experiment with a courier service between the two cities and drew in Bigfoot Wallace and Henry Westfall as associates. But Skillman saw larger opportunities: he wanted to establish a stage line with a mail contract.

In the skimpy records of the time, conflict has persisted on who first applied for such a contract. When J. Evetts Haley published his landmark *Fort Concho and the Texas Frontier* in 1952, he had evidence that the formidable Richard Austin Howard had joined Henry Skillman in that application. Wayne R. Austerman, doing research in Washington for his 1985 book on *The San Antonio-El Paso Mail,* concluded that it was Bigfoot Wallace who joined Dick Howard in that first bid to the Post Office Department.

Somehow the government had envisioned that both Eagle Pass, far to the southwest on the Rio Grande, and Presidio del Norte, deep in the Big Bend of that river, should be included on that route. It was an impossible gambit, but the Howard-Wallace bid bravely proposed to service it once every two months, "through in thirty days," at $25,000 per annum. They also proposed a sensible alternative: to leave out Eagle Pass and Presidio, taking the direct route between San Antonio and El Paso, for $18,000. The postmaster general disallowed that bid, as being both extravagant and not in accordance with the terms of the advertisement.[2]

At this point Henry Skillman moved in on the scene. Austerman showed that Skillman did not try to negotiate at long distance. The grizzled, flamboyant plainsman boarded a steamer on the gulf and went to Washington as a lobbyist. Although all the original mail contract papers have been lost from official files, Austerman found that the capital's *Daily National Intelligencer* lived up to its name on September 22, 1851, providing the intelligence that on September 20 Henry Skillman had signed a contract with Postmaster General Nathan K. Hall to establish mail route No. 6401, from Santa Fe through El Paso and then by the lower road (i.e., Howard's Well and Las Moras) to San Antonio. He was to get service under way by November 1851 and continue to run until expiration of the contract June 30, 1854. It was the fruition, after more than sixty-five years, of Pedro Vial's lonely scout between those cities in 1786–87.[3]

While Dick Howard was waiting for word on his bid for the contract, he spent at least part of 1850 assisting Lt. W. F. Smith on the first survey of the Texas Colorado River from Austin to its mouth on the Gulf of Mexico.[4] Having been denied the contract by the Post Office Department, that splendid scout dropped out of the Trans-Pecos milieu where he had made such signal contributions. Henry Skillman established himself during the next two to three years as the prime mover and innovator of stage and mail operations along the San Antonio to El Paso and Santa Fe road.[5]

An equally famous line had had its advent in 1858: the Butterfield Overland Mail, which ran from St. Louis through Sedalia, Missouri, to Fort Smith, Arkansas, then across present-day Oklahoma

down into Texas to Fort Chadbourne, across to El Paso, and through
New Mexico and Arizona to San Francisco. Covering 2,795 miles, it
was the longest animal-drawn conveyance route in United States history, and perhaps the longest regularly scheduled such service the
world has ever seen.

The Butterfield Mail neither traveled along nor intersected any
part of the Texas Chihuahua Road; however, one single performance
must be recorded here, for it adds another perspective to the same
Henry Skillman who, in heroic role, appears so often in the earliest
years along the road to Chihuahua.

During the last week of September 1858, on its first run all the
way west, the Butterfield Mail was under pressure to set a good record.
The new Concord coach had as its only *through* passenger the special
correspondent of the *New York Herald,* Waterman L. Ormsby, who
manfully bore the ordeal of passage all the way from St. Louis to San
Francisco in order to file his dispatches on the dramatic event.[6]

When the coach-and-six came clattering down through Castle
Gap and across the flats to Horsehead Crossing of the Pecos at 3:30 on
the morning of September 26, Captain Skillman was waiting at the
primitive station to take up the reins as the next driver. Correspondent
Ormsby saw him as "a Kentuckian . . . of magnificent physique, over
six feet tall," the very picture of a plainsman: flowing blond hair and
beard, dressed in buckskin, festooned with bowie knives and revolvers.
He had but recently made the move from the San Antonio-El Paso line
to the Butterfield, and was ready to go.

The coach lurched out of the station corral at 4:30 that morning,
Skillman up on the box with the skein of reins firmly grasped in his
great battered hands. The Butterfield road did not cross the river there
but turned up the east side, the same route that Loving and Goodnight
followed with their cattle drives in later years. It was at that time
called "Pope's new road," for Capt. John Pope, who had had the miserable assignment, in the years just past, of drilling a series of wells
for the army — and the general public — up this dreary route.[7]

At 10:00 that night Skillman drove the coach into the new station at Emigrant's Crossing, sixty miles above the Horsehead. They
paused only for a meal and fresh mules, pushing on another sixty miles
to a station occupying Pope's old camp, near the crossing that bears his
name. This was a relatively commodious structure of stone and adobe,
"the only substantial habitation in the 436 miles between Ft. Chadbourne and the first settlements below El Paso." [8]

Here they finally crossed the Pecos, which got no better notice from Ormsby than from any other observer of those days. After breakfast next morning on Delaware Creek, having used cow chips as fuel for a cooking fire, they pointed toward the purple-hazed mass of the Guadalupe Mountains. In the late afternoon, under the looming slopes of Guadalupe Peak, the big Concord coach pulled up at the log corrals and stone station called the Pinery (now Pine Springs on U.S. Highway 180). With a fresh team but durable Henry Skillman still on the reins, they pulled off in the dusk down the rutted Emigrant Road across the desert that Robert S. Neighbors had scouted out almost ten years before. Sometime that night they met and paused for greetings with the first eastbound stage, which had left San Francisco September 15.[9]

Caked with alkali dust, the passengers as bone-weary and stiff as the driver himself, they pulled up next afternoon at the Hueco Station, planted among the weird stone outcroppings of the Hueco Tanks. The famous sheltered pools were dry; a drouth was on. The station tender showed the wayfarers two eight-gallon kegs, saying, "That's all we have left for a dozen men and as many head of cattle." [10] Presumably, he spared the travelers enough to wet their whistles.

And so they arrived at Franklin Station, across the river from old El Paso del Norte,

> with the rugged Captain Skillman still on the wagon seat and manfully playing the lines. He had cracked the whip across the alkali flats and plateaus, and on the darkest nights "whirled along on the very brink of the precipices with perfect safety," from the time of their departure at 4:30 on Sunday morning, until they arrived at Franklin at 5:00 on Thursday morning, September 30, 1858, without relief or rest, ninety-six hours later. Even in the brave annals of Texas, Skillman ranks as quite a man.[11]

Indeed he does, and he deserved a better fate than that which the United States Army, whose roads he had so notably helped to open, meted out to him six years later.

In the last half of the 1850s, trade and development along the Chihuahua Road west of San Antonio settled down to a bustling, profitable routine, always marred, however, by the sporadic and fierce onslaught of the Comanches, Apaches, Lipans, and Kiowas.

In the spring of 1855, when J. M. West and eighteen-year-old James Pearson Newcomb teamed up to establish the *San Antonio Her-*

ald, listing themselves together as "publishers and proprietors" in the masthead, they wanted, of course, to put their best foot forward. In their first issue, the lead story, bearing the earmarks of Newcomb's style and philosophy, in large type occupying all the first column of the first page, was headlined "The Indians — The Peace Policy." It read, in part,

> The Indians have been the greatest drawback against which Texas has had to contend. Every year they have ravaged our frontier, murdering our citizens, and robbing them of their stock and other property . . . Anything calculated to terminate, or render less frequent the depredations that have prevented the settlement of our frontier, will be hailed with delight not only by our frontier settler but by every well-wisher of the State, for nothing would tend more to promote the interest and prosperity of the state . . .
>
> To effect this much-desired object, the General government has determined to adopt the "peace policy" toward the Indians of Texas, as it has done toward those of other new States . . .
>
> The truth is, the Indians have been treated inhumanely for years . . . until they find themselves in a barren waste where they can neither live by the chase, nor the cultivation of the soil . . . This being the condition of the Indian, it behooves the white man, who reduced him to it, to relieve his sufferings and ameliorate his condition . . . [12]

The government's "peace policy" was perhaps as well-intentioned as were the editors' admonitions to the settlers on the frontier — and as ineffectual. The United States Army was already committed to the construction of forts to protect the traveler and the settler.

Returning to the work of his boundary survey in 1854, Maj. William H. Emory traveled with a well-armed escort from San Antonio to El Paso. Of this trip he wrote in his monumental *Report:*

> We did not see an Indian on the route, although, in front and in rear of us they were committing depredations along the whole road. At Cantonment Blake on the Devil's River[13] they waylaid and killed a couple of soldiers; at Live Oak [soon to become Fort Lancaster] they drove off, in open daylight, all the animals of the military post temporarily established at that point. At Fort Davis we found they had attacked a party and killed a sergeant and a musician; just beyond, at Dead Man's Hole, they attacked the mail party, and would probably have handled them severely, had not another party coming in the opposite direction, joined them at the critical moment.[14]

Beyond Castroville, Quihi, New Fountain, and D'Hanis, the establishment of Fort Inge on the Leona River (two or three miles south of present-day Uvalde) had made possible the settlement of the surrounding Frio, Sabinal, and Nueces Canyon country. General Worth had sent out Capt. Sidney Burbank of the First United States Infantry to camp at the place on March 13, 1849, apparently as a tentative occupation. But when Lt. W. H. C. Whiting was detailed in the summer of 1849 to make a survey for an arc line of forts on the western frontier of Texas, and in his findings included the site of Fort Inge as a key point on that arc, it was officially established, with Capt. Seth Eastman, also of the First Infantry, as its first commandant.[15]

The fort stood on a handsome location, overlooked by the strange conical mound, 150 feet high, known as Mount Inge. An interesting geologic study in itself, the mound is composed entirely of chunks of purplish rock known locally as "Uvalde phonolite," ranging from a few inches to several feet in diameter, tumbled irregularly together as if dropped from the sky. It served admirably as a lookout post, commanding many miles of surrounding territory.[16] The army built the fort at the foot of the mound on a crescent of level land extending to the banks of the sparkling Leona River. The flat, fertile terrain was ideal for gardening and for grazing, while wood for fire and for construction was plentiful up and down the banks of the creek.[17]

W. W. Arnette, taking a contract to furnish hay for the post, had pitched his tent nearby in February 1852. He found five families living in the vicinity along the Leona.[18] The Wool Road passed by the gates of the fort and forded the Leona at that point. A few miles farther west, nearing the Nueces, the Wool Road split off to the southwest, while the Chihuahua Road ran on west to Las Moras.

Three towering frontiersmen, all close friends, settled early in that general area. Ed Westfall, six feet three or four inches tall, brown-haired, blue-eyed, beloved by all the Uvalde country, and so absolutely fearless that he was a legend in his own time, built his cabin on the Leona south of Fort Inge.[19] Henry Robinson, tall, with flaming red hair and beard, homesteaded at Chalk Bluff, up the Nueces Canyon.[20] Somewhat to the southeast, Bigfoot Wallace lived at his remote cabin in the community that now bears his name; he rode with the Overland Mail, changed horses at Fort Inge, and often fraternized along the road with his two tall sidekicks. A history of Uvalde County asserts that "there were very few Indian trails taken up without one of the three old scouts being along to pilot the expedition through the prickly pear,

mountains, or cedar brakes, and sometimes the three were together." [21]

Other families, reassured by the presence of the fort and of those
intrepid frontiersmen, moved into the fertile bottomlands of the lower
canyons, homesteading at Waring, at Sabinal Station, and at Patterson
community. Reading W. Black and Nathan L. Stratton as partners
bought land along the Leona two miles above Fort Inge in March of
1853, establishing a community they called Encina but which became
the flourishing town of Uvalde. [22]

Massacres, skirmishes, and pitched battles with the Indians in
these foothills of the Edwards Plateau were numerous. Perhaps one
notable affray, involving all the classic elements of lonely homesteaders
at the mercy of the Comanches, army intervention, and a long-range
chase, can serve to epitomize them.

Around Ranchero Creek, about three miles east of Sabinal Station
and twenty-odd miles east of Fort Inge, John Davenport and John and
Doke Bowles, father and son, had settled with their families. The John
Davenport homestead, located at the point where the great road to the
west crossed the creek, began early to serve the wagon trains as they labored past, providing a campground and incidental provisions.

On October, 28, 1859, John Bowles and John Davenport, riding
separately some miles west of their homes, were ambushed, riddled
with arrows, and scalped by a party of Comanches from the headwaters
of the Llano, far to the north. Davenport's body was discovered first by
Doke Bowles. When it became apparent that John Bowles was missing, neighbors instituted a search, but his body was not found until
later, in a remote thicket near Guide Hill. [23]

The settlers, organizing a posse, sent a courier twenty miles west
to Fort Inge, asking Lt. William B. Hazen, then in command of the
fort, to send reinforcements to join them at the mouth of Frio Canyon.
Hazen sallied out on the morning of October 30 with one noncommis-
sioned officer and eight men, all mounted, from Company F. Among
the settlers who met him at Frio Canyon were the sutler W. W. Arnette, Doke Bowles, Clabe Davenport, brother of the slain John Davenport, John Q. Daugherty, William Thomas, Frank Isbell, Everett
Williams, and John Kennedy — a party altogether of about forty-two
men bent on vengeance.

The chase that ensued was epic even for those legendary days of
the hill country. Doke Bowles led the party up Frio Canyon as guide
and chief tracker, with the understanding that Lieutenant Hazen

would take command when the Indians were sighted. Catching up with the fleeing Comanches required more than two days, and some seventy-five miles of trailing, but the trackers did surprise them in camp on the morning of November 3. The posse attacked immediately, killing four of the Indians on the spot, but in their return fire Lieutenant Hazen was knocked off his horse by a heavy ball that pierced his breastbone, passed through his chest, and lodged near his backbone. Some of the soldiers stayed with Hazen and sent for help, while Doke Bowles took command and led the remainder in pursuit. He was mounted on a racehorse known as Fuzzy Buck, famous in the western country and lent him on the spot by W. W. Arnette.

The tale of that chase up the headwaters of the Frio and into the Llano country has become one of the prime legends of the area. Fuzzy Buck would continually outrun all the other settlers' horses, so that Bowles could come up alone within range of the fleeing war party, discharge his weapons, and then have to turn back. His fellows, meanwhile, would have freshly loaded guns waiting for him; Bowles would seize them and return to the chase.

According to the story, "When the battle came to an end for lack of ammunition, there were only three Indians who trudged to the top of a hill in the distance, and slid off their horses to the ground." In the hyperbole of the legend, "dead Indians were scattered many miles back to where the battle first commenced." When the fighting finally broke off, the pursuers and pursued were in the high country at the head of the North Llano River, nearly 200 miles by trail from Sabinal.[24]

The army managed to bring a wagon up to where Lieutenant Hazen lay with a hole through his chest, and took him out to the new hospital at Fort Clark, where he finally recovered from his massive wound. Promoted to captain for his part in the affray, he survived to become chief signal officer of the army.

John Davenport's widow remained at her place on Ranchero Creek and with the children managed as best she could. Her house was a few hundred yards above the creek crossing where the Chihuahua Road ran on west. Wagon trains often camped there at the spring, and Aunt Mary Davenport, as she was known, soon found herself supplying eggs and other foodstuffs to the passing freighters. This proved so popular that she eventually kept a store of sorts in her house, and the patronage aided materially in keeping her family together. It was the only place to trade, for some years, between D'Hanis and Uvalde.[25]

Forty-two miles west-northwest of Fort Inge, the army had established Fort Clark on July 30, 1852. The site, at the headwaters of Las Moras Creek, was leased from Samuel A. Maverick for twenty years at $50 a month, "with the privilege of taking from the tract as much hay, fuel, stone, and timber as may be required for the use of the post." That tract extended from the head spring some eight miles down the Las Moras, the breadth varying from one and a half to two miles. Lt. Col. W. G. Freeman, on his inspection tour August 1, 1853, found the permanent installation still under construction, with six officers and fifty-six men living in tents and engaged in the building work. The assigned force nominally included two companies with a small medical unit. Altogether, however, Colonel Freeman found that "Neither company has more than half its complement, and the two united on parade hardly formed more than a respectable platoon."

Fort Clark served as the western outpost of the United States Army until Fort Bliss was reached, 475 miles to the northwest. Despite its rudimentary state, Colonel Freeman recognized Fort Clark as "a point of primary importance, being the limit of arable land in the direction of El Paso, and from its salient position looking both to the Rio Grande and Indian frontiers." He wrote that "it ought to have a strong garrison of horse and foot, and it is well fitted for a Cavalry station, timber for building being convenient, and an abundance of excellent grazing in the immediate vicinity."[26]

As earlier noted, Fort Davis was established in Limpia Canyon September 3, 1854. On the Pecos River, Fort Lancaster, alongside Live Oak Creek, was not formally occupied until August 20, 1855, though army units had frequently camped at the site. Army engineers had already chipped and hacked out on the mountainside the remarkable steep wagon road down Lancaster Hill to the fort's site in the Pecos Valley. Camp Hudson at the Second Crossing of the Devil's River appears in history in 1857; Fort Quitman, the loneliest of posts, where the El Paso Road first reaches the Rio Grande, was established September 28, 1858; and Camp Stockton, later Fort Stockton, was activated at Comanche Springs March 28, 1859. So developed the chain of military installations that protected the westerly stream of traffic to El Paso and Chihuahua, along with the settlements that would cluster around the posts.[27]

Lieutenant Whiting's concept of another chain of outposts, to screen the arclike western frontier of settlements, brought about the development of Fort McIntosh at Laredo, Fort Duncan at Eagle Pass,

Camp Wood on the upper Nueces, Fort Mason near the Llano, Fort McKavett on the San Saba, Fort Concho at present-day San Angelo, and Fort Belknap on the northern prairies.[28]

As for that breakneck road down Lancaster Hill, which motorists a century later, coming westward down the long grade on old U.S. 290 toward Fort Lancaster and Sheffield could still see plainly from across the canyon: army engineers' records on how and exactly when it was carved out have not been found.

The white gash slanting steeply down the north side of the canyon wall was already there in 1855, however, for a tow-headed German immigrant lad named Peter Jonas documented it with his own bitter experience. His testament was written half a century later in the labored, unschooled way of a man who had never become comfortable at writing in an adopted language.[29]

Peter Jonas was born October 12, 1839, in Nassau, Germany. He immigrated with his parents to Texas in 1846, settling near New Braunfels. The father, soon widowed, took up freighting and often carried the boy along on his trips, so that Peter learned to drive the big wagons himself before he entered his teens. Hard times then put him on his own; he was driving for other freighters by the time he was fourteen.

In his autobiography, Jonas recorded that when he was sixteen, he "went to work for Capt. Pope, who started on an expedition to the Pecos River experimenting in boring Artesian wells." John Pope was that professional soldier, competent but violently irascible, who at that time had been directed by Secretary of War Jefferson Davis to drill a line of exploratory water wells across the Trans-Pecos. Some grateful associates thought the ill-tempered Pope had been exiled to the desert as a way to get rid of him.[30] The lonely, frustrating assignment did not break him — he became a brigadier general in the Civil War — but it did bring out the worst in his temperament, as Peter Jonas's experience shows:

> I had a falling out with Capt. Pope near Ft. Lancaster where I quit him. We had 60 wagons. 40 of them were gov't wagons and 20 were his own 10-mule teams wagons. I was driving one of his 10-mule teams we was going up a very steep and rocky hill. Our team got up the hill first. [At] about sundown Pope ordered all to come down with our whips to help the balance up the hill. We seeing there was too many men and being in one anothers way, there being 80 Teamsters and about 75 Mechanics and Laborers, so my-

self and three others concluded to stay with the wagons and cook
supper for our Mess Mates, having fires started and being at work
cooking when Cap't Pope came up to the top of the Hill and
seeing us and giving us a very severe cussing and calling me a little white-headed son of a ————.

Pope put the boy under arrest and made him walk all night with
the sentinel at the point of a bayonet. Next morning Peter Jonas told
the captain he was quitting his job.

Pope looked at me very cross and commenced cursing me again as he
did at the Hill and says to me I will give you 10 minutes to get out
of camp. I went down to the wagon and [started] throwing out my
things. My old friend Ed Froboese called me saying to come to
breakfast. I says to Ed I don't want any breakfast. [When Ed learned
why] Froboese jumped up and said if you have to leave I will stay
with you, and six more of my friends were ready to go with [sic] so
the Seven went and reported to Pope and told him they would stay
with me.³¹ When he gave them all 10 minutes to get out of camp we
then went [back] to the Post Ft. Lancaster intending to stay there
until some trains of wagons might come along and bring us back to
San Antonio which might some times happen in 4 or 6 months those
days, but luckily about the third day a Mr. Waldeck came along.

The eight young teamsters started to join up with Waldec, but
for some reason not made clear in Jonas's narrative they switched instead to "an outfit from N. M. under command of Capt. Clayboarin
[sic] 5 wagons and escort of soldiers." Unfortunately, the vindictive
Pope apparently got a word in with "Capt. Clayboarin," for

. . . after we got about six miles from Ft. Lancaster, he stopped the
wagons and made us all get out and walk 35 miles. [That would
have been to Howard's Well] next day 45 miles [to Beaver Lake]
next day after that 25 miles but crossing Devil's River about ten
times, to Camp Hudson.

The footsore lads finally reached Fort Clark, 150 miles from Lancaster
Hill, where they separated themselves from "Capt. Clayboarin" and
his dubious hospitality, hitching a ride into San Antonio "with some
Mexican carretas." The importance of Peter Jonas's memoir is that it
gives the only known description, in any detail at all, of how laden
wagons got up that cruel grade at Lancaster Hill. Dozens of men with
bullwhips concentrated in turn on each straining team, brutally lash-
ing the mules up the ledgy ascent.

One other story about that incredible hill survives, this one about the downhill run. It took place as late, perhaps, as 1870, but as told here the story enhances the picture of the most imposing piece of road construction achieved by army engineers in Texas before the Civil War.

Henry W. Daly tells a highly colored story of his experiences as a stage driver for Ben Ficklin in the late 1860s and early 1870s.[32] He makes clear that the stages going west usually followed the road from Fort Concho to the Pontoon Crossing on the Pecos, but places this incident specifically on the lower road and on in to Fort Lancaster:

> From a driving standpoint the most dangerous piece of road east of the Pecos was over Lancaster Hill. Later this was given up in favor of a detour, but during my time at the reins we crossed the hill. Near the crest the road entered a defile of rock so narrow that two teams could hardly pass. Then came a long steep incline cut in the hillside, after which the road, following the contour of the mountain, turned left at almost a forty-five degree angle. This point was always a source of anxiety because the rains cut great ruts across the roadway. It was best to take this turn at a walk, because the lead mules would be virtually out of sight before the coach started to change direction. Shortly beyond this was a right hand turn, not so sharp as its predecessor, then another incline: hillside on one hand and space on the other. Snuggled at the bottom was Lancaster Station and an abandoned army post.
>
> We had just entered the defile at the summit . . . when with deafening yells a swarm of Indians leaped down on all sides. Had I hesitated they would have had the mules by the bridles.
>
> Throwing out my lash and taking a fresh grip on the reins I dashed through the gap. On the incline Indians began to pepper us with arrows. The air seemed black with them. But as luck would have it young Jim Spears [a road agent for the stage line] happened to be inside the coach and he directed the fire of the passengers.
>
> As we thundered toward the turn I believed my last moment had come, and I may say that that is the only time I have ever had that feeling. A half-naked Indian, leaping down from the bank, deflected my thoughts for an instant. As he lunged at the bridle of one of the lead animals I threw out my whip and caught him squarely in the face. The next I knew the mules were careening around the turn. The wheels left the ground and the whole coach seemed to swing out over space. I could see the harness tighten and strain. Then we hit, on two wheels, careening so that I had to grasp the seat. It required some seconds for me to realize that we were actually on the road, and to this day I don't see how we got there. I do not think it would have

happened again in a thousand times. The Indians continued to pour arrows into us, but once beyond the second turn we could see the guard at the station, aroused by our firing, coming to the rescue. The Indians fled. Taking stock of our casualties, we found that two passengers had been painfully wounded. The coach and mules were so full of arrows that they resembled pin cushions. I had two arrows in my back.

"Daly," said Jim Spears, "that would have been a hair-raising run without any Indians. How in hell did you manage that turn?"

"Mr. Spears," said I, "the mules managed it." [33]

And what of Indianola, at the far opposite end of the Chihuahua Road, in those last days before the holocaust?

Indianola had prospered. Under the headline "Indianola, A City," its local paper had trumpeted in early 1853: "The *Bulletin* has the pleasure to announce that the bill to incorporate Indianola as a city has passed both houses of the legislature and become a law." [34]

At about that same time Col. W. G. Freeman had landed at Indianola to start his inspection tour of the Eighth Military Department. Freeman found that the Indianola Depot, which he inspected on the day of his arrival, was used by the quartermaster and subsistence departments of the army. Indianola itself, he noted, "contains some 600 inhabitants and is a place of considerable trade. All supplies coming by sea for the principal depots at San Antonio and Austin are landed at this point and conveyed hence by wagons, the distances to the places named being, respectively, 140 miles W.N.W. and 160 miles N.N.W." [35]

Army facilities included five warehouse buildings, a blacksmith shop, and a stable, built on leased ground, plus "a wharf, 250 feet long, on which is laid a railway . . . connected with the land, and for the exclusive use of the wharf and the lease on the ground, the Government pays a monthly rent of $80." [36]

By 1860 the population had grown, from the 600 people found by Colonel Freeman in 1853, to a total of 1,469, while Port Lavaca up the bay had 810.

In the fall of 1858, the *Indianola Courier* was reporting that "hereafter we will have two steamers a week by Berwick's Bay route, and two by way of the Mississippi River, from New Orleans, making four steamers a week." [37] At the end of the decade the waterfront boasted two impressive T-head wharfs, according to a panoramic lithograph "drawn from nature" by Helmuth Holtz.[38]

The impact of four steamers a week, or more, shows in this comment from an Indianola newspaper in December 1858: "This week has presented a stirring scene of business activity in the loading and discharging of vessels — long trains of wagons, carts, and drays blocking off the streets, depositing their freights of cotton, hides, wool, pecans, corn, etc. and filling up with boxes, barrels, bales, and crates for the vast interior." [39]

In agricultural products alone, Indianola exported, in the twelve-month period ending September 1860, 35,825 bales of cotton, 1,412 bales of wool, 449 barrels of sugar, 613 barrels of molasses, 21,685 head of cattle, 42,599 hides, and 273 horses.[40] To tally a gross figure on movements of silver coins, bullion, and other metals is impossible, but the records of individual trains indicate that the total value ran into the millions of dollars per year by 1860.

[12]

Civil War
Hiatus

The sprawling Commonwealth of Texas — which had welcomed annexation with open arms only sixteen years before, joined its new parent nation two years later in lusty battle against Santa Anna, then for a dozen years devoted its energies toward opening and stabilizing the Rio Grande segment of the American frontier — now turned precipitously toward secession and fratricide.

Sam Houston, the old lion of San Jacinto, elected as governor of Texas in 1859, struggled to stem the tide of secessionist sentiment, but his voice was drowned out.

What were the issues in Texas? Obviously, the most emotional and simplistic one sprang from the determination of Northern abolitionists to free the slaves. The evidence suggests that in Texas the reaction provided another illustration of uninvolved people being roused to a lather of indignation by the shrewder few with heavy financial stakes. Texas was not essentially a great slave-owning state. Though there were, by the census of 1860, some 182,566 slaves in Texas, their ownership was confined to about five percent of the white population, or about 20,000 persons, and only 335 whites owned as many as fifty slaves. Furthermore, most of the slaves were concentrated in the eastern and deep southern counties.[1]

In those areas the stakes were indeed high. Many Texas planters, prior to the abolishment of slavery, had mortgaged their land to buy more blacks, or had mortgaged slaves to buy land, and it was the foreclosure of these mortgages which left many of them ruined after the war. In 1860 the assessed value of slaves in Texas was $64 million, about one-fourth of the total value of all property assessed.[2]

San Antonio, with 7,743 free citizens, had only 591 slaves, yet some of the most violent spokesmen for the slavery issue lived there. To a large degree the old Texians, under skillful manipulation, were simply reacting typically as they always did to any threat of compulsion from "outside." No better example could be offered than that of Dr. John S. (Old Rip) Ford. That staunch frontiersman, a firebrand always ready for a fight, was a solid citizen who took part in every public issue from the first days of the Republic in 1836 to the final throes of Reconstruction in the 1880s. The record does not indicate that he ever owned a slave.

Besides his many other avocations, Ford was for a long time the editor of the *Texas Democrat,* later the *Texas State-Times,* in Austin, a forum in which he unhesitatingly spoke his mind, often with some extravagance. Here and in his memoirs he always took a strong and unequivocal stand for slavery, deeming it sanctified by the scriptures. He particularly resented abolition as "an unjust effort to deprive [Southerners] of their property [and] to take it for nothing." He thought that the election of Lincoln as president "proved beyond all doubt that the aggressive Yankees intended to destroy the South's most cherished institution for their own economic gain."[3]

But Ford felt just as strongly about another reason that Texas should secede, one bearing heavily upon the fortunes of the new roads to the west, which he had helped to open. Rip Ford had campaigned happily sixteen years before for annexation by the United States because he felt that great republic had the strength and intent to stabilize the frontier. Now Ford and many other Texans, despite the chain of nineteen forts manned by more than 2,000 soldiers, believed the United States government had taken a lackadaisical attitude toward providing protection for the Texas frontier. Ford felt that this was in itself "ample cause to sever . . . connections with the Union."[4] The Texas secession ordinance and declaration of causes, as finally written, insisted that inadequate frontier protection as much as abolitionism and economic coercion justified Texas in leaving the Union.[5]

Actually, many honest and patriotic Texans were stampeded into the secessionist movement by the manipulations of the notorious Knights of the Golden Circle. This was a racially chauvinistic secret society that in the mid-1850s had backed the filibusters, such as William Walker, in their expansionist activities in Central America. It had faded with that movement, but in 1860 and 1861 spread again like a prairie fire across the South, with special fervidness in Texas. The Society, according to H. H. Bancroft,

> became a power in the land. By its influence the sentiments of the people were revolutionized; from its fold were drawn the first armed rebels in Texas, under the famous Ranger Ben McCullough [*sic*]; it furnished the vigilance committees; and to its members were charged murders and incendiary acts committed during the war.[6]

Bancroft was careful to add "So says Newcombe," thereby vitiating to some degree the objectivity of his description, for the record of James Pearson Newcomb's career shows that he was himself a chauvinist on the other side. Nevertheless, the fact of the destructiveness of the Knights of the Golden Circle stands unchallenged. The group appealed to unsophisticated backwoodsmen by its promise of secret deeds of derring-do, but how it duped such solid public figures as Ben McCulloch, with his lifetime of brave and dedicated service, is almost incomprehensible.

In an award-winning study researched a century after the Civil War, Roy Sylvan Dunn concluded that

> The Knights of the Golden Circle seemed to synthesize the diverse ambitions, fears, and frustrations that had plagued the South since the 1830's . . . It brought together men who desired adventure, fame, and fortune. It appealed to those who feared the influx of foreigners and the spread of Roman Catholicism. It offered a weapon to Southerners who resented the unrelenting, often abusive efforts of the abolitionists . . . The KGC was a reflection of the times when men could feel but could not think.[7]

Heavily infiltrated by the KGC, the Secession Convention on February 1, 1861, voted its will 169 to 7 over the stunned opposition of Governor Sam Houston.[8] It also set up a Committee on Public Safety headed by John C. Robertson, ostensibly to steer the secession movement pending ratification in the statewide referendum called for February 26. A review of the committee's proceedings and reports shows clearly that its primary purpose was to get rid of United States troops stationed in Texas and to deal with any armed resistance that might be met.[9]

With San Antonio the seat of military power in the Southwest, the men selected by the Committee on Public Safety to serve in that city were in a specially strategic position. The bold actions they took in the next two weeks established Confederate control of the state, but the coup was cataclysmic to frontier life and to the teeming traffic on the roads west.

The three men who actually served were Thomas J. Devine, Samuel A. Maverick, and Phillip N. Luckett. Devine was a forty-year-old lawyer, practicing in San Antonio; Luckett, twenty-six, was a physician from Corpus Christi, believed to be a card-carrying KGC; senior member Sam Maverick needs no further introduction. James H. Rogers was also named as one of the commissioners but did not serve.[10]

Ironically, as his wife Mary recorded, Maverick had come to the new colony of Texas a quarter century before in order to escape the atmosphere of South Carolina,

> where the doctrines of nullification and ultimate Secession were aggressively espoused by an overwhelming majority of the ruling class . . . But all doctrines and issues of the former time bloomed into life about him when Texas became a member of the Union. Creeping beneath the shadow of the manifold blessings of the Union, came the bitter and unceasing strife. At last [Maverick] came to believe the strife was forced on us, and that there was before us an "irresistible conflict" which we could not escape no matter where we turned.[11]

For a man who had worked so devotedly to build up protection for the frontier, Maverick's mission now must have been painful, for the committee's first objective was to dismantle the Federal military establishment in Texas, evacuate the chain of frontier forts, seize the treasure of their arsenals, and oust the 2,328 officers and men of the Eighth Military Department, United States Army. It was a staggering assignment for these three civilians and the handful of hard-riding Minutemen whom they mobilized, but they accomplished their mission within three weeks, before even the foggiest plan had been designed for what might be put together to fill the void.

This signal victory for the South — and debacle for the Union — could not have been brought about had not a most pliable instrument been at hand in the person of Bvt. Maj. Gen. David E. Twiggs, commanding, Eighth Military Department.

The general, in his ready compliance, formed one element of a troika which almost overnight precipitated the revolution in Texas. The other two elements were the Committee on Public Safety and a strike force of a few hundred "minute-men," heavily infiltrated with Knights of the Golden Circle. When the zero hour came, February 15, 1861, under cover of night, Ben McCulloch's men were parceled out and stationed at key locations in the city, ready to overwhelm any action that might be initiated by the small force of 160 army troops in San Antonio.

To describe how the army was ousted from Texas in early 1861, two accounts are offered here. First, one of the more remarkable documents, right out of the *res gestae,* was placed upon the record in June 1861, when Maj. J. T. Sprague, United States Army, appeared before the New York Historical Society in New York City to recite his version of the harrowing days he had but recently experienced in San Antonio. Sprague, a genuine veteran of the ante-bellum frontier in Texas, was the same Eighth Infantry officer who had headed the second military expedition to El Paso in April 1850, following that of Major Van Horne the preceding year. His paper, though strongly partisan, presents considerable evidence to support the thesis of the KGC's dark manipulations to move the state into the Confederacy.[12]

Second, another of the few observers of the confused scene in San Antonio who made any record of impressions was a militantly loyal woman, Caroline Baldwin Darrow, wife of General Twiggs's confidential clerk, Charles Darrow. In her "Recollections of the Twiggs Surrender," published twenty years later from notes made at the time, Mrs. Darrow recited a virtual hour-by-hour narrative of the crises, developments, and melodramatic incidents swirling about the plazas and narrow streets of the beleaguered little city.[13] Dr. Sylvan Dunn's study, "The KGC in Texas, 1860–1861," also focuses on these developments.[14]

The statewide election for ratifying or rejecting the ordinance of secession went overwhelmingly "for": 46,129 to 17,697. When Sam Houston, as governor, and his secretary of state, Ebenezer Cave, refused to take the oath of allegiance to the new Confederacy, the Secession Convention summarily ousted them from office.

The Committee on Public Safety had found General Twiggs more than submissive in agreeing, step-by-step, to the committee's objectives: to dismantle the Federal military establishment in Texas, evacuate the network of nineteen frontier forts, and oust from the borders of the state the men and officers of the Eighth Military Department. Twiggs took the ultimate step on February 18, responding to the committee's relentless pressure with a note:

> . . . I now repeat that I will direct the positions held by Federal troops to be turned over . . . provided the troops retain their arms and clothing, camp and garrison equipment . . . and such means of transportation . . . as may be necessary for an efficient and orderly movement of the troops from Texas . . .[15]

It was the most traitorous act by a general officer of the armed forces in the history of this nation. In contrast, honorable men like Robert E. Lee and Albert Sidney Johnston removed themselves from the Union army rolls *before* doing any damage to the United States.

Twiggs left Texas through Indianola, landing in Louisiana, where he accepted a commission as major general in the Provisional Army of the Confederacy. When news of his capitulation reached Washington, the secretary of war moved swiftly, on March 1, dismissing him from the army "for his treachery to the flag of his country in having surrendered . . . on the demand of authorities in Texas, the military posts and other property . . . under his charge." [16] Broken in health and spirit, David Twiggs did not long remain in the post he had so dearly bought. He returned to his home in Augusta, Georgia, where he died on July 15, 1862.

One by one, across Texas, between February 21 and April 25, all the camps and posts were closed down and abandoned, their soldiers streaming down the hard-won roads through San Antonio and down to Matagorda Bay, where evacuation turned into a shambles.

The new Confederate government moved to establish in San Antonio a military command structure for Texas similar to the one the United States Army had maintained during the previous fifteen years. A succession of Southerners, mostly Texans, commanded and staffed this skeletal Department of Texas for the next four years: Earl Van Dorn, Henry McCulloch, P. O. Hebert, and finally James B. Magruder. During the last year of the war, the department headquarters were moved to Houston.[17]

The way Texans went about their Civil War was nothing if not imaginative. Shortly after the expulsion of the Federal troops, word circulated among the settlements that a great "buffalo hunt" was being organized for the western plains — a strange activity to be undertaken when strife with the Colossus of the North was just commencing. The invitation was pressed, nevertheless, for adventurous young men, equipped with horse, saddle, and heavy rifle, to join up with John R. Baylor at his camps, either on the northern outskirts of San Antonio on the Salado, or west of town on León Creek. The boys got the idea that a big buffalo hunt was a solidly patriotic venture, and they began to drift into the camps from all directions, with as motley an array of weapons as had been seen on the frontier.

All was business, however, as soon as they reported. It turned out that John R. Baylor was the same surly, pugnacious man who two years before had harassed patient, durable Robert S. Neighbors while he sought to contain the Indian tribes of the northern Texas frontier on their designated reservations. Many believed Baylor fomented the plot that resulted in Neighbors's murder.[18]

Baylor had emigrated to Texas from Kentucky at the age of seventeen. A veteran Indian fighter from the Comanche campaigns of 1840, he belonged to "the only good Indian" school, and he practiced his learning with zeal. Baylor went from the Rolling Plains to the Secession Convention in Austin, took part in Ben McCulloch's coup against the Union army, got his commission from the new Confederate government, and stayed to fight the Yankees. Under direction of the new Department of Texas, Lieutenant Colonel Baylor, CSA, would take half the Second Regiment, Texas Mounted Rifles, west to El Paso on a covert, unpublicized mission.

This was to be the first stage of a grand design to seize New Mexico and Arizona, and eventually push the Confederate flag to the Pacific Coast, so as to deny all the West, and especially California's gold, to the Union. It was one of the most daring projects undertaken by the South, and it probably would have won the war for the South had it succeeded.

But while John Baylor labored through the month of May in the mesquite thickets of the Salado to whip his raw recruits into a fighting force, no firm plan had been perfected for the more massive backup he would have to have after extending himself in the wastes of New Mexico. It would be July 8 before the War Department in Richmond even named the man to take up the job.[19]

On that date it commissioned as brigadier general Henry Hopkins Sibley, a West Point graduate who had been serving as brevet major with the United States Army in New Mexico. Sibley had resigned his Federal commission May 13 and made himself available to the Confederacy. His new orders as brigadier were to proceed to San

Antonio and organize a brigade of three more mounted regiments and a battery of howitzers. With this force he was to invade the territory of Arizona, which at that time still included the territory of New Mexico, to drive all the Federal forces from that department.[20]

Meanwhile, John R. Baylor had learned from old Trans-Pecos hands that there was neither water nor forage enough at many key spots along the Chihuahua Road and the branching road up to El Paso to support at one time even his limited force of some 700 men and their mounts. He made the wise decision, therefore, to deploy his companies spaced out in several groups, some days apart.

He started Maj. Edwin Waller, Jr.,[21] out ahead, in charge of an advance force of six companies. Waller dropped off two companies to garrison abandoned Fort Clark, and proceeded on to the Devil's River, where he learned from travelers that Fort Bliss, with its Federal stores, was standing abandoned, across the Rio Grande from El Paso del Norte. Major Waller immediately sent a detachment of one hundred men on forced march up the deserted road. The small force was amazed and relieved to find the Confederate flag flying over Fort Bliss.[22]

Genial, unflappable James Wiley Magoffin, erstwhile Santa Fe trader, American consul at Chihuahua, sutler to the United States Army, and unfailing host to any distinguished traveler who came up or down the roads, had some years earlier established himself at "Magoffinsville," a tract which included the original grounds of Fort Bliss. The army had evacuated that post on March 31, in accordance with Twiggs's orders. After waiting a decent interval to see whether any other move would be made against the fort, Magoffin simply ran up the Confederate flag on the parade ground. He had enlisted Simeon Hart, who operated the only flour mill in that part of the West, and J. F. Crosby, district judge for all of western Texas beyond the Pecos, to hold the fort with him until help should arrive. The remainder of Waller's forces did come in by stages over the next several days.[23]

Though Baylor's half-regiment had numbered about 700 men when he left San Antonio, he had distributed some 400 of them along the way, including Bliss, as he came up the road. He pared the remainder down to a selected 250, while they rested a few days and trained at Fort Bliss. Then, on July 23, Baylor moved this strike force up the river from El Paso, crossed at San Tomás, and proceeded toward Mesilla, which, with a population of about 2,500, was the largest town in the valley and the second largest in the Arizona Territory. Within the next two and a half days, this feisty warrior had met and rebuffed a

Yankee force twice the size of his own, followed up by capturing the entire Union outfit, and had occupied Mesilla,[24] proclaiming himself governor.

Though New Mexicans, with their strong traditional ties to colonial Spain, generally mistrusted Texans, a sizeable block of Confederate sympathy did exist, especially among Anglo-American settlers. Most of it was centered at Mesilla in the Rio Grande Valley. The *Mesilla Times,* in its issue of August 3, blazoned: "ARIZONA IS FREE AT LAST!"

Far away to the southeast in San Antonio, the new General Sibley had just reported and was barely starting to organize the regiments that were to support Colonel Baylor and continue the drive westward. Unlike hard-driving Gen. John E. Wool, who had needed only six weeks to put together a force of similar size for the 1846 campaign against Santa Anna, Henry Hopkins Sibley took from August 1 to the end of October to get even the first of his regiments on the road. One reason was that he got no help at all from the Confederate command in Richmond. His call for volunteers, to rally at the same camps where Baylor had made up the first contingents, brought a motley crowd of farmers, frontiersmen, and townsfolk: but they were anxious to fight and brought such homely weapons as they had.

The men placed in command positions included some of Texas's more notable citizens: William Polk "Gotch" Hardeman; James Reily, who had been minister to the United States from the Republic of Texas; William Read Scurry; Tom Green; and William Steele, one of the few top officers in Sibley's Brigade to survive the war and remain in public life.

The expedition as finally organized comprised the Fourth, Fifth, and Seventh Mounted Rifle Regiments, a battery of six howitzers, and the brigade headquarters staff. Reily's Fourth Regiment got away from San Antonio on October 26, 1861, followed a week later by Tom Green's Fifth. Brigade headquarters marched out November 18, and Steele's Seventh Regiment brought up the rear on November 20.[25] They took their westering course out the Chihuahua Road, following the golden gleam of their strike for the Pacific Coast. Of the more than 3,000 men in all who marched west, less than 1,800 ever returned.[26]

The expedition did get through to El Paso without major incident, and on to Mesilla to join up with self-proclaimed Governor John R. Baylor.

Shortly before Sibley's arrival at Mesilla, Baylor had made the first of two violent mistakes which stained his whole career. Ironically enough, the young editor of the *Mesilla Times,* Robert P. Kelley, who had so ecstatically welcomed Baylor's forces, had within a few weeks disagreed with him on handling of the Volunteer Arizona Guards. He trenchantly urged that Baylor should move north and engage the Federal commander, Col. E. R. S. Canby, who was assembling large forces at Fort Craig, only 117 miles upriver from Mesilla. Baylor had no intention of engaging so large a force. On December 12, Kelley criticized him violently in the *Times.*

The two men quarreled, then had a disgraceful brawl on the street in Mesilla. Kelley died later from Baylor's pistol shot through the throat, inflicted while he lay sprawled on the ground, but the people of Texas never got the whole story, at least in their generation.[27]

On December 20, upon the brigade's arrival, General Sibley issued a proclamation to the people of New Mexico and Arizona, declaring that all former federal taxes were abolished, assuring the people of his friendship, inviting Union soldiers to join with him, and promising political rights and liberty to everybody.[28]

But Indians were not included in that Utopian concept. Colonel Baylor, confirmed as military governor of the territory, was moving energetically to consolidate his position by more drastic means. Alarmed by the extent of Apache control through his territory, Baylor turned on the Indians with unbridled ferocity. In a March 20, 1862, letter to Capt. Thomas Helm of the Arizona Guards at Tucson, he said:

> You will . . . use all means to persuade the Apaches or any tribe to come in for the purpose of making peace, and when you get them together kill all the grown Indians and take the children prisoners and sell them to defray the expense of killing the Indians. Buy whiskey and such other goods as may be necessary for the Indians, and I will issue vouchers to cover the amount expended. Leave nothing undone to insure success, and have enough men around to allow no Indian to escape.[29]

A copy of those orders reached the capital at Richmond while Baylor was back in Texas on what he expected would be only a short visit. The savage and treacherous approach he took in his letter was too much for the professional soldiers and statesmen in the Confederate command. Jefferson Davis quietly removed him from office.[30]

Even as Sibley's campaign was getting under way in New Mexico, he initiated a probe of northern Mexico's intentions vis-á-vis the

South that could have realized Stephen F. Austin's original concept of the Chihuahua Road as an artery of commerce all the way to the Pacific — if it had succeeded. He detached Col. James Reily temporarily from his regiment to proceed as an envoy of the Confederate government to Ciudad Chihuahua.

Arriving there in mid-January, Reily placed several proposals before Governor Luis Terrazas. His first request, that the governor give his blessings to favorable trade concessions, was readily granted. As to an understanding for mutual crossing of the border in hot pursuit of marauding Indians, that was politely rejected. Next Reily proposed that, in the event the United States should undertake to send Union troops across the state from the West Coast, the governor should resist it. Don Luis parried that issue, saying that he personally would oppose such a move, but that the Supreme Congress of Mexico would appropriately make that policy decision.[31]

Reily went on to Hermosillo, capital of the state of Sonora, for talks with Governor Pisquiera. The substance of his discussion there is not known, but in his report to Richmond, Colonel Reily, an inveterate optimist, hints at their grandiose objective: "We must have Chihuahua and Sonora. With [them] we gain Southern California, and by a railway to Guaymas render our State of Texas the great highway of nations!" It was seventy years before such a railroad was built from Texas through Presidio del Norte and Ciudad Chihuahua, eventually not to Guaymas but to Las Mochis; it was too late then to capture the tide of empire.

Nothing materialized from Reily's mission. He returned promptly but under great difficulties to New Mexico. Nevertheless, the whole concept of his undertaking, and the proposals put before the two Mexican governors, shed some light on the vainglorious aura surrounding the Confederate leadership in the early months of the War Between the States.[32]

The thread of continuity in Sibley's campaign can be kept by noting only three salient developments: victory at Val Verde, defeat at Glorieta, and retreat to Texas.

Sibley took his command up the Rio Grande Valley in January, finally bringing his force of about 2,600 men into confrontation with about 3,800 Union soldiers under his own brother-in-law, Col. E. R. S. Canby, outside Fort Craig. In the battle which came to be known as Val Verde, the Sibley Brigade won a clear victory, driving Canby's forces in disorder back into the fort.[33]

That was the apogee of Sibley's campaign. He made the mistake of bypassing Fort Craig, which was well stocked with military supplies and might have provided him with logistic support. From there on, everything was downhill. He did push on north for a month, occupying Santa Fe on March 23. From that old town he deployed Maj. Charles Pyron's battalion of 500 men toward Fort Union, up the Chihuahua-Santa Fe Road through Glorieta Pass. Colonel Scurry, who was still marching his regiment up from Bernalillo, was to bypass Santa Fe and go directly to join Pyron at Apache Pass in lower Glorieta Pass.[34]

Unbeknownst to the Confederates, the Union army had already sent their First Colorado Volunteers, under Col. John P. Slough, south from Denver into New Mexico, aiming to occupy Santa Fe. Slogging through heavy snow in Raton Pass, they learned that Santa Fe was about to be taken by Confederate troops. Consequently, they changed their line of march to Fort Union, where they picked up reinforcements and moved out toward the upper approaches of Glorieta Pass. Advance elements of the Confederate and Union forces ran head on into each other in the Pass, engaging in a skirmish with minor casualties before each retired.[35]

Scurry, marching into the lower reaches of the Pass, worried about the danger of his wagons getting into such close quarters. He chose to drop his train at the foot of a high bluff known as Precipitous Mountain, leaving about 200 men to guard the 80 wagons and 200 mules and horses.[36]

When Union scouts reported to Colonel Slough how Scurry had left his supply train behind, Slough dispatched Maj. John Chivington with about 400 men to make an arduous bypass of the mountain to cut off the wagons.[37] Meanwhile Scurry, having joined up with Pyron, moved forward through the crest of the Pass and came face to face with Slough's main force just west of Pigeon's Roost, near noon on March 28. There the old Santa Fe Trail ran along the very narrow bottom of a deep gorge, where the slopes were covered with boulders and cedar.

In this rugged terrain, the battle was joined. It was an exhausting fight, lasting five hours, with the opposing forces deployed up the slopes, each struggling to wrestle its batteries into position. Casualties were not high: 28 killed, 48 wounded on the Union side; 36 killed, 60 wounded among the Confederates.

Again the Union army was the first to retire, dropping back to a place called Kozlowskie's Ranch. The Confederates were too worn out to pursue. But the crushing blow had already fallen, not only for Scurry but also for all the rest of Sibley's Brigade. By early morning that day, Chivington had reached a point on the bluff's crest above the encamped wagon train. From his vantage point, undetected, he could see that only a handful of men remained to guard the supplies; actually, all but seventeen had pulled out to join what they deemed the more valorous action in the Pass.

Chivington sent only two companies, at first, whooping down the steep slope upon the wagons and the *caballado*. The seventeen guards, after one look at the yelling horde bounding down the cliff, took to their horses in the direction of Santa Fe. Chivington's men burned every wagon; their only casualty was one man killed when an ammunition wagon blew up in his face. Some 200 mules were captured and bayoneted on the spot. The Confederate brigade as a whole lost most of their rolling stock and their principal supply of ammunition, rations, and baggage. For a half century afterwards, a pile of rusting wagon tires marked the spot at the foot of Precipitous Mountain where Sibley's grand design fell apart.[38]

Choosing not to press his advantage, Colonel Slough marched his Yankee forces back to Fort Union. But Scurry had to bring word to General Sibley, resting in Santa Fe, that though the battle was won, the logistic capabilities of the campaign, woefully limited from the beginning, were now lost indeed.

Unable to keep his forces adequately supplied with military essentials, Sibley had to make the bitter decision to retire completely from New Mexico. Brother-in-law Canby pursued and harried him toward El Paso.[39] For a good part of the way Sibley and his regiments, now almost entirely dismounted through the deterioration of their animals, struggled through the hideous Jornado del Muerto, losing most of their remaining supplies. A disorganized, exhausted force straggled into Fort Bliss over a period of days in late April and early May. Sibley had left Colonel Steele and his regiment at Doña Ana with orders to hold back Canby's army.[40]

One of the vagaries of the wartime economy in the West was that, in midst of the sweeping depredations made by Apaches, and terrible hardship all around, a stagecoach to San Antonio was still running, occasionally. This was the last gasp of George H. Giddings's historic San Antonio-San Diego Overland Mail.[41]

The June 5, 1862, issue of the *San Antonio Herald* prominently displayed a letter from a correspondent who signed herself only as

"Mollie." The talented and observant writer, after holding forth on the delights of the upper Rio Grande Valley, with its harvest of grapes and other delicacies, noted that she left El Paso May 17 and made these observations:

> . . . We came by stage, and although we were traveling alone, in a wild Indian country, a woman and unprotected, under the hottest sun that ever shone, our journey was made pleasant and very comfortable. In the first place, we had premium drivers and conductors — men who handled their reins and managed their teams with skill, who guard with true courage all that is consigned to their care, and who, although cut off from civilization, are capable of exhibiting the most delicate and solicitous attentions, the most profound respect for the presence of a lady.
>
> . . . We passed the entire First Regiment upon the road at different points. Major Hampton was encamped at the Muerto. The Major is in wretched health. Colonel Hardeman was at the Limpia Canon. The men were suffering terribly from the effects of heat; very many of them are a-foot, and scarcely able to walk from blistered feet. They were subsisting on bread and water, both officers and men; many of them sick; many ragged; and all hungry; but we did not see a gloomy face — not one! They were all cheerful, for their faces were turned homeward! How many pale, sick, hungry faces have we seen brighten as they repeat the glad sound! Citizens of San Antonio, will you not give them a warm and hearty welcome? Will you not open your bosom and feed and strengthen them? They will come to you, hungry and weary, needing your care . . .[42]

In that same issue of the *Herald,* the citizenry also heard from Colonel Reily, whom Sibley had released to push on ahead and make preparations for the brigade's return to San Antonio. Reily addressed a public appeal to Bexar and other nearby counties to prepare facilities for the returning units, to gather clothing and supplies, and insofar as possible send wagons and teams out the road to meet the returning warriors.[43]

So it was that, as the first of the brigade's companies limped along the rocky draws between Howard's Well and Beaver Lake, on the morning of July 3, they met a supply train of six wagons sent from San Antonio. The clean water, clothing, fresh food, and coffee, and such simple luxuries as tobacco, combs, and soap that the wagons yielded, brought a high point of pleasure and relief to the tattered men on their weary trek. Then, as they neared San Antonio, from D'Hanis on, families and friends came out to succor and greet the survivors. The units trudged in, from late July until the last of August.[44]

Of the 3,700 men whom Sibley took out of San Antonio in the summer and fall of 1861, with heady visions of extending the Confederacy to the Pacific, scarcely 2,000 ever reported back. Most of those who did survive in condition for active service were eventually moved into the long and fruitless campaigns at Galveston and in Louisiana and Arkansas. Tom Green, William Read Scurry, and James Reily died leading valiant charges against Union foes, and scores of their men died with them.

As for Indianola and the other towns on Matagorda Bay, the southern end of the Chihuahua Road, traffic was as disrupted and chaotic throughout the war as on the western reaches.[45]

Far out to the West, the old settlements at La Junta de los Rios were witness to the final work of Henry Skillman, who had made the whole sweep of the Trans-Pecos and New Mexico his theater of adventure for twenty years.

Born in New Jersey in 1814, Henry Skillman had spent his boyhood in Kentucky,[46] and by 1842 had been drawn into the Chihuahua trade through New Mexico. Therefore, as a wagon-master, he had been on hand in 1847 to be recruited for the Traders' Battalion.

In the aftermath of the war with Mexico, Skillman gravitated back to the Rio Grande Valley in New Mexico, where he was available when Lt. W. H. C. Whiting needed him in 1849 for the mission downriver to Presidio. So well and favorably known by them was Skillman that Billy Whiting's first reference to him in his journal was that "today I secured the services of the brave Captain Skillman as a guide and member of my party." [47]

Skillman's remarkable ride through Presidio and east, to rejoin Whiting on the Pecos, took him to San Antonio for the first time. In the late summer, he made another forced ride, this time from San Antonio to El Paso, arriving in mid-September to expose the manipulations of the notorious Parker H. French.[48]

Skillman spent the decade of the 1850s as one of the most notable of Texas pioneer stagecoachmen, first with his own line from San Antonio all the way to Santa Fe, then for a time as driver for Giddings's San Antonio-El Paso Overland Mail, and finally as the West Texas driver for the Butterfield line. Later he was agent for that line in El Paso. There was even a station named for him on the Butterfield route, twenty-five miles below Pope's Crossing of the Pecos in Loving County.[49] Then the Civil War brought its chaos and ruin into the Southwest. During the period of Baylor's and Sibley's adventure in New Mexico, Skillman seems to have served as driver or escort to the "Confederate States Mail," serving Mesilla, El Paso, and San Antonio, organized by George Giddings as a gap-stop following the demise of his Overland Mail.[50]

When General Sibley withdrew his brigade, the line of forts closed as he retreated. Soon afterward all semblance of mail and stage operations shut down, partly because there was no protection from the Indians and even more convincingly because while Texas was Confederate, New Mexico — with El Paso tacked on — and all points west were Union, and there was no legal basis for communication.

When Col. William Steele pulled the last Confederate troops out of Fort Bliss in July 1862, the post stood vacant and desolate.[51] Finally, Gen. James H. Carleton, commanding the California Column, gingerly moved some Union elements under Col. E. E. Eyre down the river valley to take over Fort Bliss on August 20, 1862.[52] At that time, all the remaining Confederate sympathizers in Franklin-Coons-Magoffinsville, with Skillman among them, had to cross the river into old El Paso del Norte.

In that little colony of expatriate Southerners, the duty fell on Henry Skillman and a small band of his friends to keep open some degree of communication and courier service with Confederate headquarters in San Antonio. With Fort Davis and the other frontier forts standing open to the wind and prowling Indians, Skillman found his best route, horseback, to be down the Mexican side of the Rio Grande to Presidio, and then along the Chihuahua Road to San Antonio.

General Carleton established Maj. William McMullen of the First California Infantry downriver at the old Spanish fort in San Elizario, as a buffer to the south. McMullen, a real worrier and in a constant dither of anxiety about the possibility of Rebel incursions from farther down the river, kept plying General Carleton, far to the west in New Mexico, with those apprehensions. He was especially upset by a rumor, gleefully planted by Henry Skillman, that John R. Baylor was raising an army of 6,000 men to reinvade New Mexico. Thus matters drifted along for a year and a half in this remote little theater of minor operations, while the Great War east of the Mississippi held the public's attention in dread preoccupation.[53]

Finally, in the spring of 1864, Carleton decided that Henry Skillman, serving the Paso del Norte colony of rebels as their courier, had roamed the Trans-Pecos with impunity long enough. He chose Capt. Albert H. French, First Cavalry, California Volunteers, to scout out Skillman's pattern of activity in the Big Bend country and, if possible, to put an end to his work.[54]

French left San Elizario on April 3, 1864, with twenty-five enlisted men, a chief scout and interpreter, George Kohlhaus, and two guides, Miguel Garcia and Pedro Japie [Guipia]. His movements for the first eight or nine days are not of record, but the evidence indicates that he moved across from the Chinati country to intersect the Chihuahua Road somewhere in the neighborhood of San Esteban.[55]

French moved down the Alamito Creek section of the road and found sign that at least two bodies of horsemen had passed toward the river within the fortnight. He judged there were some eighteen to twenty horses and mules tracks, quite fresh; therefore, he made his marches with great caution, keeping spies out in advance, until on the afternoon of April 14 he reached what he called "Cottonwood Springs," fifteen miles from the river. That was, of course, Alamo Spring, later the site of the Hernandez *rancho*. There, on the bole of one of the great cottonwoods, he found an inscription indicating that Captain Skillman had reached that place the third of April.

Sending his "intelligence guides"[56] ahead once more, French moved slowly to within six miles of the river, unsaddled, and waited as dusk fell. After dark his scouts returned with news that they had located Skillman and his party in camp "at Spencer's Ranch, near the crossing." French crept on down to the river during the evening, found a deserted ranch house on the banks, and left his horses there with a guard, "one mile from the rebel camp."[57]

Stealthily, then, French and his twenty-seven men stole in upon the unsuspecting camp. Legend has it that, unaccountably, Skillman and his nine men had gone to sleep without posting a guard, leaving the coals of their campfire to guide the enemy upon them. French surrounded the camp at half an hour after midnight, April 15. Creeping closely with several of his men, he barked an order for surrender at the sleeping forms. With the reflex action of the frontiersman, but betrayed by his fatal incaution, Skillman grabbed his carbine and reared up in his blankets, bellowing his defiance, wild-eyed, the famous gray-streaked blond beard and locks all tousled. French fired point-blank; Captain Skillman fell back on his blankets dead. One, perhaps two others tried to resist, and the surrounding party opened fire, killing one more Confederate outright and mortally wounding two others. Four were taken prisoners without harm; two men, of whom one was wounded, escaped in the confusion and dark and got across the river.[58]

Nine of Skillman's horses and mules stampeded during the firing and confusion into the nearby hills, but French recovered five horses, four mules, all of the arms, provisions, forage, and camp equipage. Best prize of all, he retrieved the packet of mail which Skillman was bringing to the Paso del Norte colony. Unable to remove the fatally wounded men, French reported they "were properly cared for," which one would hope meant that the people at Spencer's Ranch tended them until they died. French alleged that he found Captain Skillman had been collecting customs on salt and other items at Spencer's Ranch, which at that time was the only establishment at the crossing opposite from Presidio del Norte. Some of the captured Confederates told French that it had been Skillman's intention to leave for Eagle Springs, on the road between Fort Davis and Fort Quitman, to spy out the country around El Paso.

But Henry Skillman's work was done; French's exultant report makes no mention of whether he even buried the great trailsman and his slain comrade. Perhaps he did, in the new little cemetery where a village to become Presidio was beginning to grow up around Spencer's Ranch.[59] Or perhaps they left him where he fell, beside the Chihuahua Road he had served so well.[60]

Henry Skillman's name has been kept alive only at Bloys Camp-meeting Ground in the Davis Mountains. Established in 1890 by Dr. W. B. Bloys, a Presbyterian home missionary who had come to Fort Davis in the eighties, the annual August meetings have drawn cowboys, ranch folk, businessmen, and an interdenominational clergy together in spiritual regeneration for more than ninety years. And it is located in Skillman's Grove, a lovely glade of live oaks and cedar trees dotting the meadows of black grama grass in a valley among the Fort Davis foothills, sixteen miles west of Fort Davis.[61] A plaque erected at the entrance to the Bloys Campmeeting Ground, on State Highway 116, identifies the spot as Skillman's Grove, named for the great plainsman.

Years before French trailed him down at Spencer's Ranch, Henry Skillman had had to stand off an Indian ambush, alone, in this grove. When he had run off the last Apache, he looked about and found that the place was good. He decided it would be his own. The rush of pioneer expansion kept him adrift, but time after time as he posted through the glade, the wheels of his big coach crunching the yellow gravel, he would say to a passenger beside him on the box: "That's where I'm a-going to settle down, when this is all over." [62]

In the last years of the Civil War, a curious calm settled upon the frontier insofar as Indian depredations were concerned. There were, of course, separate incidents of outrages committed against isolated homesteads, often where the family had been left unprotected by able-bodied men, most of whom were drawn into the Confederate service; these were few, however, in relation to the terror of earlier and of later days. The passage of stagecoaches and wagon trains had also been entirely suspended.

Nevertheless, the state government — not the Confederate government — did undertake to keep an elaborate system of state militia in the field, operating as Minutemen units on rotating duty. This structure went through several mutations in the course of the four years. Virtually up to the collapse of the Confederacy, the state, though plagued by draft-dodging and desertions, was trying to keep the militia in the field. [63]

One major bloodletting which was tragically unnecessary did occur, involving a large body of Indians and brought about by some bumbling, well-meaning militiamen of the Middle District, Frontier Regiment. Few Texans today have heard of the Battle of Dove Creek, but it must be ranked along with the Council House Fight in San Antonio as among the needless tragedies that helped exacerbate natural tensions and extend the Indian wars in Texas through a full half-century — longer than in any other part of the nation.

The shambles at Dove Creek occurred in January 1865; to understand it at all, one must look back even forty years before the Civil War. About the time Moses and Stephen Fuller Austin were carving out an area on the coastal plains of Texas for their colonies — the second and third decades of the century — another in-migration, unheralded and unbeknownst to most European Americans, was occurring in northeast Texas.

Agrarian Indian tribes, including Delawares and a large body of Cherokees, had been pushed farther and farther southwest out of the Mississippi River basin by the fiercer nomadic tribes and by land-hungry whites. The Cherokees had been relentlessly dispossessed in the south and transported to Arkansas and "The Territory"; many of them filtered down across the Red River and into the primeval glades of northeast Texas.

From far to the north came by stages a curious people, the Kiwig-ipawa, which meant "he stands about" or "he moves about." [64] He did both, that cross-grained, introverted aborigine, who wanted only to be left alone and who knocked down his wigwam and moved on away rather than be assimilated. The white man had corrupted his name to "Kickapoo," and it has been hard for later generations, who have heard the name mainly in connection with lugubrious medicine-show reme-dies and cartoons, to take him seriously. Starting in distant Wisconsin, the Algonquin Kickapoo was so mauled and harried southward by the Indian Confederacy of the Illinois that by the time he reached the Red River he had, for simple survival, "studied war" and become a prickly, suspicious warrior. Some of the subtribes settled in northeast Texas be-side the remaining Caddoes; others turned west before they crossed the Red River and tried a stand in eastern Oklahoma, that part of the ter-ritory that had been set aside for in-migrating eastern agrarians.

As early as 1850 these unhappy migrants were on the move again; now the Seminoles, the dispossessed ones from Florida, were with them. Out on the western Texas frontier, along the banks of the Llano River, Indian Agent John Rollins in April 1850 encountered the char-ismatic Wildcat, known among his own people as Coacoochie, chief of the Seminoles. [65] Wildcat told Rollins that he was in the process of moving some of the Seminoles and Kickapoos across Texas to Mexico, because they had not been able to live peaceably with the Creeks in the territory. The agent told Wildcat he must take his people back north of the Red River, but Wildcat smoothly dissembled.

Rollins didn't know it then, but the subtle Wildcat was operat-ing an underground for runaway black slaves. Over a period of many months, and through a complicated series of maneuvers, he sparred with Seminole subagent Marcus Duvall in the territory; came near bringing down upon himself the wrath of the Texas Rangers and the United States Army; and negotiated in great aplomb with the Mexican government. Withal, he successfully executed his coup, without bloodshed, moving several hundred Kickapoos, Seminoles, and the black slaves of some of the wealthier Seminoles clear across western Texas and into Mexico at Piedras Niegras.

During this time the beauteous raven-haired journalist Jane Caz-neau, with her husband Gen. William L. Cazneau, was engaged in founding the town of Eagle Pass across the Rio Grande from Piedras Negras. She interviewed Chief Wildcat and was taken with his poli-cies. She wrote that a beautiful location about thirty miles above Eagle Pass was assigned to his people [by the Mexican government], after converting them one and all into full and entire citizens of the "golden republic" . . . The Seminoles' black slaves, of whom Wildcat himself owned several, were legally accommodated into the Mexican system which disavowed slavery but propagated a system of peonage that had little more to recommend it.

Jane Cazneau averred that the chief and his brother The Bear were made, respectively, the judge and the sheriff of their new municipality, and were promised commissions in the Mexican army as well. But, she said, the chief's "predilections were evidently with the Americans. He kept his hunting camp as near our settlement as possible, ranged in amity the passes that covered it, and in many ways was a willing and useful guard.[66]

Making due allowance for Mrs. Cazneau's bias as a salesperson for the Eagle Pass frontier, the facts remain that Wildcat and his protégés were peaceably settled across the river. There is no record that either the Seminoles or the Kickapoos engaged in any significant raids across the border before the end of the Civil War in the United States.

All this amity was dissolved in terror and hatred at Dove Creek. In the late fall of 1864, a second large band of Kickapoos under the leadership of Chiefs Nokouhat, Pecan, and Papequah moved from their Kaw River reservation in Kansas toward the storied haven in Mexico, acting upon invitation of the Mexican Kickapoo chieftain, Machemanet. They were being pressed, in Kansas, to take up arms for the Union side in the great conflict, and the Kickapoos wanted no part in the white man's internecine slaughter.

Some 700 of them, including a number of Potawotomies, started their emigrant march, with written permission from the Kansas reservation.[67] They encountered no problems in getting through Oklahoma, but realizing that Texas was an active part of the Confederacy and that Texans were a chancy lot at any time, they undertook to skirt the settlements and avoid any collision by keeping far out on the border after crossing the Red River.[68]

If only they had been able to get a little further, all might have been well, and rivers of postwar blood might have been spared. But one evening late in December, Capt. N. M. Gillintine of the frontier militia, on a scout out of Erath County with twenty-three men, found himself gazing at an enormous trail beaten out in a southwesterly direction. They followed the trail down to a campsite, which the men judged to be not over two days old. The size of the encampment, with hundreds of campfires and remains of ninety-two wigwams, was enough to stir the back hair of farm boys who had lived through Comanche raids. If there had been a real plainsman among them, though, he could have immediately seen, from the wigwams and other sign, that this was no Comanche or Kiowa war party.[69]

Gillintine hurried back to the settlements, spreading the alarm that 500 or more hostiles were moving down the frontier. His figure may even have been an underestimate, but hostility was furthest from the minds of the Kickapoos as they proceeded on their cautious way, grazing their herds on the scanty forage as they moved.

Capt. S. S. Totton of the Frontier Militia's District No. 2, which was commanded by Maj. James Erath, organized the pursuing expedition.[70] The attacking party has in later accounts been called "Texas Rangers," [71] and it is true that these wartime militiamen were sometimes in their day referred to as "rangers" or members of "ranging companies." But that term was used in the old generic sense by which the word has been used since the earliest New England colonial days. There was no Texas Ranger organization during the Civil War, and it would unjustly burden an organization that has had more than its share of vituperation to label it with blame for the Dove Creek fiasco.[72]

Totton sent word out to the militia units to gather at Meridian on December 19. The scattered companies finally made rendezvous on or about Christmas Day at Camp Salmon, organizing into a battalion of 325 men and officers. Totton learned at this point that the Confederate army wanted in on the show, had started Capt. Henry Fossett with a small party on the trail, and asked Totton's militia to meet him at Fort Chadbourne.

Totton chose to ignore that directive and struck cross-country to where Captain Gillintine had first cut the big trail, in order to be sure that he could find and follow it himself. Fossett cooled his heels for a few days at abandoned Fort Chadbourne while volunteer units drifting in from other army companies brought his force to over 160. Then he aimed at the reputed direction the migrating horde had taken, and actually struck their fresh trail in brush country known as the Big Shinnery, on about January 4. Fossett and his troops thought, from the signs, that there must be several thousand Indians altogether.[73]

On January 7, 1865, Fossett's scouts, who had been ranging far ahead, returned to report that the Indians had gone into camp on Dove Creek, at its confluence with Spring Creek, sixteen miles southwest of the present site of San Angelo.[74] By chance, on that very same day, the Kickapoo travelers had been engaged in some good-neighborly relations with the first real settlers in all the Concho River basin: R. F. Tankersley and family, who had homesteaded the year before at the head of the South Concho Springs. About New Year's Day, some of the trekking Kickapoos had made a friendly visit to the Tankersley Ranch and learned that several of the settlers' horses had strayed from the range. On January 7 a delegation of the migrating Indians went back to the ranch, driving the strayed horses they had encountered on the trail.[75] Such were the "hostiles" whom Totton and Fossett were pursuing so lustily.

The weather had been consistently bad and cold, alternating between rain and snow, throwing Totton's battalion far behind in following their portion of the days' old trail. But their scouts and Fossett's did get together on that day of January 7, agreeing on a rendezvous point overlooking the Kickapoo campsite.

After an all-night forced march, Totton brought his battalion up with Fossett, who was fuming to attack, early in the morning of January 8. The militiamen and their mounts were exhausted and hungry; Totton had left his pack train and all supplies except ammunition far behind.

The two commanders conferred alone for a few minutes, held no council of war with their staffs, distributed no orders, and made only the vaguest formation for a line of battle. They simply gave the command "Forward!" and started a headlong cavalry charge on tired mounts across three miles of open country.[76]

It is easy to imagine the astonishment and dismay of the Kickapoos as they saw this motley array of armed whites come charging down the wintry slopes upon them. From the whites' standpoint, it was the way old Texians had won battles against odds, all the way from San Jacinto and Plum Creek to Val Verde and Galveston. But the difference was that of a Sam Houston or a Ben McCulloch, as compared to these insecure militiamen and jaded soldiers, burdened with guarding a huge frontier in the waning days of a war that was already lost.

The battle was lost too. In short, the Texans plunged into those creekside thickets and came up against a force twice their number, with benefit of cover and actually better-armed than the poor lads who came down upon them. And the Texans were badly beaten.[77]

They fought bravely all day there in the creek bottoms and on the hillsides, but had to withdraw at dusk, leaving their dead and carrying such of their wounded as they could. They had left, also, a record of having shot in cold blood, apparently with Captain Fossett's tacit consent, an old man who came forward under a white flag to parley, as well as one child and a Kickapoo woman also under a white flag.

Their most agonizing ordeal came in the week following as, with many dismounted and carrying their wounded on improvised litters, they struggled through a snowstorm, virtually without food, to reach the nearest settlements. The Texans had lost twenty-two dead and twenty wounded on the day of the battle; several more died on the trail — making the Dove Creek tragedy the worst of the Texas frontier period in terms of Anglo-American combatant forces lost in one engagement against Indians.

Evidence found later at the campsite indicated that the Kickapoos had precipitately abandoned much of their gear, food, and utensils as they fled. They evidently made a long arc westward, out beyond the settlements, then south, until they showed up at Piedras Negras, more than 200 miles distant, just one month later. There they told F. G. Huntress on February 8, in an interview published in Austin February 22, that they had lost twelve killed and eight wounded in the fighting at Dove Creek. Texans' estimates had been as high as eighty Indians dead.[78]

The damage went much deeper than the number killed, however. The Kickapoo tribesmen had lost forever any remaining shreds of faith in Anglo-American integrity. Anglo-Americans had given them safe conduct to Mexico but had ignored the protective promise and attacked them in force without cause or warning, shooting their messengers of peace. It was as simple as that in the Kickapoo mind.

The story they brought to their hundreds of kinsmen in Nacimiento Canyon bore fruit within the year and for years to come in terrible retributory raids against homesteads, freight wagons, stagecoaches, or any other unwary travelers along the lower Rio Grande reaches of the Texas frontier. In that light, the Dove Creek Battle had a massive bearing on the postwar fortunes of the Chihuahua Road.

The fact that from late 1862 until early 1866 no wheeled vehicle moved between San Antonio and El Paso or Presidio has been mentioned. The nearest to a recorded exception to that general statement appears in this tantalizing excerpt of a letter from Capt. Charles Atkins to Lieutenant Collins at Austin:

The boys are all gone up the El Paso road, to meet a company of men

coming through from California. They encountered some Yankees
this side of Presidio and were badly used up, losing ten men killed,
wounded and missing. Three of them came in last night. I sent up
an ambulance for the wounded, and a wagon with provisions, for
they had nothing to eat but their horses.[79]

Who were the "men coming through from California"? Who were the
"Yankees this side of Presidio"? So little is known of what went on
west of Fort Clark during the latter part of the war that this letter must
stand almost without context to interpret it.

The great fratricidal war ground to a halt in the spring of 1865;
the dismantling of the Confederacy began at Appomattox in April
when Robert E. Lee handed his sword to Ulysses S. Grant. The last
land battle of the war was fought — and won — characteristically by
Col. Rip Ford, at Palmito Ranch near Brownsville on May 13. "Old
Rip" didn't know the war was over and lost, until one of his Yankee
prisoners told him.

Gen. Phil H. Sheridan, United States Army, commander of the
Military Division of the Southwest, took Gen. E. Kirby Smith's sur-
render of the Trans-Mississippi Department, Confederate States of
America, including the Department of Texas, at Galveston on June 2.
Later that month, General Sheridan assumed military command of the
division, with Gen. E. R. S. Canby, Sibley's old nemesis on the Ari-
zona frontier, now commanding the Department of Louisiana and
Texas within that division.[80]

Weary, sick, and wounded Confederate soldiers, sometimes leading the bony nags that would have to plow the weed-grown fields, filtered back to their farms throughout those spring and summer
months.

The Reconstruction government, cautiously generous under President Andrew Johnson, clamped its expectable strictures upon the activities of most of the shattered cities of the South. Remarkably, San
Antonio, site of so many bloody battles in the century before, had
heard not one military gun fired in anger during the Civil War. Many
families in the farming areas of South Texas had been ruined by the loss
of their slaves, their principal capital. San Antonio, at one with all the
Confederacy, had given a dreadful toll in casualties suffered on distant
fields among its men and youths.

Of all cities in the Confederacy, however, San Antonio was "the
most important town which had free and unblockaded access to the

trade marts of Mexico [through Piedras Negras and Matamoros] and through it to the outside world of supply." [81] This access to Mexico kept the stores better stocked than elsewhere, and hard money, from the cotton trade, was relatively plentiful. Therefore, one student of the era ventures the conclusion that "San Antonio came out of the war far richer than it entered it." [82]

[13]

Re-constructing
Under Reconstruction

As the states of the shattered Confederacy groped their way toward reestablishing a peacetime economy in the waning months of 1865 and early 1866, a curious anomoly existed along the Chihuahua Road. A fraction of the way up its path from the Gulf of Mexico to the capital city of Chihuahua lay San Antonio, the largest city in Texas, with ten to twelve thousand inhabitants. It was physically undamaged by war; its trading houses had prospered in the extralegal cotton traffic with Mexico; their entrepreneurs were itching to get the whole world of business moving again.

Down on the coast, though, Indianola's wharfs were burned; bridges were down; and the twenty-seven miles of the San Antonio and Mexican Gulf Railroad from Lavaca to Victoria lay in ruins from defensive destruction by Confederate forces. The United States Army, exhausted by war, was at first indifferent and desultory in rebuilding depot facilities in Lavaca and Indianola.

San Antonio's only surviving newspaper, the *Herald,* operating on a triweekly basis, reduced from its prewar daily, was maintaining a careful deference toward the occupying Reconstruction authorities. It reported on August 29, 1865:

Late and reliable information from Lavaca informs us that no vessels have arrived from New Orleans except on government account. The consequence of this is that all produce is very high. Flour ranges at from $14 to $16 in specie and $17 to $20 in currency. Mr. [James] Taylor, the collector, has arrived, and it is to be hoped the Port will soon be open for business, though it is anticipated some little time will elapse ere the business of the lower country can be fully restored.

To the west of San Antonio an even greater vacuum existed. One West Texas pioneer and student of the frontier, Alice Jack Shipman, wrote more than half a century ago that

after the first year of the Civil War, the Big Bend district passed into the hands of the Indians, and with the exception of small settlements at Presidio and Franklin [El Paso] it is doubtful if there were any Americans at all living within the boundaries of Texas west of the Pecos River . . . The Indians did little raiding . . . until the close of the Civil War, because there were no inhabitants left and travel was abandoned. [1]

The Indians, whose perennial raids across the Trans-Pecos down into Mexico had been considerably hampered by the U.S. Army's chain of forts in the 1850s, had four years of almost complete freedom during the war to resume their old plundering down across the Rio Grande. The Mescalero Apaches, from their strongholds in the Davis Mountains and other high fastnesses, and the Comanche Plains Indians, who swept down the great trail that bore their name, ravaged mercilessly throughout Chihuahua. After the Treaty of Guadalupe Hidalgo in 1848, which promised American protection from Indian incursions, many great *haciendas* had been able to rebuild tremendous herds of cattle and horses. Now, at the end of the Civil War, they were painfully depleted — in many cases completely wiped out. "A great demand for cattle arose in Mexico," Mrs. Shipman wrote, "and good prices were offered. These prices tempted the cattlemen in Central Texas to drive great herds over the Chihuahua Trail." [2]

A virtual shopping list of opportunity therefore presented itself to that restless breed of men who wanted to see wheels rolling westward once more, with trade goods to bring new life into the settlements and military supplies for the reestablishment of army posts. Silver beckoned to be hauled from Chihuahua's mines, ranches needed to be restocked in Mexico, stage lines had to be refurbished, and, finally, hordes of bankrupt, dispossessed, or disenchanted Civil War veterans needed wheels under them to move their families, their steel-shared Georgia plows, and their corn-husk beds to new land in the West.

The men of San Antonio and other towns along the road were sensitive to every one of these fruitful channels of activity. As quickly as the disrupted economy permitted, they moved to take advantage of the demands.

Some of the earlier activists had passed from the scene. Maj. George Thomas Howard, who had successfully intertwined his trading operations into his genuinely devoted military and public service from 1840 until the beginning of the Civil War in 1861, at last went under in that conflict. Major Howard had lost his longtime partner, Duncan C. Ogden, by death on March 11, 1859.[3] Despite increasing bad health, Howard volunteered for service in the Confederate army and was commissioned as brigade quartermaster of the subdistrict of the Rio Grande. Ill and overweight, operating painfully over South Texas and often into other parts of the Confederacy, he was successful in providing cattle for the Confederacy and negotiating cotton exchange contracts with Mexican sources.[4] Throughout the war, though, he was corresponding anxiously, bitterly, with his brothers and employees in San Antonio, trying to hold together his properties.[5] His biographer said, "Major Howard fought against the Union, and lost — his store, his cart contract, almost his home. In the long run, the Civil War cost him his life."[6]

Four months after the end of the war, the San Antonio newspaper carried the dreary note that an auction sale of furniture would be held at the home of Maj. George T. Howard.[7] By the following year, Tom Howard, who had taken part in every significant development in San Antonio since the revolution of 1836, was back in his hometown, Washington, D.C., negotiating with an alienated government. He died there in bed, August 6, 1866.[8] His widow, Mary McCormick Howard, for the remainder of a long life tried valiantly to piece out a living in San Antonio from the fragments of the major's shattered empire.

Though in the first postwar months no regular wagon trains ran to the coast, and none whatsoever toward the West, the earliest opportunity to put some of San Antonio's wagons back into service came in providing feed for the occupying army's horses and mules. In September, Col. C. G. Sawtelle, assistant quartermaster for the Department of the Gulf, was advertising for sealed proposals to carry various military goods and specifically forage for the forces in Austin, San Antonio, and elsewhere. A stinger was added in the specifications: "No bids will be entertained from persons who have belonged to the Confederate Army, unless accompanied by sufficient evidence that the bidders have taken the amnesty oath [as stipulated by] the President of the United States June 17, 1865." [9]

Apparently enough old Confederates swallowed their pride and met those terms, for by December the army released information that about 150,000 bushels of corn had been brought into the post at San Antonio since August, and the newspaper noted with relish that about 1,000 bushels daily were still moving into the city for that purpose. At least one familiar name, that of George Giddings, the famous prewar stagecoachman and freighter, was indicated in the editor's comment that "the principal contractors have been Messrs. Giddings, Lane Thornton, Knox, and Hancock & Reynolds." [10]

New faces were appearing on the South Texas business scene. One of the earliest stirrings of new enterprise was evinced when two express firms announced the same day, August 29, 1865, that they were open for business in the handling of goods and money for express shipment. Neither of these appeared to survive, for nothing more was heard from them. But these announcements were followed in less than a month by the appearance of Dan Murphy, the Fort Davis storekeeper who had made a fleeting effort to maintain a stage line from Fort Davis to Presidio and Chihuahua in the last days before the war. When the Confederates evacuated Fort Davis in 1862, he had come down the road with them to San Antonio. Murphy now announced that he had opened an "Express Train" between San Antonio and Indianola, that he would provide a semiweekly express of three wagons to run through in three and a half days between the two cities, and that in San Antonio he would "office at P. Garahy's old stand on the northwest corner of Main Plaza." This was not in the true sense a stage line; Murphy had no contract to carry United States mail. [11]

Mr. Murphy appears to have flourished, at least for a while, since the editor of the *Herald* mentioned him favorably from time to time for bringing exchange papers in from the outside world. On one occasion the editor expressed the sentiment that Dan Murphy was to be "thanked for bringing up from the coast delicacies of which our people have been deprived for so long: oranges, apples, and potatoes . . ." These were displayed at the store Murphy had established at "Garahy's old stand." [12] In so small a note one senses something of the austerity of life on the frontier in those earliest Reconstruction days.

This was the half-century when a town's destiny was measured by whether it did or did not, or would soon or would not, have a railroad serving it. The railroad was more than a status symbol, more than a mere convenience. Plenty of hard evidence was at hand to prove that the Iron Horse on rails could haul freight at a fraction of what it cost to haul it by ox-cart or mule-drawn wagon on muddy or sandy roads or across the waterless desert. For instance, the standing rate for movement of freight by wagon across Texas was about one cent a mile per hundred pounds, subject to violent variations upwards when conditions were unfavorable, but never appreciably less than that figure. It was common knowledge, however, that in mid-century America the railroads could move the same freight for less than half a cent per mile. Indeed, this prospect was more than vindicated after the first railroads were finally completed to San Antonio, when the International and Great Northern submitted a low bid of $1.25 per 100 pounds for shipment of government supplies from St. Louis to San Antonio — a distance of more than 800 miles.[13] This difference could and did build a new kind of economy. Though the old freight wagon was absolutely essential to opening up a new land, it was taken for granted, even as the traffic boomed, that the wagon was obsolete and transitory before the first whip cracked over the backs of mules straining to turn the six-foot wheels.

On Matagorda Bay, shortly before the war began, construction on a little rail line had been started from Indianola up the coast toward Lavaca and Victoria. Describing it more exactly, it would have joined the San Antonio and Mexican Gulf line from Lavaca to Victoria about six miles north of the port town at a point called Clarks — if that line itself had been completed. But S. G. Reed, the veteran railroad man who compiled A History of the Texas Railroads, garnered evidence to show that the San Antonio and Mexican Gulf had never actually run a locomotive along its right-of-way before the Civil War, and that the feeder line from Indianola had only the ties laid out along the right-of-way, with no iron on them.[14]

Now the cry became: when could this first section of the road be restored and completed, and how soon might western Texas dream of having the road extended?

Preoccupied as it was with Reconstruction, the United States Army recognized that its own interests would be served by providing rail facilities, if only to relieve some of the public pressure. Surely, then, there was a degree of cause and effect represented in two September developments. First, Gen. Phil Sheridan and his commandant of the newly recreated Department of Texas, Maj. Gen. H. G. Wright, with headquarters at Galveston, visited San Antonio about September 1, then angled back to Indianola "for the purpose of looking at the military situation there." [15] Second, the *Victoria Advocate* passed word back to San Antonio on the ninth: "work on the railroad between Victoria and the coast is proceeding finely [*sic*]. One and a half miles of track is laid." [16]

Indianola was already waking up from its wartime and early Reconstruction paralysis. Though due allowance should be made for hometown hyperbole, evidence of this awakening was shown in a long letter from an unidentified correspondent of that port city, appearing in the *San Antonio Tri-Weekly Herald* in October. It told of ships coming and going, of the sweet music of hammer and saw, mule-skinners' imprecations, and steamboat whistles. One important specific was added:

> a magnificent wharf is now being constructed at this place, second to none in the South. At its terminus in the Bay there will be twelve feet of water. It is supplied with a T-rail upon which horse cars are placed for the purpose of discharging freight very rapidly — also sufficiently wide for drays [carts] to operate with facility. [17]

The letter contained, also, a suggestion that all this new hustle and bustle would be accelerated by the completion of the railroad line by the army up to Lavaca and on to Victoria.

Another step forward in modern communication which western Texas businessmen anticipated gleefully was the completion of the "USM" telegraph line from Houston to San Antonio. The *Herald* reported regularly, beginning in August 1865, on its progress up toward Austin and thence through San Marcos and New Braunfels. In early September the editor indulged his optimism: "I suppose it will be three weeks or a month before it reaches San Antonio." [18]

For once, such a forecast was not far off the mark. On October 28, 1865, the lead position in the editorial column of the paper was occupied by this dispatch:

The Telegraph

Ed. Herald — The line is completed and we are happy to inform you that we are ready for business. C. H. Spellman

Immediately beneath, the editor enthusiastically greeted the advent, endorsing the management of the San Antonio terminal facilities under

Charles Spellman, who had opened the "electric telegraph" office in the Menger Hotel. Editor Logan called to his readers' attention the first two actual telegraphic news dispatches, relayed from Houston, appearing in another column, and promised regular instantaneous news coverage from all parts of the nation and abroad.[19]

Aside from satisfying the reading public's appetite for the latest word, the new service bolstered the business community in keeping it abreast of market and financial developments. Scarcely two weeks later, the week of November 15, the paper had found that the more adequate news sources and general business stimulation brought by the telegraph connection had made possible its return to daily publication, suspended since the beginning of the war.[20]

During those weeks of autumn 1865 a modest new publication, the *San Antonio Express,* appeared on the San Antonio scene, at first welcomed fraternally by J. D. Logan, the *Herald*'s editor.[21] The amity soon dissolved, however, and as with most rivals in nineteenth-century journalism, they were after each other, hammer and tongs.

From time to time citizens of Texas were reminded that the military occupation, which had its benevolent side in such operations as the reconstruction of Lavaca's railroad, was essentially still a police state. About the first of November, upon orders of General Sheridan, the army summarily arrested five or more well-known San Antonians who no doubt had considered themselves safely back into peacetime routine, and dispatched them to New Orleans.[22] Three of these men had figured prominently, back in 1861, in the Committee on Public Safety's deal with General Twiggs to break up the United States military establishment in Texas: Judge Thomas Jefferson Devine, Col. P. N. Luckett, and Maj. Sackfield Maclin. The first two were members of the three-man special committee; Maclin a secession-oriented officer who, while still holding his United States Army commission, had negotiated pliably with the committee under deputation from Twiggs, then renounced his commission and moved smoothly into the Confederate command.

Word filtered back to San Antonio during the next two months about the detention of these men at Fort Jackson near New Orleans. They were never brought to trial, though Judge Devine was twice indicted for treason. Speculation ran that they were all arrested because they had fled for a time to Mexico after the collapse of the Confederacy. Samuel A. Maverick, the third member of the committee, had stayed imperturbably at his duties in San Antonio, and so did not suffer these belated indignities. In January, though, the others were released, one at a time; when Judge Devine arrived in San Antonio he reported that only a Dr. Gwin was still being held.[23]

Gen. Phil Sheridan, who had ordered the arrest and detention of these citizens, with no specifications against them, was indeed preoccupied with what he considered his overriding concern: the "reconstruction" of the wayward states which lay under his authority. So overwhelming were the obligations in protecting the freedmen, both against their own inexperience and improvidence and against the hostility of some white elements, and in supervising the erection of a new civil structure, that Sheridan and his staff largely ignored the increasing clamor for pacifying the frontier.[24]

As early as September 1865, a gesture had been made toward frontier protection by assigning Lt. Col. Wesley Merritt to provide a show of strength in western Texas. Merritt had been breveted up to major general in the heat of the war, but was now commanding Ninth Cavalry forces in the Texas District at his permanent rank. J. D. Logan interviewed Merritt and reported that "the general has authorized me to say to our citizens on the Indian border that it is the design of the Government to give them perfect protection and that it will be done." But, Merritt cautioned, the forts would not be reopened. Instead, the ex-major general described how he would send "heavy detachments to scour the whole frontier country" and thereby keep the land clear of Indian depredations.[25] Of all tactics used to cope with the Indian problem, that method proved to be the most useless.

Three days after the army's promulgation of policy, a letter reached San Antonio from J. M. McCormick in the Uvalde area: three parties of Indians had swept into the community within plain view of the walls of abandoned Fort Inge. Little Henry Robinson, out gathering wood near his home, was killed by a rifle ball through his heart. "We need protection from these savages," Logan editorialized. "Many of the border settlers have left their homes and moved to other settlements for safety."[26]

No further protection was given than whatever fruitless sweeps Colonel Merritt may have mounted. Official records of the United States Army show no actual army combat encounters with Indians in the eighteen months between the Civil War and Christmas Eve, 1866.[27]

More than enough encounters occurred between the Indians and

the hapless citizens, however. A typical instance was on January 27
and 28, 1866, when a party of eight savages ranged through Medina
County, just west of San Antonio. They struck first up the Hondo
Creek, above Harper's Ranch, where they butchered a young man
named George Miller. They showed up next at Quihi, on the Chihuahua Road thirty miles out of San Antonio, stealing a herd of horses
from the Saathoff homestead. Their final appearance, verging toward
San Antonio, was at Castroville; after a feint, they were run off and dispersed.

The *Herald* morosely concluded "there is no utility or safety in the
present mode of defending the frontier. A thorough and radical change
is demanded." [28]

One compilation shows twenty-four settlers killed by Indians in
1865 within the area eighty miles from San Antonio west and north,
representing about fourteen separate incidents. In 1866 fourteen died
in the same area, in thirteen different attacks; and in 1867 eighteen in
that area plus nine Mexican drovers in one attack outside Eagle Pass.
The contemporary compiler insisted that this was only a partial tally,
that many more were killed who were never reported. [29] By 1868 a
Uvalde County jury had gathered evidence that Indians, mainly Kickapoo, had killed at least sixty-two persons in that one county in the last
three years, besides many others wounded. [30]

The same situation prevailed all the way north and east along the
frontier in a great arc through the Concho River country and beyond as
far as Denton in extreme North Texas. At Denton, citizens from there
and from surrounding counties in a mass meeting sent word to the
governor that unless help arrived they would abandon their homes. In
April of 1866 a Waco newspaper asserted that upwards of four-fifths of
the outlying homesteads stood deserted. [31]

These attacks along the northern and northwestern border came
principally from Comanches and Kiowas, but the settlements to the
southwest of San Antonio faced a new enemy. The story that the migrating Kickapoos had brought down to their brethren in Mexico
about their treatment at Dove Creek had united them all in an unremitting guerilla war against the settlements in the Uvalde country and
down onto the *Llanos Mesteñas* or Mustang Plains of South Texas. The
plunder from their warfare was profitable, for the merchants and poli-
ticos of Santa Rosa and other towns within the Mexican border provided a ready market. [32]

But as outraged reports piled up on Governor J. W. Throckmorton's desk, forcing him to implore the military to provide substantive protection, Gen. Phil Sheridan earned the lasting hostility of border Texans by his single-minded approach to Reconstruction. He was convinced that the governor and his petitioners were deliberately overrating the frontier situation. He wrote Gen. Ulysses S. Grant, the army chief, late in 1866 that "the mainspring of the whole movement is to get the United States troops from the Interior of the State . . . It is strange that over a white man killed by Indians on an extensive frontier the greatest excitement will take place, but over the killing of many freedmen in the settlements nothing is done." [33]

Because of this total lack of protection during all of 1865 and well into 1866, no wagon trains or stagecoaches moved out of San Antonio westward toward El Paso or Chihuahua. Possibly there was one exception. Records in Presidio County indicate that George Crosson, who had first come to the Big Bend at the beginning of the Civil War, did take a train west from San Antonio to Chihuahua for James Walker sometime in 1865. Tradition says that he commanded twenty wagons with twelve to sixteen mules to the wagon. On the return trip he brought back mainly bullion. [34]

Service to Eagle Pass, which lay southwestward down the river, and on to Monterrey, got under way first. The service was initiated in January 1866 by young August Santleben, who had just been mustered out of the United States Army on October 28, 1865, in San Antonio.

Santleben had carried the weekly mail on horseback, from Castroville to Bandera and back, for his father, who had the contract. That was in 1859 and 1860, when Santleben was fourteen, giving him some basis for claiming to have been the youngest mail carrier in the United States. He continued that service for a year and ten months, making about a hundred round trips of sixty-four miles each. His father's contract was canceled in 1861 as the war broke out. As the elder Santleben engaged in freighting cotton in that new and profitable wartime enterprise with Mexico, young August drove an ox-cart for him for a year, from Columbus in southeast Texas through Helena to Eagle Pass. [35]

This snail-paced mode of transportation hardly suited an adventurous seventeen-year-old on the turbulent wartime frontier. August left his father in September 1862, crossed the Rio Grande, and lived by a variety of enterprises there for more than a year. During this time, as an occasional driver for private parties, he learned the roads to Monterrey, Saltillo, and San Luis Potosi, as well as the river routes inside

Mexico all the way to Matamoros, making acquaintance with many of
the colorful Anglo-Americans then doing business in the Mexican border cities.[36]

Among long-lasting friendships he formed at this time were those
with Thomas B. MacManus, later customs officer at Eagle Pass; the
Groos brothers, Fred, Carl, and Gustav, operating a freight business to
Eagle Pass and a cotton yard at Piedras Negras before they got into the
banking business in San Antonio; and Capt. Adolph Muenzenberger,
who later became Santleben's partner. All this background was invaluable to ambitious August Santleben, age twenty, when the war was
over and he could launch his own career in transportation.

After a brief visit in Castroville, Santleben put in his bid for a
post office contract to carry the mail from San Antonio to Eagle Pass.
He was politically right for the time, for he had just put in two years'
honorable combat service in the Union army. He was probably the only
prospective bidder with that qualification who also knew anything
about the Eagle Pass country. And he certainly was qualified as a
driver. He got the contract on January 1, 1866.[37]

A rare contemporary photograph from the *San Antonio Light*
collection shows the young German on his high-wheeled ambulance, ready to start his Eagle Pass round trip in early 1866.[38] The
rig, its hooped canvas top covering three seats for six passengers, is
drawn by six mules — four abreast in the lead, two more abreast at
the wheel, though Santleben later related that he ordinarily used
only two mules to draw this particular outfit.[39] The picture shows
that a crowd had gathered around the conveyance in front of Kapp
and Muenzenberger's at the corner of Laredo and West Commerce
streets.

Here the twenty-one-year-old Santleben launched his Eagle Pass
and Monterrey adventure. With round hat cocked back on his curly
locks, perhaps a short corncob pipe stuck between his teeth, and sen-
sible boots planted firmly on the dashboard of his very own ambulance,
he anticipated a chancy road ahead of him and a fortune to be made. In
August 1867, Santleben took Capt. Adolph Muenzenberger as partner
and extended his operations into Mexico, establishing the first stage
lines into Monterrey from the Texas border. His perils, escapades, and
successes of the next two years took place far to the southwest of the
Chihuahua Road. Santleben came back, however, brash and full-
fleshed, into the history of the Chihuahua Road before the decade was
over.

It is important to look at how this man's story came to be preserved as the only detailed primary-source account of life along the trails to Chihuahua. August Santleben lived a full seventy years, and during the last half of these he was a settled, respected man of affairs and city official in San Antonio. Fortunately for posterity, sometime before 1910 he and Isaac Dunbar Affleck got together to publish the old freighter's memoirs.

Affleck's father Thomas was a Scottish beekeeper and entomologist from Dumfries. He had emigrated with his wife to Washington, Mississippi, where their son was born in 1844. They traveled on to Texas in 1858 to establish Glenblyth Plantation near Brenham, Isaac's home for the rest of his life. Starting at the age of seventeen, the young Affleck served with gentlemanly aplomb — a manservant to attend him — in Company D of Terry's Texas Rangers during the Civil War. He did not marry until he was thirty-two; Mary Foster Hunt of Kentucky was already well known as a nature poet when she married Affleck. Himself a student of politics, science, and Texas history, Affleck's contributions appeared frequently in the Texas press. He too became an entomologist, specializing in study of the Texas agricultural ant — the familiar "cut-ant." His findings are recognized and cited in H. M. McCook's *The Natural History of the Agricultural Ant of Texas.*[40]

It is a broad jump from the life of the ant to the life of the hardy wagon freighter, and just how Affleck and Santleben got together is not known. By coincidence they were almost exactly the same age, Affleck being but four months the elder. August Santleben had no formal schooling, and there is nothing in his career to suggest that he developed any skill at writing. To cite I. D. Affleck as "editor," as the volume they produced does, must be a considerable understatement.

The book checks out remarkably against all other sources that can be correlated. No basis exists for seriously challenging any essential facts in his narratives or geographical descriptions. To be sure, Affleck's Scottish ear for Spanish as pronounced by a German was not always acute; for instance, he rendered as "Leon Seto" the Leoncita Spring southwest of Ft. Stockton, thereby making the name incomprehensible, since *leoncita* means little lion.[41] And it surely must have been Affleck's own unfamiliarity with the Trans-Pecos that led the book to say the Fort Lancaster crossing of the Pecos was "a few miles above the present site of the wonderful steel bridge on the Sunset Railway that spans the river a height of three hundred twenty-one feet above . . ."[42]

Such cavils are misleading; the book the two men produced under the uninformative title of *A Texas Pioneer* is a marvelous record of life in one of the least-known aspects of the frontier, unique in its authoritative detail and wealth of incident. It covers his experiences on the Texas frontier from the time his father handed him over the rail of a sinking ship in Galveston Bay, as a five-month-old infant, to the time forty years later when the linking of the rails at Shumla, near Roy Bean's Langtry, put to an end forever the era of wagon freighting. Had Affleck and Santleben not collaborated, any future generation's concept of what it was like out there on the Chihuahua Road would be a bare-bones skeleton indeed.[43]

After Santleben's first run down to Eagle Pass was under way, the *Herald* told excitedly of an attempt to establish traffic once more on the big roads west:

Transportation for El Paso

. . . that old transportation man, Major Bethel Coopwood, proposes to be the pioneer in opening the far-famed El Paso and Chihuahua route. Here is a chance for any enterprising merchant who has got the goods . . . The Major offers to transport them in a mule train, with fine wagons, on ten days notice . . .[44]

Bethel Coopwood did not get traffic moving in the form offered above, but he did eventually, during that yeasty year of 1866, get a stage and mail service of sorts moving between San Antonio and El Paso. Although he did not last very long in that effort, he had the imagination and brashness to encourage others to follow.[45]

The "old transportation man" was not yet thirty-nine when the San Antonio paper took notice of his proposal, but he had been around. At nineteen he went to Texas to get in the Mexican War and fought in a cavalry regiment in Mexico. In 1854 he was admitted to the bar in California. Settling later in the Rio Grande Valley of Texas, he established himself as a lawyer while at the same time improving his knowledge of the Spanish-Mexican culture along the border. He married Josephine Woodward in 1859; they became the parents of fourteen children. He was, nevertheless, able to detach himself from these home ties long enough to fight for three years in the army as a captain of cavalry, starting with service in Sibley's New Mexico campaign. Toward the end of the war he "spent a year in Coahuila."

As soon as ex-Confederate officers could be sure of getting amnesty, he was back in the San Antonio area negotiating for the purchase of the surviving camels at Camp Verde. During the same period, while he was trying to get the El Paso mail running again, he was also busy promoting the camels for various desert enterprises in Mexico and the Far West. When no one seemed interested in the big beasts for serious work, Coopwood sold most of them in small parcels to circuses, experimenters, and sentimentalists.[46]

When he finally got out of the stage-line business, Bethel Coopwood settled back into his law practice and his study of the Spanish era along the border. Against his early career as something of an adventurer, it is illuminating to find that thirty years after the Civil War, when a few earnest academic types founded the Texas State Historical Association, Judge Bethel Coopwood became one of its most enthusiastic fellows. During the early years of the association's *Southwestern Historical Quarterly*, he contributed scholarly treatises on the founding of Mission de la Bahía[47] and on the route of Cabeza de Vaca through Texas; [48] even up to the year of his death in 1907 he was writing book reviews for the *Quarterly*. He had earned a place as one of the *aficionados* of the Chihuahua Road, from La Bahía on the south through La Junta de los Rios in the west.

In those hardier days of 1866, shortly before Bethel Coopwood finally got his mail contract,[49] a very substantial mule-drawn freight train in two parts did get under way on the road from San Antonio to El Paso. All the fears of Indian attack and hardship were vindicated in their experience.[50]

The owners were newcomers to the commercial transportation scene, John and James Edgar, but frontiersmen and veterans of both the Mexican War and the Civil War. Each brother organized a train of twenty wagons and two hundred mules. The forty wagons were loaded with merchandise and supplies consigned to El Paso — a realization of the venture Major Coopwood had yearned to initiate two months earlier.

Available records yield no date on the Edgars' departure from San Antonio, but it must have been about or just before the first of April. The two outfits did not try to travel together because they knew there would not be enough forage and water at many points for 400 animals. John Edgar was several days ahead of his brother's train when he reached Limpia Canyon in the Davis Mountains. At that always-dangerous point, Wild Rose Pass, where the canyon walls close in on the road, the train was surrounded and brought under siege by Chief Espejo and a large band of his Mescalero Apaches.

The Indians were not in sufficient force to overwhelm the wagon train, so Espejo tried to bargain. Fortunately, John Edgar knew the ways of the Apache when they tried to parley, and he refused to listen. The Indians faded away into the canyon; Edgar, fearing that the band might well ambush him further up Limpia Creek, seized the opportunity to turn his train around and make the best speed possible back toward the Pecos.

A courier from his brother's train met them on the road with tidings of disaster. Pulling up onto the plains from the Pecos toward Escondido or Tunas Springs on April 22, they had been enveloped by a terrific rainstorm which turned into sleet and snow as a blue norther howled down upon them. Weather like this was entirely unexpected in the last week of April. James Edgar's remuda of 200 mules huddled together that night for protection; by morning near a hundred of them were frozen or smothered to death.[51]

The remaining hundred could not move all twenty wagons in the heavy mud, but James had been able to get some of them into the empty walls at Fort Stockton, sending ahead the courier who had met his brother. John, with his train, pulled on into Stockton. They regrouped, recruited their animals for several days, and got under way once more. This time they negotiated Wild Rose Pass successfully, at last reaching El Paso but with a much-depleted train of wagons and freight.[52]

Meanwhile, there were developments at the coastal end of the road. W. T. Mitchell, named as superintendent for the San Antonio and Mexican Gulf Railroad, announced as of April 1, 1866, that "the road, having been recently turned over to the company by the United States military authorities, is now being put in condition for the prompt and speedy transportation of freight and passengers between Victoria and Lavaca . . . Trains for the present will be run regularly four times per week."[53]

The railroad system was beginning to make its contribution to the movement of goods, mail, and people into the vast interior of the Southwest, and even this first small link was a noticeable stimulus. Opening up transportation from the coast did not solve the problems on the far frontier, of course. The early experiences of the Edgar brothers with their first trains, and those of the Coopwood mail line, served only to highlight the travail of the settlers themselves. So great was the outcry in the face of the Federal army's stubborn indifference that the Texas legislature, even though dominated numerically by Reconstructionists, passed a bill to provide for 1,000 state militiamen to be stationed on the frontier. This and some prodding from President Andrew Johnson finally stung General Sheridan into action.[54]

"Little Phil" could not abide the prospect of state troops commanded by ex-Confederate officers operating in a conquered territory where he held supreme jurisdiction, so he simply vetoed the act of the legislature. But he did counter that action by sending an inspection team into the troubled areas to determine whether there was any validity in the exasperating clamor.[55]

The result of the inspectors' finding was such that even Sheridan, the hard-lining Reconstructionist, was finally pushed to reopen some of the forts east of the Pecos. In December 1866 the Fourth Cavalry rode in and reoccupied Fort Mason near the Llano River in Kimble County, Camp Verde under the crest of Bandera Pass, Fort Inge on the Leona in Uvalde County, and Fort Clark at Las Moras Springs; and early in January the Sixth Cavalry settled in at Jacksboro, thus establishing a line once more from North Texas across the Texas Colorado River nearly to the Rio Grande along the border line of farm and ranch settlement.[56]

All of this looked impressive on paper and in official conciliatory statements, but the war-weary officers who filled the command billets were less than enthusiastic about actually tangling with Indians, while the whole Trans-Pecos country was ignored.

These reluctant steps by the military in the early months of 1867, toward meeting the problems of the frontier, took place against a background of almost anarchic conditions in the state government. The administration of Governor J. W. Throckmorton, with a legislature too heavily leavened by ex-Confederates to meet the hardening standards of the Federal government, fell into special disfavor for failing to ratify the thirteenth and fourteenth amendments. Finally, through the Congressional Reconstruction Act of March 2, 1867, Texas again lost its statehood and reverted to the role of a "conquered province" under military rule. Throckmorton remained for a while as provisional governor but was unsatisfactory to General Sheridan, who summarily removed him on July 30, 1867, as "an impediment to Reconstruction," installing former governor Elisha M. Pease in his place.[57]

Meanwhile, a new venture, evoking memories of the remarkable cattle drives to California in Gold Rush days, had appeared along the trail to Chihuahua. As mentioned earlier, the entire Civil War hiatus since 1862 had left the Rio Grande frontier wide open and unchallenged for Comanches and Apaches to raid at will into Mexico, more than decimating the herds of the great *haciendas* in the states of Coahuila and Chihuahua. Even before the end of the war, one effort to meet the obvious market for cattle was made. W. A. Peril later claimed that "in 1864 I went down into Mexico with a herd, passing near the head of the South Concho River, by way of Horsehead Crossing on the Pecos, to old Fort Stockton, on to Presidio Del Norte on the Rio Grande." Though the Comanche Trail had seen thousands of horses and cattle plodding up *out* of Mexico as Comanche plunder, this may have been the first time that a herd of Texas Longhorns passed *down* through the Big Bend.

In 1868, though a hungry market still existed for rebuilding Mexican cattle herds, no other supplier in Texas had dared venture across the Trans-Pecos with a herd. Now, however, some Central Texas ranchers, glutted with cattle and with no way to reach United States markets, were determined to make a try for Mexico. Capt. D. M. Poer, son of Ira Poer of San Antonio, came down from the Concho country with more than a thousand head of Longhorns, through Castle Gap and the Horsehead Crossing of the Pecos to Fort Stockton. Ten miles west of the fort, after watering at the León hole, the herd lined out across the great basin between the Davis Mountains and the Glass Mountains, on the old Chihuahua Road.

Captain Poer's herd did not stop in the Big Bend; he took them right down Alamito Creek to Presidio del Norte, pushed them across the Rio Bravo after paying custom charges, and on into Chihuahua State. He brought them finally to the enormous *hacienda* at Aldama operated by Don Luis Terrazas, thirty-third governor of the state and the best-known in the long line of his famous family.[58]

In that same year of 1868, W. O. Burnam and a party of twenty-five neighboring cowmen left Burnet County on the Colorado for Chihuahua, herding more than a thousand head of cattle to trade for sheep. They spent two months on the trail and "never saw a white man."[59]

According to general statement by local observers in the Trans-Pecos area, additional thousands of cattle were driven down this road into Chihuahua in the late 1860s, but records are scarce to identify those who made the drives.

Through at least half of 1867 the Kiowa, Comanche, and Apache remained free to range without impediment west of the Pecos, as did the Kickapoo and Lipan on the lower reaches of the Rio Grande in Mexico. They all struck through the lackadaisical line of frontier installations whenever they chose. Governor Throckmorton's last summary, issued in August 1867, showed that in the twelve-month period just closed, the Indians had killed 162 Texans, wounded 24, and carried 43 into captivity. These figures did not include any from Wise and Young counties, which were among the worst ravaged.[60]

At long last, a year and a half after he had assured the San Antonio editor that the frontier forts would not be reopened, fresh-faced Lt. Col. Wesley E. Merritt, with four troops of the Ninth Cavalry, marched into desolated Fort Davis on Limpia Creek to reactivate it on July 1, 1867. The Ninth Cavalry was one of two mounted regiments which by that time were composed of black troopers under white officers. Merritt and his successors developed the Ninth into one of the better outfits on the frontier.

At Fort Davis the army eventually brought in about 200 civilian carpenters, masons, and laborers to help with constructing a permanent post, partly of stone, partly of adobe, such as the prewar commanding officers pleaded be built.[61]

Hard on the heels of the cavalry and the artisans came private-venture citizens to resettle the town of Fort Davis and the beautiful country around it. One of the very first was Dan (Pat) Murphy, to re-open his store. As already noted, Dan had been trying to operate an express line from his temporary base in San Antonio to Indianola. His wife, Sarah, a native of County Derry, Ireland, had died late in 1865 at the age of thirty-three, leaving her husband with "a numerous and interesting family of young children." [62] Dan Murphy prospered as a storekeeper in Fort Davis, and he married the widow Brady, his first wife's sister, who already had four daughters with the same first names as Dan's daughters. It is not surprising that their home was "the scene of lively social affairs for both Army and civilian folk." [63]

Fort Stockton was reactivated about the same time as Fort Davis, and Fort Quitman followed in 1868. The immediate effect of the three installations, manned this time with cavalry instead of the prewar infantry, was to make civilian traffic along the El Paso Road, and comcomitantly most of the Chihuahua Road, at least reasonably feasible once more. The presence of a solidly permanent post at Fort Davis, in the very gates of Limpia Canyon, at last pried Espejo and other Mescalero Apache groups from their stubborn lodgement in the Davis Mountains. In no sense, however, could it be said for at least another twelve to fourteen years that security from the Indian threat had come to the Trans-Pecos country.

The Scotsman Ed Hall, former customshouse officer in old Presidio del Norte and later husband of Juana Pedraza, had engaged in freighting all along the Chihuahua Road before the war, but he had long ago been wiped out by assassins' bullets.[64] His successor as title-holder at Fort Leaton, John Burgess, along with his longtime neighbor John Davis, took up the freighting business, perhaps just before Fort Davis was reopened in 1867. Wagons and cart trains began to venture through from Ciudad Chihuahua.[65]

All these stirrings of new business prompted the federal government about 1867 to send Sgt. Maj. Moses Kelley, a veteran of the Union army, down from El Paso as a deputy under W. W. Mills of that city, to open a customshouse for the United States at Spencer's Ranch, across from old Presidio del Norte. It is said that he made the trip down from El Paso by boat along with John Burgess, Young Bill Leaton, and Juan Ochoa.[66] No doubt Kelley took over the more informal function of toll collector performed by William Russell and during the war allegedly by Henry Skillman. Kelley became a popular and effective representative of the United States government in that remotest of outposts.[67]

Soon after Fort Davis and Fort Stockton reopened, John Burgess won a contract from the Department of Texas to haul materiel for those establishments. At the same time, the ranches along the river at Presidio were supplying corn and beef for the forts, and even grinding corn and selling it competitively there against the mills in San Antonio. Burgess is said to have had a routine of off-loading at the two forts the supplies that he had brought up from San Antonio, then proceeding to his headquarters at El Fortín, where he would refurbish the wagons and recruit his mules on the lush grazing along the river. Back in shape, he would load the train with the local produce, which in season of course included La Junta's famous melons and fruit, and haul it down the line to Forts Davis and Stockton on the way back in to San Antonio. That may sound like a pretty ordinary routine, but the round trip was 900 miles by wagon over some of the wildest and loneliest country in North America.[68]

San Antonio on October 9, 1867, had welcomed a courtesy visit from Bvt. Maj. Gen. J. J. Reynolds, the new commandant of the Fifth Military District who had succeeded Maj. Gen. Charles Griffin.[69] On November 5, to the great glee of *Express* editor James P. Newcomb, General Reynolds brusquely removed from office the entire slate of Bexar County and San Antonio municipal officers, replacing them with hand-picked, suitably Union-oriented appointees. The grounds for this police-state action were claims that the Rebel-dominated state legislature had set up election procedures that allowed hundreds of unqualified voters to pack the ballot boxes for unsuitable officers. Editor Newcomb's joy at this long-delayed victory over the elements which had run him out of town six years before was not lessened by the fact that Reynolds now installed him as one of the city aldermen.[70]

Traffic up from the Gulf Coast to San Antonio was encumbered not by Indians but rather by three other factors: the paralysis caused when epidemics of cholera and yellow fever swept the lowland cities; by some of the wettest weather the coastal plains had ever seen; and by bitter conflicts in Karnes and Goliad counties between die-hard Southern elements and the hard-lining radical Republicans.

With the rebuilding and modernizing of the large new wharf in late 1865, Indianola had experienced an early rebirth of trade. A new journal, *The Indianola Times,* appeared to chronicle the town's progress, and in June of 1866 it declared that the city was "thronged with wagons and Mexican carts, and immense quantities of lumber go up country . . . A wholesale merchant told us yesterday that . . . he was shipping more goods into the interior than at any previous time . . . We are all OK and next fall will be still more so." [71]

But the port cities along the gulf had a tragic year ahead of them. In late fall 1866 through the fall of 1867, yellow fever and cholera raged out of control in New Orleans and southern Louisiana, where the doughty explorer-scout-surveyor Richard A. Howard, as well as Maj. Gen. Charles Griffin and the young son of former Texas governor A. J. Hamilton, were among hundreds who succumbed.[72] The scourge spread to Houston, Lavaca, Indianola, and on to Corpus Christi. An indication of its impact was reflected in a note in the *Express:* "A private letter to Mr. William Chrysler from a gentleman in Lavaca says the yellow fever is becoming more malignant and nobody thinks of business. The writer speaks in the most desponding [*sic*] terms of affairs in that town."

A week later the *Express* had a more sanguine view: "The city of Indianola has entirely recovered from the illness. Yellow fever has left and the hospital is deserted." This optimism seemed premature. In mid-October long delays in mail delivery from the coast were attributed to the yellow fever epidemic, though that seemed to have been in the final stages, for there were no more references to the epidemic after that.

At the same time, nature mounted another blow against the movement of trade, in the form of the longest season of heavy rains that old-timers could remember, with accompanying coastal storms. The rainy weather, starting in August 1867, held up mail and freight delivery from the coast. Occasionally thereafter, through the fall and winter, the roads dried up enough to let freight traffic through, as in October when the San Antonio editor reported that "a large number of wagons freighted with goods arrived in the city yesterday and there was a general waking up of business." All winter, though, the bad weather prevailed, climaxing in a storm on Matagorda Bay which was an augury of the disasters that lay ahead. "We sympathize with our neighbors at Indianola in their terrible affliction," editorialized New-comb of the *Express*. "Eighty thousand dollars utterly swept out of ex-istence, in one of our western cities, is hard to spare."

In February the newspaper found it "a lamentable fact that a train from Indianola, a distance of one hundred fifty miles, has been out twenty-eight days. We have been unable to find out whether this delay is in the Mexican Gulf and San Antonio Railroad, or on the wagon road."

Traffic moved briskly at times in the spring and summer of 1868, but the heavy rains set in again in the fall, making the roads sodden and all but impassable. The demand for goods at almost any price sent freight rates skyrocketing for a time in January 1869 to $3 per hun-dredweight from Indianola to San Antonio.

The newspaper reported on January 26 that transportation to the coast had become "a dead lock [*sic*], no teams have arrived for weeks, which are on the road somewhere, if not under the ground. Merchants have daily looked for their goods, hoping against hope that they will [*sic*] be in time for the Christmas trade, and now it's nearly February, and they have not heard from the anxiously expected teams yet." Two days later these delays were specifically attributed to the heavy rains. And on February 19: "Dull. We mean by using the word dull that there is a stagnation in every department of trade . . . in this city of narrow sidewalks and streets." By March 13 the paper was crying that "it now costs our merchants $8 per barrel for flour for transportation from the Coast to this city. What are we to do? We will have to give up flour and go back . . . to munching corn bread."

The situation began to mend in a long-range trend around the first of April 1869. The oft-jaundiced eye of the *Express* editor cleared a bit to observe that businessmen were "taking courage again. Trains laden with spring goods come up from the coast every day and trade is looking up." Again, a few days later, he found that freight rates were beginning to ease off: "A good many carts left for the coast on contract of $1.50 per one hundred pounds. The highest price paid last week was $2.00 per one hundred pounds." In Indianola, nine vessels arrived to discharge cargo between April 30 and May 5, while five ships departed the harbor between May 1 and 6. Throughout May, trains had moved briskly in both directions; a similar rate of port traffic was maintained in June.[73]

The third element harassing freight movement between the Matagora Bay ports and the interior, from 1867 halfway through 1869, was lawless factional strife. This persisted in its most violent forms through Karnes, Goliad, and DeWitt counties, which lay athwart the main wagon roads.

The strong Radical element that gained control of Congress in 1866 had held that the new government in Texas and those in several other southern states were unconstitutional, having created themselves without the sanction of the Congress. It also claimed that the leaders of these governments were rebellious and did not guarantee protection of life and property.

The Congressional Reconstruction Act of March 2, 1867 — a particular affront to Texas since it was enacted on the anniversary of the original Texas Declaration of Independence — withdrew statehood from all the offending states and left Texas a "conquered province" governed by military rule. Along with his actions in ousting municipal and county officers, General Sheridan removed Governor Throckmorton from office July 30, 1867, appointing Elisha M. Pease as military governor in his place.[74]

These acts fanned passions among the extreme elements on both sides. Overt repression by Radicals, open defiance by die-hard Confederates, dark deeds under the cover of night, all became common features of community life throughout the state. So, when editor James P. Newcomb of the *San Antonio Express* is quoted in the following passages, simply because he was perhaps the most frequent commentator in the contemporary press of Southwest Texas, the reader must remember that Newcomb was himself among the most biased of Radical partisans, spurred not only by his genuine grievances of the past but the more by his own vaulting ambition for political power.

Rioting occurred in Helena, county seat of Karnes County, in early August of 1867, almost at once after the abrupt removal of Governor Throckmorton. Newcomb's analysis was that the trouble developed as "two Germans, Michael Eilerhoh and Peter Lorens were cruelly beaten . . . by the inhabitants because they had taken out their first naturalization papers, or in the parlance of the country wanted to 'make damned Yankees out of themselves.' "[75] One day later, using his favorite epithet "Hell-ena" in his headline, Newcomb declared that "the people of Karnes have attracted the attention of the whole country by resistance to the authority of government." He observed that residents of "Hell-ena" were apparently concerned about the slowness of immigration, but that that had "a strange appearance coming from a section of the country whose people made it too hot for a man such as William Leland of New York to live in; who drive away the agents of government; whip men for being 'damned Yankees'; and the perpetrators go unpunished." [76]

A story of troops stationed at Helena to quell disturbances related in a report by Newcomb in the *Express* on November 19, 1867:

> Major General [*sic*] Geo. W. Smith left this city on Saturday noon with a strong scout of men to look after Yorktown and Helena. The Major [*sic*] is the right man to look after these rebel districts and we hope he will be successful in capturing some of the peculiar inhabitants of that region in order that their conservative sentiments may have a fair investigation before a military commission. [77]

At any rate, with the arrival of the cavalry, according to the local historian, "the people lived a new life. The soldiers stayed eight months . . . New order was established, new officials were elected, and life in general went on peacefully." [78]

In far West Texas, the Indians were still an ever-present terror. Jarvis Hubbell, survivor of the midnight raid upon Henry Skillman's camp at Presidio in 1864, came to a hideous end early in 1869 in the wastelands between Van Horn's Well and Fort Davis. Judge Hubbell, having business in Fort Davis, limped down to the stage station at Overland Street in El Paso on an early January day to buy passage south. He found that for some reason the little stage wagon then assigned to the El Paso-Fort Concho run could carry only one passenger that day; perhaps urgent freight occupied the remaining passenger space. At any rate, a recently discharged soldier from the Thirty-sixth Infantry had bought the one seat. Hubbell pleaded that his business in Fort Davis was of a pressing nature, and the soldier "yielded his place . . . after the most earnest solicitation." [79]

The coach rolled out on time, about the fifth day of January, 1869, with driver James Basse on the box and Jarvis Hubbell inside as passenger. Two days later the soldier caught the next stage out. All went well until they reached a point about nine miles out the road from Van Horn's Well toward Eagle Spring. Far from the road they sighted the abandoned, wrecked hulk of the earlier stage wagon. Hurrying on, they were shocked to find a man's head, severed from the body, lying beside the road; a little further on, an arm; and the poor abused torso of the driver Basse.

Shaken by these dismembered findings, the two travelers halted the stage, encamped, and made coffee to regain their composure. The soldier realized that but for the judge's earnest solicitations he himself would have been in that ambush, and he felt impelled to try to find out what Hubbell's fate had been. He and the driver took two mules from their coach, mounted them, and rode back to the deserted stage. They found it stripped of its curtains, cushions, and baggage, riddled with bullets and bristling with arrows, and blood everywhere. At first there was no sign of Jarvis Hubbell, but as the men rode out a little way on the Indians' trail, they found a man's slipper. The soldier recognized it at once: when Hubbell had talked to him that day in El Paso, the judge was wearing that slipper to favor a sore and swollen foot.

Forced to conclude that the Indians had murdered Hubbell and carried his body away, the two men returned to their own stage and hurriedly resumed their journey. According to the soldier's story, related when he reached San Antonio some days later, they had gone down the road scarcely two miles when

> their ears were suddenly saluted by the most hideous yells and a party of twenty-five or thirty Indians made a charge upon them, but upon the soldier and the driver opening fire upon them they halted, endeavoring to draw [the travelers'] fire; about this time the eyes of our travelers were greeted with a most pleasant sight, for a scouting party of the Colored Cavalry came in sight, their attention having been drawn by the firing.[80]

No trace of Jarvis Hubbell's body was ever found. A canyon in the general area where the attack occurred came to be known as Basse Canyon, and was again the scene of tragedy more than a decade later.[81]

By mid-summer 1869, the hunger for new goods in opening up the fastnesses of the West had overridden Reconstruction's stagnation and the hazards of travel imposed by the Indians, with a flood of wagons moving from one end to the other of the Chihuahua and El Paso roads.

[14]

The Men,
the Teams, the Wagons

A wide diversification of people, vehicles, and animals carried the freight in the fading years of Reconstruction and the boom times that followed. The people came from every quarter.

Even El Paso, still just a village on the far border of civilization, was putting some outfits on the road: trains operated by Gabriel Valdez, brother-in-law of James Wiley Magoffin; Inocente Ochoa; and Isaac Lightner plodded the long, slow road to San Antonio or Chihuahua City. Other old El Paso hands known in the trade were Alexander Daguerre, William T. Smith, and Mariano Varela.[1]

John Monier of San Antonio, credited with being the first freighter to convert to the use of mules before the Civil War, was still very much in business up and down the length of the Chihuahua Road.[2] Born in Alsace-Lorraine in 1833, John Claude Monier had arrived in Texas with his parents as part of Castro's colonists about 1844. He got into freighting in the earliest days that the road was open, working at first out of Castroville, and was reputed to have been the first North European freighter to take mule-drawn wagons over the road to Chihuahua.[3]

Philip Monier, ten years younger, went to work as a freighter for his brother John at the age of sixteen, in 1859. With the big surge of postwar business, however, he formed his own line in 1870, carrying freight in all directions out of San Antonio, often as a government contractor, until put out of business by the railroads in 1883. He was one of those who used from ten to fourteen mules on his great wagons, driving them four abreast. Another much younger brother, Joseph, born in Castroville in 1855, joined his elders as a freighter after the war. Each died at about the age of eighty: John in 1912; Philip in 1921; and Joseph in 1940.[4] The family name is still prominent in the business life of San Antonio today.

Another of the best-known freight lines based in San Antonio was that of Edward Froboese, Sr. Born at Wanfried, Hesse-Nassau, Germany, on July 23, 1834, Froboese was educated at Rinstein College in preparation for medical studies at a university. A nasal affliction brought about deafness, and though he eventually received surgical treatment which partially restored his hearing, his academic career was frustrated. The disappointed lad joined the tide of German migration to Texas in 1852, landing at Galveston and moving inland to La Grange. There the scholar who had aspired to be a doctor began his new life in Texas working on a farm at eight dollars a month. By 1853 he was a cowboy, driving a herd of cattle from Meyersville, near Victoria, to San Antonio.

Family history says that in October 1854 Ed Froboese joined "Captain Henry's" Ranger company in San Antonio.[5] Because of Indian raids in the hill country, his company was ordered to Fort Martin Scott, an oft-deserted post two miles south of Fredericksburg on Barron's Creek.[6] They spent the winter on scouting expeditions. Apparently, it was following that tour of duty that Froboese, turned twenty, joined Captain Pope's party as a teamster.

Froboese next went into the service of the United States Quartermaster's Depot as a teamster, making regular trips from San Antonio to Indianola for army supplies. Later he took a job as teamster with a private freight train, probably that of Maj. George T. Howard, moving government supplies up the frontier to Fort Mason, Fort Chadbourne, and on beyond. His last work as a hired teamster was in 1859, hauling buffalo hides out of Wichita County, when it still had no permanent settler.

At the start of the Civil War, Ed Froboese conducted a wagon train to Monterrey, Mexico, for Charles Elmendorf, Sr. — his first experience in the land across the Rio Grande. With a few hundred dollars saved from that contract, he established his own freight line along the frontier in the cotton trade with Mexico. A year later, with Louis Scheihegen as partner, he started a wagon train running to Monterrey. During this period he often struck off on personally conducted freighting expeditions to distant points in Mexico. One of his most unusual assignments was to take $250,000 in gold through the rebel Mexican lines to meet the payroll of the Emperor Maximilian's troops.

A staunch Union adherent and Republican throughout his career, Froboese had no difficulty at the end of the war in returning to San Antonio to set up a business. He established a large livery stable on West Nueva Street, on the east bank of San Pedro Creek. For thirty years this served as his base of operations, first for his freighting lines and later for local drayage. His home during all this time was directly across Nueva Street from his stable.[7]

Ed Froboese was a solid citizen, knowledgeable in his handling of animals and vehicles, dependable in his relations with his fellow man, of whatever race or faith.[8]

Closely associated with Froboese in his freighting years was Mariano Frescas, his wagon-master, born in San Antonio in 1835. Mariano's granddaughter, Josephine Lanham, related that in the course of his frequent drives to Chihuahua he "met, courted, and soon married Zeferina Campa, in the year 1865 . . . bringing her to make her home with him in San Antonio, nearby to his place of employment . . . just around the corner on Laredo Street . . . present site of the Bexar County Jail."[9]

The granddaughter recalled that Ed Froboese also met, married, and brought to San Antonio a *señorita* from Ciudad Chihuahua: Eusebia Campa, who bore him several sons. After her death in 1883, Froboese married Maria Madrid, who had accompanied him and his bride to San Antonio from Chihuahua and served as governess to their sons. Josephine Lanham adds that

> Mr. Froboese's wagon-trains transported many families, including my mother's grandmother, Mama-grande, together with an aunt, and two uncles (of the Campa family) from Chihuahua to San Antonio, all settling in the same and nearby surroundings, living united, and whether related by blood or marriage, or not related at all, coming from Chihuahua they considered themselves related as "comadres compadres, primas and primos."[10]

The same intense pride felt by the descendants of Don Mariano Frescas concerning the part he played as a freighter on the Chihuahua Road is reflected in the inscription on a large granite monument standing today in San Antonio's San Fernando Cemetery No. 2. It is at the grave of Ramón Hernandez, born in Chihuahua in 1829, died in San Antonio, March 3, 1908. In bas-relief across the face of the gray granite, a train of wagons, each drawn by ten mules, comes out of the mountains along a trail bordered by cactus and lechuguilla. The text beside the picture says "In memory of Ramón Hernandez, Sr., first trail blazer and transportation wagon freighter in the Southwest." [11]

Unfortunately, there are very few references on the public record concerning the freighting activities of this esteemed man, who settled in San Antonio about 1868. [12] While the tombstone legend spoke of his early trailblazing, which would imply he started freighting before the Civil War, the *Express* as late as July 1875 noted that "the train of Ramon Hernandez consisting of eight large wagons drawn by ten mules to each wagon, arrived in the city this morning from Cuero . . ." [13] Therefore, he may have been active in the business for twenty years or more.

Ramón Hernandez lived well into the twentieth century. How he occupied himself in his later years is not known, but he had earned a secure place in the community. Upon his death, his funeral services were conducted at the cathedral and "the procession was long and comprised the oldest and many of the most prominent citizens of San Antonio [with representatives of] . . . the Ladies Catholic Society, the Amigos del Pueblo, and the San Fernando Society." [14] But not a word was said in his obituaries about his work as a freighter. So quickly had the city forgotten a commerce that had figured so largely in its building.

The recollection, however, was strong and compelling within the Hernandez family. A quarter-century after the funeral, in the mid-thirties, one of the sons journeyed all the way back from Alaska, where he was a prosperous businessman, to fulfill a mission. He looked up Luis Rodriguez, who headed a local monument works and whose sculpture adorns many of the public buildings of San Antonio. Rodriguez related Hernandez's instructions: "I want you to make a beautiful monument to my father. Its principal feature is to be a Chihuahua wagon train, with this inscription [he dictated the legend the stone now bears] . . . I don't want the work which my father did ever to be forgotten." Luis Rodriguez carved the picture himself. [15]

Then there was Anastacio Gonzales, who was a blacksmith by trade, but being ambitious had progressed from repairing freight wagons to owning them himself and engaging in the Chihuahua trade.

Young Gonzales had a small but comfortable home at the corner of Salinas and Laredo streets, an area now occupied by a church. When he became affianced to a girl in the neighborhood, he started construction on a substantial stone house on a lot adjoining his small home, intending this as a more suitable place for his beloved. But a dreadful fate awaited him at Howard's Well.[16]

The freighting firm of Adams & Wickes was one of the few operating along the Chihuahua Road which bore Anglo-Saxon names. It flourished from 1869 until the middle of the seventies as the largest contractor with the United States government for hauling supplies from the gulf and to the distant line of forts on the frontier. During that relatively brief period, the two protagonists of the line managed to get themselves into some dubious deals that reached near scandalous proportions. But they played the wagon-freight business for what it was worth and got out before the decline began, moving on to greater riches in the real estate business.[17]

Harden B. Adams, the first of the partners on the Texas scene, was a native of Plainfield, New Jersey. He had left school at the age of seventeen and taken passage by ship to Texas, no doubt intending to make his way to the California gold fields. At Lavaca where he landed, however, he met John James, the loyal San Antonian and indefatigable land developer, who took him to the Alamo City. The 1850 census showed Adams a resident of San Antonio, listed as a clerk at the age of nineteen. He was apparently padding his age a bit to enhance his employability. During the decade of the 1850s he was in Mexico for a while but was back in San Antonio before the outbreak of the Civil War. He joined the Confederate army in 1861. At war's end he had won a major's maple-leaf for service in the Quartermaster General's Department.

Broke when he mustered out of the service, Adams headed back to San Antonio, where on April 17, 1866, he married Flora Kate Jones. He went to work in the brokerage business with James H. French, the railroad promoter, and James Minter. Less than a year later, by March 14, 1867, the relationship between Adams and J. H. French was reversed: Adams was an agent for the government, purchasing horses at Sappington stable from James H. French.

Then the door of opportunity swung wide for the thirty-four-year-old Adams: Edwin de Lacy Wickes hit town, and he was loaded. Five years older than Adams, Wickes had made a fortune in Chicago real estate during the early boom of that city. Why he should choose to cast his lot with San Antonio at that precarious time in its history is not on record. Whatever the reason, his judgment from a material standpoint was good, because he continued to prosper, and Harden Adams prospered with him.

They established the firm of Adams and Wickes, early in the year 1868, with the primary purpose of securing government hauling contracts; and the indications are that the huge amounts of freight they transported over Texas roads in the next decade were almost exclusively army goods. The press took notice of their activities with such observations as "[y]esterday, Adams & Wickes train of 20 wagons pass through the city loaded with government freight for the . . . forts and posts on the frontier . . ." [18]

Almost from the beginning of their operations, a tidy relationship developed with Bvt. Maj. Gen. J. J. Reynolds, regular colonel of the Twenty-sixth Infantry and commandant of the Texas Department, who during those years was reconstructing Texas in the radical Union image.

The nemesis of this comfortable trio — Adams, Wickes, and Reynolds — turned out to be Col. Ranald S. Mackenzie, commander of the Fourth Infantry. That humorless, dedicated, and incorruptibly honest soldier was beginning to build a reputation at that time on the northwest Texas plains as one of the few effective Indian fighters in the army.

Mackenzie's biographer, Ernest Wallace, traced the brash young colonel's awareness of General Reynolds's peculations with Adams and Wickes in their contracts for delivering forage and wood. When Mackenzie balked at going along with deals which would have endangered his men, Reynolds filed court-martial charges against him. In the upshot, however, the army command found no basis for prosecuting Mackenzie. Instead, they let him proceed with his famous plains campaigns, transferred Reynolds to hazardous duty in the Far West, and replaced him, in command of the Department of Texas, with Brig. Christopher C. Auger, an able and nonpolitical officer. [19]

Adams and Wickes survived the sorry affair with equanimity; it had received little or no open publicity. They were still successful in getting army contracts, but a greater danger than scandal was afflicting them on the roads to the frontier forts. Indian depredations against their wagon trains were eating up their profits.

As early as August 1868, one of their trains, on the return leg of

a trip from San Antonio to Fort Davis with army supplies, was involved in a brush with Indians. A member of the party reported upon
their arrival in San Antonio that near the "Riffles" on the Pecos,
wagon-master Ashley and several of his teamsters had discovered and
attacked a group of about twenty Indians.[20]

On June 12, 1869, an Adams and Wickes train, westbound near
the Devil's River under a wagon-master named Browington, was
charged suddenly by a band of about fifty Comanche warriors. They
succeeded in driving off and capturing about eighty mules — a sting-
ing loss.[21] On the twentieth of that same month another Indian attack
against one of their trains near Howard's Well caused the death of one
teamster and the loss of 150 mules.[22] Near Fort Mason, February 24,
1870, the Adams and Wickes wagon-master was killed by Indians.[23]
In February 1871 the firm told the newspapers about "an attack in
force upon one of their trains three miles west of Fort Mason."[24]

Peter Jonas of New Braunfels in 1868 was a dozen years older
than the tow-headed rebel lad Captain Pope had booted out at Fort
Lancaster. Now Adams and Wickes recruited him as wagon-master. In
the rough-and-ready autobiography he wrote years later, Jonas related
that in 1868 he

> . . . dropped everything and came to San Antonio and took charge
> of one of Adams & Wickes wagon trains and started to Eagle Pass
> . . . The train was made up out of all kinds of mules which had been
> bought up here and there, some old, some poor and no account and
> 60 wild ones, and I had a hard time making the trip but got true
> [sic] all right, after coming back from that trip I turned in all the no
> account old mules, and the firm by this time having a large number
> of wild mules on hand, I taken another lot of wild mules in place of
> the old no account ones and by doing this I made a fine train out of
> a bad one.
>
> Next I was sent to Fort Mason Fort Griffin and to Fort Richard-
> son with my regular train and 10 additional teams to take and dis-
> tribute Cannons and Gattlong [sic] guns to the diverent Army Posts
> the first Gattling Guns ever came to Texas . . .
>
> After returning [from an East Texas trip] was send to El Paso
> again, which pleased me the road El Paso allways good but then
> was much more danger from Indians on that road, but we hardly
> ever feared any danger. My men were all Mexicans 14 men and
> myself, we were pretty well armed. The Mexicans are not afraid of
> Indians at all, and they are generally very good Mule drivers.

They had to drive their team during the day and stand guard at night with the mules . . .

I made one trip going from here by way of Fort Concho to New Mexico moving troop to Fort Selton [Selden] . . . This trip took over 6 months from the Time I left here until I got back, on this trip at El Paso on the way back the Indians took 17 mules and the Bell Mare from me, myself and six of men followed the Indians up to the Oregon [Organ] Mountains in New Mexico but I could not overtake them. This was the only trouble I had in all my travels during the time I ran Wagon Trains . . . A number of other Wagon Master were attacked and lost their entire herd . . .[25]

There is no way of knowing how completely the newspapers were able to report upon Indian depredations, so Adams and Wickes may have suffered even more than appears upon the record. That which was reported, however, seems enough to have been insupportable. Possibly the fact that neither of the principals in the firm had working road experience in wagon freighting or in fighting Indians contributed to their losses, through failure to enforce discipline on the road or to have an adequate contingency plan against Indian attack. Certainly men like Santleben or Monier, inured to the road through years of seasoning, did plan ahead and prepare their drivers in every possible way.

For whatever reason, Adams and Wickes sustained more than their share of losses in the lives of their men, their mules, and the goods they handled. All their neatly finagled contracts could not counteract those losses.

In terms of the number of teams, wagons, and men which the firm put on the road, however, they certainly must have outranked any other operator in Texas. Their huge corrals and wagon yards lay along Austin Street, then called the Old Austin Trail, northeast of the main center of town, which was clustered about its plazas. One source written in 1932, long before the present expressways carved the area into segments, said that "the yards covered the area bound by the present streets of Oak, Van Ness, Hackberry, Crosby, to Austin."[26] Van Ness and Crosby streets are gone today, but the context indicates that the area, comprising at least half a dozen city blocks, ran along Austin up to where Interstate Highway 35 crosses Interstate 37.

Peter Jonas graduated in the later years of the wagon freight era from simple drover and then wagon-master to operator of a large store and saloon on Austin Street immediately adjoining his old employers' yards, while his brother Edgar had charge of the corrals and maintained his paying office in Peter's store.[27]

Adams and Wickes did have foresight in one respect: they could see what would happen when the railroads, building steadily up from the coast, reached San Antonio. Therefore, in about 1875, they began to reduce their rolling stock and moved smoothly into the real estate business. In the *San Antonio Herald* of March 5, 1875, they were advertising 2,500 city lots for sale in San Antonio as well as property in other counties. They had an interest, also, in a twenty-league grant lying athwart the route of the International Railroad — later International and Great Northern — which was building toward San Antonio. They had climbed aboard the Iron Horse.[28]

Not all the other early wagon freighters settled down to make a career of it. Many took a wagon or two into the traffic when cash was scarce on the farm, or they hired out for a while as drovers. One of those was Grenade Drake Gilliland. Born in Talledega, Alabama, in 1826, Gilliland was the son of a Methodist minister. He migrated to Texas in 1838 in a covered wagon, settling near Lockhart. A biographical sketch says that he later "drove a freight oxen wagon from old Indianola to San Antonio, carrying supplies brought in by ships to the port, Indianola, Texas, once a port of entry for commerce to and from the old west as far away as Chihuahua, Mexico."

On the line between Wilson and Atascosa counties, below San Antonio, "Uncle Drake" Gilliland founded an extensive ranch that is still in the family. He surveyed the site for the first Atascosa County Courthouse in Pleasanton; and as Acting Grand Master for the Texas Masonic Lodge, A. F. & A. M., he laid the cornerstone of the Wilson County Courthouse at Floresville on February 22, 1884. He helped establish the Methodist Church in South Texas, and two of his grandsons were Texas Rangers. His descendants today have only two material souveniers of his earlier life: his branding iron and the heavy trace chain from his ox-drawn freight wagon, used on the Chihuahua Road more than a century ago.[29]

Other short-timers show up unexpectedly here and there. Col. Tom C. Frost, founder of the banking dynasty in San Antonio that bears his name, operated wagon trains out of Cuero on one branch of the Chihuahua Road for a time. Others appear only as names in the recollections of old-timers. Charles Barnes of the *San Antonio Express* staff at the turn of the century added these: A. Talamantes, Henry Bitter, Louis Oge, Charles Guergin, Jesus Hernandez, Enoch Jones.[30]

Political upheaval on the border drew August Santleben out of the stagecoach business and into full-time wagon freighting to Chihuahua. Santleben was always discreet in his discussion of political connections, but he says enough to make clear that he and his partner, Captain Muenzenberger, had enjoyed a very good situation at the Eagle Pass-Piedras Negras crossing of the international boundary. The United States customs officer at Eagle Pass was Thomas B. MacManus of the well-known family based near Chihuahua City, while across the river the Mexican officials were Nicholas Gresanta and his assistant Pedro Morales. These men, said Santleben, "were all my intimate friends whose personal influence and official powers were exercised in the interest of the line whenever an opportunity offered." [31]

Those opportunities offered themselves frequently. The success of the pioneering stagecoach and express line had depended upon special privileges granted by the Mexican government to stimulate trade. The most important of these was an exemption from tariff charges on all goods — except money. On legal tender a municipal duty of two percent was collected in Monterrey, and an export duty of ten percent was levied by the Piedras Negras customs officials. According to Santleben, his coach was never checked or delayed by government officials "on either side of the Rio Grande."[32]

But all good things come to an end. Santleben and Muenzenberger were forced out of business in August of 1869 "on account of sudden changes in the custom-house officers at Eagle Pass and Piedras Negras, because the removal of our friends naturally affected our business . . . Our net profits were large and we hated to give up the line, but we were compelled to do so." [33]

Thomas MacManus, the helpful customs officer on the Eagle Pass side, was called in to duty at customs headquarters in Washington. Adolph Muenzenberger moved to Santa Rosa, Mexico, to engage in mining and milling. Santleben, in the settlement of the partnership, retained the mules, and he brought them to San Antonio to undertake a new direction in business.[34]

August Santleben was now twenty-four years of age, single, solvent, with a decade of transportation experience already under his belt — experience wherein he had "encountered all the dangers and difficulties on the route successfully" and therefore felt "competent to grapple with larger undertakings." With all these advantages working for him, Santleben did not hesitate to invest his profits in the business of freighting.

He made the plunge by buying six of the large, heavy wagons

which he himself called "prairie schooners," augmenting his mule *re-muda* to have ten mules for each wagon plus a few extra for emergencies. Hiring experienced drivers, he placed Theodore Lamberson, who had worked with him in Mexico, in overall charge of the train, as wagon-master.

The new enterprise got under way in September 1869 with a contract from A. I. Lockwood, the San Antonio banker, for hauling a cargo of wool to the docks in Indianola. The train ran into the last of the two-year period of wet weather on the coastal plains, so that under constant rains and encounters with high water, the wool got wet. The young freighter was slapped with $1,200 damages on the wool, which he had to pay to Lockwood, plus some $600 in claims on other goods. That took all the profit out of his first job. Undaunted, Santleben simply resolved to expand the scope of his operations all the way to Chihuahua and in so doing to increase the number of wagons in his train.[35]

Santleben's memoirs throw light upon how Indianola emerged to be the focal point for freight to northern Mexico during the seventies:

> Goods were then moved through Texas from Indianola under bond. The guarantee was exacted by the Federal custom house officials to insure prompt transportation through the United States to the Mexican border, where the duties were paid, and all bonded freight for Mexico was shipped from that point until 1877 . . .[36]

One of the big bonded warehouses which received and held the off-loaded import goods at Indianola was that of the brothers August and Valentine Heyck, commission merchants. From their bays August Santleben loaded his wagons in December 1869 for his first trip to Ciudad Chihuahua and south to Parral, a one-way journey of 1,150 miles. He had to make heavy bond, payable to the United States Treasury Department, to insure that the goods would move promptly and without tampering through United States territory.[37]

Santleben did not mention which of the several alternate routes he took up from the coast to San Antonio; but since it was a wet winter, after coming through Helena he probably bypassed the Carvajal Crossing of the Cibolo, staying on the east side and using Plummer's or Peacock's Crossing of that creek to go up through the "Sandhills Country" of Wilson County, ideal in wet weather. This would bring him back to the main road along the San Antonio River near the mouth of Calaveras Creek, and then into San Antonio.

Since this was to be his first venture into the state of Chihuahua,

Santleben employed a new wagon-master, Eutemio Megarez, born and reared in that state. The entire route beyond Fort Clark was new to Santleben, but he was fortunate in falling in with Ed Froboese, who was taking a train to El Paso. They could, therefore, travel together through the worst of the Indian country as far as Fort Stockton.

Nine miles beyond Fort Stockton, at the León water-hole, Santleben bade farewell to Ed Froboese and turned southwestward toward Presidio del Norte. His is the first postwar account of that portion of the road. The only new feature he introduces, in addition to those mentioned by Julius Froebel in 1853, is a watering place he called "El Alamita" [*sic*] twenty-five miles down Alamito Creek from San Esteban Springs. Here, as he said, and as later maps show, John Davis was to establish a ranch in 1870 or 1871.[38]

Without event, Santleben took his train down to the Rio Bravo and to the little settlement Spencer had founded, which was by 1869 beginning to be called Presidio. Old Presidio del Norte, across the river, had been officially renamed Ojinaga in 1865 for Gen. Manuel Ojinaga, governor of the state and martyred hero of the Juarez revolution.[39] Santleben observed that "the river at that point is always fordable, except when the water is high, and then the passage is made on ferry-boats." [40]

He submitted an inventory of his freight for inspection by "Captain Mose" Kelley, the U.S. customs officer, then forded the river into Mexico, where his train was placed under guard until Mexican inspectors had verified his manifest and the duties on the bonded goods were paid. He was gratified to find, on this first experience at La Junta de los Rios, that he was courteously treated by officials of both governments.[41]

Taking the only feasible road for wheeled vehicles, up the east side of the Conchos River, Santleben's train touched at each of the landmarks detailed sixteen years earlier by Julius Froebel: Rancho de la Mula, Chupadero, Julimes, and Bachimba. He found, as did every traveler, that the little water-seep at Chupadero, in the middle of an otherwise totally dry passage of ninety miles "was scarcely sufficient for [his] teams." [42] Unlike others, though, Santleben learned fast. On later trips, to ensure an ample supply, he posted a couple of men ahead by six hours, with digging tools, to make a little dam below the rock ledge where the water seeped, so that a pool would be ready when the teams arrived.

Bachimba, across the Conchos River from the fine springs at Julimes, was the seat of the MacManus family, of whom Thomas had been his great and good friend at Eagle Pass, so August Santleben stopped there to pay his respects.

The final hurdle, in crossing a spur of the Sierra Madre and on into the capital, was the Cañon del Ojito, a narrow pass between the plain of Machimba and that of Mápula, where Indians had often ambushed even large parties of travelers.[43] The freighter traversed it this time without incident, and so came down across the windswept plain to the city of Chihuahua, where the first sight was the towers of the cathedral rising dramatically against a great backdrop of mountain ramparts.

Wagon trains were now putting up at the facilities on the outskirts of the city known popularly as the Mesón de Maceyra, built a year or so earlier by Felix Maceyra when he initiated his express service through Eagle Pass.[44] The nearest equivalent in Texas to Maceyra's *mesón* was the San Antonio wagon-yard of the latter half of the nineteenth century, such as that operated by George Stumberg two blocks south of the courthouse; but these were relatively modest enterprises.

Santleben preserved a word picture of the Maceyra caravansary. It occupied the whole of a large plaza, walled, with stalls around the inner perimeter, sufficient for stabling 600 animals, with a cement feed trough to accommodate them all. The plaza offered space for four trains of heavy wagons, perhaps fifty of the great vehicles, to drive inside and be quartered.

In the center of the plaza stood its most distinctive feature, a huge stone granary, in the shape of a bottle, standing reputedly seventy-five feet high. Up the steps which wound around the outside, corn was carried by hand, in baskets, and deposited through a hatch on top. When the tower was filled to capacity with 5,000 *fanegas,* or about 15,000 bushels, it was sealed with adobe mortar, making it airtight and thus protecting the train from weevils. Grian could be taken out, as needed, through an iron door at the bottom.[45]

Such a granary as this became the prototype for the strange pyramidal or conical concrete granaries which now dot the landscape of Mexico, built under government subsidy in recent years. At that time, however, it provided a sure and welcome source of grain, unique in northern Mexico, for the thousands of teams of mules and oxen plying the roads into the capital from El Paso, Ojinaga, and the southern reaches of the Republic of Mexico.

La Mesón de Maceyra charged a moderate fixed fee for sheltering a wagon train, but since it was a private enterprise, the prices charged for provender for the teams were subject to the open market price. Santleben recalled that in a normal season the price of a *fanega* of corn (three bushels) ranged from $2 to $3; but in a droughty season or when the country was gripped by civil war, the cost might skyrocket. In the season of 1873, a time of political upheaval, he had to pay $12 a *fanega* and found it scarce at any price.[46]

On this first of many journeys to Chihuahua, August Santleben extended his trip about 175 miles southward to Hidalgo del Parral. His route lay roughly along that of the present main highway: back to Bachimba and up the valley of the Conchos to cross the river at what was then known as Santa Rosalía (now Ciudad Camargo).[47] Santleben traveled then in a large arc south and west through Jimenez to the mining center of Hidalgo del Parral. He found the entire road after leaving the MacManus Ranch at Bachimba to be "bad and hard on the teams." [48]

When he reached Parral, Santleben loaded his train with crude copper ore and with bars of pure silver, consigned to him by F. Stalfort of that city. He hauled it back to Chihuahua and delivered the silver to the mint operated there by Henry Müller, or Mueller, who was licensed to strike coinage for the Mexican government.[49]

Ten days later Müller turned back to Santleben $185,000 in newly-minted Mexican pesos, which were accepted at that time in the United States as legal tender equal in value to the dollar. With that sizeable sum of money, destined to cover debits for goods purchased in the United States, and all of the copper ore, which was consigned to firms in Texas, August Santleben led his train back to San Antonio without misadventure.

Such were the men who pushed the wagons through on the Chihuahua Road. But what was the rolling stock that carried the freight, in that period before the Iron Horse made them obsolete?

The pioneering vehicle on the road, of course, was the primitive Mexican *carreta*. Some years ago, in a nook outside the Witte Museum's Transportation Hall at Hemisfair Plaza in San Antonio, stood the ruin of one of the original Mexican *carretas*, perhaps the only original one still remaining in Texas or the southwestern United States. The curators hoped then to get it rehabilitated, but its fate was uncertain.

Today, however, faithful in every detail to the actual ponderous carts that rolled on the Chihuahua Road, a huge replica dominates one courtyard within the great adobe pile known as Fort Leaton or El Fortín. Three miles down the Rio Grande from Presidio, the once crumbling ruin was handsomely restored in the 1970s by the Texas Parks and Wildlife Commission as a museum of Chihuahua Desert culture. Its superintendent, Luis Armendáriz, is a direct descendant of John Spencer, the original settler on the east bank of the river at Presidio.

Armendáriz found that the best and almost only source for authentic detail on the *carretas* was August Santleben's passage in *A Texas Pioneer*. Craftsmen of the Junta de los Rios area followed the specifications closely.

The first impression one gets upon viewing this ponderous vehicle is its overwhelming size and weight. The huge *carreta* was put together with locally hewn timbers, mainly *alamo,* that is, cottonwood, which when seasoned is almost indestructible. Santleben felt that the most remarkable feature "was the absence of metal in all its parts, which were fashioned almost exclusively of cottonwood timber and fastened together with wooden pins and thongs of rawhide." [50] It moved, of course, upon two wheels, about seven feet high, and each wheel was composed of but three great slabs of wood, hewed and fitted to the proper dimensions, thus forming the complete wheel — twenty inches thick at the middle and ten inches at the rim. Each such wheel must have weighed over 500 pounds. These wheels turned on an axle hewn from live oak or pecan wood, squared through its length to eight inches, but at each end rounded to form a spindle which tapered from seven inches in diameter at the inner shoulder to six inches on the outer. [51]

The frame, as much as six feet wide and fifteen feet long, was of heavy timbers mortised and pinned together and secured firmly to the axle with wooden pins and rawhide thongs. The rawhide, of course, was applied when wetted and was bound in place under great tension to form, when dried, a plastic shell which would hold and last for decades. [52] Other slabs formed the floor of the bed, while heavy standards set vertically into the frame supported a roof which was thatched with straw. The tongue, a rough cottonwood pole, sometimes thirty feet or more in length, passed over the entire frame and axle and was secured at each point by the same pins and rawhide lashings.

In Mexico these original *carretas* formed the basis for heavy transport through most of the nineteenth century. Santleben saw many of them used in the state of Chihuahua for hauling grain to market from such *haciendas* as the 2,000-acre farm of the Cordero brothers, and those of Frank MacManus, Gustav Moye, and others. Such carts as these made up the train which Julius Froebel joined to come down the road from Chihuahua to San Antonio in 1853. The *carretas* based around San Antonio were smaller than the Chihuahua carts, lighter built and drawn by no more than three yoke of oxen, sometimes only one. They formed the basic rolling stock for the cart trade which occupied so many drovers in San Antonio; and they were the principal vehicles which drew the jealousy and violence of Karnes and Goliad folk in the deplorable "cart war" of the 1850s. [53]

One should understand that the substitution of four-wheeled wagons and of mules, for carts and oxen, was no sudden, final transition. Nick Eggenhoffer, the splendid illustrator whose drawings have enlivened the pages of many a Western story and book, compiled and illustrated with loving care a reference book on the vehicles that moved the frontier ever westward in the nineteenth century. Eggenhoffer traced how the Conestoga wagon, developed in the Conestoga Valley near Lancaster, Pennsylvania, was originated in the middle of the eighteenth century, used in Braddock's ill-fated campaign, and in the revolution twenty years later. It became the standard vehicle for moving goods along the "National Pike" that crossed the mountains beyond the Cumberland Gap and wound on westward. With "undercurved body and overhanging ends," it was a graceful outfit that seized the imagination of the people. [54]

The army wagons that John E. Wool brought up the road from Lavaca in 1846 were a lighter, modified version of the Conestoga, with less of the undercurve and overhang. Similar versions were being used in the late 1840s and 1850s on the Santa Fe Trail. The early wagons of Ben Coons, Maj. George T. Howard, and Thomas Monier, before the Civil War, were no doubt along those modified lines that were coming to be called "prairie schooners." [55]

The enormous demand for wagons in the Civil War, as met most lavishly by the Union forces, meant that thousands upon thousands of vehicles, their teams, and their drivers were put through a proving ground that was the whole mid-continent, over every type of terrain, in flood and in drought, blizzard to baking heat, deep mud to choking dust, to say nothing of the havoc wrought by bullet, cannonball, and shrapnel. Out of this torture emerged the six-mule army wagon, which was, as Nick Eggenhoffer has observed, "the wagon supreme, a vehicle that seemed to call for no improvement . . ." [56] Though it had straight

sides, it still showed its heritage from the Conestoga in the slight up-
sweep at both ends, the perky, slanting tool box fitted to the front
end, and the big feed-trough for the mules across the rear. But this fine
vehicle, the favorite of a generation of emigrants, ranchers, and those
who went a-hunting the buffalo, was not large enough, nor heavy
enough, for the grueling Chihuahua Road, where the whole margin of
profit for a trip might rest upon the extra pounds that could be loaded
on one wagon-bottom. The bed of the army's wagon, according to
Quartermaster Department spec's quoted by Eggenhoffer, was
"straight, three feet six inches wide, two feet deep, 10 feet along the
bottom, 10 feet six inches at the top, sloping equally at each end . . ."
Such a vehicle with six large army mules in harness could carry 3,000
pounds across open country on firm ground.

    Contrast this with the giants of the road which August Staacke,
the wagon merchant of San Antonio, was bringing into the trade by
1869 from the builders Wilson and Childs of Philadelphia. The hind
wheels of these wagons, described Santleben,

> measured five feet ten inches in height, and the [iron] tire was six
> inches wide and one inch thick; the front wheels were built like
> them; but they were twelve inches lower. The axles were of solid
> iron, with spindles three inches in diameter, and all the running
> gear was built in proportion for hard service. The wagon bed was
> twenty four feet long, four and a half feet wide, and the sides were
> five and a half feet high. Wagon bows were attached to each, and
> over them two heavy tarpaulins were stretched, which hung down
> the sides, that thoroughly protected the freight. On these covers the
> train owner's name was painted, and beneath, a number, from one
> upwards, to distinguish the wagons, in which freight was loaded as
> it was entered on memoranda. The woodwork of these wagons was
> painted a deep blue and the iron work black.[57]

    These monsters, twice as long and twice as deep as the standard
army wagon of the day, carried 7,000 pounds as their average load behind ten small Mexican mules. Therefore, with only one driver and the
ten thrifty little mules for the three-and-a-half-ton load, as compared
with one driver and six heavy mules for the army's one-and-a-half-ton
load, Santleben felt that the comparison demonstrated the efficiency of
the Texas freighter's favorite vehicle.

    During this same period, freighting interests in northern Mexico
developed their own line of wagons to keep pace with competitors from
north of the Rio Grande. These so-called "Chihuahua wagons" were

more clumsily built than those from the United States, Santleben mentioned, "with frames twenty-four feet long, without sides, resting on a heavy running-gear with three and a half inch axles and enormous wheels with tires six inches wide and an inch thick." But they were capable of carrying 10,000 pounds, Santleben claimed, citing as an example that "a train of twelve wagons, each drawn by fourteen mules, distributed in three sets of four working abreast and two to the tongue, would transport one hundred and twenty thousand pounds of freight with ease over the roads in Mexico." [58] Among the largest of these operators were David and Daniel Sada of Monterrey and John Gargin, an absentee owner living in San Antonio. But Santleben reserved his highest praise for one "Rocky Garady . . . who owned and ran a train of twelve wagons, with fourteen mules to each, that was known as the finest outfit in Mexico, and I am sure that their equal could not be found in the United States." [59]

Perhaps it was Santleben's German sense for orderly, disciplined conduct that attracted him to these trains, for he noted that "the same drivers were employed continuously by train-owners in Mexico . . . and that they were subject to strict obedience as *peons,* and discipline was rigorously enforced." [60]

The mules, raised on the owners' home ranches, also became well-disciplined, an aspect that stood in sharp contrast to the wild, unbroken beasts that more often than not were available to American freighters as well as the stagecoach lines. Many a traveler told how fresh teams brought up to the stage at an isolated station had to be fought into place to be harnessed. A man had to hold each mule's bit until the driver got in place on his lofty seat and arranged the reins in his hands to his satisfaction. Then, at a signal, each hostler released his mule, the driver gave a great whoop, and the mules dashed wildly out of the corral with the coach careening behind them.

On the other hand Santleben averred that in a Mexican wagon or cart train (and he admitted the same as to his own train)

> . . . the mules, on account of long service, were easily controlled and became trained to routine movements. This was seen when it was time to hitch up, after the *caporal* [the number two man of the train, in charge of the mule herd] walked to the center of the corral among the loose mules, where he cracked his whip and ordered them to their places. Inside of five minutes every mule, sometimes as many as two hundred, would stand in their proper positions, backed

up against the wagon with their heads toward the *caporal,* ready for
the bridles which the drivers placed upon them.[61]

Dry specifications as to length of wagon beds, size of wagon
wheels, thickness of their tires, the way the mules were hitched, do not
convey the visual impact which these big, bustling trains had upon
their observer.

Santleben had his own love affair with the wagons throughout his
life. He — or perhaps his alter ego I. D. Affleck — felt that

> the prairie schooner was a humble pioneer that plodded its way
> slowly over plain and mountain, yet it was appreciated in its day,
> and its arrival at its destination was greeted with far more interest
> than that manifested when a modern, up-to-date steam train arrives
> at its station. Their rarity, and because they were the main depen-
> dence in the West for the transportation of goods, always insured
> them a warm welcome . . .[62]

James Pearson Newcomb, fiery editor of the *San Antonio Express,*
had become secretary of state in Austin under Radical Republican
Governor E. J. Davis in late 1870. The reporter who succeeded him in
writing copy for the paper had a sharp eye for the picturesque aspects
of the freight traffic crowding the streets of his city. On a spring day in
1871 he noted that "A Mexican *carreta* passed through our town yesterday, laden with freight, and perched upon its top sat one of the
hurdy-gurdyists who, about this time of year, begin to make their appearance in our city." [63] Earlier, Newcomb had observed that "an immense train of regular Mexican carts, numbering forty-eight and as
large as good-sized log houses, passed down Commerce Street." [64]

H. H. McConnell, serving in the Sixth United States Cavalry in
1868, recorded this impression of a Mexican wagon train:

> After leaving New Braunfels we overtook a Chihuahua train loaded
> with cotton goods en route to Mexico, and it was the finest outfit of
> its kind I had ever seen, and was evidently used by persons of some
> consequence. One of the firm accompanying it was splendidly
> mounted on a black horse he told us had cost a hundred doubloons.
> His dress was dark velvet, the jacket and pantaloons ornamented
> with silver buttons, his saddle literally plated with silver, and he
> wore an elegant pair of silver-mounted pistols, his whole appearance
> much like that of the traditional bandit as seen on the operatic stage.
> His train consisted of thirty wagons, each carrying ten thousand
> pounds and drawn by twelve to fourteen mules, besides which a herd
> of three hundred extra mules was driven by the *vaqueros.*[65]

It remained for Sidney Lanier, the gentle Georgia poet, to render the artist's impression of the Chihuahua trade at the crest of its activity. Lanier, suffering the ultimately fatal effects of consumption, which he had contracted as a prisoner in the dank hulk of a Yankee prison ship during the Civil War, visited San Antonio in 1873. He spent several months in the city, leaving a treasure of his impressions recorded in a comprehensive survey that began with the sentence "If peculiarities were quills, San Antonio de Bejar would be a rare porcupine." He captured one of those quills one afternoon as he loitered on the bridge above the sparkling waters of the river:

> . . . one may take one's stand on the Commerce Street bridge and involve oneself in the life that goes by this way and that. Yonder comes along a train of enormous blue-bodied canvas covered wagons, built high and square in the stern, much like a fleet of Dutch galleons, and lumbering in a ponderous way that suggests cargoes of silver and gold. These are drawn by fourteen mules each, who are harnessed in four tiers, the three front tiers of four mules each, and that next the wagon of two. The "lead" mules are wee fellows, veritable mulekins; the next tier larger, and so on to the two wheel mules, who are always as large as can be procured. Yonder fares slowly another train of wagons, drawn by great white-horned oxen, whose evident tendency to run to hump and fore-shoulder irresistibly persuades one of their cousinship to the buffalo.[66]

[15]

The Prime Days of
August Santleben

During the three to four years, 1869 into 1873, when August
Santleben was carving out a place for himself as one of the prime
freighters on the Chihuahua Road, he had to work through the worst
days of the Indian trouble on the frontier. The dismal harvest was garnered from Montague County on the Red River to Starr County in the
Lower Rio Grande Valley.

When General of the Army William Tecumseh Sherman was finally drawn, by the flood of protests and pleas passing through the
Texas governor's office, to make his own personal inspection of the
frontier, he came full of skepticism. But when he and his staff narrowly
escaped being massacred by Kiowa warriors on May 18, 1871, while
traversing Salt Creek Prairie near Jacksboro, his eyes opened to the
very real burden of Indian depredations.

These warriors in ambush, headed by Chiefs Satank, Big Tree,
and Satanta, listened to their medicine man's counsel and let the great
white man pass unrecognized and unharmed, only to pounce upon and
destroy, a few hours later, an innocent wagon train. They killed six
drovers at once, chained the wagon-master, Samuel Elliott, between
the wheels of his wagon, and burned him alive there, along with all the
other wagons and their freight. One survivor stumbled late that night

254

into Fort Griffin, where General Sherman was spending the night with Col. Ranald S. Mackenzie.[1]

As Sherman listened to the man's account, the image of the screaming freighter chained to the flaming wagon burned itself into the mind of the army general. Reflecting no doubt with Henry Ward Beecher that "There but for the grace of God was William Tecumseh Sherman," his whole attitude toward the war in the Southwest was changed. He concluded at once that he must take drastic action, and he did.

One result was that it launched the young Colonel Mackenzie on his unremitting campaigns against Kiowas and Comanches on the northwestern plains over the next two years.

In the spring of 1872, the most ghastly massacre of the postwar years on the Texas frontier was perpetrated at Howard's Well, the key watering place on the Chihuahua Road. August Santleben, as always barely escaping disaster himself, played a kind of Greek chorus to the tragedy. He was returning in early April from having delivered a train-load of government freight at Fort Davis, when he decided to risk a new venture: hauling salt from the natural deposits of the Pecos country down to the markets at San Antonio. He took his empty wagons on the longer route by Horsehead Crossing. After fording the Pecos River there, he turned upstream about fifteen miles and about two miles east of the river, to reach salt-encrusted Juan Cardona Lake.[2]

Scooping up the salt deposits along the lakeshore to bulk-fill his wagons took three days; during this time Santleben's *caporal* discovered that they were being shadowed by a band of at least thirty Indians. The freighter therefore took extreme precautions, sending his full strength of men to ride herd on the mules during their evening excursions to water at the Pecos, posting heavy night guards around the corralled wagons, and "sidelining" the mules while they were turned out to graze awhile before being driven into the corral for the night.[3]

Thereby thwarting the Indians, Santleben got his wagons filled, traveled down the river only five miles until he discovered the wagons were badly overloaded, and threw out 2,000 pounds of salt from each. Properly lightened, the train moved smartly on down the Pecos, past Pontoon Crossing, and in a couple of days all the way to the favored camp at Live Oak Creek near the ruins of Fort Lancaster. To the group's dismay, the *caporal* reported seeing the Indians continuing their stalk from across the river.

The train got a predawn start the next day, making the run

through broad arroyos to reach Howard's Well by late noon. As they were pulling out from the water hole after the dinner stop, Anastacio Gonzales, the ambitious young man who was building a new house for his bride in San Antonio, drove up from the south with a train of six wagons.

The men were friends; Santleben paused in his ambulance to visit, while his wagons pulled out. Santleben was acutely conscious of the Indians who had been shadowing him for days, and he counseled Gonzales on the danger. The more experienced man said he urged Gonzales "to use every precaution to avoid an attack, because I was satisfied that the same Indians were hovering in the neighborhood, and . . . possibly they would make an assault upon his camp if they saw they could do so with impunity." [4]

After this chat, and aware that his wagons were getting ahead of him, Santleben bade his friend goodbye, slapped the reins on the rumps of his mules, and started down the road toward the Devil's River. He was the last man to converse with the ill-fated party.

According to Santleben's information, only a few hours later Lt. Frederick L. Vinson of the Ninth Cavalry, scouting in the neighborhood with some black troopers, saw heavy smoke rising from beyond the hills.[5] Hastening on to trace it, they came down upon Howard's Well too late, finding only a scene of carnage. Their deadly job done, the Indians had fled with their loot.

Just as with the unfortunate teamster 300 miles to the northeast at Salt Marsh Prairie the year before, these savages, whoever they were, had tied Anastacio Gonzales to the wheels before they burned his wagon. His charred body still lay among the smoldering fragments, the poor twisted arms chained to the scorched iron tires. Other bodies were scattered in the coals.[6]

Lieutenant Vinson set out at once to track the marauding party and the captured mules. Santleben learned at Fort Clark only that when the soldiers caught up with the Indians, a fight occurred in which Vinson and several soldiers were killed.[7] The army's "Chronological List of Battles, Actions, etc." simply cites the two units of the Ninth Cavalry that were engaged: Companies A and H, "near Howard's Well," and the date, April 20, 1872.[8]

Santleben always believed that Anastacio Gonzales, overly anxious to press on up the road, ignored his friend's warnings, stopped at the well without forting up into the traditional corral — and paid the price. His most poignant monument was the almost-completed stone house on the corner of Salinas and Laredo streets in San Antonio. His grief-stricken widow would never allow the structure to be touched; when Santleben wrote his memoirs almost half a century later, she was still living in the original little cottage beside the bare walls her lover had put up for her.[9]

Unfortunately, the two San Antonio newspapers were at that time polarized in their attitudes toward the United States Army. The *Herald,* with lingering loyalty to the Southern cause and ill-disguised contempt for all things Federal, took the opportunity to vent their spleen upon Col. Wesley Merritt, who had been heading south that day on the road and apparently had sent Lieutenant Vinson and party out ahead as a scouting screen.

The *Express,* on the other hand, fiercely protective of the Union establishment, closed ranks, printing only a signed letter from a civilian at Fort Clark, which contained nothing derogatory toward the army's performance.[10] There are virtually no other sources, so it has been impossible to make a valid assessment of the army's part in the matter, or even to decide how many people were killed that unhappy day at Howard's Well.

The reports range from Santleben's account — that nine teamsters including Gonzales had been killed — to the Crockett County Historical Commission's claim that there were seventeen in the wagon train. Neither figure contained the casualties suffered by the army: Vinson and at least one other. Deaths on the white man's side, then, were from eleven to twenty. The tragedy must stand as the worst single postwar event of the Indian depredations on the Texas frontier. As to survivors, the *Express* account clearly describes three — a woman and two wounded men. One other contemporary account is not easily dismissed. Sidney Lanier, the poet and essayist who observed the San Antonio scene in 1873, wrote this thumbnail sketch from a stroll on Commerce Street:

> Do you see that poor Mexican without any hands? a few months ago a wagon train was captured by Indians at Howard's Wells; the teamsters, of whom he was one, were tied to the wagons and these set on fire, and this poor fellow was released by the flames burning off his hands, the rest all perishing save two.[11]

Perhaps other factors were working toward the same end, but during the decade ending in 1881, in human terms it can be said with confidence that two men did more than all others to bring about an

end to the Indian wars on the Texas frontier. They were disparate
types: Ranald Slidell Mackenzie, brilliant, cold, remote, a brevet
major general in the Union army when he was twenty-four; John Latham Bullis, not quite a year younger than Mackenzie, unassuming,
warm, not disturbed that he was still a second lieutenant after years of
success on the frontier.

The two men shared the capacity to press an attack, once the
commitment was made, ferociously and with unswerving determination to succeed. This they did, time after time after time, the one with
an entire regiment at his command, the other with a handful of black
Seminole scouts.[12]

Their campaigns along the Rio Grande border and into Mexico
had the ultimate effect of making the Chihuahua Road, and almost all
of West Texas, at long last safe for traffic and settlement. By 1873
Mackenzie was recognized as the officer best fitted to deal with the inflammatory situation that had developed along the Rio Grande. He
was ordered to move his Fourth Cavalry down from the Northwest
frontier to Fort Clark on Las Moras Creek.

Under General Sherman's orders, Phil Sheridan came out to the
new command in early April of 1873, reviewed Mackenzie's regiment
with approval, then was closeted with him for two days of intense
planning. The upshot was Mackenzie's famous — or infamous, some
would say — raid into Mexico to destroy the Kickapoo and Lipan villages at Nacimiento Canyon near Remolina, on May 18, 1873.[13]

This remarkable imperative served to bring the very junior officer, John L. Bullis, directly into association with Mackenzie, for in
putting together his task force for the strike, the latter realized he
needed Bullis and his hard-riding, fearless black Seminole scouts to
supplement his regular army troops. And he was familiar with Bullis's
record in leading small contingents of these hardy men. When Mackenzie called Bullis up to Fort Clark from Fort Duncan down the river,
he and the thirty-four black Seminoles he brought with him were
honed for action.

Mackenzie's strike with five chosen companies of regular army
cavalry, Bullis and his scouts, and four civilian scouts — 415 men in
all — has been termed "the most daring and arduous exploit in the annals of Indian warfare." The story of Mackenzie's exploits was told and
retold in the latter years of the 1800s. In 1965 Ernest Wallace published the most complete story of the colonel's career; while in 1986

Richard Thompson's new work, *Crossing the Border with the 4th Cavalry,* focused on the raid itself and its implications. [14]

The raid accomplished its ostensible purpose: it broke the back of Kickapoo and Lipan aggression, though smaller raids continued sporadically to give trouble. Sheridan and Sherman kept their word: Mackenzie was protected from any official cavilling at his boldness.

Mackenzie was not left long in command at Fort Clark. His unique capacities were needed again on the Staked Plains. In the summer of 1874, he joined the concerted Red River campaign against the Comanche and Kiowa tribes on the Llano Estacado, capped by his stunning attack down the cliffs on Palo Duro Canyon. The most far-reaching effect of that rout was Mackenzie's cold, calculated destruction of more than a thousand of the Comanche ponies he had captured, which put that major segment of the tribe afoot at the onset of winter.

Mackenzie's brilliant exploits continued for several years after he and his Fourth Cavalry had been transferred across country to Montana. His remarkable career came to a tragic conclusion when he suffered a mental breakdown at his last post, in San Antonio, in 1883. In early 1884 a medical board in New York had the dismal duty of bringing him before it, hearing the evidence, and over Mackenzie's anguished protests, retiring him, barely forty-four, on disability "contracted in the line of duty." [15]

Bullis remained on station at Fort Clark, though he was seldom there. Most of the time he was in the field, ranging through the Rio Grande Valley or up in the Big Bend, on preemptive strikes. That was the distinctive tactic he developed: to stay mobile, try to anticipate where the Lipan or the Kickapoo would strike next, and be there to strike back. When he struck a static camp or village, it was always at the break of day — the same format Mackenzie had used in his vastly larger operations. During those years on the Texas border, Bullis led his black scouts on at least twenty-five expeditions, some lasting as long as five months out there on those bleak deserts. And he never lost a man. [16]

He shared every hardship, faced every danger at the head of the column, and worked diligently for his men's welfare back at the post. Years later one of those old black scouts, Joseph Phillips, reminisced:

> The scouts thought a lot of Bullis. Lieutenant Bullis was the only officer ever did stay the longest with us. That fella suffered just like we-all did out in the woods. He was a good man. He was an Injun fighter. He was tuff. He didn't care how big a bunch dey wuz, he

went into 'em, every time, but he look after his men. He didn't stand back and say "Go yonder"; he would say, "Come on, boys, let's go get 'em." [17]

The people of Texas appreciated Bullis too. When he was finally due for a transfer, the communities where he had operated got together and had a handsome sword forged specially for him, engraved with scenes reminiscent of his exploits, and carrying the legend: "Bullis, the friend of the frontier."

With border tension relieved in the mid-1870s by the dissipation of the Kickapoo and Lipan menace, the southern part of the frontier turned with renewed vigor to more orderly traffic along the roads and the settling of homesteaders moving always westward.

August Santleben, at the age of twenty-five, had married Mary Anna Obert from Boerne, in Kendall County, on December 30, 1870. By February of 1874 he felt easy enough about conditions on the frontier to persuade his wife, with their baby daughter Sophie, and a neighbor girl as companion, to accompany him on a trip to Chihuahua. [18] The family traveled in Santleben's personal ambulance, along with his wagon train.

The trip westward was not as free of Indian disturbance as Santleben had hoped. At Fort Clark they had news of increased Indian activity and were, therefore, heartened when they fell in at San Felipe Springs with a party of seven well-armed Easterners, under leadership of a Dr. Livingstone, and on their way to California on a prospecting trip.

Making their way through the Devil's River Canyon country, they caught up with Colonel Mackenzie's command, [19] a large body of soldiers, accompanied by a group of black Seminole scouts, ten wagons, and a hospital ambulance. They traveled not far apart on up to Beaver Lake, where Mackenzie established a base camp, planning to send scouting parties out toward the headwaters of the Concho, up the Pecos, and across toward the Rio Grande, hoping to intercept the rumored raiders. With some reluctance Mackenzie allowed Santleben to move on out toward Howard's Well before the soldiers had time to accomplish their reconnaissance.

The wagon train had proceeded scarcely two miles, in early afternoon, when Livingstone's party, ranging a mile ahead with six pack mules, was attacked by a band of forty Indians converging from both sides on the road. They killed a man named Black at once; another suffered a severe leg injury; and the raiders hazed away and captured all the pack mules. The survivors brought the wounded man back to Santleben, who rushed him to Mackenzie's command for medical treatment. The surgeon amputated the man's leg, but the hapless adventurer died that night. He was buried on the shore of Beaver Lake, while Santleben's men found and buried Black among the rocks where he fell.[20]

The five survivors of Livingstone's party, bereft of their supplies, continued their journey with Santleben, but tragedy still stalked them. One of the group was an eighteen-year-old named Head Boone from St. Louis, who by now had all he wanted of adventure and was anxious to get back home to his mother. Four nights later they were camped some miles from Lost Pond, a valuable water hole which travelers usually missed and because of this had been given its Spanish name, Escondido, or "hidden." It lay in the wastelands between Howard's Well and Live Oak Creek. That evening the poor distracted lad, Head Boone, fumbling in the dark with the gear attached to his saddle, accidentally discharged his shotgun into his body and died within the hour.

Mrs. Santleben, who had become attached to the boy, sorrowfully superintended his burial next day on a hill overlooking Lost Pond. The men dug a deep grave in the soft stone, buried him there with such ceremony as they could command, and set up a slab of stone engraved with his name.[21]

Reduced to four, Livingstone's party was not yet free from danger and alarms. As the train proceeded upriver from Fort Lancaster, near Pecos Springs, Livingstone and one of his companions again moved out ahead and over a small mountain. They ran face to face into a group of Indians, who were as badly startled as they, and both parties fled in opposite directions. Livingstone and his friend came pell-mell back toward the train, yelling "Indians!" with every jump. Santleben, expecting an immediate attack, hastily swung his wagons into corral formation, but nothing developed. The trip west was without further incident; presumably Livingstone left the train at Fort Stockton and continued on his journeys toward California.

At Chihuahua, Santleben off-loaded his freight and spent fifteen days collecting his return cargo: copper and hides, plus $150,000 in Mexican pesos, consigned to Heyck Bros. at Indianola. The trip back was peaceful until they passed the empty walls of old Fort Hudson, at the Second Crossing of the Devil's River, and approached Dead Man's Pass in the course of an all-night drive.

Mrs. Santleben, little Sophie, and the girl companion were trying to sleep in the bed of the ambulance, buttoned up within its all-around canvas curtains. The ambulance, driven by one Wiley Miller, was preceded by Santleben's lead wagon, in which he was riding, along with two passengers picked up at Presidio. It was this lead wagon, Santleben recalled, which carried the great sum of money. He had placed Mrs. Santleben's ambulance immediately behind so that he could be at hand in case of emergency.

This proximity was of no avail that night, however. The *caporal* and his men were driving the herd of spare mules down the road when some sudden alarm spooked the animals; they scattered in all directions. The herders, shouting "Indians!" to alert the train, sped in pursuit of their mules. Excitement rippled down the length of the train at the word of Indians, but pure panic seized the ambulance driver, Wiley Miller; he simply abandoned his seat and dived into the bushes beside the road.

The team of two mules drawing Miller's ambulance panicked also, turning from the road and stampeding into the darkness. Poor August Santleben, from his heavy-laden wagon, could only watch helplessly as the ambulance, bearing its precious cargo — his family, locked inside the curtains — careened toward a canyon with a forty-foot precipice. In blessed relief, some of the alert outriders saw the emergency, galloped alongside the mules, and drew them to a halt practically on the verge of the precipice.

Though the *caporal* and his herders insisted the alarm was indeed caused by Indians, Santleben was convinced that some prowling animal, perhaps a panther or a bear, common in that area, had caused the alarm. The mule herd was rounded up and Santleben, thankful that his family had been saved from harm, even forgave defecting Wiley Miller.[22]

One might have expected Mary Anna Santleben to remain close at home after these successive emergencies on what was supposed to be a quiet journey to Chihuahua. But she was not daunted; she tried it again the next year, with a new infant daughter Charlotta and the older Sophie, and a young woman, Amelia Stienle of Castroville, as companion.

This time Santleben had let his train get on the road six days ahead of him. Taking the late start and driving the ambulance carrying the women and children, now drawn by horses, the indefatigible freighter undertook to catch up with the train before it reached the Indian country beyond Fort Clark. Pushing through at night as they approached the Nueces River beyond Uvalde, he was attended only by a man named Faustino, riding horseback alongside the ambulance. Suddenly, from the darkness they were jumped by three armed men, one of whom got ahead of the team, the other two springing toward the ambulance shouting, "Hands up!"

In reflex action, Santleben snatched his pistol and fired one shot at the man ahead in the road, then another at one of the two alongside the vehicle. The noise and flashes of the pistol fire spooked the horses; they dashed forward as the highwaymen opened fire. The robbers, on foot, were unable to pursue and could only fire a volley in frustration before the ambulance rounded the next turn. Santleben estimated that some twenty shots were fired altogether. He did not know whether he hit either of his assailants, and found that only one of their bullets had taken effect, shattering a spoke on a wheel. He was pleased that his wife went through the crisis "cool and collected," though the girl companion was badly frightened and the escort rider Faustino fled into the night.

The rest of the trip, after joining up with the wagon train, was without special excitement, marked only by one incident on the return leg, on Alamito Creek above Presidio, apparently near San Esteban Springs.

> Mrs. Santleben walked off a short distance from camp to look for moss-agates, that were abundant in that country, and in the high grass she discovered two complete human skeletons. None of the bones had been disturbed, and they were bleached white. Evidently they had been there a long time, and nothing could be found in the vicinity that suggested the cause of their death; nor could we tell whether the remains were of white men or Indians.[23]

Indian attacks, gun-shot accidents, runaway teams in the night, ambush by highwaymen, confrontation with forlorn skeletons while on a quiet walk — if one wonders what the life of women was like during these years on the frontier, this sample from Mary Anna Santleben's experiences should provide an answer. The wives' role on the trail may have been passive, but if they remained "cool and collected," their part as helpmate provided the moral backing the men needed.

In the course of a late 1874 trip, the freighter was in Ciudad Chihuahua, ready to leave for Texas, his wagons heavily loaded with goods, plus a large sum of money in silver pesos. At this juncture, a passing aberration in the currency situation almost caused Santleben's downfall.

Merchants throughout Mexico had an oversupply of small silver five- and ten-cent coins, found to be unpopular with the low-income *poblanos* accustomed to copper. At the same time, small change happened to be in great demand in Texas; as much of the Mexican five- and ten-cent pieces as could be obtained was commanding a ten percent premium. But the Mexican government maintained a prohibitory export duty on coinage that canceled out any profit that might have been made from legitimate movement of the silver pieces into the United States. The pressure was on to find ways to smuggle the stuff across the border.[24]

This set the stage for a play that put poor August into a predicament comically reminiscent of Joseph's brethren in the Bible story, when, bringing wheat back from Egypt to a famine-stricken Canaan, they were caught with the Pharaoh's silver cup buried in one of the bags of grain.

Santleben drove his wagon train down from Chihuahua City without incident to La Mula, that desolate outpost forty miles from Presidio. A customs officer stationed there made his usual cursory inspection of the loaded wagons and was ready to pass them on when the *alcalde* of the hamlet intervened, evidently acting on a tip. He pointed out one certain bag of beans, dramatically demanding that it be opened. Upon inspection, it proved to contain a large quantity of contraband five- and ten-cent pieces.

Mortified and enraged to be found in such a situation, the eminently proper Mr. Santleben was hustled off down the road under guard by customs officials to Presidio del Norte, where a judge formally charged him with smuggling money out of the country. His predicament was doubly acute since he faced not only a long term of penal servitude, but also the confiscation of his entire train. Among the consignments on that trip was $180,000 in silver Mexican dollars, on which the ten percent had been properly paid but which was nevertheless subject to confiscation if Santleben were found guilty. He would, of course, be responsible for the loss.

Released on bond, he spent a miserable sleepless night agonizing over his prospects. Next morning, to his surprise, his trial was called promptly; his friends, both those in Presidio and a group traveling with him, rallied behind him. Santleben made a spirited defense, proving that the bag in which the coins were found was part of a large consignment placed in the wagons by merchants in Chihuahua, and that he could not have known of the presence of the money. Backed by the testimony of his friends, he somehow convinced the court that persons unknown had imposed upon him and used the train for illicit purposes. He was honorably acquitted, only the contraband money being confiscated. Henrico Peña, the Mexican customshouse official, good-humoredly waved him on through inspection, and August Santleben, with his sanitized wagonloads of merchandise and legal silver pesos, took to the primitive ferry across the Rio Grande with vast relief.[25]

Part of his entourage was a company of popular Chihuahua musicians, Professor Manuel Manso and his stringed orchestra troupe, traveling to San Antonio for engagements. This exotic group did not pass unnoticed through the rude new town of Presidio on the east bank of the Rio Grande. James Clark, a junior customs officer for the United States, welcomed them and spread the word, as Santleben moved on with his party to camp twelve miles up the Alamito Creek.

That evening, when the Santleben train was drawn up into its usual circular corral, the campfires sparkling within, there came the sound of hoofs — causing an instant alert. But then came the crunch and rattle of light wheels, accompanied by friendly halloas, and a merry crowd dashed up to the circle of wagons. It was James Clark, the customs officer, in an ambulance with his wife and two other young women, escorted by six youths of the town, on horseback. Inspired by the presence of the orchestra, they were ready for a frolic, and Santleben, not yet thirty years of age, just delivered from the threat of Mexico's noisome prisons, was equal to the occasion. After supper, he spread several heavy tarpaulins on the smooth ground inside the corral circle.

With the brilliant western skies arching overhead, Professor Manso's musicians tuning their instruments, and the coyotes perhaps answering from the dark hills looming nearby, they were all set for a dance. Besides Manso's troupe, several members of the Loza family from San Antonio were traveling with the train, and they joined in the festivities, along with the ten lonely young people from Presidio, and surely at least some of Santleben's trail-worn wagoneers. With candles set upon the broad iron wagon tires to illuminate the improvised dance floor, the exuberant young folk danced the *schottische* and the Mexican hat dance. Surely, as Santleben remembered it,

nothing similar to our frolic on that occasion was ever seen in that wild region, and probably its like will never be witnessed again, as the wilderness . . . cannot be greatly improved. Everyone had entered into the spirit of the occasion and their pleasure found utterance in expressions of delight [until], as day was dawning the *caporal* drove in the herd to be hitched . . . After breakfasting with us, Mr. Clark and his party returned through the uninhabited country to their homes.[26]

During these last years before the railroads connected the United States and Mexico, one of the more effective ambassadors of goodwill traveling up and down the Chihuahua Road was Dr. Frank Paschal. A son of the early San Antonio pioneer Franklin La Fitte Paschal, and brother of a later mayor of the city, George Paschal, he had spent his early youth in Monterrey, thereby learning the language and the customs of the people. After graduating from the Louisville Medical College, he returned to San Antonio as a very young man to become associated in the practice of his profession with the redoubtable Dr. George Cupples. He chafed somewhat, however, in the subordinate position under the strong-minded Cupples and decided to cast his lot with the city of Chihuahua, where there would be less competition. His obvious talents earned him a warm welcome among the people of that city, and within two years he had established a solid practice.

He journeyed then to San Antonio to marry Ladie Napier and bring her back to their new home. The young couple took the stagecoach by the upper road to Benficklin, or Fort Concho, then west by Horsehead Crossing to Fort Davis. Awaiting them was an ambulance with four mules, a driver, and a horseback escort, ready for the journey down Alamito Creek to Presidio and up the Conchos River to Chihuahua.

Ladie Napier Paschal was at once accepted into the heart of the people along with her popular husband. August Santleben vouchsafes that

> the doctor soon became the leading physician, with an extensive and lucrative practice, but his services were not withheld from the poor, and he was greatly assisted in his charitable attentions by Mrs. Paschal, who devoted much of her time to this work. Many indigent people were relieved by his skill as a surgeon, and quantities of medicine were generously distributed to them free of cost.[27]

August Santleben made no direct claims concerning his own public relations success, but his memoirs strongly reflect his achievements in this field. In the mid-1870s, when he was shuttling his slow train over these incredible distances several times a year, a goodly number of Texans took opportunity at one time or another to come along for the ride. He mentions such San Antonio notables as Gus Mauermann, later chief of police in the city, Ernest Paschal, Fred Miller, Tom Nelson, Henry Laager, and Judge Netterville Devine, son of the Judge T. J. Devine who had served as one of the three Confederate commissioners.

Netterville Devine made his round trip when he learned that Santleben would be coming back, on that occasion, by the upper road through the Concho River country of Texas, where the great herds of buffalo were then at their flood tide. The party, traveling by ambulance at the head of the wagon train, reached Chihuahua City just at a time when Don Luis Terrazas was giving a brilliant masquerade ball in the Governor's Palace.

Santleben and Judge Devine received special invitations to attend; they procured suitable costumes for the occasion and joined a glittering crowd of the state's notables, other foreign visitors, and Dr. and Mrs. Paschal. Santleben remembered the event with obvious pleasure, and it must indeed have been a high point for the sturdy trader, who only thirty years before as an infant in a German immigrant family had been handed over the rail of a sinking ship in Galveston harbor.

On the return trip to San Antonio, his train loaded with hides, copper, and Mexican silver coin, Santleben diverted from his usual route at Fort Stockton. He went up, by way of Horsehead Crossing, through Castle Gap, across the West Texas rolling prairies, through Central Station, or Centrila, and up to the headwaters of the main Concho River — buffalo country.

In those brief seasons, just before the monstrous commercial slaughter of the late seventies got under way, it appeared to the observer that all the bison in the world must surely have gathered there in the headwaters of the Concho and its tributaries. To Santleben they appeared to be innumerable.

Judge Devine, along with Jack Berry and Henry Vonflie, wagon-masters in the train, found no sportsman's satisfaction in their first round of simply firing into these tranquil herds. Netterville Devine got more than he bargained for in excitement, though, when he assayed to tramp out ahead of the train and do a bit of Indian-stalking for a fine bull specimen. He found one small herd isolated from the main body and was creeping cautiously toward it, trying to get within range, when he happened to look about and saw a group of Indians, on foot, stealthily approaching over the prairie.

He immediately realized "the hunter was being hunted, and as he disliked the idea of figuring as game for Comanche sportsmen who coveted his scalp, he . . . made a hasty retreat. Fortunately he had a good start, and he improved the time by running at full speed on a bee-line until he reached the train." [28]

Santleben recalls this incident as occurring in 1874, the same year Colonel Mackenzie was sweeping the high plains northward in his decisive campaigns against the Comanches. But, as Devine's experience showed, the Indians were still irresistibly drawn to hover on the flanks of herds they deemed to be their own, and hunting on the part of intruding Anglos did not become safe until several years later.

Other hazards still attended the passage of wagon trains through western Texas. In 1875 Santleben had his closest scrape with non-Indian robbers. He was camped again on the Alamito Creek road east of Presidio, only a few miles from the place where his party had enjoyed the merry all-night frolic the year before. Again, he had silver along with his freight — this time $150,000 in Mexican coinage.

He took his usual thorough precautions: corraling the wagons tightly, leaving only a space to drive the mules in, with a guard party named for each watch for the night. The mules were grazing quietly on the nearby slope on a mountain, under the watchful eyes of the *caporal,* his herders, and one of the wagon-masters. Only the clear intermittent notes from one bell in the herd, sounding in the hush of the desert night, betrayed the presence of the train in that remote canyon.

In the second watch, after Vonflie and his men had come in and retired, Santleben himself, a young man named Timps, and three Mexican drovers were on guard, sitting outside the corral near the two wagons containing the trove of money. Without warning, a shot fired outside the train broke the stillness, followed by the sound of booted men running over loose rocks toward the camp from the east. August Santleben leaped to his feet and fired his rifle in the direction of the attack. His companions followed suit, and the assailants returned the fire with a volley, apparently having taken cover among the rocks. Within moments Vonflie and his men within the corral, aroused from their sleep, had joined Santleben outside to form a force of twelve men against the unseen enemy. Both sides were firing briskly at the flashes of the opposing men's guns.

The *caporal,* meanwhile, had herded his mules together at the first alarm, and with his men came hazing them down the slope toward the wagon corral. Avoiding the line of fire as best he could, he stampeded them through the gap into the circle of wagons, but by that time the battle in the darkness was over. Through the remaining hours of the night a tense vigilance gripped the entire wagon party, for they fully expected a renewal of the attack, which from the tactics followed was clearly not by Indians.

Dawn came without further alarm. In the first light Santleben and some of his men ventured out to scout the area. They found the rough depression where the attackers had holed up to return the fire, with cartridge cases scattered all about, and located the spot where the unknown party had tied their horses — a large number. But not even a drop of blood was to be found on the rocks as earnest that their return fire had taken effect. They only retrieved "a couple of old hats, a gourd of water, and a few trifles of less value as trophies of our victory." [29]

Through Santleben's grapevine intelligence, he later learned that the gang which attacked him numbered about forty desperadoes of the border country who had learned of the large silver shipment he was transporting. They had planned to approach the camp in two groups from different directions and attack simultaneously when the signal gun was fired. One salient, however, had found the *caporal* and his guards between themselves and the camp as they slunk in, and in trying to get around them were delayed and out of range when the signal came. This half of the robber band never got into action at all, thereby making it possible for the freighters to stand off the attack.

This constituted the only serious attempt ever made against Santleben's wagon train. His constant vigilance and the alertness of his men, always well-armed, no doubt had established a reputation for him in the border underground. A large enough gang might have overwhelmed a Santleben train, but any prospective assailant probably realized that a high percentage of the attackers would end up dead.

On a trip to Chihuahua in the spring of 1875, Santleben was drawn into a fascinating involvement with a huge meteorite shown him near the capital city. He ended up by loading the 3,000-pound mass on one of his wagons and hauling it back to the railhead at Luling, Texas. His idea was to get it displayed at the Centennial Exposition in Philadelphia, which was under preparation at that time. Unable to deal directly with authorities at the exposition, and under the pressure of urgent practical business matters, he rather naively shipped it blind to Philadelphia, asking that it be shown for fee in some exhibit. He never heard anything from his prize until after the exposition was over, when word came to him that the official Mexican exhibit had preempted his meteorite for its display and when the exposition closed, had given it to "the British Museum." Santleben was deeply disturbed, but could do nothing about it.

A century later, this author tracked down the location of the meteor to our own Smithsonian Institution in Washington, which has had it ever since 1877. The ton-and-a-half chunk of almost pure iron had come from a crypt in the Casas Grandes ruins of northern Chihuahua State, and today it is one of the chief items in the meteorite section of the museum. The history of how it got there is a bizarre and intricate one.[30]

By early 1876, when August Santleben again pulled out of the Luling railhead laden with freight for the Chihuahua market, the arrival of the Gulf, Houston and San Antonio railway in San Antonio was clearly imminent. Santleben shared a belief with other observers that it would be a great many years before the rails moved west beyond that city, which was designated as the terminal point. Knowing the roughness of the terrain as he did, through the hundreds of miles west and northwest to the borders of the state, he simply could not envision a feasible roadbed being laid across those silent wastes. And even if it were feasible from an engineering standpoint to build a railroad on to El Paso, Santleben felt "that the Indians would destroy the track as fast as it was built, and cause it to be abandoned . . . It was a wild and inhospitable region that promised to be a desert for ages."

The energetic freighter was conditioned, therefore, to welcome with enthusiasm a proposal which awaited him in Chihuahua City. Wholesale merchants in Chihuahua were ecstatic about a possible railroad terminus at San Antonio. Their problem in tapping market resources of the United States and Europe through Indianola, Texas, or Independence, Kansas, during all these years had been the snail's pace at which goods moved and the unpredictability of delivery. This required them to send out cash as much as a year before they could expect the goods it purchased to be sold. To ensure having enough stock on hand to meet sales demand, these wholesalers were required to place very large orders at a time.

After interviewing a number of the most prominent merchants and realizing the seriousness of their intent, Santleben

> proposed to them that if a certain number of merchants in the city
> would obligate themselves to import 72,000 pounds of merchandise every month, exclusive of heavy machinery, and export all

their remittances and freight through me, I would start thirty-six small wagons with five mules to each. I explained that I intended to divide the wagons equally into three trains, and that each wagon would be capable of hauling two thousand pounds of freight; that after the line was established the trains would run on schedule time and make the trip to Chihuahua in thirty days, by leaving San Antonio on the first and fifteenth of each month, and return in the same time after leaving Chihuahua on the seventh and twenty-fourth of each month.[31]

The freighter also agreed to provide wagons such as had never before been seen on the wagon roads of the West: specially constructed with roofs to protect the merchandise from weather and from pilferers. Santleben worked out the terms of a contract with the merchants, whose only further stipulation was that the contract could be dissolved in the event a railroad should be completed at any time within ten years. This gave the freighter no concern, for the construction of such a railroad was, as he said, beyond his conception.

He was riding a wave of exultation when he left Chihuahua, for he saw that at last he had within his grasp the most advanced concept for freighting that had ever been negotiated on the American frontier. As soon as he reached San Antonio he looked up Ed Froboese, laying before him the grand plan developed and contracted with the Chihuahua merchants. Froboese was glad to join in the enterprise as a full partner. The two men went for an interview with Col. Tom Frost.

The reason for approaching Frost on the freighting proposition was that, along with his several other interests at that time, he was agent in South and West Texas for the Mitchell Wagon Company. Santleben had to have a vehicle much lighter and faster than the cumbersome prairie schooners then in use. They knew Mitchell was making a reputation with an adaptation of the army wagon. The two men asked Frost to find out, by quickest means possible, how soon, and for how much, thirty-six wagons could be delivered, built to the buyers' specifications. A message went back to Tom Frost from the Mitchell factory, giving a satisfactory quotation on the price and delivery time for the new model of wagons.

At almost the same time, however, a doomsday message came from the West. Messrs. Kedelson and Degetau of Chihuahua sent the almost unbelievable intelligence that the state of Chihuahua had let a contract for construction of a railroad from Ciudad Juarez, the new

name of El Paso del Norte, to Chihuahua City. Furthermore, the road
was to be finished in three years.[32]

That railroad was undertaken in prospect of connecting with the
Southern Pacific, at that time already building across the southwestern
United States from San Diego to El Paso. The Mexican road was to be
a major, northern sector of the government's *Ferrocarriles Nacionales de
Mexico,* and was to continue from Chihuahua southward to Mexico
City. Governor Luis Terrazas had been authorized to proceed with construction of the section between Juarez and the state capital. Although
completion came three years later than projected, Santleben knew he
was fortunate to have learned of the plan in time to save him from ir-
revocable commitments. But the wagon freighter had seen the handwriting on the wall; railroads from east and west soon crowded in on
his doomed way of life.

[16]

The Coming of
the Iron Horse

Nothing in twentieth-century experience has been comparable, in the way of enthusiasm and gleeful anticipation of prosperity, with the passions which accompanied the advent of the railroad across frontier lands in the nineteenth century. The automobile, the airplane, and finally travel in space have each touched the American spirit in different ways, but they came in more sophisticated days, to a people surfeit with the marvels of science. The Iron Horse, on the other hand, first evidence of technology, demonstrably changed the face of the land as it progressed, scattering the Indian tribes before it, bringing all the goods and goodies of industrial society to those lonely people who had pushed ahead into the raw frontier.

As early as 1854, only five years after the first Anglo scouts had found their way across the Trans-Pecos country to El Paso, promoters filed a firm bid with Governor Elisha M. Pease in Austin to build the Great Pacific Railroad, otherwise known as the "Mississippi and Pacific Railroad." It would proceed from the eastern boundary line of Texas "to a suitable point on the Rio Grande, at or near the town of El Paso." [1] This was a bold proposal by southerners to fulfill the dream raised by the opening of an apparently feasible route through the area of the Gadsden Purchase in southern New Mexico. It would give the states of the South first access to the new empire gold was building on the West Coast.

But the Great Pacific Railroad was never built by those backers. Before any appreciable amount of iron was laid on any roadbed, the gathering storm of the Civil War had brought the project to a standstill, and the promoters had to wait until Reconstruction days to back another railroad project.

Then, with revolutionary zeal, railroad fever seized the folk of central and western Texas throughout the seventies and half of the eighties. Along the historic roads leading up from the gulf through San Antonio, and on toward the Pacific, people watched in dread concern, on the one hand, toward the west the fateful campaigns against the Indians, and looked eastward, with equal preoccupation, toward the erratic progress of railroad crews laying down the roadbed, the wooden ties, the iron ribbons that brought the bright future ever nearer.

"Railroads! Railroads! Railroads!" cried the *San Antonio Express* in 1871, "are what San Antonio needs to make her a second Chicago." [2]

And even then, railroads were slowly on the way. That persistent little enterprise, the San Antonio and Mexican Gulf, had finally gone into operation from Lavaca to Victoria in 1866. Some government freighters began taking on their goods at Victoria, but since the larger tonnage was still going to Indianola, most wagon trains continued to run to that point. The S.A.&M.G. almost at once began to have financial and other problems. By one means and another, reducing service to triweekly, the road stayed in operation until 1870, when the United States government foreclosed to satisfy a $45,000 judgment. The government then promptly sold the line to Charles Morgan and Henry S. McComb. They announced plans both to extend the line westward and also to integrate it with their Indianola Railroad, which by fits and starts was at long last getting its line completed from that town up the coast some fourteen miles to join the S.A.&M.G. at Clarke, a few miles north of Port Lavaca. The sponsors built depot structures, shops, and yards at Indianola to connect with Morgan Line's wharfs. Morgan bought and rebuilt two locomotives in Mobile, had them brought overland to Victoria, and himself piloted one of them triumphantly into Indianola. [3]

The *Express* noted that from the railhead in Victoria to San Antonio the freight by wagons was now "nine bits [about $1.12] for ox-wagons and $1.25 for mule teams." But according to the *Express* the

Indianola *Bulletin* was reporting exorbitant charges for the thirty-odd-mile haul by rail up from the port to Victoria, leading that journal to conclude that Charles Morgan "seems to be absolutely devoid of all bowels of compassion." [4] In broader perspective the fact seems to be that Charles Morgan was in a very tight financial squeeze, needing all the cash flow he could muster. [5] When the consolidation of the two small lines was approved by the Texas legislature April 22, 1871, the new enterprise appeared under the ambitious title of Gulf Western Texas and Pacific Railroad Company. As Morgan's biographer says, "the name . . . left little doubt as to its purpose — to link the Gulf and Western Texas with the Pacific." [6]

The franchise gave Morgan authority to extend the line as far west as the Rio Grande, so he started at once on a roadbed up the east bank of the Guadalupe River from Victoria. By March 3, 1873, it had reached the settlement of Cuero, transforming it into a railroad town and county seat of DeWitt County. [7] But the line never got any further.

The larger rival port area of Galveston, along with Harrisburg and later Houston, had of course not been idle through all these years in getting railroad service extended into western Texas. Before the war, the Buffalo Bayou, Brazos and Colorado had completed its line as far as Alleytown, two and a half miles east of the Colorado River. [8] The people of Columbus, on the west bank of the Colorado, were bitterly disappointed when the builders chose not to try to bridge the Colorado. Instead, the railroad turned north up the east side of the Colorado toward La Grange and Austin.

The war brought all that to a halt. In the early days of Reconstruction, the B.B.B.&C., though beset with financial difficulties and twice sold and reorganized, did build on across the Colorado to establish a railhead at Columbus in 1870. In January 1870 Thomas W. Peirce entered upon the fortunes of that line in a move that ultimately assured the emergence and completion of the second transcontinental railroad, the Sunset Route and Southern Pacific.

Peirce was a Boston businessman who had developed wide-ranging interests in Texas long before the Civil War. By 1861 his firm had fifteen packet ships handling cotton, sugar, and hides between Galveston and Boston. As early as 1857 he had become a director of the Houston and Texas Central Railroad. [9] After the war he expanded his railroad interests by taking over the B.B.B.&C. in the belief that rail line would ultimately reach from the gulf to the Pacific.

For two years Peirce was only one of a number of associates in the new line, including Jonathan Barrett, also of Boston, and John Sealy, the guiding spirit of Galveston finance. By the end of 1872, however, Barrett had resigned and Peirce emerged as the dominant figure, a role which he maintained throughout the following decade.[10] His first and driving aim was to get the road built on through to San Antonio before some other road got there. The Gulf Western Texas and Pacific, nearing Cuero, and the International, building into Austin, both posed that threat.

The twelfth Texas legislature, on July 27, 1870, had given Barrett, Peirce, and associates a franchise to reorganize the B.B.B.&C. under a new name — Galveston, Harrisburg, and San Antonio Railway Company, with the privilege of extending the road to San Antonio and then to a terminus on the Rio Grande.[11]

Peirce organized a highly competent staff to push the process of expansion and new construction. Maj. James Converse was superintendent of construction for the new line west from Columbus, with Capt. R. G. Polk as his assistant. An outbreak of yellow fever in the construction camps caused delay at the outset, however, and it was April 1873 before the work actually began to move forward. After that, progress was rapid; not even the financial panic later that year delayed it. Schulenberg became the railhead in the summer of 1874.[12]

During those days of ferment, with three railroads all pointing toward San Antonio, the quaint old stagecoach and the wagon freighters were fair game for the public and the newspapers. In February of 1872 the *Express* in San Antonio offered this item:

> The mail came in from the Salado [six miles southeast of the city] all safe and sound but without any passengers or the driver. They had imprudently alighted for a moment at the creek and the horses didn't wait for them . . . even the horses realize the unsatisfaction with the mails . . .[13]

A few weeks later, noting that ten or twelve mule-drawn wagons laden with cotton had come through on their way to Mexico the editor sighed: "Wagons are a great improvement over the carts, but it will be a greater step forward when the snort of the Iron Horse shall wake up our western prairies."[14]

The capital city was soon to be served by the International, which through a merger with the Houston and Great Northern became the International and Great Northern. Galusha Aaron Grow, the Pennsyl-

vania politician, former Speaker of the United States House of Representatives, came to Texas in 1871 as new owner of the International
and presided over its expansion. [15]

Charles Morgan, who in a flush of prosperity in 1872 had bought
out H. S. McComb, now ran into a renewal of financial crisis. The
1875 Indianola storm cost him sorely; government support for extension beyond Cuero dried up; and by 1876 Morgan had given up his objective of reaching San Antonio by rail. Cuero remained "the *de facto*
western terminus of the G.W.T.&P. with wagon and coach connections to the interior." [16]

An Eastern journalist visiting San Antonio in 1874 was shocked
to find some merchants who actually were reluctant to see the railroads
arrive, fearing that they would lose the trade west of San Antonio. [17]
Nevertheless, the number of citizens being dragged unwillingly into
the Railroad Age must have been small. In the late summer of 1873,
the people of Bexar County had voted 1,566 to 46 favoring a subsidy
of $500,000 to Peirce if he got the G.H.&S.A. — the eventual Sunset
Route — operating into San Antonio by March 1875, with a bonus of
$50,000 for every month he could beat that deadline. Peirce fully ex-
pected in 1873 to achieve that objective, but the yellow-fever epidemic, the shortage of labor, and the inevitable hazards of keeping a
timetable in an unorganized society, conspired to frustrate him. [18]

Nevertheless, as the deadline month arrived and the railhead had
only reached Luling — fifty miles distant and named for Peirce's wife
— the San Antonio paper was not discouraged. The editor twitted the
railroad builder: " 'Doctor' Pierce [*sic*] is feeling our pulse. We hold
his paper for $200,000 [*sic*] and yet we are not happy. Our city has
railroad fever . . ." [19]

Despite the looming threat of railroads, seaborne freight through
Indianola, connecting with wagon freighters, remained dominant
throughout most of the 1870s. No complete log of maritime shipping
at Indianola survives, after two overwhelming hurricanes, but the *San
Antonio Express* published periodic reports as they became available. For
instance, the paper noted that in four days, from January 12, 1870,
through January 15, eleven ships had arrived at Indianola and that on
January 15 three ships had cleared that port. Again, from January 29
through February 5, seven ships had arrived and six had departed. [20]

The effect of that shipping at the port showed up in San Antonio
when the newspaper, in mid-February, 1870, observed that "freight

trains of all descriptions entered town from the coast, bringing goods from New York, New Orleans and other points. Other trains left the city for the upper country and Mexico."

Still, the restless towns of the interior felt keenly their isolation from the more modern facilities, railroads and highways, which other parts of the country were enjoying. Across the Great Plains to the north, the transcontinental Union Pacific railroad had been in operation to San Francisco for months, since the golden spike was driven at Promontory Point, Utah, on March 8, 1869. Wells Fargo and other express companies were rapidly shifting their movements to the rails, providing service that dazzled those parts of the country still dependent on stagecoaches and miry, unimproved roads.

In January of 1871, the *Express* editorialized:

> The *Indianola Bulletin* reports quite an accumulation of freight at that place, which would indicate that transportation is scarce. This will account to many of our merchants for the non-arrival of long-expected goods. Both San Antonio and Indianola are just hungry for a railroad.[21]

The freight-wagon operators were, of course, individual free agents; there was no instrument, by government fiat nor by associative agreement, for regulating their rates nor the way their wagons should be distributed to the various centers of commerce. Furthermore, the wagoneers were completely at the mercy of road conditions.

The public had long belabored the city fathers in San Antonio about the sorry state of the wooden bridge that spanned the river on Commerce Street — the only secure ingress to the business area from the world to the east. The state-appointed city administration, headed by Mayor W. C. A. Thielepape, did take one innovative action. The newspaper heralded the action on April 28, 1871: "We learned that Mr. Santleben has arrived in our city, in precedence of his train, which is bringing the new iron bridge. The bridge will be here next week, and will be promptly placed in position." [22]

Santleben tells of the project with much satisfaction, not only because he got an unusually large compensation for the contract, from Indianola to San Antonio, but also because he took delight in accomplishing difficult tasks. "Some of the material," he relates, "was forty feet long, and so heavy that it could be transported only on the largest wagons. Fourteen wagons were required to haul it, and I received a total of $3,250 for freighting it." [23]

Gustave Schleicher, the German civil engineer and railroad promoter who later served in Congress, erected the new structure where Houston Street crossed the river.[24] The opening of this sturdy-structured bridge, the first iron span of any size in western Texas, contributed to the development of Houston Street, which had been a mere muddy lane. It soon became a major business artery.

In 1871 a resurgence of cotton purchases by moneyed interests in Mexico brought a new aspect to some of the freight movements. The *Express* reported in October that "We noticed a long train of Mexican carts yesterday . . . and ascertained that they were destined for Seguin for cotton and that they had come from Mexico [to transport it back] to that land of prickly pear, revolutions, and specie dollars." But those "specie dollars" from Mexico remained the exciting flux that kept the channels of commerce running. August Santleben had continued to haul frequent shipments of specie out of Chihuahua, reaching his all-time peak in 1876 with a load of $350,000 in silver cartwheels. As early as 1871, the port of Indianola was glowing with the effects of the trade. Its newspaper reported in March that a ship departing for New Orleans "carried $96,000 in bullion. When it is taken into consideration that this valuable freight was brought all the way from Mexico on wagons and without a guard, it will convince our Northern friends that Texas is in a quiet and peaceable condition." [25]

Big trouble brewing on the frontier might have made that claim of peacefulness somewhat exaggerated, but the wagon trains still crawled up and down the long road, and in increasing volume. In early November of 1871 the San Antonio newspaper found that "Commerce Street is encumbered with wagons from the coast bearing Christmas supplies" and by the end of that month: "Our merchants, the clerks and assistants are literally overrun with business and freight is coming in and shipments are to be made for the holidays."[26] Main Street led south from Commerce Street to Castroville Road, turning westward toward Mexico. In December the newspaper found that area blocked with Mexican carts carrying cotton from Central Texas. At this point the editor raised the cry in his columns, evidently an echo from astonished spectators on the street: "and still they come!"[27]

By October of 1873, steam trains were running regularly into Cuero from Indianola and Port Lavaca on the Gulf Western Texas and Pacific, and freight could be delivered to San Antonio by wagon from Cuero for seventy-five cents per 100 pounds.[28]

It was plain that the wagon freighters still carried the stuff of commerce. For instance, on one day, July 23, 1876, Ramón Hernandez's train of ten wagons left for Fort Bliss; Severiano Calderon's train of ten wagons pulled out for Fort Stockton; and Maximo Cardenas's eight wagons followed, bound for Fort Davis.[29]

When the indefatigible writer-artist team of Edward King and James Wells Champney visited San Antonio in 1874, King marveled at the frenetic activity of the wagon-freighting business:

Most of the houses and blocks in Commerce and other principal streets are two stories high — sometimes three — and there are some fine shops — one or two of them being veritable museums of traffic. It is from these shops that the assortments are made up which toil across the plains to the garrisons and to Mexico; and a wagon-train, loaded with a "varied assortment," contains almost everything known to trade. Through the narrow streets every day clatter the mule-teams, their . . . drivers shouting frantically at them as they drag civilized appliances toward Mexico. These wagoneers lead a wild life of almost constant danger and adventure, but they are fascinated with it, and can rarely be induced to give it up.[30]

Hungry as he might have been for the coming of the Iron Horse, the flood of wagon traffic caused the reporter in September 1876 to evoke once more the old greeting: ". . . And still they come! is the morning cry as trains of freight wagons arrive in the city." [31]

But the great day was close at hand. San Antonio would have its railroad.

The prospects had seemed precarious throughout 1875 and most of 1876. Colonel Peirce had failed to claim his golden fleece in March 1875; the half-million-dollar subsidy voted by Bexar County to be paid the G.H.&S.A. if it reached San Antonio by the given date was forfeited. His railhead was still between Luling and Kingsbury, at least fifty miles out of the Alamo City when the deadline expired. But Peirce's magnetic personality, the steady progress westward he continued to make, and the tantalizing shrinking of the remaining gap led the people of San Antonio and Bexar County to listen to the colonel's final plea for assistance.

Bexar County called another election for January 29, 1876, this time to give the railroad $300,000 upon completion into San Antonio, of which $100,000 could be advanced when work had progressed to the point that the county officials could be assured of final realization.

The long history of failures and of shady dealings on the part of many railroad promoters had by now made many citizens wary of new propositions. When the ballots were counted after the election, 2,694 people had voted for the bond issue, a majority of 58. By that narrow margin the Railroad Age was assured for West Texas, because Colonel Peirce and his associates desperately needed the cash to finish their job.[32]

The railroad had other help, of course. Between 1873 and 1877 the State of Texas had granted the Galveston, Harrisburg & San Antonio 1,432,960 acres of its public lands toward construction of the 128 miles of road from Columbus to San Antonio.[33] Rejoicing landowners along the route, speculators, and promoters of new settlements donated practically all of the right-of-way between the two towns, plus about $40,000 in cash.[34] For a brief time in 1876 the last interim railhead was at Marion, a village which today is virtually on the edge of Randolph Air Base, a major Air Corps-Air Force facility in the twentieth century.

That last-gasp head-of-the-rails had its traditional fling. For instance, a report datelined Marion related that

> two men, Truthfull James and Joe Somebody, set up a saloon in a four-by-six shanty and . . . employed a man to tend bar for them. The second day after their opening the gentlemanly (?) barkeeper fled for parts unknown, bearing in his trousers pocket all the collateral of the firm, who were thus disenabled from continuing the calling they had assumed. The place of business is now dull and dreary looking.[55]

In December 1876, Colonel Peirce and some of his staff entered San Antonio, with considerable fanfare, to present their credentials for the suggested advance of funds. On the twenty-first of that month a team of county and city officials went with the colonel and his retinue to inspect the status of the work as it crossed the Cibolo Creek only twelve miles out of town. The colonel got his $100,000 to lubricate the closing of that final link.[36]

A month later, in the grip of winter, the *Express* observed: "The poor teamsters, bad weather is worst on them. The roads between here and Marion are as bad as they could be, and there is not a particle of grass within a half mile on either side of the road!"[37] And that was about the last time the papers had to write about the hardships of wagon freighting east of San Antonio.

By February 7 the newspaper could announce that "the 19th is to be the day! Visitors from New York, Galveston, Houston, and Austin are to come on the first train,"[38] and the town was launched on a dizzying whirl of preparations for the greatest gala San Antonio had ever seen.

Before his death in 1870, Sam Maverick had set aside land at the junction of Austin and Sherman streets, to be donated as the site for depot and lots when the railroad did reach the city.[39] That farsighted man, who had worked toward getting a railroad into San Antonio since the last of the 1840s, did not live to see rails west of the Colorado on any main trunk line. But when the railhead, coming in town from the northeast, stopped at Sherman Street to erect a temporary depot and to lay out yards, on nine acres of land the Maverick family donated, the elder Maverick's vision paid off. The station, nine blocks north of the present Southern Pacific depot, attracted a boom in building all along Austin Street, and the Maverick properties there boomed with it. Sam Maverick's son Willie put up a lumberyard and store building at the terminal.[40]

On February 15 the first freight train pulled into the yards, with Colonel Peirce in the cab, heaving fuel under the boiler, alongside John Sullivan, the engineer. August Santleben participated in the opening and unloading of the first freight cars at the temporary depot.[41]

By the morning of February 19, Alamo Plaza was festooned with streamers and Chinese lanterns, focusing upon the balcony of the Menger Hotel, where the speakers' stand was set up. A trainload of excursionists was steaming toward the city from Galveston and Harrisburg. To give it proper welcome, Colonel Peirce had brought into San Antonio, just ahead of time, the first private car ever seen in Texas. The *Express* editor, as one of the guests invited to board the car, described it as

> one of that class known to railroad men as a President's car . . . of the very finest make such as railroad magnates choose, taking the best in their travels. It was built by the St. Louis and San Francisco Railroad Company, having every attachment necessary to convenient and comfortable travel, such as a state room, drawing room, sleeping berths, kitchen, and provision apartment. The engine that pulled the train bore the name of Barrett, after Jonathan Barrett, one of the trustees of the road.[42]

In one bound, the sturdy pioneers of San Antonio, as they stepped up to the carpeted opulence of Colonel Peirce's private car, moved into the Railroad Age, abandoning forever the cramped and jolting journeys on stagecoaches, the plodding wagons that brought their freight. The men who took that historic step at noon on February 19, 1877, should be rescued from the oblivion of a century-old newspaper story. They were, per the editor's listing:

> Messrs. [Harden B.] Adams, [Frederick Jacob] Waelder, [Major] Minter, J. V. Dashiell, W. B. Young, N. O. [Nate] Green, [Willie H.] Maverick, detailed to meet the excursionists; with Messrs. Sweet of the *Herald,* Hauschke of the *Frei Presse,* and the editor of this paper [Frank Grice].[43]

Others on this car as it moved out toward Marion included, of course, "the hero of the occasion," Colonel Peirce,[44] with his chief engineer of the road, Maj. H. B. Andrews, other staff members, and several army officers.

The westbound excursion train from Galveston pulled into Marion at 4:30; Peirce's private car was cut out of the eastbound train and assembled with the other, after suitable greetings. Aboard the visitors' train were Texas Governor R. B. Hubbard and virtually his entire staff of state officers, including Adj. Gen. William B. Steele, a San Antonian. Also on board were the Galveston mayor and eight aldermen, plus 180 other visitors from that city; the mayor of Austin with eighty from there, and a scattering of representation from other towns. Houston was not mentioned. The *Express* writer painstakingly recorded the names of more than 250 of these guests. Not one woman was on the list.

When the train chugged into the eastern environs of San Antonio, the visitors saw a remarkable gathering along the right-of-way. As remembered by Capt. R. G. Polk, assistant engineer of construction for the Galveston, Harrisburg, & San Antonio:

> The advent of the train created unusual interest among the people for miles around and in the country tributary to San Antonio even to the Rio Grande. They came to see it by all kinds of conveyances, from the meek and patient burro to Mexican carts drawn by oxen yoked by their horns, on horseback and afoot. They assembled on each side of the railway tracks, on the hills east of the city, the aged and gray, children in arms, gazing in wonder at the puffing locomotive and the train of cars following.[45]

The members of the official excursion party debouched upon the new platforms at the temporary San Antonio depot, only to be overwhelmed by a mass of San Antonians estimated at eight thousand.

Plans for a speech of welcome by Mayor James H. French had to be abandoned; all the welcoming party could manage was to hand the principal guests into the waiting carriages and get the procession up-town under way.

Night had fallen; torch-bearers led the parade, followed by an army band, infantry, the Alamo Rifles, and cavalry, then the guests in their carriages, followed by thousands of marching citizens.

The news writer admitted that the scene in front of the Menger Hotel, with 8,000 folk packed beneath the lanterns and torches, "beg-gard description," but he tried anyhow, his rhapsodies mounting to a noble climax: "The bows and bars of brilliancy threw their shining glamour over a dense throng of the fair of San Antonio fair." In that setting Mayor J. H. French appeared upon the balcony to introduce Governor Hubbard, who, in a "brief but eloquent" address, sought to do justice to the occasion. The racing pencil of the reporter caught florid phrases:

> The sections of East and West had already been bound together by love, by the ties of citizenship, but this was a consummation by iron arms drawing the people more closely together as regards the in-terests of commerce as well as of feeling — cemented, never to be di-vided . . .
>
> San Antonio was at last connected by rail with the settled re-gions of the East, and it was the great duty of the hour to develop her section . . . We could rejoice upon the near approach of that day when Texas would have 2,000,000 of people, and when it would be rated with New York and Pensylvania as one of the most populous States in the Union. Our sections being connected would also bring us together in blood. The bright-eyed boys of East Texas would find sweethearts here, and marry the rosy-cheeked maidens of the West . . .

Mayor French then introduced the Honorable Galusha A. Grow, former Speaker of the House in Congress, entrepreneur extraordinary, and president of the International and Great Northern Railroad, still building toward San Antonio. This colorful gentleman was perhaps not so astonishing in his rhetoric as the governor — or perhaps the re-porter's hand had become cramped — for the newspaper notes were more succinct on the second address, which focused largely upon the thought that

> . . . Ours was perhaps the largest city on the continent today that had remained so long without railroad connections, and upon the ex-

treme Western bordere of the Nation, we had waited long and pa-
tiently, but not in vain, as the present demonstration proved, for the
completion of a railroad to our city.

At the conclusion of the long day of celebration, "the assemblage,
slow to dissolve, wore away by small degrees, all returning to their
homes most perfectly satisfied with the events of the day and hour." [46]

[17]

Twilight for
the Wagons

Four days after San Antonio's great railroad celebration, the *Express* editor had had time to pull back and get a little perspective on the new age his part of the world had entered. He wrote that

> . . . no longer does the weary freight wagon crawl into San Antonio bearing its few hundred pounds of weight. But instead the iron horse now rushes in upon us, comfortably bearing hundreds of persons and tons of burden . . . We visited the railroad depot last evening, and while there, in steamed a long train of cars laden with all manner of freight. [It] has been deposited in the freight depot and [many] were busily engaged . . . distributing it to the respective consignees, the charge being 35 cents per thousand pounds.[1]

This overnight transformation in the handling of goods from the East did not mean that wagon freighting was killed off at once toward the West. The very next day after the reflections above, the *Express* remarked, "Strangers who see trains of wagons filled with hides [might have] . . . a belief that all the cattle creation of the Southwest has been put through a skinning process lately." [2] Much of this traffic in hides came from northern Mexico, where there was still no railroad service to tap the markets for live beef.

286

And, of course, for almost five years to come the merchants of Chihuahua City continued to need their goods. Though they could now get them off the train at San Antonio, Chihuahua City was still more than 700 miles away, and only wagons could close that gap.

At the same time, the constant pressure from business to speed up deliveries across West Texas and into Mexico had to be accommodated. The first step in that direction was the opening of the so-called new Military Road, in a nearly direct line from the first crossing of the Devil's River to Fort Davis. This could cut out the big loop which proceeded around by Howard's Well, Live Oak Creek at Fort Lancaster, the Pecos River itself up to Pontoon Crossing, then west to Tunas Spring, Comanche Springs at Fort Stockton, the León water holes, and Leoncíta Spring before reaching the Burgess Springs at the site of present-day Alpine — all for the sake of access to those successive water holes.

This New Military Road is still called with good reason "Bullis' Road" by old-timers in the Big Bend.[3] It was a great time-and-miles saver indeed — that is, in a wet season when San Francisco Creek and Sanderson Draw had plenty of water holes. But in dry seasons it was useless for slow wagon freighters, who had to have water nearly every twenty miles, with perhaps one or two longer stretches if they were separated by several days. The general route of the road was developed by Lt. John L. Bullis in his expeditions across the Big Bend during the 1870s, probably most definitively in an assignment between May 1 and the fall of 1879. Capt. W. R. Livermore and his assistant, F. E. Butterfield, both engineers, followed in late 1879 and early 1880, establishing astronomically determined positions to which the new road was tied.[4]

The fact should not be forgotten that the New Military Road, scouted out by Bullis and engineered by Livermore, laid down the basic route which made possible only three years later the transcontinental railway and a succession of highways which have followed it. At no point across the Big Bend is the railroad more than five miles from the soldiers' road.[5]

For those who have no opportunity to follow the route of that road on Livermore's map, a few landmarks should be noted. After leaving the springs at the head of San Felipe Creek, always the hinge where the Chihuahua and El Paso Road began to swing northwestward, the new route crossed the Devil's River a mile or so below the ford established by Whiting in 1849. Here, just as the later gravel highway of

the early 1900s did, and all the successively broader and straighter
ones which have followed, the Military Road struck off across the high
rocky uplands, cut by deep arroyos, which the early wagon trains had
never been able to negotiate. When it reached the canyon of the Pecos,
it descended the canyon wall on a long slant, forded the rock-bottomed
Pecos within a mile of its junction with the Rio Grande, and climbed
back out again up the cliffs.[6]

Only twelve or fifteen miles beyond, where the Pecos swings
back very closely to the Rio Grande, Bullis's three black Seminole
scouts had won their Congressional Medals of Honor a few years earlier, saving their leader's life. To the west, on the Rio Bravo itself,
was Eagle Nest Crossing, where in a steep defile a creek bearing the
same name runs down to the river and makes possible a horseback
crossing. It was here at Eagle's Nest that part of Wildcat's Seminole
tribe crossed into Mexico on their home-seeking trek down from the
reservation in the 1840s.[7] The rowdy railroad camp called Vinegaroon was to spring up here on the east bank of Eagle Nest Creek
within a couple of years, to be succeeded almost at once by Roy
Bean's Langtry on to the west a little way.

But in 1880 there was nothing there except the golden eagle sailing the updrafts of wind on the Rio Grande Canyon, and a *tinaja* called
Coe's Spring in the rocky basin where the trail circled the head of Eagle's Nest Creek.

From there the road led thirty miles from Eagle's Nest to Meyer's
Spring — a day and a half by laden wagon. As always, water was the
controlling factor; Bullis had had to divert the road some miles north
of the shortest course just to get the precious water at Meyer's Spring
— there was no other dependable source within a long day's travel.
Then came a dreary march westward, past the site of present-day Dry-
den, until the road descended into broad, grassy-bottomed Sanderson
Canyon.

Pleasant water holes were scattered along this huge drain in the
right time of the year, but in other months it might be totally dry and
impracticable for mule-drawn vehicles, while at still other times sudden floods came washing down the canyon, rendering it altogether impassable for weeks at a time. Only the drilling of deep wells made possible the ultimate establishment of the town of Sanderson, some years
later, as a division point on the Southern Pacific; the huge, wooden-
wheeled Eclipse windmills that supplied the railroad's water tanks
stood spinning there beside the road until late in the 1930s.[8]

Bullis's road continued on up Sanderson Canyon until it played out, then took a tributary called Maxon's Creek and followed it due west to Maxon's Spring, at its head and very close to the present Southern Pacific right-of-way. Then, in extremely rough country, it threaded up Peña Negra Creek, across Peña Blanca, leaving Camel's Hump or Horse Mountain off to the south, and finally to Peña Colorado (Rainbow Bluff or Rainbow Springs).

Col. Ben H. Grierson, commanding the Headquarters District of the Pecos at Fort Concho, had on August 13, 1879, directed the commanding officer at Fort Stockton to move two companies of the Twenty-fifth Infantry to Peña Colorado and establish there a cantonment to guard that section of the new road being developed. They built adobe-and-stone huts, roofed with grass and adobe, taking advantage of the fine springs beneath the novaculite ledge which crowns the cliff and gives the place its name.[9]

Lt. Charles Judson Crane commanded one of the two companies of the Twenty-fourth Infantry which relieved the original two companies on July 6, 1880. He remarked years later in his reminiscences that there was not a single dwelling on the 150 miles of road between San Felipe Springs at Del Rio and Peña Colorado, when he traveled through there in 1880.[10]

Beyond Peña Colorado, the road came out on open antelope plains, with Iron Mountain and the Glass Mountains to the east and the Del Norte Mountains capped with Mount Ord to the west, leading up in a grand sweep to the juniper groves, which at that time graced Altuda Pass. In that pass, as Lieutenant Echols had found when he felt his way through with his camels in 1860, one can look out to the northwest and see the unfailing landmark of the Davis Mountains area: Mitre Peak, standing up sharp and clean like a bishop's mitre. But first, for water, the road had to go down by Ramsey's Draw and reach Burgess Springs.[11] There it rejoined, at last, the Chihuahua Road coming from Fort Stockton and the León water holes.

At that time, another road was making its own shortcut to Presidio. It was known as the "Cut-Off Road." No one knows for sure who laid it out, though Lieutenant Echols followed some of that same general route with his camels, out of Camp Stockton, in 1859 and 1860. Travis Roberts, who has spent a long life on lands that lie athwart the Cut-Off Road south of Marathon, said:

I was told by an old Mexican whose mother was raised at Presidio, that she had told him the cut-off road from Presidio to Fort Stockton, she thought was started by a few travelers around 1850. Perhaps to the tiny nearby settlement of St. Gall, since Fort Stockton was not established until the late 1850's.[12]

Its purpose seems apparent from a look at Livermore's Military Map of the Texas Frontier, where it shows up clearly: it would save some miles by not going farther north than necessary, but, more importantly, it would save taking a heavy wagon up over mile-high Paisano Pass before going down into Alamito Canyon.

This Cut-Off Road left the main Chihuahua Road and started across the prairies a little west of due south, out of Fort Stockton, just as Echols and Hartz had done with their camels in 1859, and just as U.S. Highway 385 does today. The road entered the eastern foothills of the Glass Mountains, leaving Sierra Madero to the left and Six Shooter Draw to the right. It came through those hills and down over the escarpment, no doubt as Highway 385 does today, into the wide flat known as Big Canyon, which drifts gently toward Marathon. Of course Marathon wasn't there at all then, but only five miles on southwest from its future site was Peña Colorado, or Rainbow Springs, with its good water. In later years the army post, and on the hill across the springs the Halff Bros. Store, made a cozy little settlement.[13]

The statement can confidently be made that the section of the Cut-Off Road below Rainbow Springs was by all odds the loneliest, wildest, probably most picturesque wagon trail on the entire southwestern frontier. It struck almost directly southwest from the Springs' arched bluff, aiming at Del Norte Gap twenty miles away across Maravillas Draw. This huge draw seldom boasted any water holes in that section of its long course down to the Rio Grande, but if the freighters coming north from Mexico were short of water, they and other wagonmen knew Monument Spring, about ten miles before reaching Peña Colorado. At the base of a long escarpment bordering the road on the north side, a dry arroyo — Monument Creek — breaks through. A half-mile up the rocky bed of that draw, Monument Spring trickles from under a ledge to provide a series of shallow ponds of fine water before the flow disappears in the thirsty desert. The drovers would unhitch their teams from the wagons, down on the flats, and lead the mules up to that providential water. It was the first dependable water source from far beyond Del Norte Gap.[14]

For freighters going *toward* Mexico, after they crossed the wide, rocky, and dry flats of Maravillas Draw, the road climbed up to Del Norte Pass, a wind-gap in the Cochran Mountains barrier. It is steep and narrow, with 5,500-foot hills bulking on either side of the pass. The road emerges quickly, though, to open country beyond. The pass was the key to getting across to the Alamito Creek country. Leaving the dark mass of Elephant Mountain to the north, the trail ran down long slopes to Calamity Creek Wash, where there was no water. But five miles beyond, at the mouth of Dark Canyon, with Butcherknife Hill standing as a landmark across Calamity Wash, was Chopwind Spring, as essential to that road as Howard's Well was to the old main road.

Still on a general southwest bearing, the road skirted below Turney Peak and McKinney Mountain, on the north, with Straddlebug Mountain to the left, until upon turning due west across Crystal Creek it entered a pass which Livermore's map called "Blunt's Gap" (sometimes called Jordan's Gap). This lay between Church Mountain on the north and Cerro Boludo on the south. The road emerged from that pass into the broad valley of Alamito Creek, striking the main Chihuahua Road at Peñitas, a mile or so above the springs at the Davis *rancho,* where the thirsty traveler might be favored with a touch of native peach brandy if he found Old Man Davis in a mellow mood.

When the railroads made it to West Texas and the need for wagon-freighting tapered off, most of the Cut-Off Road fell into disuse. The section from the new rail siding at Marathon through Peña Colorado and Del Norte Gap did serve as part of the Marathon-Terlingua road until the late 1930s. From the Terlingua mines, heavy covered wagons of the Conestoga type carried out quicksilver, shipped in seventy-pound clay flasks bedded down in hay, to meet the Southern Pacific at Marathon. Even today, on the Catto-Gage ranch seven or eight miles from Peña Colorado, far out on gravelly flats one may see the twin wagon-wheel ruts of the Cut-Off Road pointing faintly but clearly to Del Norte Pass, a notch on the horizon, and to Presidio beyond.

Despite the imminence of railroad linkage in the late 1870s, the freight still had to move by wagon, and the hub city of that commerce, San Antonio, was feeling the pressure in physical terms. A typical wagon train moved with 100 to 120 mules, or oxen, under harness, and a reserve *remuda* of forty or more. If there were but ten trains within the environs of the town at one time — arriving, unloading, moving out, or simply standing by for the next trip — that alone meant upwards of 2,000 big, hungry beasts, demanding forage, demanding water, and burdening the streets and corrals of the town with their manure. But there were, in addition, of course, all the animals kept by small carters with two to half a dozen each; plus the livery stables; the army, still based downtown; and every homeowner who aspired to his own means of transportation — another couple of thousand, certainly, maybe 5,000 altogether.

This situation, incomprehensible to the urban dweller in the latter half of the twentieth century, was so much taken for granted then as to draw no comment. It nevertheless had its obvious effects upon the olfactory sense, upon the insect problem, and, in a city with minimal or no sewer systems, upon surface drainage. The lovely San Antonio River wound its shaded way through the downtown area, where the best homes still had canvas-walled bath-houses erected in the water, which must have been lethal traps indeed.

About the only recorded reaction to the overpopulation in draft animals, however, was impatience with congestion on the streets. Commerce Street was then, and so remained until the 1890s, hardly half as wide as now, and the somewhat crooked thoroughfare was still unpaved.[15] Main Street, running south from Commerce Street past San Fernando Church to the principal area of wagon yards and livery stables, was equally inadequate. Small wonder, then, that the *Express* in November 1875 noted a collision and resulting tangle between a Mexican cart and a ten-mule prairie schooner on Main Street, observing sourly that "carts are a nuisance since controlling oxen on our narrow streets is a difficult job."[16]

The town somehow transcended these problems. The journalist Edward King was certainly a seasoned traveler, yet he had been able to say in 1874, after several weeks' observation:

> San Antonio now has the reputation of being the healthiest town on the American continent . . . The local proverb says, "If you wish to die here, you must go somewhere else." . . . So certain are consumptives and other invalids to be cured in the city and surrounding region, that retreats and quiet residences for people to enshrine themselves in during recovery are going up in all quarters."[17]

Salubrious or not to the everyday citizen, the route of the Chihuahua Road remained subject to catastrophes of nature, from such mass disasters as the hurricane at Indianola to lonely accidents made the more poignant in a single life. Describing the braking system on heavy freight wagons, August Santleben had mentioned that "occasionally accidents happened to a brake and the heavily loaded wagon would become uncontrollable, with the result that mules and driver were often crushed to death under the wheels." [18] Perhaps one such tragedy the freighter had in mind was that of the devoted family man Don Mariano Frescas, on Edward Froboese's line.

Somewhere in the Big Bend country "halfway between Texas and Chihuahua," Don Mariano was driving a twelve-mule wagon one frosty morning in the winter of 1877. As the train descended a steep hill, a mule slipped on the thickly frosted rocks. The fall jerked the reins from Fresca's hands, the brakes would not hold on the icy road, and the wagon went out of control. Don Mariano was thrown from his seat; as he fell to the road, one of the ponderous iron-shod wheels passed over his body.

When the pandemonium of thrashing, screaming mules and careening wagon had been quieted, mourning fellow drivers prepared the crushed form of their comrade for burial. The *carreros* scraped a grave at the top of a rocky hill by the roadside and laid him to rest under a large, rough cross bound together from small branches. Flintstones bordered the grave and a board from the broken wagon said only "El Compañero Frescas" — Frescas, Our Companion — to remind the passing drivers on their journeys. [19]

During a whole decade following the Civil War, the port city of Indianola had moved steadily ahead. True, the railroad from Galveston and Houston, building out toward San Antonio, was taking an increasing percentage of trade, but the gross volume of freight was increasing even faster, so that Indianola was still enjoying growth in business. Morgan's little rail line, connecting his shipping docks with the trunk road to Victoria, for a while strengthened the port's competitive position.

There had been a portent of disaster on October 3, 1871, when an onshore gale caused the tide to rise higher in the streets than anyone ever remembered. Along with the tides came a fire that, fanned by the gale, ran out of control, gutting a block or more of buildings. The steamer *Mississippi* ran aground, though she was later salvaged; most of her large cargo of goods was ruined. [20] This foretaste of what a storm might do was quickly forgotten as Indianola forged ahead.

From about 1,500 at the end of the Civil War, the population by 1875 had grown to more than 6,000. Although the huge plants for slaughtering cattle to salvage their "hides and tallow' had seen their best days, as live cattle moved up the new mid-continent trails in greater volume to railheads connecting with eastern markets, brisk business still flourished at the plants for canning the giant sea turtle, for killing and dressing turkeys, and for experimental marketing of canned beef. Confident predictions held that Indianola, with its salubrious climate, would become as popular a resort town as Galveston.

In mid-September, 1875, "at the height of her prosperity," Indianola was crammed with visitors, court officials, and subpoenaed witnesses attending a district court trial growing out of the shooting of Billy Sutton and Gabe Slaughter in the Taylor-Sutton feud, only a year earlier. On Wednesday, the fifteenth of the month,

> the storm which was known to have been gathering in this latitude, and which had been prognosticated by the heavy banks of clouds that for some days had hung over this section, commenced, a heavy northeast wind being its most prominent distinguishing feature, accompanied by an almost steady rain. It was early noticed that the bay was being rapidly filled, but . . . no uneasiness was felt . . . the wind, which had increased to a gale, was confidently expected to decrease in violence as the sun went down, and the citizens of Indianola slept undisturbed . . .[21]

Far from abating, the storm by the next morning had steadily increased in violence to true hurricane intensity, called in those days a "cyclone." All the eastern side of the town lay submerged as the tide ran in angry torrents across Main Street and began to fill up the prairie areas behind the port.[22]

> By noon the water had increased to several feet in depth, and was pouring through the cross streets like a mill race. It now was evident that there no longer existed any hope to save property from destruction. Life, and life alone . . . was worth struggling for . . . The current rendered it impossible to retain footing for an instant without assistance, and life lines were stretched along Main Street, across the torrents. Boats, loaded with women and children, were drawn by ropes up Main Street to the upper part of the town, which was thought to be the safest.[23]

As the storm increased in intensity, heavy timbers broke loose from the wharves and the shipways and came surging through the town on the flood. Before the afternoon was over, most of the buildings along the bay front had succumbed to the storm; it soon became clear that even those on the highest ground, which were now crowded with refugees, could not long withstand the growing pressure.

In what the *Victoria Advocate* called the "Night of Horror" which followed, one building after another, filled with terrified refugees, either collapsed or broke loose from its foundations, under the attack of wind, wave, and floating timbers.

> The water was filled with buildings in all stages of demolition, hurrying rapidly westward into the Bayou and out on the prairie beyond. Clinging desperately among the debris, and with it being swept away, were dozens of persons who had been precipitated into the flood by the falling of the houses they occupied . . . Near the lower part of the reef one building carried with it thirty-one people, men, women, and children, and with it were carried into and across Powderhorn Lake. Eleven only survive, leaving twenty-one [*sic*] to be added to the list of missing.[24]

After midnight the tragedy was compounded when the eye of the hurricane passed, the direction of the gale shifting to drive the impounded waters, built up inland, racing back across the stricken town.

> The immense power of the cyclone and terrible rush of water at this stage can be comparatively judged by the fact that the water which consumed eighteen hours in its passage to the west, required only about one-third as long to return . . . Buildings which had stoutly withstood the deluge from the east were swept into the bay by the returning water . . . Many persons were carried out into the bay clinging to pieces of the wreck or on hastily constructed rafts.[25]

The morning of September 17 dawned upon a scene of utter desolation as the storm blew itself out. Only eight buildings remained intact in the town where 6,000 persons had dwelt. Half a dozen steamers and large sailing vessels had been driven ashore and lay broken up, and dozens of smaller craft lay scattered far inland. A party which came down horseback on Sunday from Victoria found the railroad line broken and scattered, the entire roadbed, ties, and track in places wiped out with whole sections of steel rail thrown a half-mile or more into the lake by the ferocity of the tides. Distraught survivors picked their way among the debris, searching for some sign of their lost ones, whole long rows of bodies lay in one of the remaining buildings, gathered there in hopes of identification before mass burial.[26]

The *Advocate* assembled for its account of the disaster on September 24 a list of 123 persons already known dead or still missing at that time. As more facts came to hand, 270 bodies were finally counted and estimates of the death toll ranged upward to more than 300.[27]

To a degree, the town tried to rebuild and come back. Morgan constructed new docking facilities, particularly to accommodate the beef shipping industry. As early as October 11, barely three weeks after the storm was over, the Cuero newspaper reported that the G.W.T.&P. railroad from the coast had been repaired; that there were once more three steamers per week into Indianola, and that "the town is crowded with mule wagons and oxcarts bringing in cotton and hides and carrying out freight for San Antonio and intermediate towns." [28]

But the bulk of the survivors were afraid to return to that town on its vulnerable, low-lying shell reef. Before the port could fully regain its vitality, the trunk line of the Sunset Route had been completed into San Antonio from Galveston, and Indianola's days of glory were over.

S. G. Reed, whose father was killed in the final Indianola storm of 1886, says "Of the many ghost towns in Texas, none lived longer, none throve better, none died as tragic a death as Indianola." [29]

Beyond doubt, the man who entered Texas as an infant in a lifeboat from a sinking immigrant ship looked back with most pride upon his years along the hard, lonely roads of the frontier. August Santleben claimed that between 1865 and 1880 he "traveled a greater number of miles as a mail contractor and when staging and freighting than any other man living."

To back up this claim, he broke his career down into three periods. From January 1, 1866, until June 20, 1867, as a mail contractor between San Antonio and Eagle Pass he drove seventy-eight round-trip weekly stage trips of about 335 miles each — or 25,740 miles. From August 1, 1867, until June 30, 1869, he drove the stage from Eagle Pass to Monterrey: forty-eight round trips of 1,050 miles each — or 50,400 miles.

From 1869 until 1880 — most of it before 1877 — Santleben ran his train of freight wagons from Texas seaports to Chihuahua City, as well as to frontier posts in Texas. He believed that a reasonable estimate of his travels during this time, from the seat of his ambulance, his freight wagon, or the saddle, would be 50,000 miles. These three enterprises added up to over 126,000 miles of hard going.

The value of freight that he hauled ran into the millions of dollars, and he also claimed that he hauled more hard money out of Mexico during that period, on stages and wagons, than any other person, the majority of the specie going to firms in Europe.

Though I risked my life continually on these travels and jeopardized all the property I possessed, besides much that was entrusted to me by others, I generally reaped a reward that compensated me for all the dangers and hardships I encountered. Although I sustained many losses in various ways on my own account . . . I can truthfully say that not one of my customers who entrusted money and merchandise to my care, or the Federal government under my mail contracts, ever lost a cent through my negligence.[30]

Thirty years after his last freighting trip to Chihuahua, August Santleben was a widower, his wife Mary Anna having died on April 11, 1911. Of his seven children, including two who were adopted, only little Charlotta, who made the last trip with him to Chihuahua, had preceded the mother in death. His autobiography had been published the year before and was well-received; his friends were legion; his children were about him.

At eleven o'clock on a mild September evening he had stepped outside his bedroom, at his home on North Flores Street, and was standing on the second-story gallery as he removed his outside clothing to prepare for bed. Some coins fell from his pocket; he stooped to recover them and tripped on his clothing, struck the railing on the porch, and tumbled head first to the ground fifteen feet below. He lay there two hours before his family heard his groans.

Attended by Dr. Frank Paschal, whose practice in Ciudad Chihuahua he had so much admired almost forty years before, August Santleben lingered through alternating periods of lucidness and coma from Thursday evening until death came from brain concussion on Monday morning, September 11, 1911.

Among his pallbearers were former Mayor Marshall Hicks and Judge Netterville Devine, who had hunted buffalo with him along the meadows of the Concho River in 1874. After services at the First Presbyterian Church, he was laid to rest September 19 in the Odd Fellows cemetery on East Commerce Street.[31]

The man who had so successfully guarded millions of dollars of other people's money across the hazards of the Chihuahua desert was ironically brought low at his home by a handful of his own small change.

[18]

End of
the Trail

Any traveler in 1880 or early 1881 on the El Paso Road west of
the Davis Mountains might well have been caught up by the last
bloody convulsions of the Indian wars in Texas. During those months
the Apaches killed two stage drivers, three passengers including a retired general, two immigrants by wagon train, at least a dozen soldiers, and an equal number of Mexican sheepherders, farmers, and
other citizens along the Quitman reaches of the Rio Grande.

The killers may have been a remnant squad of Victorio's Mimbres
Apaches who split off into Texas while Victorio and the main body of
his tribe were being harried to extermination in Mexico in the fall of
1880. Whoever they were, these fugitive marauders were finally
stopped for all time, when Texas Rangers from two companies of the
Frontier Battalion, under Capt. George Wythe Baylor, caught up with
them in the Diablo Mountains, south of Guadalupe Peak, at dawn on
January 29, 1881.[1]

At the time those last Indians died on the bluffs of the Sierra Diablo early in 1881, each of the three principal Texas towns along the old
wagon road west — Indianola, San Antonio, and El Paso — was in a
different state of flux.

An itinerant correspondent for the *San Antonio Weekly Express,*

calling himself Hans Mickle, had visited Indianola a year earlier and
forwarded a long, melancholy description of the town as it stood then,
four years after the first devastating hurricane. He found unmended
evidences of the storm on every hand, hulks of buildings standing vacant, deep bayous scoured by the storm cutting across unbridged principal streets. He estimated that of 6,000 people who had lived in the
busy port city of 1875, scarcely a thousand remained, and they were in
a despondent state of mind, still haunted by the horrors of the storm,
and seeing no future ahead for the town.

Of even greater import to them than the storm, Mickle said, was
the destruction wrought by Charles Morgan as he struggled for his own
survival against the main trunk railroads bypassing his port. Unable to
fight them, he had joined them, thereby diverting the life-sustaining
port traffic away from Indianola and Port Lavaca. Though Morgan had
died, discredited, in 1878, Mickle in 1880 still saw the Morgan interests personified in the name, with his hand at Indianola's throat, throt-
tling away her life.[2]

San Antonio had much sympathy for the port which had fed her
with freight for thirty years, but the Alamo City no longer depended
on Indianola. Her fortunes were now joined with the railroad industry,
and she was prospering mightily. San Antonio's population has been
estimated at 14,900 when the Sunset Route reached there in 1877;[3]
by 1880 it was 20,500; and in the 1900 census, 53,291.[4]

At first the principal new development lay in the area along Austin Street, where the G.H.&S.A. or Sunset Route had established its
depot and yards. The railroad had put up at the corner of Austin and
Sherman streets a long, wooden depot structure, two-story at the
front.[5] A railroad hotel stood at Austin and Tenth streets, a block from
the depot. Boardinghouses, pretentious saloons, grocery stores, and
other shops blossomed out on Austin Street all the way from Fifth
Street — now McCullough — to Twelfth Street, where the expressway
interchange now starts.

After twenty years of driving freight wagons and stagecoaches,
Peter Jonas had retired in the early 1870s to start a little saloon beyond
the Adams and Wickes yards on the old Austin road. In 1879 he
moved to a site at 701 Austin, where he had shrewdly brought five lots
before the railroad boom reached its peak. There he built "one of the
finest stone buildings in the Southwest . . . and shortly thereafter
added a huge dance hall in the rear. In the stone structure he opened a
saloon and boarding house."[6]

Boardinghouses were particularly in demand because the workers who manned the drays, the trains, and the railroad shops had to live close by their work. Call-boys or messengers would ply the neighborhood to notify the men when their services were needed.[7]

The advent of the telephone marked another great stride in communications, and there is a piquant aspect to the thought that a wagon-freighter may have pioneered this technological advance in San Antonio. Santleben claimed to have

> introduced the first instruments that were ever put in operation in San Antonio. The line was a private enterprise and the wire was stretched from our [drayage] office in a nearly direct line to the freight office of the Galveston, Harrisburg, & San Antonio Railroad by passing it over buildings and attaching it to trees and other objects. One phone was in our office and the other was attached to the desk of our shipping clerk in the depot, Mr. Ed Dieselhorst . . . They were not as perfect as those now in use, but they answered our purpose equally as well and certainly gave satisfaction . . .[8]

This exclusive access to Alexander Graham Bell's miracle did not last long. In mid-March 1881, one Logan H. Root made a low-key advent into San Antonio. He approached the city fathers and explained his mission: he wanted not money, subsidy, nor anything of that nature but the blessing of the city fathers in his putting a few poles around town to string wires for a proposed little system of telephones. The new enterprise of which he was president, back in St. Louis, was conducting similar experiments in New Orleans, Houston, and other towns, but Root was positive the innovation would be especially successful in San Antonio. The firm he represented was a fledgling enterprise called Southwestern Telegraph and Telephone Company. No one had reason then to dub it "Ma Bell." [9]

Apparently under the aegis of Root's firm, a telephone exchange did go into operation only two months later. The man in charge was J. K. Dunbar and the exchange was located on the second floor of a building at 278 West Commerce Street.[10] He was reputed to have a hundred subscribers when he started on June 17. The *Express* five weeks later listed "all the [new] connections for week ending July 23, 1881," all twelve of them, and suggested that subscribers clip the item out.[11]

By 1883 the exchange had 300 subscribers, and the railroads began to use the system to replace the call-boys and messengers. Rail-

road men could now reside elsewhere in town, get their calls by telephone, and ride the horsecars to work. [12]

The International and Great Northern Railroad had reached San
Antonio in February 1881, building its depot across town on West
Houston Street. At that time the new street railway system built a line
along Houston Street from the I.&G.N. to Avenue C — now Broad-
way — and out that avenue to Tenth Street and the Sunset depot. All
these influences tended to disseminate the new population from the
pressure point on Austin Street. Its glittering days faded while the city
as a whole continued to thrive. [13]

From San Antonio, with its 21,000 people in 1881, for 600 miles
north and west there was not a town with as many as a thousand people. But then the twin towns of El Paso stood on either side of the Rio
Grande at the Pass of the North. The old town of Paso del Norte (to
become the city of Juarez in 1889)[14] had perhaps 10,000 people in
1881. On the Texas side, the sometime village of Franklin, gradually
becoming El Paso, had still counted its population at 736 in 1880,
while its sister town downriver, Ysleta, claimed 1,700. Then railroad
fever seized El Paso full flush in 1881.

Although the railroad giant C. P. Huntington had been building
his Southern Pacific Railroad eastward ever since 1877 across California, Arizona, and finally New Mexico, toward El Paso, the impact did
not fairly strike the little town until late 1880. An interview with
"Judge Allen Blocker [sic] of El Paso," published by the *San Antonio
Express* in January 1881, told what happened when the Railroad Age
became a reality as Southern Pacific rails were laid down the Rio
Grande from Old Mesilla toward the pass. At the same time, the At-
chison, Topeka and Santa Fe and the Texas and Pacific were approaching from the east — and in northern Mexico the *Ferrocarriles Nacionales*
were rushing their rail line to connect Juarez with Ciudad Chihuahua:

> The scene at El Paso just now beggars description. The fact that
> three [sic] great railroads are practically there has caused a world of
> people of all classes, nationalities, and colors to rush to the locality
> from all quarters of the globe . . . It is generally believed that El
> Paso is to be a great city, and hence speculators have come into the
> country seeking investments for their millions . . . El Paso's three
> railroads . . . rapidly approaching . . . now draw all the provisions
> for their hands at El Paso . . . Judge Blocker [sic] says that all the
> country produce is bought up in advance, and that all the land in the
> vicinity . . . has been bought up by speculators. Blocks worth $25

and $50 six months ago, for which the judge is agent, are now held
at $800. All the land from the Hart's Mill, a mile north of town, to
a point about five miles below, has been purchased for town purposes
by eastern capitalists who will lay it out in blocks and realize handsome profits when the town commences to develop into a city. [15]

It is strange that the El Paso on the east side of the river either was unaware of or ignored the reality of the fourth railroad nearing completion from old El Paso del Norte to Ciudad Chihuahua. It had its own
very substantial significance, but nothing on the record indicates any
excitement around El Paso.

A brash history of the Southern Pacific Railroad reported, concerning that company's advent, "suddenly, on May 19, 1881, here
they were in El Paso, which was a sun-baked village of adobe houses,
of cantinas where the beer was warm and the tequila plenty hot." [16]

Huntington had been planning all along to connect his Southern
Pacific line at El Paso with the Texas and Pacific at El Paso, coming
across Texas from Dallas and the upper Mississippi Valley. And Col.
T. W. Peirce had been stalled for more than three years at San Antonio. His charter granted him the right to extend "to the Rio Grande,"
and that had generally been assumed to mean a point somewhere on
the Lower Rio Grande, such as Eagle Pass. [17] But he still had his youth-
ful dream of a road that would bind the gulf to the Pacific.

Huntington, too, had come to realize the advantages of a more
southerly route from El Paso eastward. Sometime in 1880, he entered
into negotiations with Colonel Peirce. About all Peirce had to offer was
a railhead in San Antonio with a line reaching back to the Gulf of Mexico — in addition to an organization that could put an effective construction crew on the job almost at once. That was enough to attract
Huntington.

On December 3, 1880, the public learned in San Antonio that
the G.H.&S.A. had obtained right-of-way for an extension westward, [18] but no one could say for sure just where the new road was
going. The secrecy under which negotiations proceeded generated the
wildest of rumors. Therefore, when the *Express* interviewed Judge
Blacker of El Paso in January 1881, the judge was quoted as saying he
had been informed

> by an officer of the Southern Pacific that his company had been
> trying to purchase the G.H.&S.A. from Colonel Peirce but that the
> Colonel had fixed his price at twenty million dollars which was re-
> garded as too steep. [19]

As late as March 1, the public was still in the dark as to the real facts:

> It is now reported that the Sunset will not own a mile of road west of San Antonio, that the efforts of Colonel Peirce to consolidate with the Southern Pacific have failed, and friends of the [Jay] Gould interests are fastening their clutches on the stock of the Peirce road.[20]

As the agreement actually evolved, Peirce and his cohorts appeared in a corporation called the Southern Development Company, which was owned and financed by Southern Pacific, and which was to build westward to meet Huntington's eastward-building line somewhere between El Paso and San Antonio. "Payment for the work," says S. G. Reed, "was to be made in first mortgage bonds, second mortgage bonds, and capital stock of the G.H.&S.A." [21] In other words, in order to achieve his dream of a link with the West, Peirce was mortgaging and putting up as collateral the actual stock of the G.H.&S.A. And these were indeed later acquired by Southern Pacific.[22]

Firm news of the extension to El Paso broke in San Antonio only when construction started in late March 1881. A flurry of orders put scores of wagons and teams to work for a while delivering material for construction teams to lay out the new line around the south side of the city and starting west.

As work moved ahead on this final link in the southern transcontinental railway, Colonel Peirce's crews shaped up the roadbed through Castroville and on across the mellow clay loam of the scrub mesquite pastures to Hondo, D'Hanis, and Sabinal Station. Always the base of the Edwards Plateau hill country lay just to their right, the coastal plains spread to their left, and they followed within a few rods of the wagon road Col. Joseph E. Johnston had surveyed in the summer of 1849. It was along here that young Policarpo Rodriguez, second scout under Richard Howard, of Johnston's expedition, had led out with the thrill of the trailblazer:

> I would go ahead to find the marks of our survey and then come back to guide the teams. When the prairie was smooth and open, the colonel gave the teamsters orders to follow me and not turn to the right or left; and I led them in a perfectly straight line. When you looked back from the front, you could see but one wagon — the one in front. You could see the white trail through the clay soil for miles and miles as straight as an arrow. The troops followed on behind us.[23]

Such was the heritage which the scouts, the surveyors, the soldier work battalions, the freight wagons, and the stagecoaches left for the railroads of the late nineteenth century and the great expressways of the mid-twentieth century. Those trails follow the ghosts of Jack Hays, Billy Whiting, Policarpo Rodriquez, Richard Howard, Henry Skillman, John L. Bullis, and Philip St. George Cooke across the wide desert wastes toward the beckoning West.

Wooden ties were laid on a skinny wooden bridge across San Felipe Creek and almost to the banks of the Rio Grande by June 22, 1882, the new railhead there creating the town of Del Rio where only irrigated farms had been before. A few miles beyond, at the crossing of the Devil's River and continuing for more than fifty miles to the far side of the Pecos River, lay the most difficult stretch for construction the engineers experienced along the entire Sunset Route.

From the Devil's River Canyon to the Pecos Canyon, the road had to bridge limestone chasms and to wind torturously through rocky arroyos; then it had to tunnel down to flood level in the canyon of the Rio Grande to cross the mouth of the Pecos River on a precariously low causeway; and tunnel out again, in late 1882, to high ground. (The famous Pecos High Bridge, 325 feet above the river, was not built on an upstream shortcut until 1891–92.) [24]

Meanwhile, construction by Huntington's crews eastward from El Paso progressed rapidly since there were no rivers to cross. Not one constant-flowing stream in the entire 350 miles from El Paso down the Southern Pacific route to the banks of the Pecos exists. The line "reached Sierra Blanca, 90 miles, on December 6, 1881; Marfa, 104.1 miles [farther] on January 16, 1882." [25] From the new village of Marfa the railway rose to join the Chihuahua Road in Paisano Pass, the highest point on the entire Southern Pacific Railroad between New Orleans and Portland, Oregon: 5,074 feet above sea level. Twelve miles downhill and east from Paisano, the Iron Horse could take water from Burgess Springs — a whistle stop that became Pat Murphy's Murphysville, then the cowtown of Alpine, and now the seat of Sul Ross University. From there, almost mile for mile to the banks of the Pecos, the route was the New Military Road, scouted out by John L. Bullis and surveyed by W. R. Livermore in the late 1870s. [26]

During those few months, Colonel Peirce's crews had blasted and chipped their way for some twelve miles up the west bank of the Pecos River and through another tunnel to get beyond a ridge. The nearby construction camp, a rowdy mixture of Chinese laborers, Irish track-

layers, and every kind of teamster, was known as Vinegaroon, sometimes confused with Roy Bean's Langtry and the Jersey Lilly, which
were to blossom a little later a couple of miles westward up the track.

The two construction crews, the one from the west and the one
from the east, finally targeted in on a meeting point "at the east end of
the second bridge . . . about three miles [sic] west of the mouth of the
Pecos." [27]

The day of fulfillment was January 12, 1883. Because of the re-
moteness of the area, the total lack of any accommodations for
hundreds of miles in either direction, there were no large crowds of excursionists. Nevertheless, while Huntington himself did not undertake the journey from California, great men of both railroads were
present, to send fine phrases of felicitations echoing down the canyon
on whose brink they stood.[28] But the magic of the telegraph wires, already strung, captured those words for citizens waiting all along the
railway route from New Orleans to San Francisco, and their content
was worthy of the occasion.

It was Col. Thomas W. Peirce's day. A dressed cedar tie had been
laid at the junction-point, with holes tapped to receive the special solid
silver spikes wrought for the occasion. Folding his hands upon the long
handle of a sledge hammer, he lifted his eyes to the bright skies of
western Texas and began:

> In the majestic presence of these great canyons of the Rio Grande,
> which impress and awe me with the majesty of the great Jehovah,
> and which speak more eloquently than words, the insignificance of
> man, and on the other hand, man's significance in his great
> triumphs over the forces of nature, of which we have abundant evi-
> dence all around us, I proceed to drive this spike which connects by
> rail the waters of the Pacific with those of the Gulf of Mexico. This I
> do in the Great Presence and in the fulfillment of the promise made
> to myself when visiting Texas in early youth in search of health, to
> be at least instrumental in this great achievement which assists to
> bind the different sections of our country more closely together, and
> to make our continent the highway of the nations of the earth. May
> God in His Providence make this great work redound to the interest,
> comfort, and civilization of mankind . . .[29]

As he spoke, he had hammered home the silver spike. James
Campbell, the superintendent of Southern Pacific lines east of El Paso,
alternating with Maj. James Converse, who had had charge of

G.H.&S.A. construction since its earliest days, now drove down the spike at the other end of the tie. Campbell had his say:

> Gentlemen, we stand at this chasm, the work of the Great Architect of nature, now bridged over by the hand of the mechanic . . . Gentlemen, it is an easy matter to come here in our special cars, fitted up with all the comforts of life, and carry off the newspaper honors of this occasion, but we must not ignore those who have borne the brunt of the battle and hardships of the field. We must not forget the men commanded by Captain Hood, walking on this scorched desert in a hostile country, setting stakes for the great army of graders, under the chief of all railroad builders, S. K. Strowbridge [*sic*].[30] Again, we see these men hanging over these immense lime walls, giving orders for the construction party. Then we have J. K. Flanders and Charles Comstock, the chief of bridge builders . . . When I look back over those vast deserts and lofty hills that we have crossed, and see that it has been but a few years when there was not a track to be seen, save that of the red man, or some wild animal, where there are now tracks of steel, on which thousands of wheels revolve, bearing on their axles the wealth of an enterprising and mighty nation, I feel as if I would draw away and give a lifetime in contemplating this scene . . .[31]

Then that veteran road-builder who is remembered today only in the name of the little town of Converse east of San Antonio had the last words:

> May the completion of this line of road become as a band of friendship, and of commercial interest as lasting as steel, connecting the hearts of the people of the Gulf states with those of the Pacific, whose interests are identified with each other, and may the projectors of the great Southern Pacific railway all live to realize and enjoy the fruits of their labor in completing this great national highway . . .[32]

Though he had not bothered to come to the Texas desert for the celebration, C. P. Huntington, chief of those "projectors" of whom Converse spoke, had not been idle. According to Reed, "Huntington had in the meantime acquired the Texas and New Orleans R.R. company from Houston to the Sabine River, the Louisiana Western, and soon thereafter the Morgan's Louisiana and Texas R.R. Co., Lafayette to New Orleans, and the Morgan line of steamers between New Orleans, New York, and Texas."[33]

On the day of the driving of that silver spike, a familiar name emerged in El Paso to put in focus the impact of the railroad's completion upon the subject of this story. The mayor of El Paso exchanged felicitations by telegram with Mayor James H. French of San Antonio, himself a longtime proponent and official of early railroad ventures. But the mayor of El Paso was Joseph Magoffin, son of that genial host, Confederate patriot, entrepreneuer, and early wagon-freighter, James Wiley Magoffin of Magoffinsville.[34] And this later-day Magoffin now sent his message to San Antonio down the long thin thread of wire beside the El Paso and Chihuahua Road: "This is the day we have so long looked forward to, when by the driving of a silver spike the ends of the G.H.&S.A. railroad are united . . . Let us now . . . run by rails from both ends to a general prosperity . . . and say farewell to the old wagon train and stagecoach times." [35]

Alamo Springs, off Alamito Creek and not far from the Rio Grande, fed this huge cottonwood. In the background is Victoriano Hernandez's large adobe home, now in ruins. Union scouts found graffiti on one of these trees that put them on the trail of Henry Skillman.

— Photo by author, 1973

The great guide and scout José Policarpo Rodriguez (Polly), with his large family and a dedicated congregation, built this sturdy stone chapel on Privilege Creek near Bandera after he had become a Methodist preacher (about 1882). The chapel was recently renovated and rededicated by his descendants.

— Photo by author, ca. 1975

The original Howard's Well Stage Station, used as such in the late 1870s, probably up to 1883. About a half mile from the actual Howard's Well, it stands on higher ground, which made a better roadbed. Note vertical palings holding adobe plaster.

— Photo by author, 1972

Justin Swift, middle, with two local boys who showed us what they and their parents declared was the real Howard's Well — dressed up with masonry walls, but in a logical location on the slope bank of the draw.

— Photo by author, 1972

The rocky, open area at bottom indicates the bed of the Chihuahua Road. Old U.S. Highway 290 to Fort Stockton comes down opposite side of canyon, with Pecos River running below hills at top.

— Photo by author, 1979

Looking up the steep incline of Lancaster Hill. The clump of hills at top shows "defile" at crest, where Henry W. Daly related that his stagecoach was attacked by a swarm of Indians. He escaped only by plunging his mules and vehicle down the precipitous road at breakneck speed.

— Photo by author, 1975

The author on the steep slopes of the Chihuahua Road at Lancaster Hill, near Shef-field, Texas. The boulders in the foreground were part of the retaining walls first put in place about 1853 by army engineers.

— Photo by Justin Swift, 1975

Joe King and Travis Roberts walk beside the wheel marks of freight-wagons on the Cut-Off Road, southwest of Peña Colorado, near Marathon. These ruts, now faintly visible lines, have persisted in the hard desert soil for nearly a hundred years.

— Photo by author, 1974

Antelope Springs (or Ojo Berrendo) *on the original Frank Mitchell ranch southwest of Paisano Pass. The Mitchell windmill stood in this clump of trees. This scene is precisely as described by Julius Froebel, German traveler, in 1853.*

— Photo by author, 1973

Limpia Creek in Wild Rose Pass, Davis Mountains. The creek and pass were named by Lt. W. H. C. Whiting in the first Anglo penetration of these mountains in 1849.

— Photo by author, 1973

Texas State Historical Marker at Horsehead Crossing on the west bank of the Nueces River. The clay bank at the upper left is the east bank of the river. Today's steep shores would not have permitted wagons crossing.

— Photo by author, 1973

Where it all started: Ciudad Chihuahua. The city of more than 300,000 is an amalgam of ancient tradition and bustling commerce. Towers of the eighteenth-century cathedral are seen at right, while a telecommunications tower counterposes it on the left.

— Photo by author, 1973

It took centuries for Roman chariots to wear ruts into the stone streets of Pompeii, but Texas-based wagon trains ground out these ruts in the softer tuff of St. Esteban Terraces in only a quarter-century.

— Photo by author, 1973

As a levy laid on by the church, a fraction of the silver pouring from the mines of Santa Eulalia built this cathedral in the heart of Ciudad Chihuahua (mid-eighteenth century).

— Photo by author, 1979

Crossing of the Santa Fe-Chihuahua Trail and the North Mexican ferro-carril, *which spelled the end of wagon-freighting in the 1880s.*

— Photo by author, 1973

Crossing of the Sacramento River near Chihuahua City. Along the base of the foothills in the middle distance, Alexander Doniphan and his Missouri Regiment, with the Traders' Battalion, although outnumbered four-to-one, won their stunning victory in 1847 over the Mexican army.

— Photo by author, 1979

Replica of the famous Mexican carreta *that opened up the Chihuahua Road and was used until past the 1850s. Occupying one of the courtyards in restored Fort Leaton near Presidio, this faithful scale model was built by local craftsmen following specifications detailed in August Santleben's book,* A Texas Pioneer. *Author's wife, Anna Jane, and son-in-law Gerald Burrough of Devon, England, who is more than six feet tall, indicate size of wheel.*

— Photo by author, 1985

A last vestige of the wagon freight traffic in the Chihuahua Desert, this mule-train was photographed in 1935, hauling quicksilver up from the Chisos Mines at Terlingua to the Southern Pacific Railroad at Marathon. These Studebaker wagons were only slightly smaller than the nineteenth-century versions. The train may have been near where the road from Terlingua joined the old Cut-Off Road to go through Del Norte Gap.

— Photo by L. M. Swift, 1935

This very early photo, attributed to 1866, may be the only one extant showing August Santleben with any of his trail equipment. According to the original caption, Santleben is at the driver's seat of his first coach, leaving from Kapp & Muenzenberger's store, corner of Laredo and West Commerce, San Antonio.

From *San Antonio Light* Collection,
courtesy Institute of Texan Cultures, San Antonio

HARPER'S NEW MONTHLY MAGAZINE.

No. CCX.—NOVEMBER, 1867.—Vol. XXXV.

THE MINES OF SANTA EULALIA, CHIHUAHUA.

CARRYING ORE TO THE FURNACE.

IT requires no little philosophy to transfer | wayfarers in more favored lands. It would be
one's self from the United States to Mexico | dignifying the *mesons* and *posadas* of the cities

Gen. Lew Wallace, later famous for his novel Ben Hur, *contributed this article to* Harper's, *celebrating the rich mines lying outside Ciudad Chihuahua.*

In 1685 René Robert Cavalier de la Salle landed on the shores of Matagorda Bay while looking for the Mississippi River. This statue marks the site near the town of old Indianola. Indianola State Park is also marked as the base of operations of Cabeza de Vaca in 1528.

— Photo by author, 1973

Lew Wallace decorated his treatise with a number of free-hand sketches drawn on the spot and completed after his return to the States. This one shows his impression of the mountain range in which lay the fabled mines, seen as his party traveled horseback out from the city.

Indianola, as seen by artist Helmuth Holtz from the yard-arm of the brig Texana in 1860. The city tripled in population after that, to about 6,000. The hurricane of 1876 virtually destroyed the bustling port and killed 300 people.

Easternmost point on the Chihuahua Road. Earle Swift checks out this cistern, the only structural relic remaining above water where once was busy Indianola, the second-largest port in Texas in 1876.

— Photo by author, 1974

The "Hanging Tree" in the Goliad courthouse yard. Justin Lee Swift demonstrating. Accounts vary as to the number of convicted persons hanged here, but it is of record that several were, about 1858, in the aftermath of the "Cart War."

— Photo by author, 1974

When the Wilson County town of Lavernia learned that one route of the Chihuahua Road ran through their community, they named their main street accordingly. The late Deed Vest, then school superintendent at Lavernia, was one of the earliest scholars to revive interest in the almost-forgotten artery of commerce.

A grandson of Ramón Hernandez commissioned Luis Rodriguez, standing at left, to execute this tombstone in the 1930s for the San Fernando Cemetery, San Antonio.

Here the Chihuahua Road ran through groves of live oak and huge pecan trees, near Pecan Springs, the head of running water in the Devil's River. William S. Abbey, of the Hudspeth River Ranch, which encloses all this area, says that these tracks are actual impressions left by the oxen- and mule-drawn wagons of the mid-nineteenth century, plying between Indianola and Ciudad Chihuahua.

— Photo by author, 1973

Chihuahua Road descending Lancaster Hill to Fort Lancaster. Justin is standing on one section of retaining wall; similar section at lower left indicates gradient.

— Photo by author, 1975

The Chihuahua Road as it starts down off plateau to traverse cliff of Lancaster Hill to Fort Lancaster. It was abandoned in 1883 and has washed out since then.

— Photo by author, 1975

Wild Rose Pass in the Davis Mountains, as seen by a staff artist with Maj. Wm. H. Emory, United States and Mexican Boundary Survey, about 1853. For several years after Lt. W. H. C. Whiting's discovery of this route in 1849, the traffic to Chihuahua as well as to El Paso moved through this defile.

John L. Bullis, Texas's greatest Indian fighter, had developed tactical skills in break-
ing up Indian raids, leading a strike force of never more than thirty black Seminole
scouts, which brought him recognition as the most effective, long-time operative in the
Rio Grande area.

— Photo from Army and Navy Journal

The Joining of the Rails. This little-known ceremony, which took place January 12,
1883, on the edge of a canyon west of the Pecos River and northeast of Langtry, spelled
the end of wagon-freight traffic in the Southwest. Huntington's Southern Pacific line,
building eastward, met Peirce's Sunset line coming from the east. Col. Tom Peirce
drove the first solid silver spike to join the rails; Southern Pacific officials drove the
other spike which completed the first transcontinental railroad across the southwestern

— Photo courtesy Southern Pacific, Inc.
and Texas Parks and Wildlife Commission

Santleben's train pulling up out of Alamito Valley in the Texas Bend, ca. 1873. The strange rock shapes are of a soft volcanic stone named by geologists as "Mitchell Mesa Tuff," prevalent on the St. Esteban Terraces.

— Illustration by Roy Ann Swift Carney

The author's daughter, Roy Ann Swift Carney, based this pencil drawing on an illustration from John R. Bartlett's Personal Narrative. Bartlett's text mentions this incident only briefly, but his on-the-spot artist made the most of it.

— Drawing by Roy Ann Swift Carney

San Antonio's Military Plaza in the 1850s. The wagon trains usually rendezvoused in wagon-lots on the edge of town, but at times, as seen here, considerable numbers of the big prairie schooners engaged in the western trade would be parked on the plaza. In the background is San Fernando Church, which during all these years had only one tower. Setting for this artist's rendition is adapted from the frontispiece plate, "Military Plaza, San Antonio, Texas," "Report of the United States and Mexico Boundary Boundary Commission, by William H. Emory," 34th Cong., 1st Sess., Ex. Doc. 1351, Washington, 1857. (Reissued 1987 by Texas Historical Commission, Austin.)

— Drawing by Roy Ann Swift Carney

Notes

(For explanation of abbreviations, see beginning of bibliography.)

Introduction

1 Francisco R. Almada, *Diccionario de Historia, Geografía y Biografía Chihuahuenses* (2nd ed., Ciudad Chihuahua: 1968), 336–337.

2 *La República Mexicana: Chihuahua, Reseña Geografía y Estadista.* (Libreria de la Vda. de C. Bouret, Paris and Mexico: 1909), 17–20.

3 Lew Wallace, "The Mines of Santa Eulalia," *Harper's New Monthly Magazine* 35 (November 1867): 682–702.

4 Almada says it was in 1707; Lew Wallace makes it 1705; *La República Mexicana* suggests 1703. For more on Cabeza de Vaca, see biographies by Morris Bishop, John Upton Terrell, and autobiography trans. by Bandelier.

5 Almada, *Diccionario,* 41.

6 Wallace, "Santa Eulalia," 686.

7 Almada, *Diccionario,* 97.

8 Sir Henry George Ward, *Mexico, with an Account of the Mining Companies and of the Political Events in That Republic to the Present Day* (London: 1829, 2nd ed.), 2:28, 300–306, 581. Sir Henry dwelt at length on the almost incredible, little-exploited silver resources of Chihuahua.

9 *La República Mexicana,* 20.

10 *Dictionary of American Biography* (New York: 1936) 19:375–376. Born in Indiana in 1827. Despite a brilliant military career during the Civil War, Lew Wallace is far better known as author of the novel *Ben Hur.* After Wallace's death in 1905, Meredith Nicholson (*Reader's Magazine,* April 1927) called him "an Oriental with medieval tastes."

11 José M. Iglesias, born in Mexico in 1823, had a long career in national politics that was much intertwined with the affairs of Chihuahua. At the time of Wallace's visit, Iglesias was National Secretario de Justicia, Fomento, e Instruccion. (Almada, *Diccionario,* 260.)

12 Wallace, "Santa Eulalia." Here, as with all following references re: visit to the mines, the source is from pp. 684–702 of Wallace's article.

13 August Santleben, *A Texas Pioneer* (Waco: W. M. Morrison Press, 1967), 123–124.

14 Almada, *Diccionario,* 566. Biographical sketch of Pancho Villa.

Chapter 1.   SPANISH EXPLORERS ALONG THE ROADS

1 J. C. Kelley, "Archaeological Notes on Two Excavated Houses in Western Texas," *Texas Archaeological and Paleontological Society* 20 (1940):225; Carlos Eduardo Castañeda, *Our Catholic Heritage* (Austin: Von Boeckmann Jones, 1936), 1: 160–163; W. W. Newcomb, Jr., *The Indians of Texas* (Austin and London: 1961), 225–229; Howard G. Applegate and C. Wayne Hanselka, *La Junta de los Ríos Del Norte y Conchos,* Southwestern Studies No. 41 (El Paso: 1974), 1–13; John Upton Terrell, *Apache Chronicle* (New York: 1972), 23, 24; Elizabeth A. H. John, *Storms Brewed in Other Men's Worlds* (College Station: 1975), 194; Cecilia Thompson, *History of Marfa and Presidio County, 1535–1946* (Austin: 1985), 1: ch. 1.

2 John Upton Terrell, *Journey into Darkness* (New York: 1962), 217–218; Cleve Hallenbeck, *Alvar Nuñez Cabeza de Vaca, the Journey and Route of the First European to Cross the Continent of North America, 1534–1536* (Glendale, CA: 1949), 3 *passim.*

3 Gonzalo Fernandez de Oviedo y Valdez, *Historia general y natural de los Indies* (Madrid: 1851–1855), 3: lib. xxxv.

4 Morris Gilbert Bishop, *The Odyssey of Cabeza de Vaca* (New York and London: 1933), 14.

5 Fanny Bandelier, *Naufragios: The Journey of Alvar Nuñez Cabeza de Vaca, 1528–1536* (New York: 1905), 149.

6 *Ibid.,* 149–153.

7 *Ibid.,* 153. The actual route traversed by Cabeza de Vaca was energetically debated in at least a dozen works from 1890 throughout the first three-quarters of the twentieth century. Among the more significant of those believing he reached the Rio Grande elsewhere than at La Junta are Adolph Bandelier, *Contributions to the History of the Southwestern Portion of the United States,* Baton Rouge, 1890; H. K. Davenport and J. E. Wells, "The First Europeans in Texas," *SHQ* 22 (1918–1919). But the latecomer completing this present review casts his lot with Hubert Howe Bancroft, *History of the North Mexican States and Texas, 1531–1800* (San Francisco: 1883) 1:78, 79; Francisco R. Almada, *Diccionario Chihuahuenses* (Chihuahua: 1968), 79; J. W. Williams, *Old Texas Trails* (Burnet: 1979), 41–43, map, 8–9; and biographers Morris Bishop and J. Upton Terrell; all of whom agree on La Junta as the place of crossing. The study by Donald E. Chipman, "In Search of Cabeza de Vaca's Route Across Texas," *SHQ* 91, no. 2 (Oct. 1987), 127–148, appeared too late for consideration in the text of this volume.

8 Cleve Hallenbeck, *The Journey of Fray Marcos of Niza* (Dallas: 1949), 32; Bancroft, *North Mexican States,* 1:70.

9 Terrell, *Apache Chronicle,* 30.

10 Herbert E. Bolton, *Spanish Exploration in the Southwest, 1542–1706* (New York: 1916) with Espejo's narrative as translated therein, 273.

11 *Ibid.,* 163–167.

12 Castañeda, *Our Catholic Heritage,* 1:179; Lloyd Mecham, "Antonio de Espejo and His Journey to New Mexico," *SHQ* 30 (1926–1927).

13 Bolton, *Spanish Exploration,* 200–283; Castañeda, *Our Catholic Heritage,* 1:182–183; Terrell, *Apache Chronicle,* 57 fn; John, *Storms Brewed,* 33–36.

14 Bolton, *Spanish Exploration,* 315, ff 325; John, *Storms Brewed,* 175–178.

15 Bolton, *Spanish Exploration,* 316.

16 *Ibid.,* 317–319. Dr. Bolton lists a full bibliography on the Lopez-Mendoza ex-

pedition, including an "expediente" or collection of unpublished manuscripts, with the original of Mendoza's journal, still preserved in the Archives of Mexico at the capital.

17 Victor J. Smith, "Early Spanish Explorations in the Big Bend of Texas," *Publication II,* WTHSS (Alpine), 55–56.

18 Clayton Williams, lifelong resident of Fort Stockton and diligent historian of the Trans-Pecos, construed that Mendoza did go to Comanche Springs. [Williams, *Never Again* (San Antonio: 1969), 1:68–69.]

19 Bolton, *Spanish Exploration,* 329–330; *Texas Almanac,* 1972–73 ed., 239.

20 W. W. Newcomb, Jr., *The Indians of Texas,* does not recognize the historical existence of a tribe called the "Tejas." The nearest he comes is "Teyas," a nomadic tribe associated with the Querechos whom Coronado encountered. Newcomb says they were probably either Caddo or Apache. His bibliography is formidable. It would appear, then, that Texas got its name only from a mythological tribe.

21 Clifford B. Casey, *Mirages, Mysteries, and Realities: Brewster County, Texas* (Seagraves: 1972), 13 and 432 fns 40, 41. Grover C. Ramsey in "Camp Melvin," *Handbook of Texas* 3:139 differs with the preceding; he locates Mendoza's crossing of the Pecos at the Pontoon Crossing, some forty miles above Live Oak Creek.

22 Castañeda, *Our Catholic Heritage,* 272–273; John, *Storms Brewed,* 178–179.

23 Bolton, *Spanish Exploration,* 317.

24 Robert S. Weddle has drawn all the threads of this web of missionary zeal, political intrigue, and military probes together in his two books on the Presidio San Juan Bautista and the "wilderness manhunt" that brought about San Antonio and Presidio La Bahia. Following these, Elizabeth A. H. John developed more fully the overall relationship of these projects to European power politics and the tissue of the numerous shifting Indian nations. [Robert S. Weddle, *San Juan Bautista: Gateway to Spanish Texas* (Austin and London: 1968) and *Wilderness Manhunt, the Search for La Salle* (Austin and London: 1973); Elizabeth A. H. John, *Storms Brewed in Other Men's Worlds* (College Station: 1975).]

25 John, *Storms Brewed,* 185–203.

26 Weddle, *San Juan Bautista,* 97–100; Weddle, *Wilderness Manhunt,* 263–264.

27 John, *Storms Brewed,* 223.

28 Weddle, *Wilderness Manhunt,* 194, text and fn; Kathryn Stoner O'Connor, *The Presidio La Bahía del Espíritu Santo de Zuniga, 1721–1846* (Austin: 1966), 10.

29 H. E. Bolton, *Texas in the Middle Eighteenth Century* (Austin: 1970 reprint edition).

30 For detailed treatment of the chain of small settlements and *ranchos* down the San Antonio River, see Robert Thonhoff, "The First Ranch in Texas," *Yearbook,* WTHA 40 (1964); Robert S. Weddle and Robert H. Thonhoff, *Drama and Conflict, The Texas Saga of 1776* (Austin: 1976); and Jack Jackson, *Los Mesteños, Spanish Ranching in Texas* (College Station: 1986).

31 Henry E. Meadows, "The Chihuahua Trail, 1590 — 1914," unpublished paper in the state files of the Crockett County Historical Survey, Austin, Texas. Meadows carries the closing of the "trail" forward to 1914, because of the debacle in January of that year when "approximately 5,000 Mexican Federalist soldiers and political refugees fled Chihuahua before the forces of revolutionary Pancho Villa and made the long trek afoot, by horseback, and a few in cars, following the old Trail to Presidio and up Alamito Creek to Marfa, where they were put aboard trains for El Paso in custody of U.S. troops."

Chapter 2.   FIRST ROAD: SANTA FE TO CHIHUAHUA

1 Text copied from photo by author, in file.

2 Josiah Gregg, *The Commerce of the Prairies* (Dallas: 1933 reprint ed.), 91.

3 Max L. Moorhead, *New Mexico's Royal Road: Trade and Travel on the Chihuahua Trail* (Norman: 1958), v.

4 Gregg, *Commerce of the Prairies*, 322.

5 Col. Henry Inman's *The Old Santa Fe Trail* (first printed in 1897, reissued at Minneapolis, 1966) contains no mention of Chihuahua; Hobart E. Stocking, *The Road to Santa Fe* (New York: 1971) has two one-sentence references to the Chihuahua trade; R. L. Duffus' fine book *The Santa Fe Trail* (London, New York, Toronto: 1930) contains one passing mention of Chihuahua.

6 Francisco R. Almada, *Diccionario . . . Chihuahuenses* (2nd ed., Ciudad Chihuahua: 1968), 140.

7 Elizabeth A. H. John, *Storms Brewed in Other Men's Worlds* (College Station: 1975), 64.

8 H. H. Bancroft, *Works* 17, "Arizona and New Mexico" (San Francisco: 1889), 132, 158; also R. E. Twitdeale, *Old Santa Fe* (Santa Fe: 1925), 126.

9 See Introduction, "The Treasure Houses of Chihuahua."

10 Herbert E. Bolton's paper, "Defensive Spanish Expansion and the Significance of the Borderlands," The University of Colorado, 1929.

11 J. F. Bannon, ed., *Herbert Eugene Bolton and the Spanish Borderlands* (Norman: 1964), 47–48.

12 Noel Loomis and Abraham Nasiter, *Pedro Vial and the Roads to Santa Fe* (Norman: 1967), 262–264; *Micro-Film Edition of the Bexar Archives, 1722–1836* (Chester Kielman, comp.), Center for Inter-American studies, U. of T., Austin, General Manuscript Series 1800–1833, 1760–1800.

13 John, *Storms Brewed*, 375, 537.

14 *Ibid.*, 661.

15 Loomis, *Pedro Vial*, 267–287; John, *Storms Brewed*, 726–731.

16 John, *Storms Brewed*, 734; Loomis, *Pedro Vial*, 287, *passim.*

17 John, *Storms Brewed*, 742.

18 *Ibid.*, 742–819.

19 Loomis, *Pedro Vial*, 369–487; map of Pedro Vial's three journeys, opp. p. 267; John, *Storms Brewed*, 757–762.

20 Loomis, *Pedro Vial*, 461.

21 Duffus, *Santa Fe Trail*, 37; Hiram E. Crittenden, *The American Fur Trade of the Far West*, 2 vols. (Stanford, CA: 1954), 2:493–494

22 Donald Jackson, ed., *The Journals of Zebulon Montgomery Pike*, 2 vols. (Norman: 1966), 1:392; Duffus, *Santa Fe Trail*, 43–47.

23 Jackson, ed., *Pike*, 414–421.

24 Duffus, *Santa Fe Trail*, 46, 49; Jackson, ed., *Pike*, 1:421. The Pike journals were found by historian Herbert E. Bolton about 1906; it took him seventeen more years to get them back to the U.S.

25 Jackson, ed., *Pike*, 1:422–447.

26 Loomis, *Pedro Vial*, 461 fn 3. (For original source, see Amangual papers, Bexar Archives, Austin.)

27 San Elzeario's name, under Anglo corruption perhaps, became "San Elizario" in

the last half of the nineteenth century. It had been established only a little later than Ysleta and Socorro, a few miles upriver — the "oldest towns in Texas" — resulting from the removal of settlers in towns by the same name, far up the river in New Mexico, destroyed in the Indian uprising of 1680–82.

28 These salt lakes, not to be confused with Juan Cardona Lake on the Pecos far to the south, lie near the New Mexico border between El Paso and Guadalupe Peak.

29 Kenneth F. Neighbors, "The Report of the Expedition of Major Robert S. Neighbors to El Paso in 1849," *SHQ* 60 (April 1957), 530.

30 Jackson, ed., *Pike,* 830.

31 Jack de vere Rittenhouse, *The Santa Fe Trail: A Historical Bibliography* (Albuquerque: 1971).

32 *Ibid.*

33 Florence C. and Robert H. Lister, *Chihuahua, Storehouse of Storms* (Albuquerque: 1966), 78–79.

34 *Ibid.,* 79.

35 William Elsey Connelley, ed., *War with Mexico: 1846–1847; Doniphan's Expedition and the Conquest of New Mexico and California* (Topeka, KS: 1907), appendix F, 628. This is a much-expanded and more useful edition of John T. Hughes's earlier work.

36 *Ibid.,* appendix K, 645–646.

37 William Cochran McGaw, *Savage Scene: The Life and Times of James Kirker, Frontier King* (New York: 1972). See also Gregg, *Commerce,* 216–217.

38 Some basic readings on Alexander Doniphan's Chihuahua Expedition: Frederick Adolphus Wislizenus, *Memoir of a Tour to Northern Mexico, Connected with Col. Doniphan's Expedition in 1846 and 1847.* Printed January 18, 1848, as *Sen. Doc. Misc. No. 26.* 30th Cong., 1st Sess.; Reprinted 1969, The Rio Grande Press, Glorieta, NM; "Doniphan to Jones," March 4, 1847, *Sen. Ex. Doc. No. 1. 30th Cong.;* Justin H. Smith, *War With Mexico,* 2 vols. (New York: 1919); K. Jack Bauer, *The Mexican War, 1846–1848, "The Wars of the United States Series"* (New York and London: 1974), 153–156; and Connelley's work, fn 35.

39 Rex W. Strickland, "The Birth and Death of a Legend — The Johnson Massacre of 1837," *Arizona and the West* 18, no. 3 (Autumn 1976), 257, 287.

40 Leavitt Corning, Jr., *Baronial Forts of the Big Bend* (San Antonio: 1967), 22. Fort Leaton in recent years has been magnificently restored by the Texas Parks and Wildlife Commission.

41 When Corning wrote his *Baronial Forts* in the 1960s, he noted the conflicting accounts of Faver's origins, but emphasized Amy Greenwood's version. Mrs. Greenwood has told this writer (RLS) the same story repeatedly, she having heard it from her grandfather. Pool had acquired much of Faver's holdings in later years, and gave his granddaughter La Ciénega when she married Hart Greenwood.

42 Corning, *Baronial Forts,* 45; *The Big Bend Sentinel* [Marfa, Texas], September 1, 1950.

43 Dispatch January 2, 1848, El Paso, to *St. Louis Union,* as reprinted in *Galveston Weekly News,* May 5, 1848. Unnamed correspondent says in part: ". . . We arrived . . . on the 16th of November. Lieut. Col. Lane, with three companies, had preceded us some two weeks. On approaching the town, he sent in advance a party of some 25 or 30 men, under ——— [sic] Skillman, (brother to the bookseller opposite the Planter's House, St. Louis) who succeeded in taking prisoner the notorious Armijo . . ." Beverly Bishop, assistant archivist, Missouri Historical Society, St. Louis, in a letter to RLS, April 30, 1977,

said, "William D. Skillman was a St. Louis bookseller with a store opposite Planter's House from approx. 1845–1852." She found examples of Skillman's invoices from that period, showing address: "No. 55 Fourth St., opposite Planter's House."

44 Rex W. Strickland, *Six Who Came to El Paso* (El Paso: 1963), 36 and 45 fn 75.

Chapter 3.   SECOND ROAD: CONNELLEY'S TRAIL

1 T. U. Taylor, "Anglo-Saxon Trails Across Texas," *Frontier Times* 15, no. 6 (March 1938): 259.

2 Other doctor-adventurers who come readily to mind include Dr. John R. (Rip) Ford, Dr. Frederick A. Wislizenus, and Dr. Geo. Cupples.

3 Biographical data on Henry Connelley and family is from Wm. E. Connelley's extensive fn 65 in his expanded edition of *War with Mexico — Doniphan's Expedition and the Conquest of New Mexico, 1846–1847* (Topeka, KS: 1907 ed.), 276–282. Although the merchant-doctor's name is sometimes found spelled "Connelly," I follow his biographer's spelling, as above.

4 *Ibid.,* 280. This was the same Stephenson, either Hugh or his brother Archibald, who with a man named Riddels opened a hotel in Chihuahua City (Rex W. Strickland, *Six Who Came to El Paso* (El Paso: 1963), 35 and 45 fn 71.

5 *Ibid.,* 280.

6 Gregg, *Commerce of the Prairies* (Dallas: 1933 reprint ed.), 214; Taylor, "Anglo-Saxon Trails," 213.

7 Robert W. Frazer, *Forts of the West* (Norman, OK: 1965), 213.

8 Gregg, *Commerce of the Prairies,* 324 fn.

9 *Ibid.*

10 The curious suffix, "de la O," was used to distinguish this Gov. Irogoyen from his uncle and predecessor.

11 Gregg refers to this agreement as "the contract for a diminution of their duties." *Commerce of the Prairies,* 125.

12 Walter Fulcher (Elton Miles, ed.), *The Way I Heard It: Tales of the Big Bend* (Austin: 1959), 3–21 (ch. 1).

13 Julius Froebel, *Seven Years' Travel in Central America, Northern Mexico, and the Far West of the United States* (London: 1859), 404–408.

14 "Diario de Don Francisco Colomo," translated from Spanish in 1937 by Guadalupe Carrasco Hernandez in Marfa, Texas. Typescript was held by Mrs. O. L. (Jack) Shipman until her death, when it passed to her daughter, Mrs. Hester Vrite Van de Vere of El Paso, who let Jerry Sullivan of Texas Parks and Wildlife Department make a copy.

15 Herbert E. Bolton, *Spanish Exploration in the Southwestern United States, 1542–1706* (New York: 1916), 197–200.

16 Gregg, *Commerce of the Prairies,* 324.

17 *Ibid.*

18 Thos. M. Marshall, "Commercial Aspects of the Texan-Santa Fe Expedition," *SHQ* 20, no. 3 (January 1917):244.

19 *Ibid.,* 245.

20 *Ibid.* What is to be made of Marshall's conjecture, based on a map in G. W. Kendall's *Narrative of the Texan-Santa Fe Expedition,* opp. page 1, that the traders journeyed from Clarkesville, Texas, to Fulton on the Arkansas River? This seems in contradiction of his other conclusion that they went from Fort Towson to Shreveport.

21 *Sketch Showing the Route of the Military Road from Red River to Austin.* William H. Hunt, Engineer, 1840, drawn by H. L. Upshur, 1841, Texas State Library, Austin (also in *Sen. Ex. Doc. 64, 31st Cong., 1st Sess.*).

22 Gregg, *Commerce of the Prairies,* 324–325.

23 J. W. Williams in *Handbook of Texas,* "Chihuahua Trail," 1:337–338.

24 Gregg, *Commerce of the Prairies,* 324–325.

25 J. W. Williams, "The National Road of the Republic of Texas," *SHQ* 47 no. 3 (January 1944): 215, citing testimony by R. H. Burnet and Thomas F. Ragsdale in the *Greer County Record, 1894, No. 4, Original United States vs. State of Texas,* 1256, 1257, 1321.

26 J. W. Williams added more on the midsection of the trail in his "Marcy's Road from Doña Ana," WTHA *Yearbook* 19 (October 1943):150. The material on Marcy's Road from Doña Ana is also covered in his monumental *Old Texas Trails,* Kenneth F. Neighbors, ed. (Burnet: 1979), 220–242.

27 Edward Everett Dale, *The Cross Timbers* (Austin: 1966), 4–5.

28 Gregg, *Commerce of the Prairies,* 325.

29 Williams, "Chihuahua Trail," *Handbook of Texas,* 1:338.

30 Grover C. Ramsey, in his "Camp Melvin" piece for *Handbook of Texas,* 3:139, construed that Connelley came down to Pontoon Crossing of the Pecos, rather than to Horsehead Crossing.

31 Almada, *Diccionario,* 283.

32 Gregg, *Commerce of the Prairies,* 325.

33 *Ibid.*

34 Wm. E. Connelley, *War with Mexico,* fn on Henry Connelley, 282.

Chapter 4. THIRD ROAD: AUSTIN'S DREAM

1 For instance, neither Louis J. Wortham nor Henderson Yoakum in their lengthy histories of Texas makes any mention of a recognized need or plan for the road to Chihuahua prior to the Mexican War of 1846.

2 Eugene C. Barker, *Life of Stephen F. Austin* (Austin: 1949), 388.

3 Monograph printed (450 copies) in Spanish in Mexico D. F., *Explanation to the Public Concerning the Affairs of Texas, by Citizen Stephen F. Austin,* translated by Ethel Zively Rather, *QTSHA* 18, no. 3 (January 1905): 232–258.

4 Letter, Austin to Samuel May Williams, February 14, 1835, in Samuel M. Williams papers, Rosenberg Library, Galveston, Texas, reproduced in *The Austin Papers,* Eugene C. Barker, ed. (Austin: 1927), 3:42–43.

5 Austin, *Explanation to the Public,* 232–258.

6 Barker, *Life of Austin,* 420.

7 Austin, *Explanation to the Public,* 230.

8 Walter Prescott Webb, *The Texas Rangers: A Century of Frontier Defense* (Austin: 1935), overall context.

9 J. Frank Dobie, *Coronado's Children* (New York: 1931), 1–7.

10 Thomas Maitland Marshall, "Commercial Aspects of the Texan-Santa Fe Expedition," *SHQ* 20, no. 3 (January 1917): 242. (I have reviewed President Lamar's correspondence over this period, as preserved in the president's letters, TSA, and find no written evidence that military aggrandizement was a factor. RLS)

11 Republic of Texas, 3d Cong. 1st Sess., *Laws,* 105–106.

12 *Houston Telegraph and Texas Register,* April 6, 1840. Frontier journalists were perhaps even more freewheeling than now. The true distance is more like 700 miles, even by today's highways.

13 Republic of Texas, 5th Cong. 1st Sess., 1840–41, *House Journal,* 494, 499, 720–723; Marshall, "Commercial Aspects," 257.

14 Rena Maverick Green, ed., *Samuel Maverick, Texan* (San Antonio: 1952), 150. President Lamar's correspondence file in TSA includes a letter dated May 10, 1841, signed by Mayor Seguin, José Antonio Navarro, Wm. B. Jaques, Sam'l Maverick, and Wm. Elliott, inviting him "to attend a ball and other entertainment" at a time he might suggest.

15 *Ibid.,* 150.

16 H. B. Carroll, *The Texan-Santa Fe Trail* (Canyon, TX: 1951).

17 June 21 has been used by most historians as departure date for the expedition, but Carroll's book (19) fixes upon June 19.

18 Thomas Falconer, *Letters and Notes on the Texan-Santa Fe Expedition, 1841–1842,* F. W. Hodge, ed. (Chicago: 1963), 78.

19 This number is Carroll's reckoning, including a number of traders who took goods along by wagon.

20 Geo. W. Kendall, *Narrative of the Texan-Santa Fe Expedition* (New York: 1844), 1:120.

21 Carroll, *Texan-Santa Fe Trail,* 164–165; Noel Loomis, *Texan-Santa Fe Pioneers* (Norman: 1958), 93.

22 Kendall, *Narrative,* 2:189–190; Loomis, *Texan-Santa Fe Pioneers,* 126–127; Waddy Thompson, *Recollections of Mexico* (New York: 1846), 92.

23 M. K. Wisehart, *Sam Houston, American Giant* (Washington, D.C.: 1962), 382–385; Jack C. Ramsay, Jr., *Thunder Beyond the Brazos* (Austin: 1985), 123–126.

24 Samuel A. Maverick's journal of imprisonment in Mexico, as reproduced in Green, ed., *Samuel A. Maverick,* 173–191.

25 Julius W. Pratt, "The Origin of 'Manifest Destiny,' " *American Historical Review* 32, no. 4 (July 1927): 795–798, citing *United States Magazine and Historical Review* 17 (July-August 1845).

26 K. Jack Bauer, *The Mexican War, 1846–1848* (New York and London: 1974), 17.

27 *Ibid.*

28 *Ibid.,* 18–26.

29 General Taylor's overland movement from Corpus Christi to Matamoros impinged unintentionally but with tragic results upon the tide of immigration just beginning to flow into Texas from Germany. John Meusebach had already contracted to use all available wagons and teams on the coast for transporting his immigrants to the interior. Taylor overrode those contracts and took the wagons to move his army. This disruption left thousands of German settlers stranded on the shore at Powderhorn. (See chapter 7.)

30 Footnotes 26, 31, and 32 cite works that will provide useful background on the Mexican War with particular reference to the war in Texas.

31 Justin H. Smith, *The War with Mexico,* 2 vols. (New York: 1919).

32 M. L. Crimmins, "General John E. Wool in Texas," *Yearbook,* WTHA (Abilene) 18 (October 1942): 48.

33 "Map of General Wool's Road, 1846, Showing Line of March of the Centre Division from San Antonio de Bejar to Saltillo," M. L. Crimmins Map Collection, ECB.

34 Smith, *War with Mexico,* 267.

35 Crimmins, "Wool in Texas," 49.

36 Smith, *War with Mexico,* 509 fn 16; Crimmins, "Wool in Texas," 50.

37 Carl Coke Rister, *Robert E. Lee in Texas* (Norman: 1946), 94.

38 Crimmins, "Wool in Texas," 50.

39 Interview by RLS with Robert S. Weddle, October 1974. Weddle had exhaustively researched the old river crossings between Eagle Pass and Laredo in writing his *San Juan Bautista* (Austin: 1968).

40 Philip Van Doren Stern, *Robert E. Lee — The Man and Soldier* (New York: 1963).

41 Bauer, *The Mexican War,* 150, 204–218. General Santa Anna had returned from exile in Cuba and gained control once more of the government and the army in May of 1846.

42 Crimmins, "Wool in Texas," 17. The victory at Buena Vista was only five days before Doniphan's equally remarkable upset of the Mexican forces at Sacramento on February 28.

43 Letters from 1st Lt. W. B. Franklin and Capt. L. Sitgreaves to Maj. Geo. E. Hughes, *Sen. Ex. Doc., No. 32,* 31st Cong. 1st Sess., 48–51.

44 *Ibid.*

45 Advertisements in the *Victoria Advocate* in the late 1840s show that this ferry charged $1.50 to transport one wagon with teams.

46 *The Old Helena Foundation,* published at Karnes City, Texas, 1968.

47 Robert Thonhoff, *The First Ranch in Texas,* Southwest Texas Heritage Series, No. 1 (Karnes City: The Old Helena Foundation, 1968), 2–6.

48 Records on Lodi in Files of Wilson County Historical Commission, Floresville, Texas.

Chapter 5. Colonel Hays Enters the Trans-Pecos

1 Rena Maverick Green, ed., *Samuel Maverick, Texan* (San Antonio: 1952), 85–120.

2 *Ibid.,* 326.

3 At Brackettville, where the buildings of the old fort and army post are at this writing being converted into an exotic resort and condominium project.

4 George Cupples was a Scot surgeon with early experience on the Continent in the British medical service. He went with Henri Castro to the San Antonio area in 1844. He later related: "Without knowing it, I located the present site of Castroville and I cut the first brush there for the first clearing." [Wm. Corner, *San Antonio de Bexar* (San Antonio: 1890), 113–114.]

5 Rena Maverick Green, ed., *Samuel Maverick, Texan* (San Antonio: 1952), 330.

6 Averam B. Bender, "Opening Routes Across West Texas, 1848–1850," *SHQ* 37, no. 2 (October 1933): 116.

7 Powderhorn was the small landing which antedated Indianola by a couple of years and was on the same peninsula.

8 James Kimmins Greer, *Colonel Jack Hays* (New York: 1952). Texas A&M University Press released a newly annotated edition of this book in 1987.

9 Walter Prescott Webb, *The Texas Rangers* (New York: 1935), 72.

10 *Ibid.,* 69.

11 Greer, *Jack Hays,* 216.

12 Green, ed., *Samuel Maverick*, 352.

13 Isaac D. Affleck's MS. re: Col. Jack Hays, ECB.

14 For instance, the *Galveston Weekly News*, October 18, 1848, carried an extensive article headlined "Col Hays' Expedition," and commencing, "The Huntsville Banner has an interesting letter from Col. Lukens of the Rangers, dated at the Llano Station, giving some particulars of Col. Hays' expedition to Chihuahua," etc.

15 The Texas Concho River is not to be confused with the Rio Conchos in Mexico, which has its confluence with the Rio Grande near Presidio.

16 Actually, the "200 miles" is itself a considerable exaggeration. From San Antonio to Las Moras Creek was never more than 130 miles.

17 This and subsequent quotes from Hays are out of his report to Colonel Peter Hansborough Bell. The report was printed in the *Western Texian* [San Antonio] December 1848 (not extant), but here copied from a reprint in *Corpus Christi Star*, January 20, 1849.

18 A "Painted Rock Spring" at the head of the South Branch of the Llano appears on Livermore's "Military Map of the Rio Grande Frontier," 1881.

19 Greer, *Jack Hays*, 219–220.

20 This and following frequent quotes from Sam Maverick's journal are drawn from its presentation in Green's *Samuel Maverick, Texan*. Original of his journal is in the Maverick file, ECB.

21 Hays's report to Bell.

22 Crockett County records in files of Texas State Historical Survey, Austin.

23 Maverick's September 29 journal entry.

24 Lifelong resident of Brewster County and authority on Big Bend frontier days, Travis Roberts of the Marathon country, knew Bev Greenwood at Alpine early in this century. Greenwood told him of his journey past Indian Well with Bullis when that veteran scout was opening up the road which bore his name.

25 Ross A. Maxwell, *The Big Bend of the Rio Grande*, Guidebook 7 (University of Texas at Austin: Bureau of Economic Geology, 1968), 99.

26 Maverick's October 10 journal entry shows that Howard had resorted to making "soup" from the sotol heart for the starving wanderers.

27 Green, ed., *Samuel Maverick*, 332–333.

28 Travis Roberts consulted Mrs. Hallie Stillwell, former justice-of-the-peace at Alpine, on the pictographs sighted by Hays and party. Mrs. Stillwell, who has lived for more than half a century on the Stillwell Ranch operated by her late husband in the Maravillas country, says firmly that the only pictographs on an open canyon wall in that entire area are less than two miles from her ranch home, on Bear Creek, not far from where it runs into Maravillas Canyon.

29 Travis Roberts supports the conclusion that the Hays party passed through Dog Canyon.

30 Mary Maverick in her memoirs (*Samuel Maverick*, 322) refers to the man who "lost his reason and was lost and afterwards saved by the Indians . . . and recovered." Affleck, paraphrasing Caperton's notes in the MS biography of Hays, says that "the doctor who went crazy and was lost . . . was picked up by the Indians who, finding him insane, took care of him. Some months afterwards, it might have been a year, he came in to the settlements of Texas, to the great surprise of his wife, who had given him up for dead and was on the point of marrying another man." John Henry Brown, *Indian Wars and Pioneers of Texas* (Austin: undated), 106, tells of Dr. Wahm that "after he had been mourned by his wife as dead for over a year [he] suddenly presented himself to her, sound in mind and

body." This curious story appears to be supported by the fact that the U.S. Census of 1850, San Antonio, lists a "doctor I. L. Warm [*sic*], living with his wife, Jane, 24, and son Richard, age 1, in Dwelling 693, Enumerated Oct. 7, 1850."

31 Hays made sure that his apology, with its reasons for his trespass, was officially recorded both in his report to Bell and in his follow-up report to Secretary of War Marcy.

32 During the Gold Rush period which followed in 1849, several parties brought wagons down to Presidio, intending to go up the Rio Grande to El Paso, but finding this was impossible, abandoned the wagons and proceeded on foot with pack animals. [C. C. Cox, "From Texas to California in 1849," *SHQ* 29, no. 1 (July 1925), Cox's journal entry of July 10, 1849.]

33 See *Houston Telegraph* story, January 18, 1849; further reference in fn 41.

34 The verb "recruit" was also used by Hays and Maverick and generally by the military and plainsmen of the day to mean "recuperate" or "refresh."

35 Caperton says that a man named Peacock joined the returning party at Leaton's. Probate records in the Bexar County Courthouse, San Antonio, reflect in detail that Leaton appointed James T. Peacock as executor of last will and testament in 1851 and that Peacock served faithfully in this duty after Leaton's death. One of Ben Leaton's charges to Peacock was that he should see to the education of his sons. Perhaps Peacock was acting as caretaker for the younger boy, Bill Shepherd Leaton, on this opportune passage to San Antonio. Internal evidence among the probate papers suggests that the boy — and other children as well — were sent to school at Goliad. [Corning, *Baronial Forts of the Big Bend* (San Antonio: 1969), 77–105.]

36 Maverick's journal entry for November 10; Hays's report to Bell.

37 *Corpus Christi Star*, December 9, 1848.

38 Contemporary reporting on Hays's expedition was considerably muddied by the activities of Dr. George A. Sturges and "Colonel" John Evertson (or Everson), merchant. These two San Antonio men, with a party all purporting to be on a "mining expedition," trailed Hays as they struggled across the Devil's River and the Pecos, and toward the Rio Grande. Sturges and Evertson returned to San Antonio and released to the press alarming stories about the expedition's hardships, capped off with belittling remarks on Hays's findings. [Maverick's journal entries September 11 and 28, 1848; *Corpus Christi Star*, December 9, 1848, and January 20, 1849.]

39 Full text of Hays's report to Peter Hansborough Bell, *Corpus Christi Star*, January 20, 1849. Colonel Hays's much briefer report to Sec'y of War Marcy, *Sen. Ex. Doc., 31st Cong., 1st Sess.*, 64–65.

40 Clayton Williams, *Never Again* (San Antonio: 1969), 3:5–6; Maude Willis Traylor, "Captain Samuel Highsmith, Ranger," *Frontier Times* 17, no. 7 (April 1940): 297–302. Highsmith's own official report to Captain Bell is reproduced in Traylor's article, as originally published in Rip Ford's *Texas Democrat* [Austin], January 28, 1849, 4.

41 *Houston Telegraph* (Francis Moore, ed.), January 12, 1849.

42 *Corpus Christi Star*, January 20, 1849.

Chapter 6.   WHITING BLAZES THE WAY

1 Hays to Marcy, December 13, 1848, *Sen. Ex. Doc. 32, 31st Cong., 1st Sess.*, 64–65.

2 Van Horne to Jones, December 18, 1848. AGO records, Letters Rec'd, OFS.

3 Marcy to Worth, December 10, 1848. AGO records, Military Book 27.

4 Worth, Order No. 10, February 9, 1849. Letters Rec'd, War Department, Chief of Engineering Office.

5 José Policarpo Rodriguez, *The Old Guide*, D. W. Carter, ed. (Nashville and Dallas: ca. 1897), 18–21.

6 *Ibid.*, 18–19. Polly dictated this conversation to his amanuensis thirty-five years after the fact; he was a man careful with his facts.

7 W. H. C. Whiting, "Journal of a Reconnaissance from San Antonio de Bejar to El Paso del Norte," Office of Chief of Engineers, Washington D.C., 1849. Published in full in *Exploring Southwestern Trails*, Ralph B. Bieber, ed. (Glendale, CA: 1938). This and the following quotes and page references are from that work.

8 Geo. Washington Cullum, *Biographical Register of the officers and graduates of the U.S. Military Academy, 1802–1867* (New York: 1879), 114–115.

9 *Dictionary of American Biography* (New York: 1943), 20:136.

10 *Sen. Ex. Doc., No. 64, 31 Cong., 1st Sess.*, 7; *House Ex. Doc., No. 5, 31 Cong., 1st Sess.*, 282, 293.

11 Bieber, ed., *Exploring . . .*, Whiting's report, 30–31.

12 *Dictionary of American Biography*, 20:136. Whiting's journal was found in MS in the Office of Chief of Engineers, Washington D.C., by Dr. Bender, and was published for the first time in entirety in *Exploring Southwestern Trails*. A shorter, more formal version was submitted by Whiting to Brig. Gen. J. G. Totten, chief of engineers, from San Antonio, June 10, 1849.

13 Whiting, "Journal," 321. It is an accepted fact that no Anglo or Mexican settlement lay in all that great area.

14 This is the sixth Howard to appear in the annals of the San Antonio area in this period. He was, so far as can be told, not a sibling of either George Thomas Howard or Richard Howard.

15 Whiting, "Journal," 327.

16 Rodriguez, *The Old Guide*, 21.

17 *Ibid.*, 23.

18 Whiting, "Journal," 262–263. Crockett County Historical Association knows location of *their* Escondido Spring in Crockett County.

19 *Ibid.*, 270.

20 Rodriguez, *The Old Guide*, 22–23.

21 The extensive passages which follow are from Whiting's "Journal," 270–281.

22 Whiting did not exaggerate Gomez's fame. In 1853 Julius Froebel, visiting in Chihuahua City, was told that Gomez was "the most dreaded chief of these savages [Apache] in northern Mexico."

23 This is the spring originally called "Varilla" but later corrupted to "Barilla."

24 Policarpo says that Chino Guero (or Chino Huero) was the son of the old man whom Whiting had spared. One of the squaws was his own wife; the little boy his son; therefore, Chino Guero was determined to save the Americans. [Rodriguez, *The Old Guide*, 25–30.]

25 Travis Roberts identifies the Apache Plume as *Fallusia paradoxa*. Letter to RLS, October 29, 1976. [See *Plants of the Big Bend National Park*, McDougall and Sperry (Washington: National Park Service, 1951), 91 and Plate 74.]

26 Whiting, "Journal," 287–288.

27 Clayton Williams believed this man was W. F. de Sarz. [*Never Again*, 3:18.]

28 It is surprising to find here the slang "rubbed out" in 1849. One might have assumed it originated with the gangster era of the 1920s.

29 Whiting, "Journal," 305. For a brief, readable account of the small settlements across from old El Paso del Norte in the 1840s, and how they combined into the new El Paso on the Texas side, see Rex Strickland, *Six Who Came to El Paso,* Southwestern Studies No. 3 (El Paso: 1963).

30 Whiting, "Journal," 300.

31 *Ibid.,* 313.

32 *Ibid.,* 325.

33 Text of Persifor Smith's order establishing Fort Davis is shown by Robert Utley in *Fort Davis,* NPS Historical Handbook No. 38, (Washington: 1965), 6.

34 Whiting, "Journal," 339. Later travelers always left the Pecos at Live Oak Creek, climbing to the high ground and striking out southeast toward Howard's Well.

35 *Ibid.,* 340.

36 *Ibid.* Italics added. Whiting's text indicates he may not have realized that this was a permanent spring.

37 *Sen. Ex. Doc. No. 64, 31 Cong., 1st Sess.,* 1849.

38 Whiting, "Journal," 345.

39 *Ibid.*

40 Rena Maverick Green, ed., *Samuel Maverick, Texan: 1803–1870* (San Antonio: 1952), 345.

41 Whiting, "Journal," 349.

42 *San Antonio Western Texian,* May 24, 1849 (having heard from Lt. Smith about the journey) observed, "They [Whiting and Smith and party] have examined a large section of country of which little hitherto has been known, and have succeeded in surveying an excellent wagon road from this place to El Paso . . . The importance of this information, both for military and commercial purposes, can hardly be calculated."

43 Stephen B. Oates, ed., *Rip Ford's Texas* (Austin: 1963); Kenneth F. Neighbors, *Robert Simpson Neighbors and the Texas Frontier, 1836–1859* (Waco: 1975).

44 Neighbors, *Robert Simpson Neighbors,* 309 fn 21.

45 Greer, *Colonel Jack Hays.* Almost half of Greer's biography is devoted to this latter part of Hays's career.

46 *Sen. Ex. Doc. No. 64, 31st Cong., 1st Sess.,* 26, quotes Colonel Johnston as saying he had "twenty laborers, required to make a practicable road for our provision wagons."

47 C. C. Cox, "Texas to California in 1849" (Mabelle Eppard Martin, ed.), *SHQ* 29, no. 2 (October 1925).

48 *Sen. Ex. Doc. No. 64, 31st Cong., 1st Sess.,* 1849.

Chapter 7. AS WAGONS ROLLED

1 *Houston Telegraph and Texas Register,* January 3, 1850. This dispatch was reproduced in *SHQ* 48, no. 2 (October 1944), 263, among a group of documents compiled by C. L. Greenwood, "Opening Routes to El Paso, 1849," apparently without knowledge of a follow-up dispatch published January 30 from the same correspondent. It is necessary, because of the newswriter's ambiguous language, to correlate the two dispatches in order to understand that Coons's train was on the way *to* Indianola, rather than *from* that port.

2 *Houston Telegraph and Texas Register,* January 30, 1850, quoting dispatch from San Antonio dated January 13, 1850.

3 *Ibid.*

4 Quoted from the *Victoria Advocate* without date by Claude A. Talley, Jr., "From Sail to Rail," in *300 Years in Victoria County,* Roy Grimes ed. (Victoria: 1968).

5 Ralph B. Bieber, ed., *Exploring Southwestern Trails* (Glendale, CA: 1958), 50.

6 Clayton Williams, *Never Again* (San Antonio: 1969), 3:51.

7 Bieber, *Exploring Southwestern Trails,* 50.

8 See masthead of *Western Texian* [San Antonio] during the months starting February 1950.

9 *Western Texian,* February 28, 1850.

10 *Houston Telegraph,* January 31, 1850.

11 Talley, "Sail to Rail," 507; S. G. Reed, *A History of Texas Railroads and of Transportation Conditions in Texas* (Houston: 1941).

12 Talley, "Sail to Rail," 507.

13 *Ibid.*

14 *Ibid.*

15 *Ibid.*

16 These reports were all quoted, but without dates, by Claude Talley, "From Sail to Rail."

17 Frederick Law Olmstead, *A Journey Through Texas* (New York: 1857), 286.

18 Sulphur Springs later became Sutherland Springs, a way-station on one branch of the road from Indianola, about thirty miles southeast of San Antonio.

19 John R. Bartlett, *Personal Narrative of Explorations and Incidents in Texas, New Mexico, California, Sonora, and Chihuahua* (New York: 1854), 1:123.

20 Primary source on French: William Miles, *Journal of the Sufferings and Hardships of Captain Parker H. French's Overland Expedition to California* (Chambersburg, PA: 1851). Also Michael Baldridge, *A Reminiscence of the Parker H. French Expedition Through Texas and Mexico to California in the Spring of 1850* (Los Angeles: 1959). Also, re: French's bilking army supply sources in San Antonio: *Sen. Ex. Doc., 33d Cong., 2nd Sess. Rep. Com. No. 455,* January 30, 1855.

21 Williams, *Never Again,* 3:63–65.

22 M. L. Crimmins, "Freighting Through Fort Davis," *Alpine Avalanche,* 60th anniv. ed., September 14, 1951, 72.

23 Bartlett, *Narrative,* 1:123.

24 Bieber, *Exploring Southwestern Trails,* 51. Bieber thinks that pressure from Aubrey's financial sources in Missouri may have influenced this public reversal.

25 *Ibid.*

26 *Western Texian,* September 19, 1850.

27 *Ibid.*

28 Walter P. Webb, *Texas Rangers* (Austin: 1973), 141.

29 See John S. Ford's account of his Ranger Company in Stephen B. Oates, ed., *Rip Ford's Texas,* 142, *passim.*

30 *Houston Telegraph,* March 7, 1850.

31 J. H. Brown, *Life and Times of Henry Smith, the First American Governor of Texas* (Dallas: 1887), 378–379.

32 Sources on John Joel Glanton: Crimmins, "Glanton of San Antonio," *Frontier Times* 17, no. 7 (April 1940), 277–288; Rev. Wm. Young's letters, in *John McCullough, Pioneer Presbyterian Missionary and Teacher* by Wm. Wallace McCullough, Jr. (Austin: 1960), re: Glanton's attack on the Rev. Mr. McCullough; Samuel Emory Chamberlain,

My Confessions — The Recollections of a Rogue, Roger Butterfield, ed. (New York: 1956), 288–290.

33 This was the same Angel Trias, twenty-third governor of Chihuahua, who had fought Doniphan at Sacramento. Almada, *Diccionario,* 538–540.

34 Leavitt Corning, Jr., *Baronial Forts of the Big Bend* (San Antonio: 1967), 26–28; Williams, *Never Again,* 3:45.

35 Corning, *Baronial Forts,* 86, *passim,* re: Leaton's last days in San Antonio area.

36 *Ibid.,* 15–16.

37 Records Gr. No. 98, National Archives, Washington, D.C.

38 *Ibid.*

39 Corning, *Baronial Forts,* 31; Louise Cheney, "Old Fort Leaton," *The Cattleman* 47 (July 1960): 44, 56.

40 Webb, *Texas Rangers,* 68.

41 John Henry Brown, *History of Texas* (St. Louis: 1893), 2:322. Col. John S. Ford's memoirs, Oates, ed., *Rip Ford's Texas,* mentions a number of exploits by Chevaille in the Mexican War, with clear indication of his qualities of leadership. (See esp. p. 65.) Henry W. Barton, *Texas Volunteers in the Mexican War* (Wichita Falls: 1970) makes at least ten mentions of Chevaille, most in highly favorable context; Walter P. Lane, *Adventures and Recollections of . . .* (Marshall, TX: 1928) has a number of respectful references to the major, with whom he alternated in several command positions during the Mexican War. No separate biographical sketch of this unusual man appears to exist.

42 A. J. Sowell, *San Antonio Light,* September 27, 1921 (reprinted as "The Battle of Bandera Pass," *Frontier Times* 2, no. 8, May 1925). Sowell says "Mike Chevalier [*sic*] and Kit Ackland went with Col. Hays to California in 1848 [*sic*]." Hays actually left San Antonio with Johnston's military train in June 1849 and reached California that fall.

43 *Houston Telegraph and Texas Register,* September 13, 1850, copied from *St. Louis Union,* "15th instant."

44 Williams, *Never Again,* 3:65.

45 Herbert Eugene Bolton, *Guide to Materials for the History of the United States in the Principal Archives of Mexico* (1913), 455.

46 John Upton Terrell, *Apache Chronicle* (New York: 1972), 166–167.

47 Ralph A. Smith, "Mexican and Anglo-Saxon Traffic in Scalps, Slaves, and Livestock, 1835–1841," *Yearbook,* WTHA 36 (October 1960): 102–103, 115.

48 *Houston Telegraph,* March 7, 1850; J. H. Brown, *Life and Times of Henry Smith . . .* tells the story of Torrey's death, differing only in detail.

49 Horace Bell, *Reminiscences of a Ranger* (Santa Barbara: 1927), 186–187.

50 *Houston Telegraph,* January 30, 1850.

51 U.S. Census of Texas, 1850, Bexar County, Item No. 703.

Chapter 8. PORTS AT THE END OF THE ROAD

1 Ferdinand Roemer, *Texas, with Particular Reference to German Immigration,* English edition (San Antonio: 1935), 15; Brownson Malsch, *Indianola, The Mother of Western Texas* (Austin: 1977), 5.

2 Victor M. Rose, *History of Victoria,* original edition Laredo, 1883, republished at Victoria, 1961.

3 A. B. J. Hammett, "Don Martín de León — Empresario," article in *The Victoria Sesquicentennial Scrapbook: 1824–1974,* Henry Hauschild, ed. (Victoria: 1974), 6. [See also John J. Linn, *Reminiscences of Fifty Years in Texas* (New York: 1883).]

4 "The Last Alcalde, and First Mayor of Victoria," *The Victoria Scrapbook*, 8.

5 *Ibid.*, 8.

6 The Council House Fight, or Massacre, has been so often told as to need no further relating. One of the better eyewitness accounts is that of Mrs. Mary A. Maverick in *Samuel Maverick, Texan*. Recommended also is Rupert N. Richardson's analysis in his *The Comanche Barrier to the South Plains Settlement* (1933).

7 Texas State Historical marker installed on Welder townhouse, Victoria, April 14, 1974.

8 Maj. H. Oram Watts was the first person buried in the "Old Cemetery" now linked with Port Lavaca. [Dedication program for "Old Cemetery," also now called "Ranger Cemetery," Port Lavaca, February 26, 1974.]

9 Linn, *Fifty Years in Texas*, 341–342.

10 *Ibid.*, 343; also Z. N. Morrell, *Flowers and Fruits from the Wilderness* (4th ed., Dallas: 1886), 130.

11 Walter Prescott Webb, *The Texas Rangers* (Austin: 1973), 61–62; also John Henry Brown (who was on the scene), *Indian Wars and Pioneers of Texas*, 78–82; and the official reports of Gen. Felix Huston, *Journals of the House of Representatives of the Republic of Texas*, 5th Cong., 1st Sess., Appendix, 141 ff.

12 Paul Freier, historical column "Lookin' Back," *Port Lavaca Wave*, April 19, 1978. May now be found in Freier's *Lookin' Back, Scrapbook*, which he issued in limited circulation 1979.

13 R. L. Biesele, *The History of the German Settlements in Texas, 1831–1861* (Austin: 1930), 75, 76, 130.

14 The twenty-six-foot-deep Matagorda Ship Channel, cutting through Matagorda Island near Paso Cavallo, was not constructed by the Corps of Engineers until the twentieth century. [88th anniversary edition, *Victoria Advocate*, September 28, 1934.]

15 *The German-Texans*, unpaged brochure of the Institute of Texan Cultures (San Antonio: 1970).

16 Lois Lucille Bray, *Old Indianola, Life in a Frontier Seaport* (San Antonio: undated), 1.

17 G. G. Benjamin, *The Germans in Texas* (Austin: 1974), 44.

18 Roemer, *Texas*, 291.

19 *Victoria Advocate*, September 28, 1934, 57–62.

20 Roemer, *Texas*, 20. Benjamin, *Germans in Texas* (43) cites 400 to 700 immigrants at Indian Point in 1844; 3,000 by January 1846; and up to 5,247 by April 1846 (49).

21 Irene Marschall King, *John O. Meusebach, German Colonizer in Texas* (Austin: 1967), 5–53.

22 *Ibid.*, 53–56.

23 Roemer, *Texas*, 20–22.

24 King, *John O. Meusebach*, 85; Henry C. Armbruster, *The Torreys of Texas* (Buda, TX: 1968), 4–6, 52.

25 Marcus J. Wright, *Texas in the War, 1861–1865*, Harold B. Simpson, ed. (Hillsboro: 1965), 100–101; John Henry Brown, *History of Texas* (St. Louis: 1893), 2:322; Paul Freier, "August Buchel, Calhoun Historical Figure," *Port Lavaca Wave*, June 30, 1976; Malsch, *Indianola*, 12.

26 Roemer, *Texas*, 23.

27 August Santleben, *A Texas Pioneer*, I. D. Affleck, ed. (Waco: 1967, fac. ed.), 5.

Santleben says only thirty-five passengers survived the wreck, but Benjamin, *Germans in Texas,* 45, says "one or two persons lost their lives." Other casualty reports range between the two extremes.

28 Santleben, *A Texas Pioneer,* 6, 229.

29 The Runge brothers' bank was moved to the new settlement of Runge, between Goliad and Helena, after the disastrous hurricanes of 1875 and 1886. It finally closed during the Great Depression of the 1930s. [Notes by Mrs. Johanna Runge of Austin, Annie Doom Pickrell, ed., *Pioneer Women of Texas* (Austin and N. Y.: 1970).]

30 John S. Hadley, "Port Lavaca and Indianola," 88th anniv. ed., *Victoria Advocate,* 57–62; Malsch, *Indianola,* 37, 83.

31 Unattributed article in *Victoria Advocate,* historical edition, 1968, Sec. 3, p. 19.

32 Paul Freier, "Saluria's Prospects in 1867," column in *Port Lavaca Wave,* May 31, 1978.

33 Calhoun County, *Commissioners' Court Minutes,* A 106, p. 112; private files of R. L. Bisele, Austin.

34 Jessie Beryl Boozer, "The History of Indianola, Texas," M.A. thesis, University of Texas at Austin (1942), 27.

35 Malsch, *Indianola* (1977). Another invaluable adjunct to any study of Matagorda Bay is the late Paul Freier's compilation, "A 'Lookin' Back' Scrapbook for Calhoun County and Matagorda Bay, Texas." It is a collection of some 200 of Freier's columns in the *Port Lavaca Wave* from 1972 through 1979. Only a few processed copies were made available to libraries and Paul's circle of friends.

Chapter 9.   OBSERVANT STRANGERS ON A NEW FRONTIER

1 "Treaty of Peace, Friendship, Limits and Settlement between the United States of America and the Mexican Republic, concluded at Guadalupe Hidalgo on the 2nd day of February in the year 1848," in Wm. H. Malloy, comp., *Treaties, Conventions, International Acts, Protocols, and Agreements Between the United States of America and Other Powers, 1776– 1909,* 2 vols. (Washington: 1910), 1:1110–1113.

2 Par. 3, Article V, Treaty of Guadalupe Hidalgo, February 2, 1848.

3 Odie B. Faulk, "John Russell Bartlett and the Southwest: An Introduction," in 1965 reprint of Bartlett's *Personal Narrative* (Chicago: Rio Grande Press), 4.

4 *Ibid.*

5 *Ibid.,* 4, 23.

6 John Russell Bartlett, *Personal Narrative of Exploration and Incidents in Texas, New Mexico, California, Sonora and Chihuahua,* 2 vols. (New York: 1854), 1:13–14.

7 The clipping is quoted in Robert V. Hine, *Bartlett's West: Drawing the Mexican Boundary* (New Haven and London: 1968), 17.

8 Bartlett, *Personal Narrative,* 1:16–18.

9 Hine, *Bartlett's West,* 17.

10 John C. Cremony, *Life Among the Apaches* (San Francisco: 1868), 18–19.

11 Bartlett, *Personal Narrative,* 1:14.

12 *Ibid.,* 2:540.

13 Par. 1, Art. V, Treaty of Guadalupe Hidalgo, in Wm. H. Malloy, comp., *Treaties, Conventions . . . ,* 1:1110–1113.

14 General Pedro García Conde, Bartlett's Mexican counterpart on the Boundary Commission, was that same admired officer who planned engineering for the defenses at

Sacramento and led cavalry in that battle. He was forced to retire from the Boundary Commission because of arthritis and privations suffered in his wars against the Indians. Died December 19, 1851, before commission's work was finished. Francisco Almada, *Diccionario de Historia* . . . (Ciudad Chihuahua: 2d ed., 1968), 218.

15 Faulk, "Bartlett," 7th and 14th pages of introduction. Faulk cites here, and in other references to Bartlett-Conde controversy: "Report of the Secretary of Interior in relation to the Mexican boundary commission, July 1852," *Sen. Ex. Doc. 119, 32nd Cong., 1 Sess.*, Serial A26, 56–65.

16 One hundred miles west in New Mexico, the new line established by the Gadsden Purchase turned due south to 31°20' N, then due W again. Wm. H. Goetzmann, *Army Exploration in the American West, 1803–1863* (Lincoln and London: 1979), 195–273.

17 Almada, *Diccionario,* 334–335. Prof. Almada's treatment of the loss of Mesilla makes clear that a real crisis developed in Chihuahua as Governor Angel Trias, in power again, protested the ceding of this territory, especially since the indemnity all went to the Federal coffers of *"el Dictador"* Santa Anna of the republic.

18 Faulk, "Bartlett," 18th page of Introduction.

19 A. B. Bender, "The Texas Frontier, 1848–1861," *SHQ* 38, no. 2, 138–139.

20 Faulk, "Bartlett," 20th page of Introduction.

21 Bartlett, *Personal Narrative,* 2:533.

22 Bartlett was bitterly disappointed that the Congress, in terminating his appointment as commissioner, also withdrew support for publishing the report and the hundreds of pictures he and his staff had executed. When eventually published in N.Y. by D. Appleton in 1854, his *Personal Narrative* was in two small volumes, with the illustrations pitilessly reduced to the point that much of their impact is lost.

23 Report of William H. Emory, *House Ex. Doc. 135, 34th Cong., 1st Sess.* (Washington: 1857), 1:74.

24 The claims of a Lieutenant Love, of having navigated a twenty-foot-long boat *up* the Rio Grande through all the Rio Grande Canyons to a point near Presidio del Norte, in 1850, are simply too incredible to be accepted by anyone familiar with those canyons. This writer had his own experiences with the rapids and rockfall in Santa Helena Canyon in 1939. [See M. L. Crimmins, "Two Thousand Miles by Boat in the Rio Grande in 1850," *Bulletin* 48, WTHSS (Alpine), December 1, 1933, p. 44.]

25 Emory, *Report,* 1:74–81.

26 *Ibid.* Emory's sinister San Carlos is the same village which provided open-hearted succor to Jack Hays's starving party in 1848.

27 *Ibid.,* 88–89.

28 Paul Horgan, *Great River* (New York: 1954), 2:802–804.

29 Julius Froebel, *Seven Years' Travel in Central America, Northern Mexico, and the Far West of the United States.* The English translation from the German was published in London by Richard Bentley in 1859; it apparently has not been reprinted. The quotations which follow are from that edition. The book is quite rare, not available for checking out for leisurely reading; therefore, the lengthy quotes seem justified.

30 Froebel, *Seven Years,* 404–405.

31 Interview by RLS with Professor Francisco Almada at his home in Ciudad Chihuahua, November 1973.

32 Froebel, *Seven Years,* 406–407. "Julima" is known today as "Julimes."

33 *Ibid.,* 408.

34 *Ibid.,* 408–410.

35 Probate File 309, County Clerk's Office, Bexar County, Texas. See Leavitt Corning, Jr., *Baronial Forts* (San Antonio: 1967), 31–73, 77–105.

36 Froebel, *Seven Years,* 411.

37 *Ibid.,* 413, refers to the mineral of the San Esteban Terrace as "porphyry." In a letter from Dr. Ross Maxwell, long-time geologist of the Big Bend, he said that "Most recent authors refer to the rock as the Mitchell Mesa ash-fall tuff."

38 See illustration in this volume.

39 Froebel, *Seven Years,* 414.

40 *Ibid.,* 415.

41 Clayton Williams, *Never Again* (San Antonio: 1969), 3:126.

42 Froebel, *Seven Years,* 416.

43 *Ibid.* Re: Henry Skillman and Bigfoot Wallace, see Wayne Austerman's study, *Sharps Rifles and Spanish Mules, The San Antonio–El Paso Mail, 1851–1881* (College Station: 1985), 21–36.

Chapter 10.   OLD HELENA AND THE CART WAR

1 Sykes S. McLane, Robert H. Thonhoff, Calloway C. Crews, *The Life and Times of Thomas Ruckman,* Heritage Album Series no. 1 (Karnes City: Old Helena Foundation, 1968). Alamita Creek in Karnes County is not to be confused with Alamito Creek in Presidio County in the Big Bend.

2 Robert H. Thonhoff, series of three articles on "Historic Helena," *Karnes City Citation,* April 1, 8, and 15, 1968.

3 *Ibid.,* April 1, 1965.

4 *Karnes County News,* December 9, 1937 (50th anniv. ed.).

5 T. Lindsay Baker, "Four Letters from Texas to Poland in 1855," *SHQ* 37, no. 3 (January 1974): 381.

6 Jacek Przygoda, *Texas Pioneers from Poland* (Waco: 1971), 33–35.

7 Edw. J. Dworaczyk, *The First Polish Colonies of America in Texas* (San Antonio: 1936), 1.

8 Przygoda, *Texas Pioneers,* 34.

9 "Memorial Homecoming — Father Leopold Moczygemba," brochure published for the liturgical reinterment of Father Leopold at Panna Maria, Texas, October 13, 1974, 28.

10 Baker, "Letters from Texas," 389.

11 "Memorial Homecoming" brochure, 28. After Father Leopold had seen his little colony securely established, he moved on to broader fields of work in a long career, capped by his sponsorship of the first Polish institution of higher learning in the U.S., the Polish Seminary of Sts. Cyril and Methodius, Detroit, 1886.

12 Przygoda, *Texas Pioneers,* 41–77.

13 Thonhoff, *Karnes City Citation,* April 1, 1965.

14 August Santleben, *A Texas Pioneer* (Waco: 1967 reprint ed.), 112–113.

15 Frederick Law Olmstead, *A Journey Through Texas* (New York: 1857), 147–160.

16 Schedule I, "Free Inhabitants in San Antonio in the County of Bexar, Texas, enumerated . . . on the 21st day of September, 1850." Microfilm, Trinity University Library, San Antonio, Texas.

17 *Ibid.*

18 *San Antonio Ledger,* June 23, 1853.

19 *Ibid.*, January 12, 1854.

20 Howard Lackman, "George Thomas Howard, Texas Frontiersman," Ph.D. dissertation, University of Texas at Austin (1954), 281.

21 *San Antonio Ledger*, April 5, 1854.

22 M. L. Crimmins, ed., "W. G. Freeman's Report on the Eighth Military Dept., II," *SHQ* 50 (October 1947): 167–168.

23 *Ibid.*, 169.

24 *Sen. Ex. Doc. No. 7, 34th Cong. 1st Sess.*, Report of the Secretary of War Showing Contracts Made Under Authority of the War Department During the Year 1855, 11.

25 M. L. Crimmins, ed., "Col. J. F. K. Mansfield's Report on Dept. of Texas in 1856," *SHQ* 42, no. 2 (October 1938): 120.

26 *San Antonio Herald*, July 22, 1857.

27 Governors' Letters, Elisha Pease Collection (1853–1859), Folder 44, TSA.

28 Edwards was described by *San Antonio Ledger*, August 8, 1857, an account of the attack, as "an old citizen of this county."

29 Affidavit by C. G. Edwards before C. E. Jefferson, Governors' Letters, Pease Collection, Folder 46, TSA.

30 *Ibid.*, Folder 45.

31 Hedwig Kroll Didear, *A History of Karnes County and Old Helena* (Austin: 1969), 18.

32 Thomas Ruckman, "Memoirs," as quoted by Didear, 19.

33 J. Fred Rippy, "Border Troubles Along the Rio Grande, 1840–1860," *SHQ* 23, no. 2 (October 1919): 91. Olmstead, *A Journey Through Texas*, in a collection of newspaper articles appended to the text of his book, includes one (503–504) from the *Galveston News*, September 11, 1856, re: an alleged conspiracy for an uprising of the blacks and the retribution that was visited upon them.

34 Didear, in her *History*, referred to this scouting expedition as ". . . a mob, headed by one Colonel Wilcox [which] came down to the Cibolo boasting that they intended to sack the town of Helena . . ."

35 The *San Antonio Ledger* had reported, August 29, that "a very large train (about 100, we believe) left San Antonio during the week under the superintendence of Mr. W. G. Tobin." This member of a large family of Tobins in San Antonio had a long career in business in the city and was the father of John W. Tobin, sheriff and mayor. [*Handbook of Texas*, 3:1014.]

36 Governors' Letters, Wilcox's September 17 letter to Pease, Folder 46, TSA.

37 *Ibid.*, Paschal to Pease, Folder 46.

38 *Ibid.*, Wilcox to Pease, Folder 46.

39 *Ibid.*, Twiggs, "Special Order No. 122," Folder 46.

40 *Ibid.*, Paschal to Pease, September 20, Folder 46.

41 *Ibid.*, "Message from the Governor to the State Senate," November 11, 1857, Folder 48. The full text of this message appeared September 26 in both the San Antonio *Herald* and the *Ledger*.

42 *San Antonio Herald*, September 19, 1857.

43 *Ibid.*, September 26, 1857.

44 Copy of Bell's letter transmitted by Twiggs to Pease, Governors' Letters, as cited, Folder 47.

45 *San Antonio Herald*, September 26, 1857.

46 Walter Prescott Webb, *The Texas Rangers* (Austin: 1973), 148.

47 Governors' Letters, Pease Collection, TSA, Folders 47 and 48.

48 *Ibid.,* Folder 47.

49 *Ibid.,* Nelson to Pease, October 14, Folder 47.

50 This probably does not mean to say that seventy-five had been killed; if that were intended, it would be very much exaggerated. The number no doubt is meant to include those killed, wounded, and otherwise abused.

51 Letters of October 14 and 19, 1857, transmitted by U.S. Secretary of State Cass to Governor Pease, Governors' Letters, TSA, Folder 48.

52 *Ibid.*

53 *Ibid.,* Nelson to Pease, November 8, 1857, Folder 48.

54 *Ibid.*

55 *Ibid.,* Nelson to Pease, November 28, 1857, Folder 48; also *San Antonio Herald,* November 25, 1857.

56 *Ibid.,* Pease to Texas Senate, November 30, 1857, Folder 48.

57 *Ibid.,* November 11, 1857.

58 *Ibid.,* November 30, 1857.

59 Didear, *Karnes County,* 21.

60 *Ibid.*

61 Thonhoff, "History of Karnes," 124.

62 Governors' Letters, TSA, Nelson to Pease, Folder 49.

63 *Ibid.,* Pease to Cass, as cited, Folder 49.

64 *San Antonio Ledger,* February 13, 1858.

65 *Ibid.,* February 20, 1858.

66 *Ibid.,* March 20, 1858.

67 Thonhoff, "History of Karnes."

68 *San Antonio Herald,* March 27, 1848.

Chapter 11. HALCYON DAYS BEFORE THE WAR

1 Example: *San Antonio Western Texian,* September 19, 1850: "we understand that the people of El Paso have petitioned for a post route from this city — the mail to go through once a month."

2 J. Evetts Haley, *Fort Concho and the Texas Frontier* (San Angelo: 1952), 76. The lead title to Austerman's book is *Sharps Rifles and Spanish Mules.* See fn 5 below.

3 Re: Pedro Vial, see chapter 4, "Beginnings of the Third Road."

4 R. A. Howard's work on the lower Colorado River survey is reported in *Sen. Ex. Doc. No. 64, 51st Cong., 1st Sess.,* 1850.

5 Wayne R. Austerman, *Sharps Rifles and Spanish Mules, The San Antonio-El Paso Mail, 1851–1881* (College Station: 1985). George Giddings, Isaiah C. Woods, James Birch, Bethel Coopwood, Ben Ficklin, Frederick Sawyer, Francis C. Taylor, and Charles Bain are thoroughly presented, and justice is finally done to the work of the remarkable "agent," Jim Spears.

6 Waterman L. Ormsby, *The Butterfield Overland Mail,* L. H. Wright and Josephine Bynum, eds. (San Marino, CA: 1968), 67–78.

7 *Ibid.,* 77.

8 Haley, *Fort Concho,* 89.

9 Ormsby, *The Butterfield Overland Mail,* 90.

10 *Ibid.,* 77.

11 Haley, *Fort Concho*, 80.

12 *San Antonio Herald*, vol. 1, no. 1, p. 1.

13 "Cantonment Blake" on the Devil's River was, as its name implies, a temporary encampment. No official post was anywhere along that river until Camp Hudson was occupied at the Second Crossing June 7, 1857. [Robert W. Frazer, *Forts of the West* (Norman, OK: 1965), 152.]

14 W. H. Emory, *Report on the U.S. and Mexican Boundary Survey* (Washington: 1857–59), 1:24–25.

15 Thos. H. S. Hamersley, comp., *Complete Army Register of the United States for 100 Years (1779–1879)*, Pt. II, 138; *A Proud Heritage, History of Uvalde County*, comp. by El Progreso Club (Uvalde, TX: 1975), 10.

16 Uvalde County, *A Proud Heritage*, 10.

17 Whiting's "Report" in *Sen. Ex. Doc. No. 64, 31st Cong., 1st Sess.*, 245–246.

18 W. W. Arnette, "Reminiscences," MS, ECB.

19 Ed Westfall was besieged by Indians in his cabin on the Lower Leona June 30, 1855, and shot through by a rifle ball. He escaped and managed to stagger, over a period of three days, to Fort Inge, where under medical care he recovered. [Sowell's *Early Settlers and Indian Fighters*, 2:363 — 367.]

20 Of that trio of Indian fighters, Henry Robinson was the only one who died at the hands of the enemy. The Uvalde Historical Commission says, ". . . on May 29, 1861, two of Southwest Texas' most feared Indian fighters were ambushed by twenty hostile Indians. Henry Robinson — tall and red-headed — was so well known to the tribes that they had painted his picture on a rock near the Llano River. He and his daughter's fiance were en route to Camp Wood when the attack came. The Indians, after they had killed the two men, took both their scalps and also Robinson's flaming beard . . ."

21 "A History of Uvalde County," *Uvalde Leader News*, April 19, 1956 (centennial ed.).

22 Uvalde County [Texas]. Inventory of County Archives of Texas, Texas Historical Records Survey, WPA, No. 232, Uvalde, 1941, 6.

23 Andrew J. Sowell, *Early Settlers and Indian Fighters* (1964 reprint ed.), 1:291–294, 2:384–394.

24 Colonel Lee's official report noted only eight Indians in the raiding party. If four were killed in the first encounter, and three were seen alive at the end of the chase, that would leave only one Indian to be "scattered" over many miles. But one should not make light of the story as told; A. J. Sowell took it directly from folk who had taken part in the pursuit. His account of "Doke Bowles" is specific and direct. Robert E. Lee was far away when he compiled his.

25 "History of Uvalde County," *Leader News*, April 19, 1956.

26 M. L. Crimmins, "W. G. Freeman's Report," *SHQ* 51–54 (July 1947-October 1950), 71.

27 Frazer, *Forts of the West*, 139–164.

28 *Ibid*.

29 Oscar Haas, ed., "Autobiography of Peter Jonas," serially in *New Braunfels Herald*, July-September 1970; this excerpt on July 9. The venerable Mr. Haas, historian of Comal County, noted, "The original hand-written autobiography is in possession of Russell S. Jonas, Houston, a grandson of Peter Jonas. A copy was handed me by Wm. H. Winckler of Houston, also a grandson."

30 Dunbar Rowland, *Jefferson Davis* (New York: 1903), 3:71–73.

31 Ed Froboese's obituary, *San Antonio Express,* September 8, 1897, refers to this same incident but places it mistakenly in the hill country near Fredericksburg or Kerrville. Jonas's first-person account is the more valid one.

32 Henry W. Daly, "A Dangerous Dash Down Lancaster Hill," *American Legion Legionnaire,* December 1939, as reprinted in *Frontier Times* 20, no. 2, (April-June 1953): 172–173. Re: this hill descent, see also William A. Duffen, ed., "Overland via 'Jackass Mail,' in 1858: The Diary of Phocian Way," *Arizona and the West* (Spring 1960), 48–52.

33 This researcher has walked Lancaster Hill from top to bottom with grandson Justin Swift, photographed it, and can verify that every feature Daly describes, from the "defile" at the crest to the sharp left turn at the bottom, followed by a right turn which opens up a view of Fort Lancaster, is exactly as he rendered it. Daly may have exaggerated somewhat his experience with the Indians, but he certainly was familiar with the hill. Although the roadbed itself has been scoured down to the rock ledges by 130 years of gully-washers, a remarkable amount of the army's engineering work, including dry-laid abutments, remains visible.

34 As reprinted in *San Antonio Ledger,* March 10, 1853.

35 Crimmins, ed., "W. G. Freeman's Report," 25.

36 *Ibid.,* 57.

37 *Indianola Courier,* as reprinted in *San Antonio Ledger,* November 17, 1858.

38 "View of Indianola — Taken from the Bay on the Royal Yard on board the Barque TEXANA Sept. 1860, as drawn from nature by Helmuth Holtz." An original of this lithograph is displayed at the McNamara-O'Connor Museum, Victoria; an excellent reproduction is in Brownson Malsch's *Indianola,* 130. See photo section this book.

39 Unidentified Indianola newspaper, quoted in *San Antonio Herald,* December 25, 1858.

40 *San Antonio Ledger,* September 29, 1860.

Chapter 12.   CIVIL WAR HIATUS

1 U.S. Census, Texas, Slave Schedule. Vol. I (1860) *U.S. Census Reports,* 8th Census, Free Inhabitants in the County of Bexar.

2 John S. Hadley, article in *Victoria Advocate,* September 28, 1934. His figures are supported by the *Texas Almanac,* 1857 (Galveston: 1856), 52–57, listing number and value of slaves by each county, with a total of 103,297 valued at $52,167,838, five years before the war started.

3 Stephen B. Oates, ed., *Rip Ford's Texas* (Austin: 1963) 315 fn.

4 *Ibid.,* quotes from Ford's newspapers, not identified by dates.

5 *Journal of the Secession Convention of Texas, 1861* (Austin: 1861) E. W. Winkler, ed. (Austin: 1912), 61–65.

6 Hubert Howe Bancroft, *History of the North Mexican States and Texas* (San Francisco: 1883), 2:434.

7 Roy Sylvan Dunn, "The KGC in Texas, 1860–1861," *SHQ* 70, no. 4 (April 1967): 543–573. Dunn, then director of the Southwest Collection at Texas Technological College, Lubbock, won the first H. Bailey Carroll Award, 1966–1967, for this essay.

8 Marcus J. Wright, *Texas in the War, 1861–1865* (Hillsboro, TX: 1965), 177.

9 *Reports of the Committee on Public Safety to the Convention of the People of the State of Texas,* printed by John Marshall, State Printer, Austin, 1861.

10 *Ibid.,* 4, 9. Dunn, "K. G. C. in Texas," 561, says Phillip Luckett "may be strongly suspected of KGC affiliation."

11 Mary Ann Maverick, *Memoirs* (San Antonio: 1921), 119.

12 Maj. J. T. Sprague, *The Treachery in Texas, the Secession of Texas, and the Arrest of the U.S. Officers and Soldiers Serving in Texas* (New York: Press of the Rebellion Records, 1862); *True Issue*, February 21, March 7, 1861; *Dallas Herald*, February 27, 1861; James P. Newcomb, "Sketch of Secession Times in Texas" (privately printed: 1863), 6. These contemporary reports were confirmed later when the commissioners' correspondence was revealed: they had reported to chairman J. C. Robertson that Ben McCulloch "was joined by about 150 Knights of the Golden Circle . . ." which by their count raised the total force to about 800.

13 Mrs. Caroline B. Darrow, "Recollections of the Twiggs' Surrender," *Battles and Leaders of the Civil War* (New York: 1884–1888), 1:33.

14 Dunn, "KGC in Texas," 543–573.

15 Wright, *Texas in the War*, 194–195; *Report of the Committee on Public Safety*, 30–42.

16 War Department, General Order No. 5, AGO, March 1, 1861.

17 Harry McCorry Henderson, *Texas in the Confederacy* (San Antonio: 1955), x-xi.

18 *Ibid.*, 69; Kenneth F. Neighbors, *Robert Simpson Neighbors and the Texas Frontier, 1836–1859* (Waco: 1975).

19 Martin H. Hall, *Sibley's New Mexico Campaign* (Austin: 1960), 32.

20 *Ibid.*

21 Name as per Hall, *Sibley's . . . Campaign*, 308. Major Waller is listed once in Henderson's *Texas in the Confederacy*, 124, as Edward, Jr., and just below, on the same page, as "Edwin." Wright, *Texas in the War*, lists him twice as "Edward, Jr.," (23 and 32). George Wythe Baylor, in his reminiscences in the *El Paso Herald*, mentions him as "Hiram Waller, Jr." Oates, *Confederate Cavalry*, lists "Edward Waller, Jr.," as Major 2nd Reg. (173), later as cdr. of 13 Battalion, Texas Cavalry, (175). Nevertheless, this was certainly Edwin Waller, Jr., son of the Edwin Waller who had signed the Texas Declaration of Independence on March 2, 1836. Edwin Waller, III, grandson of the original, lived after the turn of the century in San Marcos, Texas, where he was a perpetually unsuccessful candidate for public office until his death in the 1930s.

22 Rex W. Strickland, *Six Who Came to El Paso* (El Paso: 1963), 33.

23 *Ibid.;* Henderson, *Texas in the Confederacy*, 124; Hall, *Sibley's . . . Campaign*, 10; J. Morgan Broaddus, *The Legal Heritage of New Mexico* (El Paso: 1963), 67–69.

24 Baylor's report, dated September 21, 1861, as reproduced in George Griggs, *History of Mesilla Valley* (Las Cruces, NM: 1930), 66–68. Hall, *Sibley's . . . Campaign*, 27; Baylor's "Proclamation," is reproduced in Griggs, 69–71.

25 *San Antonio Herald*, November 9, 1861; Hall, *Sibley's . . . Campaign*, 41; also Wm. A. Keleher's *Turmoil in New Mexico* (Santa Fe: 1952), 162.

26 Johnson, ed., *Battles and Leaders*, 110–111.

27 For background on the Baylor-Kelley affair, see *San Antonio Herald*, January 4 and 11, 1862, and Kelley's own account, written a few days before he succumbed to his wound, as it appears in *Mesilla Times*, January 1, 1862, its front page framed in mourning black. Photocopy of this issue may be found in the rare books archives, New Mexico State University, Las Cruces.

28 Full text of Sibley's proclamation in Griggs, *Mesilla Valley*, 74.

29 *Ibid.*, Baylor's letter, 75.

30 Hall, *Sibley's . . . Campaign*, 224 fn.

31 Letter to John H. Reagan, January 26, 1862, *SHQ* 44:167–187.

32 J. Fred Rippy, "Mexican Objects of the Confederacy," *SHQ* 22:300; Henderson, *Texas in the Confederacy,* 74–75.

33 Henderson, *Texas in the Confederacy,* 79–80. Scurry and his men captured six artillery field pieces of late model from the Yankees at Val Verde. They hauled them doggedly up to Glorieta and back to Texas down the Chihuahua Road, to fight through the rest of the war. One surviving cannon of the six stands today in the courthouse square at Fairfield in East Central Texas. [Feature series by Ed Syers, "The Devil Gun," in *San Antonio Express,* June 27-July 2, 1976.]

34 Henderson, *Texas in the Confederacy,* 80.

35 *Ibid.,* 81. John M. Chivington, the "Fighting Parson," became notorious in 1864 when he planned and carried out the massacre of over 200 Cheyennes and Arapahos, camped peacefully at Sand Creek, Colorado. See Robert M. Utley, *Frontiersmen in Blue* (New York: 1973), 292–297.

36 Henderson, *Texas in the Confederacy,* 83.

37 *Ibid.,* 84.

38 Hall, *Sibley's . . . Campaign.* RLS interview with Marlin Frettem, owner of the property at Cañoncita, including Precipitous Mountain, August 10, 1975. He said that an old resident of Apache Canyon, Gregorio Garcia, remembers when the pile of iron wagon tires still lay at the foot of the bluff.

39 *San Antonio Herald,* June 5, 1862.

40 Hall, *Sibley's . . . Campaign,* 207–210.

41 O. W. Williams, *Pioneer Surveyor — Frontier Lawyer* (El Paso: 1968 ed.), 133–134; Emmie G. W. B. Mahon and Chester Kielman, "George H. Giddings and the San Antonio — San Diego Mail Line," *SHQ* 61, no. 2 (October 1957): 238–239.

42 *San Antonio Herald,* June 5, 1862.

43 *Ibid.*

44 Hall, *Sibley's . . . Campaign,* 213.

45 See Brownson Malsch, *Indianola,* 147–183, for review of that activity.

46 Skillman's birthplace has usually been attributed to Kentucky, but Rex Strickland, *Six Who Came to El Paso,* found him listed in the 1860 Census at El Paso as born in New Jersey, 1814.

47 Averam Bender, *Exploring Southwestern Trails,* 311, and 311 fn.

48 *El Paso Herald,* April 20, 1901. Joe Hatch's account, as retrieved by Rex Strickland of El Paso.

49 J. Evetts Haley, *Fort Concho and the Texas Frontier* (San Angelo: 1952), 90.

50 Wayne R. Austerman, *Sharps Rifles* (College Station: 1985), 180–181.

51 James Wiley Magoffin never made his home in El Paso again. He died September 27, 1868, on the ranch of his son-in-law outside San Antonio. After services in San Fernando Cathedral, he was buried in the family vault on the ranch. [Strickland, *Six Who Came to El Paso,* 67 fn.]

52 Broaddus, *The Legal Heritage of New Mexico,* 73.

53 W. W. Mills (Rex. Strickland, ed.), *Forty Years at El Paso,* Carl Hertzog, designer (El Paso: 1962), 86; C. L. Sonnichsen, *Pass of the North* (El Paso: 1968), 159.

54 Mills, *El Paso,* 86 fn, *passim.* Although French is defended energetically by his friend W. W. Mills, his carpetbagger career and eventual dismal end are spelled out in Rex Strickland's notes to Mills's memoirs and in Sonnichsen's history of the city.

55 Hitherto-published accounts of French's manhunt against Skillman have apparently been based on oral folklore, without recourse to French's official report. That report

was not found on file in *Official Records of the Rebellion,* but an extract of the vital portions re: Skillman was published May 7, 1864, on the front page of the *Santa Fe New Mexican,* introduced by a gleeful letter to Carleton from Col. G. W. Bowie, commanding 5th Infantry, California Volunteers, Headquarters, Franklin, Texas, April 25, 1864. Rex Strickland pointed the writer to that account, providing the basis for this sketch of Skillman's last days.

56 Whether French meant "intelligent" as a commendatory adjective, or whether this was a corruption of "intelligence" is not clear.

57 This is French's own very clear account of his approach upon Skillman's camp. Carlysle Raht, *Romance of Davis Mountains* (El Paso: 1919), 151, has a very convincing anecdote about Dietrich Duchover visiting French from across the river in old Presidio, during the evening before French's attack upon Skillman. It simply will not fit into the context of French's official narrative. Unless French's account was pure invention, then Duchover's visit must be dismissed as unfounded folklore. Rex Strickland believed the fatal ambush took place several miles upriver from Presidio.

58 French's own account. Strickland learned that one of the men who escaped was Bill Ford, who lived to become sheriff of El Paso County. Another is reputed to have been Jarvis Hubbell.

59 According to an editorial accompanying French's report in the *Santa Fe New Mexican,* May 7, 1864, the captured mail contained instructions from General Magruder and a precise listing of the troop and arms disposition of Federal forces in the New Mexico Territory.

60 Travis Roberts tells of a discovery made in the Presidio Catholic cemetery not many years ago. When a new grave was being opened, the diggers encountered the remains of an earlier burial: a huge skeleton with the unmistakable remnants of blond hair and a long, blond beard. Roberts got the story from Stanley Cassner, who in the 1970s was living in Austin. He had been in business in Presidio and claimed to have seen the exhumed skeleton, as described. They believe it was probably the remains of Henry Skillman. [Taped conversation with Travis Roberts, August 28, 1975.]

61 Verified by a personal visit to the campgrounds, in 1976.

62 Raht, *Romance of Davis Mountains,* 337–348; Barry Scobee, *Fort Davis, Texas* (El Paso: 1963), 22.

63 W. C. Holden, "Frontier Defense in Texas During the Civil War," *Yearbook,* WTHA, No. 4 (June 1928): 16–31.

64 T. R. Fehrenbach, *Comanches: The Destruction of a People* (New York: 1974), 278–279; William C. Pool, "Battle of Dove Creek," *SHQ* 53 (April 1950): 367.

65 Rollins to Orlando Brown, April 23, 1850, Office of Indian Affairs, 1850, Letters Received, ECB, as cited by Mildred P. Mayhall, *Indian Wars of Texas* (Waco: 1965), 92.

66 Jane Cazneau (under pen-name Cora Montgomery), *Eagle Pass, Life on the Border* (Austin, as reprinted 1966 from original New York print, 1852).

67 Pool, "Dove Creek," 379; also A. M. Gibson, *The Kickapoos: Lords of the Middle Border* (Norman, OK: 1963), 200–203.

68 A. J. Sowell, *Early Settlers and Indian Fighters of Southwest Texas* (Reprint, 1964), 1:264.

69 Pool, "Dove Creek," 369.

70 Holden, "Frontier Defense," 26–27.

71 Robert M. Utley, *Frontier Regulars* (New York: 1973), 166.

72 Webb's *The Texas Rangers* does not mention the Dove Creek Battle, and his brief passage on Civil War times (219) makes clear his conclusion that the Texas Rangers were not in existence during those years.

73 I. D. Ferguson, "Battle of Dove Creek," *Frontier Times* 1, no. 10 (June 1924): 23.

74 *Handbook of Texas,* 1:516.

75 Grace Bitner, "R. F. Tankersley and Family, Pioneers of the Concho Country," *Yearbook,* WTHA 20 (October 1944): 89.

76 Pool, "Dove Creek," 37.

77 Besides William C. Pool's and J. Evetts Haley's accounts, as cited, see: Brig. Gen'l J. D. McAdoo to John Burke, February 20, 1865, *Records,* AGO's Office, Austin; Fossette to J. B. Barrie, March 12, 1865, *Texas State Gazeteer,* Austin, April 5, 1865; Judge I. D. Ferguson, eyewitness report written in 1911, published as "Battle of Dove Creek," *Frontier Times* 1 no. 9 (June 1924): 24–31; John Warren Hunter, "The Battle of Dove Creek," in *Hunter's Magazine,* 1911, reprinted in *Frontier Times* 1, no. 10 (July 1924): 17–20; contemporary coverage of battle in *Weekly State Gazette* [Austin], February 1 and February 8, 1865, including text of Captain Totton's official report.

78 F. G. Huntress letter to R. Fink, *Weekly State Gazette* [Austin], February 22, 1865. Huntress listed himself as with "Co. G, Ben's [*sic*] Reg't, T. C. . . . . Eagle Pass."

79 Capt. Chas. Atkins's letter to Lt. Collins, *Weekly State Gazette* [Austin], February 22, 1865.

80 Wright, *Texas in the War,* 145.

81 T. A. Jennings, "San Antonio in the Confederacy," M.A. thesis, Trinity University, San Antonio, Texas (1957), 119.

82 *Ibid.,* 123.

Chapter 13.   RE-CONSTRUCTING UNDER RECONSTRUCTION

1 Alice Jack Shipman, *Taming the Big Bend* (Marfa: 1926), 36.

2 *Ibid.,* 39.

3 Francis W. Johnson, *History of Texas and Texans* (Chicago and New York: 1916), 1142; Frederic C. Chabot, *With the Makers of San Antonio* (San Antonio: 1937, 2nd ed.), 341.

4 Howard Lackman, "George Thomas Howard, Texas Frontiersman," Ph.D. dissertation, University of Texas at Austin (1954), 304.

5 Papers of George T. Howard, Howard Lackman Collection. ECB.

6 Lackman, "George T. Howard," 304.

7 *San Antonio Tri-Weekly Herald,* September 28, 1865.

8 Lackman, "George T. Howard," 305.

9 *San Antonio Tri-Weekly Herald,* September 7, 1865.

10 *San Antonio Daily Herald,* December 19, 1865.

11 *San Antonio Tri-Weekly Express,* September 21, 1865.

12 *San Antonio Herald,* October 26, 1865.

13 *San Antonio Express,* May 19, 1877.

14 S. G. Reed, *A History of the Texas Railroads* (Houston: 1941), 258–259.

15 *San Antonio Tri-Weekly Herald,* September 7, 1865.

16 *Ibid.,* September 9, 1865.

17 *Ibid.,* October 10, 1865. This wharf must have been the one built by Charles Morgan of the shipping lines.

18 *Ibid.,* September 9, 1865.

19 *Ibid.,* October 28, 1865.

20 *San Antonio Daily Herald,* November 16, 1865.

21 *San Antonio Express,* October 3, 1865. The new *Express* was a joint enterprise with the German language *Freie Press fuer Texas,* H. Pollmar and August Siemering, publishers.

22 *San Antonio Daily Herald,* November 2, 1865.

23 *Ibid.,* January 29, 1866.

24 Robert M. Utley, *Frontier Regulars, The United States Army and the Indian, 1866–1891* (New York: 1973), 166.

25 *San Antonio Tri-Weekly Herald,* September 13, 1865.

26 *Ibid.,* September 16, 1865.

27 Francis B. Heitman, *Historical Register and Dictionary of the U.S. Army* (Washington: 1903) 2:426–427 (Urbana: University of Illinois Press, 1965 reprint).

28 *San Antonio Herald,* February 4, 1866.

29 August Santleben, *A Texas Pioneer* (Waco: 1967 fac. ed.), 266–267. (See fn 43, this chapter.)

30 Ernest Wallace, *Ranald S. Mackenzie on the Texas Frontier* (Lubbock: 1964), 94.

31 *Ibid.,* 23.

32 *Ibid.,* 94; Utley, *Frontier Regulars,* 166.

33 *Sen. Ex. Doc. No. 19, 45th Cong. 2nd Sess.,* 7–9.

34 Evelyn and T. C. Davis, *Spirit of the Big Bend* (San Antonio: 1948), 32.

35 Santleben, *A Texas Pioneer,* 18–22, 37.

36 *Ibid.,* 22–31.

37 *Ibid.,* 40.

38 N. H. Rose photo in Hunter Collection, Institute of Texan Cultures.

39 Santleben, *A Texas Pioneer,* 41.

40 "Isaac Dunbar Affleck," president's paper delivered by Dr. Ralph A. Wooster before Texas State Historical Association, Austin, March 7, 1975. Copy in RLS files.

41 Santleben, *A Texas Pioneer,* 102.

42 *Ibid.,* 101. Affleck/Santleben was referring to the famous original "Pecos High Bridge" which was actually eighty miles distant in a straight line, probably 120 miles or more by river.

43 The original edition of August Santleben (I. D. Affleck, ed.), *A Texas Pioneer — Early Staging and Overland Freighting Days on the Frontiers of Texas and Mexico,* the Neale Publishing Company, New York and Washington, 1910, is a collector's item today. Facsimile edition (Waco: W. M. Morrison, 1967) may be available in some bookstores. Since the book was the old freighter's sole contribution to literature, references from it will be cited in this volume simply as Santleben.

44 *San Antonio Herald,* February 2, 1866.

45 *Ibid.* Wayne R. Austerman has thoroughly covered the fortunes and misfortunes of Coopwood, Ficklin, and their associates, in providing stage and mail service to West Texas.

46 J. Marvin Hunter, *Old Camp Verde* (Bandera, TX: 1948).

47 *SHQ* 3 (1899–1900).

48 *Ibid.,* 2 (1898–1899).

49 Robert H. Thonhoff, *San Antonio Stage Lines, 1847–1881,* Monograph 29, Southwestern Studies (El Paso: 1971), 22.

50 Shipman, *Taming Big Bend,* 37; Carlysle G. Raht, *The Romance of Davis Mountains and Big Bend Country* (El Paso: 1919), 153–154.

51 Santleben says (120) that "about sixty" mules froze to death at the place called, for many years after, "Edgar's Boneyard."

52 Shipman, *Taming Big Bend,* 38.

53 The announcement about train service at Victoria is dated April 1, 1866, but Thonhoff found his first published example of it in *San Antonio Ledger,* March 2, 1867. See Thonhoff, *Stage Lines,* Fig. 26 and p. 23.

54 Wallace, *Ranald S. Mackenzie,* 23.

55 *Ibid.,* 24; Utley, *Frontier Regulars,* 166.

56 Wallace, *Ranald S. Mackenzie,* 24.

57 Charles W. Ramsdell, "Texas in the New Nation," *The South in the Building of the Nation* 3, Southern Historical Publication Society (Richmond, VA: 1909), 422; also W. C. Nunn, *Texas Under the Carpetbaggers* (Austin: 1962), 8–9.

58 Clifford B. Casey, *Mirages, Mysteries, and Realities: Brewster County* (Seagraves, TX: 1972), 19; Francisco R. Almada, *Diccionario . . . Chihuahuenses,* 523.

59 Raht, *Romance of Davis Mountains,* 157.

60 Rupert N. Richardson, *Comanche Barrier to the South Plains Settlement* (Glendale, CA: 1933), 293.

61 Robert M. Utley, *Fort Davis* (Washington: 1955), 71–72.

62 *San Antonio Herald,* October 31, 1865.

63 Scobee, *Old Fort Davis,* 71–72. Scobee, Mrs. Shipman, and Leavitt Corning all refer to Dan and Pat Murphy as separate persons. It is true that original records cited by Clifford Casey in his history of Brewster County (24) show that "Patrick Murphy, Mose E. Kelley, and Daniel Murphy served as the board of commissioners to supervise the organization . . ." of Presidio County, in 1875. Nevertheless, I am convinced that Daniel Murphy of Fort Davis was also known as "Pat," and that the shadowy "Patrick" was a lesser-known personality. See also frequent references to both Pat and Dan in Cecilia Thompson, *History of Marfa and Presidio County, 1535–1946,* Vol. I (Austin: 1985).

64 Leavitt Corning, Jr., *Baronial Forts* (San Antonio: 1967), 38.

65 Shipman, *Taming Big Bend,* 41.

66 W. W. Mills, *Forty Years at El Paso,* Rex Strickland, ed. (El Paso: 1962), 82 fn.

67 In published accounts, Moses Kelley has heretofore been referred to as a former captain in the U.S. Army. Nevertheless, Rex Strickland found army records in New Mexico which show that Moses Kelley was a sergeant major in the New Mexico First Volunteer Regiment when he was mustered out at the end of the Civil War. [RLS interview with Strickland, August 1975.]

68 Shipman, *Taming Big Bend,* 41–42.

69 Bvt. Maj. Gen. Charles Griffin had died of yellow fever in New Orleans September 15. Reynolds was named as replacement. [*Express,* September 5 and 17, October 9).]

70 *Ibid.,* November 5, 1867.

71 *Indianola Times* copied June 26, 1866, by *San Antonio Express.*

72 *San Antonio Express,* September 4, 1867; John L. Waller, *Colossal Hamilton* (El Paso: 1968), 98.

73 All the developments of 1867–1869, above, regarding freight from the coast to San Antonio, are drawn from *San Antonio Express,* September 4, 12, 14, October 8, 17, November 20, 1867; January 13, February 21, 1868; January 14, 26, 28, February 19, March 13, April 4, 14, May 11, 19, 23, 26, June 2, 13, 1869.

74 Hubert Howe Bancroft, *Works* (San Francisco: 1884–89) 16:487; Nunn, *Texas Under Carpetbaggers,* 7–9.

75 *San Antonio Express,* August 30, 1867.

76 *Ibid.,* August 31, 1867.

77 *San Antonio Express,* November 19, 1867.

78 Hedwig Kroll Didear, *A History of Karnes County and Old Helena* (Austin: 1969), 34–37.

79 *San Antonio Weekly Express,* January 24, 1869.

80 *Ibid.,* June 22, 1869, dispatch from Ft. Davis.

81 According to Jarvis Hubbell's data sheet in Masonic Lodge No. 130, El Paso, he was killed January 11, 1869, but the fact that a dispatch was filed from Ft. Davis January 14, 1869, with a full account of his murder, after subsequent searches and confusion, makes the earlier date of January 5 more likely.

Chapter 14. THE MEN, THE TEAMS, THE WAGONS

1 W. W. Mills, *Forty Years in Old El Paso,* Rex Strickland, ed. (El Paso: 1962), 137–141. In fn 29, p. 26, Strickland adds the three names shown in text.

2 Santleben, *A Texas Pioneer,* 107–108.

3 *San Antonio Light,* March 2, 1912; *San Antonio Express,* February 27, 1921.

4 Manuscript obituaries and biographical material, S. W. Pease Collection, 833 E. Guenther, San Antonio.

5 Froboese's obituary in *San Antonio Express,* September 8, 1897, says his Ranger service was in 1854 and that his company was commanded by "Captain Henry." Actually, in context with other events, it appears more likely Froboese served in 1855 in Capt. J. R. Callahan's Company, and that the confusion arose because Callahan late in 1855 associated himself with the dubious W. H. Henry on the "Callahan Raid" into Mexico. [Webb, *Texas Rangers* (Austin: 1973), 146, and Ernest C. Shearer, "The Callahan Expedition," *SHQ* 54 (April 1951): 430–451.]

6 Robert W. Frazer, "Fort Martin Scott," *Forts of the West* (Norman, OK: 1965), 135.

7 Josephine Lanham, October 4, 1972: "Recollections of Early Spanish-Speaking Settlers and Rolling of Wagons from Old San Antonio, Texas, to Chihuahua, Mexico." [She had heard me speak on this project and brought me the MS, anxious that her family be represented. MS in RLS files.]

8 *San Antonio Express,* September 8, 1897.

9 Lanham, "Recollections."

10 *Ibid.* This group of families, settled on the West Side, may have been the nucleus for the neighborhood that was called "Chihuahua."

11 Copied from the referenced monument.

12 *San Antonio Express,* March 4, 1908.

13 *Ibid.,* July 24, 1875.

14 *San Antonio Light,* March 7, 1908.

15 In 1974, when he heard this book was in progress, Luis Rodriguez came to me, told me of the monument, and led me to it. I took his picture beside it.

16 Santleben, *A Texas Pioneer,* 144.

17 Sam W. Pease of San Antonio compiled the biographical data on Adams and Wickes. [See also Chabot, *With the Makers of San Antonio* (San Antonio: 1937), 320 re: Harden B. Adams.]

18 *San Antonio Express,* March 21, 1869.

19 Ernest Wallace's summary of this scandal, in his *Ranald S. Mackenzie on the Texas Frontier* (Lubbock: 1968), 62–74, cites in fn 6, p. 74, a collection of papers, 3888 AGO 1876 (filed with 2441 AGO 1876) including Mackenzie's letters to departmental HQ, July 11 and 19, 1871; copy of charges and specifications filed against Mackenzie, etc. [See also Robert M. Utley, *Frontier Regulars* (New York: 1973), 209.]

20 *San Antonio Express,* August 21, 1868.

21 *Ibid.,* June 12, 1869; "Autobiography of Peter Jonas," Oscar Haas, ed., *New Braunfels Herald,* September 3, 1970. See fn 29, chapter 11.

22 William Corner's compilation in *San Antonio de Bejar* (San Antonio: 1890), 148.

23 *Ibid.,* 134.

24 *San Antonio Express,* February 12, 1871.

25 "Autobiography of Peter Jonas," September 3, 1970.

26 *San Antonio Express,* July 31, 1932, front page of Society and Features Section.

27 *Ibid.*

28 Manuscript file on Adams and Wickes compiled by S. W. Pease of San Antonio from contemporary newspapers, county records, obituaries, and tombstone inscriptions. In the city tax rolls for 1889 Adams was listed with tax valuations of $255,340 — a real fortune for that era. Adams died of paralysis June 4, 1895; his funeral was conducted by Dean Richardson of St. Marks Episcopal Cathedral, and he was interred in Alamo Masonic Cemetery. Edwin de Lacy Wickes died in St. Louis June 17, 1892, and was buried there. Both men died intestate; the settlement of their estates was difficult and protracted.

29 *Floresville Chronicle-Journal,* September 16, 1960, Sec. G, p. 6; interviews with Mrs. Maude Gilliland and other members of Gilliland family, 1974–75, by RLS

30 Charles Barnes, *Combats and Conquests of Immortal Heroes* (San Antonio: 1911), 135.

31 Santleben, *A Texas Pioneer,* 60–61. [For further information on this book, see fn 43, chapter 13.]

32 *Ibid.,* 60.

33 *Ibid.,* 95.

34 *Ibid.,* 97.

35 *Ibid.,* 99.

36 *Ibid.*

37 *Ibid.*

38 *Ibid.,* 100–101; "Map of Scouting Expeditions from Camps at the Chinati Mtns., Jan. 12 to May 12, 1880," 10th U.S. Cavalry, in Crimmins Map Collection, ECB.

39 Francisco R. Almada, *Diccionario . . . Chihuahuenses,* 374–376.

40 Santleben, 102.

41 *Ibid.*

42 *Ibid.*

43 See Julius Froebel, *Seven Years' Travel* (London: 1859), 405. Santleben, or Affleck, spelled "Ojito" incorrectly as "hojito."

44 Santleben (Affleck) spells this as "meson de Massarre," 164. After a lot of puzzlement, I realized that was a misspelling of "Maceyra." Almada, *Diccionario,* 316, confirms that José Felix Maceyra was active at this time in providing accommodations for freight traffic.

45 Santleben, 164.

46 *Ibid.,* 163.

47 Almada, *Diccionario,* 83.

48 Santleben, 103.

49 *Ibid.,* 104. Henry Müller, born in Germany ca. 1820, was educated there as a mining engineer and gained experience in that field. He came to St. Louis in the 1850s, but was soon called to Chihuahua to install modern machinery in the Santa Eulalia mines. He acquired large mining interests, as well as directorship of the mint, and invested the proceeds of these ventures in land, becoming eventually one of the largest landholders in northern Mexico, next to Luis Terrazas.[RLS interview July 30, 1979, with Lic. Emilio Elias Müller, great-grandson of the original Henry Müller and a former president of the *Sociedad Chihuahuenses de Estudios Historicos.*]

50 Santleben, 107. (Photo of the Fort Leaton *carreta* is in this book.)

51 *Ibid.*

52 The Mormon Tabernacle in Salt Lake City, built under pioneer conditions more than a century ago, is still held together almost entirely by similar pins and raw-hide lashings.

53 Santleben, 109.

54 Nick Eggenhoffer, *Wagons, Mules, and Men: How the Frontier Moved West* (New York: 1961) 35–55, 110–111. [This writer offers his apologies to Mr. Eggenhoffer for the similarity between the title of this chapter and the title of his book. It was the only way he could find to encapsulate the subject of the chapter.] Also see George Shumway, *Conestoga Wagon 1750–1850 — Freight Carrier for 100 Years of America's Westward Expansion* (York, PA: 1966).

55 Eggenhoffer, *Wagons, Mules,* 102–108.

56 *Ibid.,* 115.

57 Santleben, 109–110.

58 *Ibid.,* 112–113.

59 *Ibid.,* 113. "Rocky Garady" was beyond doubt Affleck's misspelling of some Spanish name.

60 *Ibid.*

61 *Ibid.*

62 *Ibid.,* 112.

63 *San Antonio Express,* May 25. An ironic aspect of Newcomb's departure from the editorial desk at the *Express,* where he so fervidly proclaimed Radical Unionism, is that he at once became messenger, as secretary of state, in negotiating the sale of the College Land Scrip which created the Texas Agricultural and Mechanical College, a splendid example of populism at its best. [See Wm. T. Hooper, Jr., "Governor Edmund J. Davis, Ezra Cornell, and the A&M College of Texas," *SHQ* 78, no. 3 (January 1975): 307–312.]

64 *Ibid.,* December 20, 1868.

65 H. H. McConnell, *Five Years a Cavalryman* (Jacksboro, TX: 1889), 186–187.

66 Sidney Lanier, "San Antonio de Bejar," an essay purchased by William Corner and printed by him in his *San Antonio de Bexar* (San Antonio: 1890), 93.

Chapter 15.   THE PRIME DAYS OF AUGUST SANTLEBEN

1 Ernest Wallace, *Ranald S. Mackenzie on the Texas Frontier* (Lubbock: 1965); Robert G. Carter, *On the Border with Mackenzie* (Washington, DC: 1935), 82. Carter, as a young lieutenant, was at Fort Richardson when the massacre took place.

2 Santleben [see fn 43, chapter 13], 141. Travis Roberts of Marathon, Texas,

points out that Santleben was describing Juan Cardona Lake. Located in Crane County, it is the same salt deposit which had been the goal of parties coming up the Alamito Creek trail from Mexico for centuries. [See map of Crane County in any recent *Texas Almanac*.]

3 For description of "sidelining" see Carter, *On the Border,* 164.

4 Santleben, 143.

5 *Ibid.*

6 *Ibid.*

7 *Ibid.,* 144.

8 Francis B. Heitman, *Historical Register and Dictionary of the U.S. Army* (Washington: 1903), 2:437.

9 Santleben, 143.

10 Summary of sources on the Howard's Well Massacre: *San Antonio Herald,* May 3, 1872; *San Antonio Express,* May 3, 1872; Heitman, *Historical Register,* 2:437; Santleben, 143–144; Sidney Lanier's essay, in Corner, *San Antonio de Bejar* (San Antonio: 1890), 141; Charles Barnes, *Combats and Conquests of Immortal Heroes* (San Antonio: 1911), 135–136; Files of Crockett County Chapter, Texas State Historical Survey, HQ, Texas State Historical Commission, Austin.

11 Lanier, *San Antonio de Bejar,* as cited above.

12 Excellent background on John L. Bullis is presented by Edward S. Wallace (not to be confused with Edwin Wallace) in "John Latham Bullis, Thunderbolt of the Prairies," I, *SHQ* 54, no. 4 (April 1951): 452–461, and II, 54, no. 1 (July 1951): 77–85.

13 For original source material on Ranald S. Mackenzie, see R. G. Carter, *On the Border with Mackenzie, or, Winning West Texas from the Comanches* (Washington, DC: 1935).

14 Richard A. Thompson, *Crossing the Border with the 4th Cavalry, Mackenzie's Raid into Mexico, 1873* (Waco: 1986). See also a review of this book by Kenneth R. Philip, *SHQ* 90, no. 4 (April 1987): 434–435.

15 John H. Dorst, "Ranald Slidell Mackenzie," Twentieth Annual Reunion Association, Graduates U.S. Military Academy, 1889, *Army & Navy Journal* 26 (January 26, 1889): 423–424; *Dictionary of American Biography,* Dumas Malone, ed. (New York: 1935) 12:95.

16 Wallace, "Bullis," *SHQ,* no. 1 (July 1951): 77.

17 Frost Woodhull, "The Seminole Indian Scouts on the Border," *Frontier Times* 15, no. 3 (December 1937): 118–121.

18 Santleben says (149) that this trip was begun in February 1873. The full context of his narrative, however, argues compellingly that it must have been 1874. He tells of accompanying Col. Mackenzie and a large body of troops westward from Devil's River toward Howard's Well, whereas Mackenzie had not reported to Fort Clark in February 1873 and could not have been on the road westward in 1873.

19 Mackenzie was apparently in the process of transferring his Fourth Cavalry to their new duties on the Northwest Frontier.

20 Santleben, 150–151.

21 *Ibid.,* 152.

22 *Ibid.,* 153–155.

23 *Ibid.,* 156.

24 *Ibid.,* 167–168.

25 *Ibid.,* 169.

26 *Ibid.,* 170.

27 *Ibid.,* 175.

28 *Ibid.*, 177.
29 *Ibid.*, 184–185.
30 *Ibid.*, 180–183.
31 *Ibid.*, 192.
32 Almada, *Diccionario*, "Ferrocariles Nacionales," 206.

Chapter 16.   THE COMING OF THE IRON HORSE

1 "Certificate of Award for Building the Miss. and Pac. Railroad," August 4, 1854, four-page statement in Gov. Pease's handwriting, Governors' Letters, E. M. Pease, 4–4/8, folder No. 9, TSA.
2 *San Antonio Express,* June 11, 1871.
3 S. G. Reed, *A History of the Texas Railroads* (Houston: 1941), 258–259.
4 *San Antonio Express,* October 21, 1871.
5 James P. Baughman, *Charles Morgan and the Development of Southern Transportation* (Nashville: 1968), 187–188.
6 *Ibid.*, 188.
7 Reed, *Texas Railroads,* 261.
8 *Ibid.*, 112.
9 *Ibid.*, 192.
10 *Ibid.*
11 Reed, "G.H.&S.A. Ry." in *Handbook of Texas,* 1:665.
12 Reed, *Texas Railroads,* 193–194.
13 *San Antonio Express,* February 7, 1872.
14 *Ibid.*, March 30, 1872.
15 Malone, ed., *Dictionary of American Biography,* 8:30–31.
16 *Ibid.*, 191.
17 Edward E. King and J. Wells Champney, *Texas: 1874* (Houston: 1974), an extract reprinted from *The Southern States of North America,* 35–36.
18 Reed, *Texas Railroads,* 195; William Corner, *San Antonio de Bexar* (San Antonio: 1890), 156.
19 *San Antonio Daily Express,* March 11, 1875. Peirce lost out completely on that first proposed large subsidy.
20 *San Antonio Daily Express,* January 23 and February 11, 1870.
21 *Ibid.*, January 6, 1871.
22 *Ibid.*, April 20, 1871. Santleben (129) errs in saying the bridge was erected in administration of James H. French. French did not become mayor until January 19, 1875.
23 Santleben, 129.
24 *Biographical Dictionary of the American Congress, 1774–1911* (Washington, DC: 1971), 663. As soon as the darker years of Reconstruction were over, Schleicher ran for Congress as a Democrat; was elected; and served until his death January 10, 1879.
25 *Indianola Weekly Bulletin,* March 27, 1871.
26 *San Antonio Express,* November 4 and 25, 1871.
27 *Ibid.*, December 10, 1871.
28 *Ibid.*, March 16, 1876.
29 *Ibid.*, July 23, 1876.
30 King, *Texas: 1874,* 110–111.
31 *San Antonio Express,* September 2, 1876.

32 *Ibid.*, February 1, 1876; Corner, *San Antonio de Bexar*, 131.

33 Charles A. Potts, *Railroad Transportation in Texas*, Bulletin No. 119 of the University of Texas, March 1, 1909, 101. S. G. Reed says the Sunset Route lost two-thirds of that acreage twenty years later.

34 Reed, *Texas Railroads*, 196.

35 *San Antonio Express*, October 1, 1876.

36 *Ibid.*, December 21, 1876.

37 *Ibid.*, January 21, 1877.

38 *Ibid.*, February 7, 1877.

39 Reed, *Texas Railroads*, 198; *San Antonio Sunday Express*, July 31, 1932. Both sources speak of Samuel A. Maverick as if he were still alive in 1877, overlooking his death in 1870.

40 *San Antonio Sunday Express*, July 31, 1932; Arthur Mayer, "San Antonio: Frontier Entrepot," Ph.D. dissertation, University of Texas at Austin, 1976.

41 Neill C. Wilson, *Southern Pacific* (New York: 1952), 73.

42 *San Antonio Express*, February 20, 1877.

43 *Ibid.*

44 *Ibid.*

45 Quoted by S. G. Reed, *Texas Railroads*, 195.

46 *San Antonio Express*, February 20, 1877. All these reflections from San Antonio's great day are drawn from the editor's four-column story, evidently written in installments as the day progressed and hand-spiked into type during the remaining hours of the night by the boys in the back room at the paper. The editor, Frank Grice, who covered the event, had come from newspaper work in Kansas City only a month earlier. His story, with other sidebar features, especially the long list of names, is a treasure trove for researchers.

Chapter 17. Twilight for the Wagons

1 *San Antonio Express*, February 23, 1877.

2 *Ibid.*, February 24, 1877.

3 Lettered clearly on two places along the trailblazing route as shown on Livermore's "Military Map of the Rio Grande Frontier, 1881" (M. L. Crimmins Map collection, ECB) is the identification, "New Military Road." Travis Roberts of Marathon, Texas, says it is still familiarly called "Bullis's Road."

4 The legend of Livermore's "Military Map" bears the following notations, among others: "Authorities . . . Astronomical Positions: Points on New Military Road, Capt. W. R. Livermore, Corps of Eng. 1878–80 . . . Points on New Military Road, Topc. Ass't, F. E. Butterfield 1878–79–80."

5 See Livermore's "Military Map" as cited above.

6 In the early 1900s, when the first graveled highway for cars and trucks was put through the Trans-Pecos country, a fine steel span named Bullis Bridge was thrown across the Pecos River almost directly above his old ford. This bridge washed out in a flood.

7 Frost Woodhull, "The Seminole Indian Scouts on the Border," *Frontier Times* 15, no. 3 (December 1937): 123.

8 I often filled my canteens, or took a drink direct from the faucet at those windmills, while knocking about in West Texas, 1930–1940.

9 M. L. Crimmins, "Camp Peña Colorado, Texas," *Bulletin No. 56*, WTHSS (Al-

pine, Texas), December 1935. "Novaculite" is the same fine-grained stone from which the famous "Arkansas whet-rocks" were derived.

10 Col. Charles Judson Crane, "Experiences of a Colonel of Infantry," *SHQ* 23, no. 2 (October 1919).

11 Burgess Spring was known earlier as Charco de Alsate and, since the turn of this century, as Kokernot Springs.

12 Letter from Travis Roberts to RLS, March 17, 1973. This writer had visited Mrs. Hallie Stillwell, justice-of-the-peace in Alpine, Texas, in her office at the Brewster County Courthouse early in 1973. When I told her of our interest in the Chihuahua Road, she said immediately: "Don't miss talking to Travis Roberts down below Marathon. And his aunt, Mrs. Nellie Davis, at Marathon. They know more about the Cut-off Road and the Military Road than anyone else alive." When I did get to visit with Travis and Mrs. Davis a few months later, I found how true Mrs. Stillwell's statement was. They were sources for virtually all of the information on the Cut-off Road.

13 Travis Roberts was born more than eighty years ago in a house which still stands on the hill above Peña Colorado's watercourse, and within a hundred yards of the Halff Brothers store. The store was operated by the same brothers, Meyer and Solomon Halff, who had a large wholesale and retail dry goods establishment on Commerce Street in San Antonio. [*San Antonio Express,* December 11, 1880, in a review of "Reliable Merchants."] Alfred S. Gage of the Gage Land and Cattle Company established his ranch along the Maravillas Draw and up to Peña Colorado shortly after the railroad came.

14 Travis Roberts took me and Joe King to Monument Spring in April 1973.

15 The first street-pavement (mesquite blocks) was laid on Alamo Plaza in March 1889. [Corner, *San Antonio de Bejar,* 438.]

16 *San Antonio Express,* November 16, 1875.

17 Edward King (with J. Wells Champney, illustrator), *Texas: 1874* (Houston: 1974) as book-length extract from *The Southern States of North America* (Glasgow: 1875).

18 Santleben, 110.

19 Josephine Lanham "Recollections of Early Spanish-speaking Settlers and Rolling of Wagons . . . to Chihuahua," dated October 4, 1972.

20 *San Antonio Express,* October 8 and 9, 1871; *Indianola Scrapbook,* G. H. French, ed. (Victoria: 1939).

21 *Victoria Advocate* (Special Hurricane Edition), September 24, 1875.

22 *Ibid.*

23 *Ibid.*

24 *Ibid.*

25 *Ibid.*

26 *Ibid.*

27 Brownson Malsch, *Indianola, The Mother of Western Texas* (Austin: 1977), 244.

28 As quoted by *San Antonio Express,* October 16, 1875.

29 S. G. Reed, writing the port city's obituary in *Handbook of Texas,* 1:883.

30 Santleben, 226–227.

31 Santleben's obituary in *San Antonio Express,* September 19, 1911, 9.

Chapter 18.   END OF THE TRAIL

1 The convoluted, intricate story of the last stand of the Indians in Texas does not exist in print in any single account. The Texas Rangers, the United States Army, and the Mexican military were all notably engaged in this final elimination of Indian violence on

the Texas-Mexican frontier, but each related its own part to the exclusion of the others. Best primary sources: Joaquin Terrazas, *Memorias del Sr. Coronel Joaquin Terrazas* (Juarez: 1905); George Wythe Baylor, "Reports" to John B. Jones, commanding, Frontier Battalion, Texas Rangers, August 20, 1880, January 16, and February 9, 1881, TSA; James B. Gillett, *Six Years with the Texas Rangers* (New Haven: 1925); Col. Ben H. Grierson's "Report" in Sec. of War Report, *House Exec. Doc. 1, Pt. 2, 46 Cong., 3d Sess.,* 1881; and archival material at the Fort Davis National Historic Site Museum, Fort Davis, Texas. Secondary compilations: Dan L. Thrapp, *Victorio and the Mimbres Apaches* (Norman: 1974); Robert M. Utley, *Frontier Regulars, the United States Army, and the Indian, 1866–1891* (New York: 1973); and Walter Prescott Webb, *The Texas Rangers* (Austin: 1973). I have attempted a reconciled account from all sources, too long for this volume, for later publication. RLS

2 *San Antonio Weekly Express,* February 19, 1880, account signed "Hans Mickle."

3 *San Antonio Sunday Express,* July 31, 1932.

4 United States Census, 1880, 1900. Houston's population in 1880: 16,500; Dallas, 10,358.

5 Photo, "The Old Southern Pacific Passenger Depot on Austin St.," Grandjean Collection, DRT Library at the Alamo, San Antonio, Texas.

6 *San Antonio Sunday Express,* July 31, 1932; also "Peter Jonas Autobiography," Oscar Haas, ed., *New Braunfels Herald,* September 10, 1970. According to Jonas's account, he entered local politics about the same time he opened his new establishments, served as alderman from 1879 to 1883, later county commissioner, and county judge.

7 *San Antonio Sunday Express,* July 31, 1932.

8 Santleben, *A Texas Pioneer,* 209.

9 *San Antonio Daily Express,* March 19, 20, 23, 1881.

10 *San Antonio Sunday Express,* July 11, 1932.

11 *San Antonio Daily Express,* July 24, 1881.

12 *San Antonio Sunday Express,* July 31, 1932.

13 *Ibid.*

14 Professor Francisco R. Almada says in his *Diccionario . . . Chihuahuenses,* 293 (roughly translated), that by the decree of July 29, 1889, Paso del Norte was raised to the status of City with the name Juárez, in honor of President Benito Juárez, who had taken refuge there in the years 1865 and 1866 during the fight between the *Intervencion Francese* and the *Imperio.* By 1987, the population of Juárez was 1.1 million (*Time,* June 1, 1987, 51).

15 *San Antonio Express,* January 14, 1881. The newspaper called the source "Judge Blocker," but this was Allen Blacker, who had been district judge at El Paso until 1880, and who later served in the state legislature. [J. Morgan Broaddus, *The Legal Heritage of New Mexico* (El Paso: 1963), 117.]

16 Neill C. Wilson, *Southern Pacific* (New York: 1952), 77.

17 Reed, *Railroads of Texas,* 196.

18 *San Antonio Express,* December 3, 1880.

19 *Ibid.,* January 14, 1881.

20 *Ibid.,* March 1, 1881.

21 Reed, *Railroads of Texas,* 197.

22 Wilson, *Southern Pacific,* 77, adds that this acquisition of G.H.&S.A. stock made legal Huntington's extension eastward beyond El Paso.

23 Policarpo Rodriguez, *The Old Guide,* D. W. Carter, ed. (Nashville: 1897).

24 Reed, *Railroads of Texas,* 197–199; Wilson, *Southern Pacific,* 78.

25 Reed, *Railroads of Texas,* 197.

26 "Military Map of the Rio Grande Frontier, 1881," by Capt. W. R. Livermore (Crimmins Map Collection, ECB), shows the projected route of the railroad as lying alongside the New Military Road.

27 *San Antonio Express,* January 1, 1883. It was actually about three miles from the Pecos, but some ten or twelve miles above its mouth.

28 An original glossy photo of the ceremony (reproduced in Neill C. Wilson's *Southern Pacific,* opposite p. 70) shows a special railroad car backed up from each direction over the spidery trestle, within a few yards of each other, with the imperfectly fitted junction between them. It is all on the edge of a yawning chasm. Colonel Peirce, in tall silk hat, is flanked by about forty-five other dignitaries, engineers, railroad hands — and three ladies standing on the platform of the car from the west. This appears to be the total of persons at the ceremony — except for the photographer himself (probably John A. G. Rabe) who stood on some elevated point about 100 feet distant to take the picture.

29 *San Antonio Express,* January 13, 1883.

30 Wilson, *Southern Pacific,* 77, says, "In general charge of construction was J. H. Strobridge [*sic,* this appears to be the correct spelling] who had built the Central Pacific over the Sierra under Crocker years before."

31 *San Antonio Express,* January 13, 1883.

32 *Ibid.*

33 Reed, *Railroads of Texas,* 198.

34 Rex W. Strickland, *Six Who Came to El Paso* (El Paso: 1963), 28. Joseph Magoffin's rambling adobe house, built in 1875, has now been restored and reopened to the public by Texas State Department of Parks and Wildlife.

35 *San Antonio Express,* January 13, 1883.

Bibliography

Abbreviations

AGO   Adjutant General's Office
ECB   Eugene C. Barker Texas History Center, University of Texas at Austin
GPO   Government Printing Office
MS   Manuscript
QTSHA   *Quarterly of the Texas State Historical Association*
RLS   Roy L. Swift
SHQ   *Southwestern Historical Quarterly*
TSA   Texas State Archives Division, Texas State Library, Austin
WTHA   West Texas Historical Association
WTHSS   West Texas Historical and Scientific Society

BOOKS

Almada, Francisco R. *Diccionario de Historia, Geografía y Biografía Chihuahuenses.* Ciudad Chihuahua: Universidad de Chihuahua. Segunda Edición, 1968.

Applegate, Howard G., and C. Wayne Hanselka. *La Junta de los Rios del Norte y Conchos.* University of Texas at El Paso: 1974. Monograph No. 41 in Southwestern Studies Series.

Armbruster, Henry C. *The Torreys of Texas.* Buda, TX: Citizen Press, 1968.

Austerman, Wayne R. *Sharps Rifles and Spanish Mules, The San Antonio-El Paso Mail, 1851–1881.* College Station: Texas A&M University Press, 1985.

Austin, Rose. *Early History of San Angelo.* "Tom Green County," by Mrs. C. S. Autrey. San Angelo, TX: 1950.

Bakanowsk, Adolph. *Moje Wspomnienia, 1840–1863–1913, My Memoirs, 1840–1863–1913.* Edited by Tadevsz. Llow, Austrian Empire: 1913.

Bancroft, Hubert Howe. *History of the North Mexican States and Texas, 1531–1800.* 2 vols. San Francisco: A. L. Bancroft & Co., 1883.

———. *History of Arizona and New Mexico, 1530–1888.* Vol. 17. San Francisco: 1889 (orig. ed.).

Bandelier, Adolph. *Contributions to the History of the Southwestern Portion of the United States.* Boston: 1890.

Bandelier, Fanny, tr. *Naufragios: The Journey of Alvar Nuñez Cabeza de Vaca, 1528–1536.* New York: A. S. Barnes, 1905.

Bannon, J. F., ed. *Herbert Eugene Bolton and the Spanish Borderlands.* Norman, OK: 1964.

Barker, Eugene C., ed. *The Austin Papers.* Vol. 3, 1834–1837. Austin: University of Texas Press, 1927.

————. The Life of Stephen F. Austin. Nashville: Cokesbury Press, 1925. Reprint, Austin: Texas State Historical Association, 1949.

————. Mexico and Texas, 1821–1835. Dallas: P. L. Turner Co., 1928.

Barnes, Charles. Combats and Conquests of Immortal Heroes. San Antonio: Guessaz & Ferlat, 1911.

Bartlett, John Russell. Personal Narrative of Explorations and Incidents in Texas, New Mexico, California, Sonora, and Chihuahua. 2 volumes. New York: D. Appleton & Co., 1854.

Barton, Henry W. Texas Volunteers in the Mexican War. Wichita Falls: 1970.

Bauer, K. Jack. The Mexican War, 1846–1848. Macmillan Series, "Wars of the United States." New York: Macmillan: 1974.

Baughman, James P. Charles Morgan and the Development of Southern Transportation. Nashville: 1968.

Beck, Warren A. New Mexico, a History of Four Centuries. Norman: University of Oklahoma Press, 1962.

Bell, Maj. Horace. Reminiscences of a Ranger, or Early Times in Southern California. Santa Barbara: 1927.

Benjamin, Gilbert Giddings. The Germans in Texas. Philadelphia: University of Pennsylvania Press, 1910. Reprint. Austin: 1974.

Bennett, James A. Forts and Forays, a Dragoon in New Mexico, 1850–1856. Albuquerque: University of New Mexico Press, 1948.

Bieber, Ralph B., ed. Exploring Southwestern Trails, 1846–1854. Glendale, CA: The Arthur Clark Co., 1938. Journals of Philip St. George Cooke, William H. C. Whiting, Francois X. Aubrey. Southwestern Historical Series No. 3.

————, ed. Marching with the Army of the West, 1846–1848. Glendale, CA: 1960. A. H. Johnson, M. B. Edwards, P. H. Ferguson. Southwestern Historical Series No. 4.

Biesele, Rudolph L. The History of the German Settlements in Texas, 1831–1861. Austin: Von Boeckmann Jones, 1930.

Biographical Directory of the American Congress, 1774–1971. Sen. Doc. No. 92B, 92nd Cong., 1st Sess. Washington: GPO, 1971.

Bishop, Morris Gilbert. The Odyssey of Cabeza de Vaca. New York and London: 1933.

Bolton, Herbert Eugene. Guide to Materials for the History of the United States in the Principal Archives of Mexico. 1913.

————. Coronado: Knight of Pueblos and Plains. Albuquerque: Whittlesey House, 1949.

————. The Spanish Borderlands. New Haven: 1921.

————. Spanish Exploration in the Southwest, 1542–1706. New York: Scribner's, 1916.

————. Texas in the Middle Eighteenth Century: Studies in Spanish Colonial History and Administration. Reprint. Austin & London: University of Texas Press, 1976.

Bowden, J. J. The Exodus of Federal Forces From Texas, 1861. Austin: Eakin Press, 1987.

Brice, Donaly E. The Great Comanche Raid: Boldest Attack of the Texas Republic. Austin: Eakin Press, 1986.

Broaddus, J. Morgan. The Legal Heritage of New Mexico. El Paso: Texas Western Press, 1963.

Brown, John Henry. Life and Times of Henry Smith, the First American Governor of Texas. Dallas: A. D. Aldridge & Co., 1887.

Brune, Gunnar. The Springs of Texas. Vol. 1. Fort Worth: 1981.

Carroll, H. Bailey. The Texan-Santa Fe Trail. Canyon, TX: Panhandle-Plains Historical Society, 1951.

Carter, Robert Goldthwaite. *On the Border with Mackenzie, or, Winning West Texas from the Comanches.* Washington: Eynor Printing Co., 1935.

Casey, Clifford B. *Mirages, Mysteries, and Realities: Brewster County, Texas — The Big Bend of the Rio Grande.* Seagraves, TX: 1972.

Castañeda, Carlos Eduardo. *Our Catholic Heritage in Texas, 1519–1936.* Vol. 1. Austin: Von Boeckmann-Jones, 1936.

Cazneau, Mrs. Jane (McManus), (Mrs. W. L.), (Cora Montgomery). *Eagle Pass or Life on the Border.* Edited with Introduction, by Robert Crawford Cotner. Austin: The Pemberton Press, 1966.

Chabot, Frederick C. *With the Makers of San Antonio.* San Antonio: Privately published, 1937.

Chamberlain, Samuel Emory. *My Confessions — The Recollections of a Rogue.* Edited by Roger Butterfield. New York: 1956. [Condensation pub. serially in *Life*, summer 1955. Undocumented, sometimes demonstrably incorrect, information on John Joel Glanton, but worthwhile in correlating other sources.]

Chaput, Donald. *Francois Xavier Aubrey: trader, trailmaker, and voyageur in the Southwest, 1846–1854.* Vol. 16. Western Frontiersmen Series. Glendale, CA: Arthur H. Clark Co., 1975.

Chihuahua. *La República Mexicana: Chihuahua, Reseña Geografía y Estadista.* Libreria de la Vda. de C. Bouret. Paris and Mexico: 1909.

Chihuahua, Ciudad Procer: 1709–1959. Universidad de Chihuahua: 1959.

Chittenden, Hiram Martin, ed. *The American Fur Trade in the Far West.* 2 vols. 1st pub. 1902. Reissued, New York 1935; Stanford, CA, 1954.

Committee on Public Safety, Reports to the Convention of the People of the State of Texas. Austin: Printed by John Marshall, State Printer, 1861.

Conklin, Roscoe P., and Margaret B. Conklin. *The Butterfield Overland Mail, 1857–1859.* 3 vols. Glendale, CA: Arthur H. Clark Co., 1947.

Connelley, William Elsey, ed. *War with Mexico: 1846–1847; Doniphan's Expedition and the Conquest of New Mexico and California.* Expanded ed. published by author. Topeka, KS: 1907.

Connor, Seymour V., and Jimmy M. Skaggs. *Broadcloth and Britches: The Santa Fe Trade.* College Station: Texas A&M Press, 1976.

Corner, William. *San Antonio de Bexar, A Guide and History.* San Antonio: Bainbridge and Corner, 1890.

Corning, Leavitt, Jr. *Baronial Forts of the Big Bend.* San Antonio: Trinity University Press. 1st printing, 1967; 2nd printing, 1969.

Coves, Elliott. *The Expedition of Zebulon Montgomery Pike.* 3 vols. New York: Francis P. Harper Co., 1895.

Cremony, John C. *Life Among the Apaches.* San Francisco: 1868. Reprint. Lincoln, NE: 1985.

Crockett County, A History of. American Revolution Bicentennial Project. Ozona, TX: 1976.

Cullum, Geo. Washington. *Biographical Register of the Officers and Graduates of the U.S. Military Academy, 1802–1863.* Vols. 2 and 3. New York: 1879.

Dale, Edward Everett. *The Cross Timbers.* Austin: 1966.

Darrow, Mrs. Caroline. "Recollections of the Twiggs Surrender." *Battles and Leaders of the Civil War.* Vol. 1. New York: 1884–1888.

Davis, Evelyn, and T. C. Davis. *Spirit of the Big Bend.* San Antonio: 1948.

Deuvall, Aurelia Flores, and Peggy A. Rodriguez. *Our Family Heritage*. San Antonio: Graphic Arts, 1975.

Dictionary of American Biography. Edited by Dumas Malone. 20 vols. New York: 1936.

Didear, Hedwig Kroll. *A History of Karnes County and Old Helena*. Austin: San Felipe Press, 1969.

Dobie, J. Frank. *A Vaquero of the Brush Country*. Dallas: The Southwest Press, 1929.

Dorst, John H. "Ranald Slidell Mackenzie." *Proceedings of Twentieth Annual Reunion Association, Graduates of the U.S. Military Academy*. West Point, NY: Library, U.S. Military Academy.

Drum, Stella M., ed. *Down the Santa Fe Trail and into Mexico, The Diary of Susan Magoffin, 1846–1847*. New Haven: 1926.

Duffus, Robert Luther. *The Santa Fe Trail*. London, New York, Toronto: Tudor Pub. Co., 1930.

Dworaczyk, Rev. Edw. J. *The First Polish Colonies of America in Texas*. San Antonio: The Naylor Co., 1936.

Eggenhoffer, Nick. *Wagons, Mules, and Men: How the Frontier Moved West*. New York: Hastings House, 1961.

Emmett, Chris. *Fort Union and the Winning of the Southwest*. Norman: University of Oklahoma Press, 1965.

Emory, Maj. W. H. *Report on the United States and Mexican Boundary Survey*. 3 vols. Washington, D.C.: C. Wendell, Printer, 1857–1859. (Texas State Historical Ass'n. has just republished this monumental work, spring of 1988, 3 vols.)

Evans, Geo. W. B. *Mexican Gold Trail, the Journal of a Forty-Niner*. San Marino, CA: 1925.

Everett, Donald E. *San Antonio: The Flavor of its Past, 1845–1898*. San Antonio: Trinity University Press, 1975.

Falconer, Thomas. *Letters and Notes on the Texan-Santa Fe Expedition, 1841–1842*. Edited by F. W. Hodge. 1930. Reprint. Chicago: 1963.

Faulk, Odie B. *General Tom Green, Fightin' Texan*. Waco: 1963.

Fehrenbach, T. R. *Lone Star: A History of Texas and the Texans*. New York: Macmillan, 1968.

———. *Comanches: The Destruction of a People*. New York: Alfred A. Knopf, 1974.

Frazer, Robert W. *Forts of the West*. Norman: Oklahoma University Press, 1965.

Frederick, James Vincent. *Ben Holladay, the Stagecoach King*. Glendale, CA: 1940.

Freeman, Douglas Southall. *Robert E. Lee*. Vol. 1. New York: Scribner's, 1935.

Friend, Llerena. *Sam Houston: the Great Designer*. Austin: University of Texas Press, 1954.

Froebel, Julius. *Seven Years' Travel in Central America, Northern Mexico, and the Far West of the United States*. Orig. pub. in German. English trans.: Richard Bentley. London: 1859.

Frost, John. *The History of Mexico and its Wars*. New Orleans: Armand Hawkins, 1887.

Fulcher, Walter. *The Way I Heard It: Tales of the Big Bend*. Edited by Elton Miles. Austin: University of Texas Press, 1959.

German Texans, The. Institute of Texan Cultures (staff). San Antonio: University of Texas, 1970.

Gibson, A. M. *The Kickapoos: Lords of the Middle Border*. Norman: University of Oklahoma Press, 1963.

Gillett, James B. *Six Years with the Texas Rangers*. New Haven and London: Yale University Press, 1925.

Goetzmann, Wm. H. *Army Exploration in the American West, 1803–1863.* Lincoln and London: University of Nebraska Press, 1979.

Green, Laurence. *The Filibuster: The Career of William Walker.* New York: Bobbs-Merrill Co., 1937.

Green, Rena Maverick, ed. *Samuel Maverick, Texan: 1803–1870.* San Antonio: Privately printed, 1952.

Greer, James Kimmins. *Colonel Jack Hays.* New York: E. P. Dutton, 1952.

Gregg, Josiah. *The Commerce of the Prairies.* New York: 1844. Reprint. 1933.

Gregg, Kate Leila, ed. *The Road to Santa Fe: the Journal and Diaries of George Champlin Sibley.* Albuquerque: 1952.

Groos National Bank, San Antonio, comp. *From Oxcarts to Jet Planes, The Groos National Bank, San Antonio, 1854–1954.* San Antonio: The Clegg Co., Printers, 1954.

Griggs, George. *History of Mesilla Valley or Gadsden Purchase.* Las Cruces, NM: 1930.

Grimes, Roy, ed. *300 Years in Victoria County.* Claude A. Tally, Jr., "From Sail to Rail." Victoria: 1968.

Guadalupe Hidalgo, Treaty of. *Conventions, International Acts, Protocols, and Agreements Between the United States of America and Other Powers, 1776–1909.* Wm. H. Malloy, comp. 2 vols. Washington: 1910. (Vol. 1, full text of treaty.)

Hagner, Lillie May. *Alluring San Antonio, Through the Eyes of an Artist.* San Antonio: 1940.

Haley, James Evetts. *Fort Concho and the Texas Frontier.* San Angelo: Standard-Times Press, 1952.

———. *Charles Goodnight, Cowman and Plainsman.* New York: Houghton-Mifflin, The Riverside Press Cambridge, 1936.

———. *Jeff Milton, a Good Man with a Gun.* Norman: University of Oklahoma Press, 1948.

———. *The XIT Ranch of Texas, and the Early Days of the Llano Estacado.* Norman: University of Oklahoma Press, 1955.

Hall, Martin Hardwicke. *Sibley's New Mexico Campaign.* Austin: University of Texas Press, 1960.

Hallenbeck, Cleve. *Alvar Nuñez Cabeza de Vaca, The Journey and Route of the First European to Cross the Continent of North America, 1534–1536.* Glendale, CA: Arthur H. Clark Co., 1940.

———, ed. *The Journey of Fray Marcos of Niza.* Dallas: 1949.

Harris, Benjamin Butler. *The Gila Trail: The Texas Argonauts and the California Gold Rush.* Edited by Richard Dillon. Norman: University of Oklahoma Press, 1960.

Heitman, Francis Bernard. *Historical Register and Dictionary of the United States Army, from organization, Sept. 29, 1789–March 2, 1903.* GPO, 1903. Reprint, Urbana: University of Illinois Press, 1965.

Henderson, Harry McCorry. *Texas in the Confederacy.* San Antonio: 1955.

Herff, Ferdinand Peter. *The Doctors Herff.* San Antonio: 1973.

Hine, Robert V. *Bartlett's West: Drawing the Mexican Boundary.* New Haven and London: Yale University Press, 1968.

Hollon, W. Eugene. *The Lost Pathfinder: Zebulon Montgomery Pike.* Norman: University of Oklahoma Press, 1919.

Horgan, Paul. *Great River: The Rio Grande in North American History.* 2 vols. New York: Rinehart & Co., 1954.

Hunter, J. Marvin, ed. *The Bloody Trail in Texas*. Bandera, TX: 1931. (Hard-cover edition called *Indian Raids in Texas*.)

————, ed. *The Trail Drivers of Texas*. Nashville: Cokesbury Press, 1925.

————. *Old Camp Verde, the Home of the Camels*. Bandera, TX: 1948.

Huson, Hobart. *Refugio: A Comprehensive History of Refugio County from Aboriginal Times to 1953*. 2 vols. Houston: The Guardsman Publ'g Co., 1953.

Inman, Col. Henry. *The Old Santa Fe Trail*. Reprint. Minneapolis: 1966.

Jackson, Donald, ed. *The Journals of Zebulon Montgomery Pike*. 2 vols. Norman: University of Oklahoma Press, 1966.

Jackson, Jack. *Los Mesteños, Spanish Ranching in Texas, 1721–1821*. College Station: Texas A&M University Press, 1986.

Jackson, Turrentine W. *Wagon Roads West*. Berkeley, CA: 1952.

James, Vinton Lee. *Frontier and Pioneer Recollections of Early Days in San Antonio and West Texas*. Published by the author. San Antonio: Artes Grafica Press, 1938.

John, Elizabeth A. H. *Storms Brewed in Other Men's Worlds — The Confrontation of Indians, Spanish, and French in the Southwest, 1540–1795*. College Station: A&M University Press, 1975.

Johnson, Francis White. *A History of Texas and Texans*. Edited by Eugene C. Barker. Chicago and New York: American Historical Society, 1916.

Johnson, Robert Underwood, and Clarence Clough Buell, eds. *Battles and Leaders of the Civil War*. 4 vols. New York: The Century Co., 1887.

Johnson, Wm. Preston. *The Life of General Albert Sidney Johnston*. New York: D. Appleton Co., 1878.

Jones, Rose Mary, ed. *La Hacienda, a History of Del Rio and Val Verde County*. Del Rio: Whitehead Memorial Museum, 1976.

Keleher, Wm. A. *Turmoil in New Mexico, 1846–1868*. Santa Fe: The Rydal Press, 1952.

Kendall, George Wilkins. *Narrative of the Texan Santa Fe Expedition*. 2 vols. New York: Harper & Bros., 1844.

King, Edward. (J. Wells Champney, Illustrator.) *Texas: 1874*. Houston: Cordovan Press, 1974. (An extract from *The Southern States of North America*, Glasgow, 1875, which was compiled from a series, 1873–1875, in *Scribner's Monthly*.)

King, Irene Marschall. *John O. Meusebach, German Colonizer in Texas*. Austin: University of Texas Press, 1967.

Lane, Walter P. *The Adventures and Recollections of General Walter P. Lane, a San Jacinto Veteran*. Marshall, TX: News Publishing Co., 1928.

Lavender, David. *Bent's Fort*. New York: 1954.

Leckie, Wm. H. *The Buffalo Soldiers, A Narrative of Negro Soldiers in the Cavalry*. Norman: University of Oklahoma Press, 1967.

Linn, John J. *Reminiscences of Fifty Years in Texas*. New York: D & J Sadler & Co., 1883.

Lister, Florence C., and Robert H. Lister. *Chihuahua, Storehouse of Storms*. Albuquerque: University of New Mexico Press, 1966.

Loomis, Noel, and Abraham Nasiter. *Pedro Vial and the Roads to Santa Fe*. Norman: University of Oklahoma Press, 1967.

————. *The Texan-Santa Fe Pioneers*. Norman: University of Oklahoma Press, 1958.

McConnell, H. H. *Five Years a Cavalryman, or, Sketches of the Regular Army Life on the Texas Frontier Twenty Odd Years Ago*. Jacksboro, TX: 1889.

McCown, Leonard Joe. *Indianola Scrapbook*. 1974 facsimile ed. of earlier 1st ed. Calhoun

County Historical Survey Committee, Port Lavaca. Printed by Jenkins Pub. Co., Austin.

McCullough, Wm. Wallace, Jr., ed. *John McCullough, Pioneer Presbyterian Missionary and Teacher in the Republic of Texas*. Austin: 1960.

McGaw, William Cochran. *Savage Scene: The Life and Times of James Kirker, Frontier King*. New York: Hastings House, 1972.

McGowan, Edward. *The Strange Eventful History of Parker H. French*. Los Angeles: 1958.

McLane, Sykes, Robert H. Thonhoff, and Calloway Crews. *The Life and Times of Thomas Ruckman*. Heritage Album Series No. 1. Karnes City: Old Helena Foundation, 1968.

Madison, Virginia. *The Big Bend Country of Texas*. Albuquerque: University of New Mexico Press, 1955.

————, and Hallie Stillwell. *How Come It's Called That?* Nomenclature of the Big Bend Country. Albuquerque: University of New Mexico Press, 1958.

Malsch, Brownson. *Indianola, The Mother of Western Texas*. Austin: Shoal Creek Publishers, 1977.

Marcy, Randolph B. *Army Life on the Border*. New York: 1874.

Mason, Herbert M., Jr., and Frank W. Brown. *A Century on Main Plaza — a History of the Frost National Bank*. Privately printed in San Antonio, 1968.

Maxwell, Ross A. *The Big Bend of the Rio Grande, A Guide to the Rocks, Geologic History, {flora and fauna}, and Settlers of the Area of Big Bend National Park*. Guidebook 7. University of Texas at Austin: Bureau of Economic Geology, 1968.

Mayhall, Mildred P. *Indian Wars of Texas*. Waco: Texian Press, 1965.

Miles, William. *Journal of the Sufferings and Hardships of Captain Parker H. French's Overland Expedition to California, which left N.Y. City May 3, 1850 and arrived at San Francisco, Dec. 14*. Chambersburg, PA: 1851. Reprinted by Cadmus Book Shop, 1916.

Mills, William W. *Forty Years at El Paso*. Edited by Rex Strickland. Carl Hertzog print, University of Texas at El Paso, 1962.

Moody, Ralph. *The Old Trails West*. New York: Thomas Y. Crowell Co., 1963.

————. *Stagecoach West*. New York: Thomas Y. Crowell Co., 1967.

Moorhead, Max L. *New Mexico's Royal Road: Trade and Travel on the Chihuahua Trail*. Norman: University of Oklahoma Press, 1958.

Morrell, Z. N. *Flowers and Fruits from the Wilderness*. Boston: Gould & Lincoln, 1872. 4th ed. rev. Dallas: W. G. Scarff & Co., 1886.

Myres, S. D., ed. *Pioneer Surveyor, Pioneer Lawyer, the Personal Narrative of O. W. Williams, 1877–1902*. 2d ed. El Paso: Texas Western College Press, 1968.

Nance, Joseph Milton. *After San Jacinto, the Texas-Mexican Frontier, 1836–1841*. Austin: University of Texas Press, 1963.

————. *Attack and Counter-Attack, the Texas-Mexican Frontier, 1842*. Austin: University of Texas Press, 1964.

National Cyclopaedia of American Biography. New York: James T. White & Co., 1898. 53 vols. with supplements.

Neighbors, Kenneth F. *Robert Simpson Neighbors and the Texas Frontier, 1836–1859*. Waco: Texian Press, 1975.

Newcomb, James Pearson. *The Alamo City*. San Antonio: 1926.

————. *Sketch of Secession Times in Texas*. San Francisco, CA: 1863.

Newcomb, W. W., Jr. *The Indians of Texas, from Prehistoric to Modern Times*. Austin and London: University of Texas Press, 1961. Texas History Paperback ed., 1975.

New Mexico Centennial, Historical Data Committee of the, eds. *A History of Las Cruces and the Mesilla Valley.* Las Cruces, NM: 1949.

Nunn, W. C. *Texas Under the Carpetbaggers.* Austin: University of Texas Press, 1962.

O'Connor, Kathryn Stoner. *The Presidio La Bahía del Espiritu Santo de Zuniga, 1721 – 1846.* Austin: Von Boeckmann Jones, 1966.

Oates, Stephen B. *Confederate Cavalry West of the River.* Austin: University of Texas Press, 1961.

———, ed. *Rip Ford's Texas.* Austin: University of Texas Press, 1963.

Olmstead, Frederick Law. *A Journey Through Texas.* New York: 1857.

Ormsby, Waterman L. *The Butterfield Overland Mail.* Edited by L. H. Wright and Josephine Bynum. San Marino, CA: 1942.

Oviedo y Valdez, Gonzalo Fernandez de. *Historia general y natural de los Indies.* 4 vols. Madrid: 1851 – 1885.

Pickrell, Annie Doom, ed. *Pioneer Women in Texas.* 1929. Reprint. Austin and New York: Jenkins Publishing, The Pemberton Press, 1970.

Przygoda, Jacek. *Texas Pioneers from Poland: A Study in Ethnic History.* Waco: Texian Press, 1971.

Raht, Carlysle Graham. *The Romance of Davis Mountains and Big Bend Country, A History.* El Paso: The Rahtbooks Co., 1919.

Ramsdell, Charles W. *Texas in the New Nation.* Vol. 3 of *The South in the Building of the Nation.* Richmond, VA: Southern Historical Publication Society, 1909.

Reed, Samuel C., Jr. *Scouting Expeditions of McCulloch's Texas Rangers.* New York: 1847. Reprint. 1970.

Reed, S. G. *A History of the Texas Railroads and of Transportation Conditions in Texas.* Houston: 1941.

Reid, John C. *Reid's Tramp, or a Journal of the Incidents of Ten Months Travel . . . Texas . . . California.* Selma, AL: 1858. Reprint. Austin: Steck Co., 1932.

Richardson, Rupert Norval. *The Comanche Barrier to the South Plains Settlement.* Glendale, CA: Arthur H. Clark Co., 1933.

———. *The Frontier of Northwest Texas, 1846–1876.* Glendale, CA: The Arthur H. Clark Co., 1963. Vol. 5 of Frontier Military Series.

Richardson, Willard, ed. *Texas Almanac, 1859.* 3rd ed., Galveston.

Rister, Carl Coke. *The Southwestern Frontier, 1865–1881.* Cleveland: Arthur H. Clark, 1928.

———. *Robert E. Lee in Texas.* Norman: University of Oklahoma Press, 1946.

Rittenhouse, Jack de Vere. *The Santa Fe Trail: A Historical Bibliography.* Albuquerque: University of New Mexico Press, 1971. 1st. ed.

Rodriguez, Policarpo. *The Old Guide — Surveyor, Scout, Indian Fighter, Hunter, Ranchman, Preacher: His Life in His Own Words.* Publishing House of M. E. Church South, Nashville and Dallas, undated, ca. 1897. Reprinted in *Old West* 5, no. 2 (Winter 1968).

Roemer, Dr. Ferdinand. *Texas, with Particular Reference to German Immigration, etc.* Translated from the German by Oswald Mueller. San Antonio: Standard Printing Co., 1935.

Rose, Victor Marion. *A Re-publishing of the Book most often known as Victor Rose's History of Victoria [sic].* Orig. ed., Laredo: Daily Times Print, undated; reprint, Victoria: 1961.

———. *The Life and Services of Gen. Ben McCulloch.* Philadelphia: 1888.

Rowland, Dunbar. *Jefferson Davis, Constitutionalist, his letters, papers, and speeches.* 10 vols. Jackson, MS: 1923.

Ruxton, Geo. Frederick Augustus. *Ruxton of the Rockies, 1820–1848.* Collected by Clyde and Mae Reed Porter, LeRoy Hafen (ed.) Norman: University of Oklahoma Press, 1950.

Santleben, August. *A Texas Pioneer: Early Staging and Overland Freighting Days on the Frontiers of Texas and Mexico.* Edited by I. D. Affleck. New York: The Neale Publishing Co., 1910. Facsimile ed., Waco: W. M. Morrison Press, 1967.

Schmidt, Robert H. *A Geographical Survey of Chihuahua.* El Paso: Texas Western Press, Mono. No. 37, 1973.

Scobee, Barry. *Old Fort Davis.* San Antonio: Naylor Co., 1947.

Scroggs, William Oscar. *Filibusters and Financiers: The Story of William Walker and His Associates.* New York: Macmillan, 1916.

Seeligson, Lelia. *A History of Indianola.* Indianola Historical Association. Cuero, TX: Cuero Record Press, 1931.

Shepherd, Grant. *The Silver Magnet, Fifty Years in a Mexican Silver Mine.* New York: E. P. Dutton, 1930.

Shipman, Mrs. O. L. (Alice Jack). *Taming the Big Bend.* Marfa, TX: 1926.

Shumway, George. *Conestoga Wagon, 1750–1850: Freight Carrier for 100 Years of Westward Expansion.* Pub. jointly by Early American Industries Ass'n and George Shumway. (York, PA: 1966).

Smith, Justin H. *The War with Mexico.* Vol. 1. New York: Macmillan, 1919.

Smithwick, Noah. *Evolution of a State.* Austin: Gammel Book Co., 1900.

Sonnichsen, C. L. *Pass of the North — Four Centuries on the Rio Grande.* El Paso: Texas Western Press, 1968.

———. *The Mescalero Apaches.* Norman: University of Oklahoma Press, 1963. 2nd ed.

Sowell, Andrew Jackson. *Early Settlers and Indian Fighters of Southwest Texas.* New York: Argosy Antiquarian, Ltd., 1900. (References used are from 1964 2 vol. reprint.)

Sprague, Maj. J. T. *The Treachery in Texas, the Secession of Texas, and the Arrest of the U.S. Officers and Soldiers Serving in Texas.* New York: Press of the Rebellion Record, 1862.

Stern, Philip Van Doren. *Robert E. Lee — The Man and the Soldier.* New York: Bonanza Books, 1963.

Stocking, Hobart E. *The Road to Santa Fe.* New York: Hastings House, 1971.

Strickland, Rex W. *Six Who Came to El Paso — Pioneers of the 1840's.* Monograph No. 3 in Southwestern Studies. El Paso: Texas Western Press, 1963.

Sumpter, Jesse. *Paso de Anguila.* Edited by Ben Pingenot. Austin: Encino Press, 1969.

Taylor, Morris F. *First Mail West: Stagecoach Lines on the Santa Fe Trail.* Albuquerque: University of New Mexico Press, 1971.

Taylor, Nathaniel A. *The Coming Empire, or 2,000 Miles in Texas on Horseback.* 1877. Reprint. Dallas: Turner Company, 1936.

Terrell, John Upton. *Apache Chronicle — The Story of the People.* New York: World Publishing, 1972.

———. *Journey into Darkness — Cabeza de Vaca.* New York: 1962.

Thompson, Cecilia. *History of Marfa and Presidio County, 1535–1946.* 2 vols. Austin: Nortex Press, 1985.

Thompson, Richard A. *Crossing the Border with the 4th Cavalry; Mackenzie's Raid into Mexico — 1873.* Waco: Texian Press, 1985.

Thompson, Waddy. *Recollections of Mexico.* New York: 1846.

Thonhoff, Robert H. *San Antonio Stage Lines, 1847–1881.* Southwestern Studies No. 29. El Paso: Texas Western Press, 1971.

Twitdeale, R. E. *Old Santa Fe.* Santa Fe, NM: 1925.

Utley, Robert M. *Frontiersmen in Blue, 1848–1865: The United States Army and the Indian.* New York: Macmillan. 2d printing, 1973.

———. *Frontier Regulars, The United States Army and the Indian, 1866–1891.* New York: Macmillan, 1973. 1st ed.

———. *Fort Davis.* N.P.S. Historical Handbook Series, No. 38. Washington, DC: 1955.

Uvalde County, History of. *A Proud Heritage.* El Progreso Club, comp. Uvalde, TX: 1975.

Walker, Henry Pickering. *The Wagon Masters: High Plains Freighting from the Earliest Days of the Santa Fe Trail to 1880.* Norman: University of Oklahoma Press, 1966.

Wallace, Edward S. *Destiny and Glory.* New York: Conrad — McCann, Inc., 1957.

———. *General William Worth: Monterey's Forgotten Hero.* Dallas: SMU Press, 1953.

Wallace, Ernest S. *Ranald S. Mackenzie on the Texas Frontier.* Lubbock: West Texas Museum Assoc., 1964.

———, ed. *R. S. Mackenzie's Official Correspondence, 1873–1879.* Lubbock: West Texas Museum Assoc., 1968.

———, and David M. Vigness, eds. *Documents of Texas History.* Austin: 1960, 1963.

Ward, Sir Henry George. *Mexico, with an Account of the Mining Companies and of the Political Events in that Republic to the Present Day.* 2 vols. London: 2nd ed., 1829.

Watkins, Sue, ed. *One League to Each Wind: Accounts of Early Surveying in Texas.* Publication of the Texas Surveyors Association. Austin: Von Boeckmann-Jones, 1964.

Webb, Josiah. *The Papers of James Josiah Webb.* Edited by Ralph A. Bieber. Glendale, CA: Arthur H. Clark Co., 1932.

Webb, James Josiah. *Adventures in the Santa Fe Trade: 1844–47.* Edited by Ralph Bieber. Glendale, CA: Arthur H. Clark Co., 1931.

Webb, Walter Prescott. *The Texas Rangers: A Century of Frontier Defense.* Boston: 1935. 2nd ed., Austin: University of Texas Press, 1973.

Weddle, Robert S. *San Juan Bautista: Gateway to Spanish Texas.* Austin and London: University of Texas Press, 1968.

———. *Wilderness Manhunt: the Search for La Salle.* Austin and London: University of Texas Press, 1973.

———, and Robert H. Thonhoff. *Drama and Conflict, The Texas Saga of 1776.* Austin: Madrona Press, 1976.

Williams, Clayton. *Never Again.* 3 vols. San Antonio: The Naylor Co., 1969.

Williams, J. W. *Old Texas Trails.* Kenneth F. Neighbors, ed. and comp. Austin: Eakin Press, 1979.

Williams, O. W. *Pioneer Surveyor — Frontier Lawyer.* Edited by S. D. Myres. El Paso: Texas Western Press, 2nd ed., 1968.

Williams, R. H. *With the Border Ruffians, Memories of the Far West: 1852–1868.* Edited by E. W. Williams. London: 1908.

Wilson, Neill C., and Frank J. Taylor. *Southern Pacific.* New York: McGraw Hill, 1952.

Wislizenus, Frederick Adolphus. *Memoir of a Tour to Northern Mexico, Connected with Col. Doniphan's Expedition in 1846 and 1847.* Reprint ed. Glorieta, NM: The Rio Grande Press, 1969.

Wood, Jerome H., Jr. *Conestoga Crossroads.* Harrisburg, PA: Pennsylvania Historical and Museum Commission, 1979.

Wortham, Louis J. *A History of Texas, from Wilderness to Commonwealth.* 5 vols. Fort Worth: 1924.

Wright, Marcus J. *Texas in the War, 1861–1865.* Hillsboro, TX: 1965.

Yoakum, Henderson. *History of Texas.* 2 vols. New York: Redfield, 1855.

INTERVIEWS BY AUTHOR

Almada, Francisco. Professor and historian. At his home in Chihuahua City, Chih., November 1973.

Davis, Nellie. April 27, 1973, at Marathon, Texas.

Frettem, Marlin. Owner of property where Confederates' supply train was destroyed in 1862. August 10, 1975, at Cañoncita, New Mexico.

Müller, Lic. Emilio Elias. Great-grandson of Henry Müller. Corporation headquarters at Ciudad Chihuahua, July 30, 1979. [Re: original Müller's interests in meteorites.]

Payne, Blas. Grandson of Isaac Payne, Seminole scout and Congressional Medal of Honor recipient. With Joe King and Travis Roberts, August 1973.

Roberts, Travis. April 26, 1973, and taped interview at his ranch near Marathon, Texas, August 28, 1975. [Re: old roads through the Big Bend and personalities identified with them.]

Russell, Willie. Direct descendant of original Presidio pioneer, William Russell. February 1973 at Casa Piedra in Alamito Creek Valley. [Re: settlements there and the later Hernandez settlement at Alamo Springs.]

Strickland, Professor Rex W. August 1975, at his home in El Paso. [Re: Henry Skillman, Capt. Geo. Wythe Baylor, Mose Kelley, the Salt War, and the settlements downriver from El Paso.]

Sullivan, Jerry. Texas Parks and Wildlife Commission staff. January 1976. [Re: Presidio and Fort Leaton.]

Vest, Dean Deed L. St. Mary's University, San Antonio. Frequent discussions, 1969–1974. [Re: his research on the Texas Chihuahua Road. He made a number of talks and wrote at least one magazine article on the subject. When he learned I was undertaking this book, he charged me only that I should give him credit for reopening study of the old wagon road, and that I should maintain the identity of the road from Indianola to Chihuahua as the Chihuahua *Road,* as distinct from Connelley's route, the Chihuahua Trail, and the one from Independence, Kansas, as the Santa Fe Trail. These debts I have tried faithfully to discharge.]

Weddle, Robert S. Author of *San Juan Bautista: Gateway to Spanish Texas.* October 1974. [Re: fordable crossings on the Rio Grande.]

LETTERS TO AUTHOR

Bishop, Beverly. Assistant archivist, Missouri Historical Society, St. Louis, Missouri. April 7, 1977. [Establishing identity of W. D. Skillman as brother of Henry Skillman.]

Clarke, Dr. Roy S., Jr. Curator, Division of Meteorites, National Museum of Natural History, Washington, D.C. [Affirming that his division holds the Casas Grandes meteorite and offering technical and historical sources on the meteorite.]

Hutchison, Dr. Robert. Director, Meteorite Collection, British Museum (Natural History) Department of Mineralogy, London. May 5, 1977. [Confirming that Santleben's meteorite had never been at British Museum.]

Maxwell, Dr. Ross. Big Bend geologist, Austin, Texas. August 25, 1975. [Re: nature of rock formations on St. Esteban Terraces, Alamito Creek Valley.]

Roberts, Travis. March 17, 1973. [Re: sources on Cut-Off Road and Bullis Road in Big Bend.]

MANUSCRIPTS (Private papers, archival collections, unpublished letters, theses)

Anderson, Thomas F. "A History of Indianola." M.A. thesis, University of Texas at Austin, 1942.

Arnette, W. W. "Reminiscences" on early days in Uvalde County. ECB.

Boozer, Jessie Beryl. "The History of Indianola, Texas." M.A. thesis, University of Texas at Austin, 1942.

Butler, Grace Lowe. "General John Lapham Bullis: Friend of the Frontier." Ca. 1920. [I made a typescript of this MS ca. 1937 from an unidentified source. A similar copy in the files of General Bullis's daughter, Mrs. W. S. Halcombe, has been drawn upon by Edward S. Wallace and others. RLS]

Cain, Alice Virginia. "A History of Brewster County." M.A. thesis, Sul Ross University, 1935.

Campbell, Fannie Faye. "Army Explorations in Texas, 1849." M.A. thesis, Southwest Texas State College, 1964.

Carmichael, Lois Miller. "The History of Uvalde County." M.A. thesis, Southwest Texas State Teachers College, 1944.

Casey, Clifford B. "The Trans-Pecos in Texas History." Alpine, Texas.

"Diario de Don Francisco Colomo," Presidio del Norte, ca. 1835–1855. Translated from original Spanish to English by Guadalupe Carrasco Hernandez, Marfa, Texas. [Jerry Sullivan, Texas Parks and Wildlife Commission, has photocopy of original; allowed RLS to copy entries from it, ca. 1974.]

Fluth, Alice Freeman. "Indianola, Early Gateway to Texas." M.A. thesis, St. Mary's University, 1939.

Governors' Letters. TSA. E. J. Davis Collection. Letters to Davis from frontier settlers re: Indian depredations.

———. Elisha M. Pease Collection, 1853–1859. Folders 9 (includes contract for building Miss. and Pac. Railroad); 44; 45; 46; 48 (includes full text of message re: violence on the road); 49.

Gregg, John E. "The History of Presidio County." M.A. thesis, University of Texas at Austin, 1933.

Howard, Geo. T. Papers of. Howard Lackman Collection, ECB.

Huntress, F. G. to R. Fink, *Weekly State Gazette* [Austin], February 22, 1865 [reporting on arrival of Seminole and Kickapoos in Mexico after attack at Dove Creek.]

Jennings, Thomas A. "San Antonio in the Confederacy." M.A. thesis, Trinity University, 1957.

Kielman, Chester V., comp. *Guide to the Microfilm Edition of the Bexar Archives, 1722–1836.* University of Texas Microfilm Publication, Center for Inter-American Studies. Austin: 1971.

Lackman, Howard. "George Thomas Howard, Texas Frontiersman." Ph.D. dissertation, University of Texas at Austin, 1954.

Lamar Papers. TSA. President Mirabeau Lamar's open letter to "People of Santa Fe." Proposed to be carried by commissioner on Texan-Santa Fe Expedition to explain purposes of Texas Republic in broaching international border without invitation. February 21, 1840.

Langner, Walter O. "A History of the Early Settlers of the Upper Frio River." M.A. thesis, Southwest Texas State College, 1962.

Lanham, Josephine. "Recollections of Early Spanish-Speaking Settlers and Rolling of Wagons from Old San Antonio, Texas, to Chihuahua, Mexico." Dated October 4, 1972, and transmitted to RLS at that time.

McAdoo, Brig. Gen. J. D., Texas State Militia, to John Burke, February 20, 1865. [Re: debacle at Dove Creek.] In AGO records.

McMillen, Kathryn Smith. "The San Antonio-San Diego, California, Mail Line in Texas." M.A. thesis, University of Texas at Austin, 1960.

Mayer, Arthur. "San Antonio — Frontier Entrepot." Ph.D. dissertation, University of Texas at Austin, 1976.

Meadows, Henry E. "The Chihuahua Trail, 1590–1914." Unpublished MS in state files of the Crockett County Historical Survey, ca. 1945. Austin Texas.

"Memorial Homecoming — Father Leopold Moczygemba." Brochure for church reunion and liturgical reinterment of Father Leopold at Panna Maria, Karnes County, Texas, October 13, 1974.

Pease, Sam W. "They Came to San Antonio, 1794–1865." [Massive unpublished typescript of obituaries and bio sketches from many sources.] Reference Section, San Antonio Public Library. Not listed in catalogs.

Perkins, George O. "The Early History of Val Verde County." M.A. thesis, Sul Ross University, 1954.

Thonhoff, Robert H. "El Fuerte de Santa Cruz de Cibolo: A Study in Historical Site Identification." August 1970. Held by author, Fashing, Texas.

————. "A History of Karnes County." M.A. thesis, Southwest Texas State College, 1963.

Tunstall, Mrs. Florida Sharpe. Memoirs. From interview with Col. M. L. Crimmins, 1940. Typescript in Crimmins Papers, ECB.

Wallace, Edward S., and Kenneth W. Porter. "Thunderbolt of the Frontier." Adapted from typescript in papers of Mrs. W. S. Halcombe, San Antonio. [Believed to have been published in an Eastern regional magazine.]

Wooster, Dr. Ralph A. "Isaac Dunbar Affleck." President's paper delivered before convention of Texas State Historical Association, Austin, Texas, March 7, 1975. Copy in RLS files.

MAPS

"Map of General Wool's Road, 1846, Showing Line of March of the Centre Division from San Antonio de Bejar to Saltillo." M. L. Crimmins Map Collection, ECB.

"Military Map of the Rio Grande Frontier." Livermore, Capt. W. R., and Topo. Ass't. F. E. Butterfield. 1881. U.S. Army Corps of Engineers. Displays all major features of Chihuahua Road and supporting military installations, from Indianola through San Antonio to Presidio and El Paso del Norte. Original blueprint in M. L. Crimmins Map Collection, ECB.

"Sacramento, Battle of." February 28, 1847. Folded insert, tipped in at page 499, Doniphan to Jones, *Sen. Ex. Doc. No. 1, 30th Cong., 1st Sess.* President's Message and reports from the Field. Textual reference by Doniphan, page 502, indicates this handsomely executed "plan of the field" was prepared by Maj. Geo. Meriwether Clark. Full-size copy in RLS files.

". . . Scouting Expedition from Camps at the Chinati Mountains." January 12–May 12, 1880. 10th U.S. Cavalry. M. L. Crimmins Map Collection, ECB.

NEWSPAPERS

(In Texas except as noted)

Alpine Avalanche, September 14, 1951 (60th anniv. ed.).

Austin Texas Democrat, January 28, 1849 (Sam Highsmith's report to Col. Bell); June–December 1849.

Corpus Christi Star, December 9, 1848; January 20, 1849 (re: Colonel Hays's expedition to Presidio).

Daily Missouri Republican, March 13, 14, and July 8, 1850 (re: Aubrey's trip, as cited by Bieber, "Exploring Southwestern Trails").

Daily National Intelligencer [Washington], October 8, 1848 (re: marriage of Maj. Geo. Thomas Howard).

Dallas Herald, February 27, 1861.

El Paso Herald, April 20, 1901.

Floresville Chronicle-Journal, September 16, 1960, Sec. C.

Galveston News, September 11, 1856 (re: alleged uprising of blacks in South Texas).

Galveston Weekly News, October 18, 1848.

Honey Grove Citizen, March–June 1888 (series of articles on Col. Jack Hays).

Houston Telegraph and Texas Register, January 3, 1850; January 30, 1850 (re: death of Mike Chevaille); March 7, 1850 (re: death of Torrey in Mexico); September 13, 1850.

Indianola Times, June 26, 1866 (re: revival of port activity).

Karnes City Citation, April 1, 8, and 15, 1965 ("Historic Helena").

Karnes County News [Karnes City], December 9, 1931 (50th anniversary edition).

Mesilla [N.M.] *Times,* January 1, 1862 (obituary of Kelley's death); January 11, 1862 (follow-up story on shooting).

New Braunfels Herald, July–September 1970 ("Autobiography of Peter Jonas," weekly serial).

St. Louis [Mo.] *Union,* January 2, 1848, as reprinted May 5, 1848, in *Galveston Weekly News* (re: Henry Skillman); June 20, 1850.

San Antonio Express, August 29, 1865; September 21, 1865; October 3, 1865 *passim* through March 17, 1872 (Reconstruction and railroads); March 30, August 2, 1872 (railroad's progress and delays); May 27, 1875 (Indianola hurricane); January 21, 1877; February 7, 1877; February 20, 1877 (celebration of arrival of first passenger train); February 19, 1880 (Hans Mickle byline story on conditions in Indianola); May 25, 1880; April 7, 1880 (revised account of Mose Kelley's death); July 24, 1881; January 1, 1883; January 13, 1883; May 4–June 1, 1902 (four-part "Memoirs of Col. Giddings"); March 4, 1908 (obituary of Ramón Hernandez); February 27, 1921 (names of old freighters); September 19, 1911 (obituary of August Santleben); April 17, 1976 (Kickapoo villages).

San Antonio Herald, July 31, 1857, *passim* through March 27, 1862; June 5, 1862 (Mollie's story); December 19, 1865; February 4, 1866; February 16, 1866; June 11, 1866; September 9, 1866; May 3, 1872.

San Antonio Ledger, June 23, 1853, *passim* through December 29, 1860; July 20, 1866.

San Antonio Tri-Weekly Herald, September 7, 1865; September 9, 1865; September 14, 1865; September 28, 1865; October 26, 1865; October 28, 1865; November 16, 1865.

Santa Fe New Mexican, May 7, 1864 (French's account of slaying of Skillman).

True Issue [La Grange, Texas], February 21, March 27, 1861 (re: ousting of Federal troops from Texas by Commission on Public Safety).

Uvalde Leader-News, centennial edition ("A History of Uvalde County"), April 19, 1956.

Victoria Advocate, May 1968 (historical edition).

Weekly State Gazeteer [Austin], February 1 and 8, 1865; March 12, 1865 (contemporary coverage of Battle of Dove Creek).

Western Texian [San Antonio], December 1848, as reprinted January 20, 1849, in *Corpus Christi Star* (full text of Hays's report to Bell); May 24, 1849; September 19, 1850; April 1, 1853; May 13, 1853.

PERIODICAL ARTICLES

Austin, Stephen F. Trans. by Ethel Zivley Rather. "Explanation to the Public Concerning the Affairs of Texas, by Citizen Stephen F. Austin." Monograph printed in Spanish in Mexico City, 1835. *QTSHA* 8, no. 3 (January 1905).

Baker, T. Lindsay. "Four Letters from Texas to Poland in 1855." *SHQ* 37, no. 3 (January 1974).

Barr, Alwyn. "Texas Coastal Defenses, 1861–1865." *SHQ* 45, no. 1 (July 1961).

Barrett, Leonora. "Transportation, Supplies, and Quarters for the West Texas Frontier Under the Federal Military System, 1848–1861." *Yearbook,* WTHA (Abilene) v. 5 (June 1929).

Bender, Averam B. "Opening Routes Across West Texas, 1848–1858." *SHQ,* 1933.

Bloom, L. B. "The Chihuahua Highway." *New Mexico Historical Review* 12, no. 3 (July 1937).

Chavez, Fray Angelico. "Ruts of the Santa Fe Trail." *Journal* of The New Mexico Department of Development (Santa Fe) 50, nos. 7–8 (July/August 1972).

Chipman, Donald E. "In Search of Cabeza de Vaca's Route Across Texas." *SHQ* 91, no. 2 (October 1987), 127–148.

Cox, C. C. (Mabelle Eppard Martin, ed.) "From Texas to California in 1849." *SHQ* 29, no. 1 (July 1925).

Coy, Owen C. "The Last Expedition of Josiah Gregg." *SHQ* 20, no. 1 (July 1916).

Crane, Charles Judson. "Experiences of a Colonel of Infantry." *SHQ* 23, no. 2 (October 1919).

Crimmins, Col. Martin L. "Fort Lancaster, Crockett County." *Frontier Times* 10, no. 1 (February 1933).

———, ed. "W. G. Freeman's Report on the Eighth Military Department." *SHQ* 51–54 (July 1947–October 1950).

———. "John Glanton of San Antonio." *Frontier Times* 17, no. 7 (April 1940).

———, ed. "Col. Robert E. Lee's Report on Indian Combats in Texas." *SHQ* 39, no. 1 (July 1935).

———, ed. "Col. J. F. K. Mansfield's Report on Dept. of Texas in 1856." *SHQ* 42, no. 2 (October 1938).

———. "Camp Peña Colorado, Texas." *Bulletin* no. 56, WTHSS (Alpine), December 1935.

———. "Two Thousand Miles by Boat in the Rio Grande in 1850." *Bulletin,* no. 48, WTHSS (Alpine), December 1933.

———. "General John E. Wool in Texas." *Yearbook,* WTHA (Alpine), 1942.

Dalton, Arthur. "History of Fort Inge on the Leona River." *Frontier Times* 3, no. 10 (July 1926).

Daly, Henry W. "A Dangerous Dash Down Lancaster Hill." *American Legion Legionnaire,* December 1939.

Davenport, H. K., and J. E. Wells. "The First Europeans in Texas." *SHQ* 22, 1918–1919.

Denham, Claude. "Frontier Problems and Amusements in Crockett County." *Yearbook,* WTHA 9 (October 1933).

Dunn, Roy Sylvan. "The KGC in Texas, 1860–1861." *SHQ* 70, no. 4 (April 1967).

Ferguson, I. D. "The Battle of Dove Creek." *Frontier Times* 1, no. 9 (June 1924). From MS written in 1911.

Fitzhugh, Lester N. "Saluria, Fort Esperanza, and Military Operations on the Texas Coast, 1861–1864." *SHQ* 51, no. 1 (July 1957).

Fulmore, Z. T. "General Volney Erskine Howard." *QTSHA* 14, no. 2 (October 1910).

Gooding, Larry. "Across the Plains in 1849." *Frontier Times* 1, no. 11 (August 1924). Reprinted from *Dallas News,* May 14, 1911.

Greenwood, C. L., ed. "Opening Routes to El Paso, 1849." *SHQ* 48, no. 2 (October 1944).

Haley, J. Evetts. "The Comanchero Trade." *SHQ* 38, no. 3 (January 1935).

Hine, Robert V. "An Artist Draws the Line." *American Heritage* 19, no. 2 (February 1968).

Holden, W. C. "Frontier Defense in Texas During the Civil War." *Yearbook,* WTHA, no. 4 (Lubbock), June 1928.

Hooper, Wm. T., Jr. "Governor Edmund J. Davis, Ezra Cornell, and the A&M College of Texas." *SHQ* 78, no. 3 (January 1975).

Hunter, John Warren. "The Battle of Dove Creek." *Hunter's Magazine,* 1911; reprinted in *Frontier Times* 1, no. 10 (July 1924).

Kelley, J. C. "Archaeological Notes on Two Excavated House Structures in Western Texas." *Texas Archaeological and Paleontological Society* 20, 1940.

Kelly, Charles J. "Notes on Julimes, Chihuahua." *El Palacio* 56.

Kinder, L. S. "A Chapter in the Life of Col. Chas. Goodnight." *Yearbook,* WTHA 6 (June 1930).

Lafferty, Jack. "The Old Chihuahua Trail." *Texas Parade* 22, no. 10 (March 1963).

McMillen, Kathryn Smith. "A Descriptive Bibliography on the San Antonio–San Diego Mail Line." *SHQ* 59, no. 2 (October 1955).

Mahon, Emmie Giddings W., and Chester Kielman. "Geo. H. Giddings and the San Antonio–San Diego Mail Line." *SHQ* 61, no. 2 (October 1957).

Marshall, Thomas Maitland. "Commercial Aspects of the Texan-Santa Fe Expedition." *SHQ* 20, no. 3 (January 1917).

Martin, Mabelle Eppard. "California Emigrant Roads Through Texas." *SHQ* 28, no. 4 (April 1925).

Nelson, Al B. "Campaigning in the Big Bend of the Rio Grande in 1787." *SHQ* 39, no. 3 (January 1936).

Nunn, Annie Dyer. "Over the Goodnight-Loving Trail." *Frontier Times* 2, no. 2 (November 1924), as reprinted from *Dearborn Independent.*

Pate, J'Nell. "United States–Mexican Border Conflicts, 1870–1880." *Yearbook,* WTHA 38 (October 1962).

Pool, Wm. C. "The Battle of Dove Creek." *SHQ* 53, no. 4 (April 1954).

Porter, Kenneth W. "The Seminole Negro Indian Scouts, 1870–1881." *SHQ* 55 (1951–1952).

Pratt, Julius W. "The Origin of 'Manifest Destiny.' " *American Historical Review* 32, no. 4 (July 1927).

Schick, Robert. "Wagons for Chihuahua." *The American West* 3 (January 1966).

Shearer, Ernest C. "Callahan Expedition." *SHQ* 54 (April 1951).

Smith, Ralph A. "Mexican and Anglo-Saxon Traffic in Scalps, Slaves, and Livestock, 1835–1841." *Yearbook,* WTHA 36 (October 1936).

Smith, Victor J. "Early Spanish Explorations in the Big Bend of Texas." *Publication II,* WTHSS (Alpine).

Stephens, F. F. "Missouri and the Santa Fe Trade." *Missouri Historical Review* 20 (July 1916).

Strickland, Rex W. "The Birth and Death of a Legend — The Johnson Massacre of 1837." *Arizona and the West — A Quarterly Journal of History* 18, no. 3 (Autumn 1976).

Sullivan, Jerry. "Fortress on the Rio Grande, El Fortin." *Texas Parks and Wildlife* 36, no. 12 (December 1978).

Taylor, Dean T. U. "Anglo-Saxon Trails Across Texas." *Frontier Times* 15, no. 6 (March 1938).

Toney, Tom. "The Indianola Story." *Texas Parade,* December 1951.

Wallace, Edward S. "General John Lapham Bullis, The Thunderbolt of the Prairies." *SHQ* 54, no. 4 (April 1951); 55, no. 1 (July 1951).

———. "General Ranald Slidell Mackenzie." *SHQ* 57, no. 7 (January 1953).

———. "General William Jenkins Worth and Texas." *SHQ* 54, no. 2 (October 1950).

Wallace, Ernest W., and Adrian S. Anderson, "R. S. Mackenzie and the Kickapoos: The Raid into Mexico in 1873." *Arizona and the West* 7 (1965).

Wallace, Lew. "The Mines of Santa Eulalia." *Harper's New Monthly Magazine* 35, no. 110 (November 1867).

Williams, J. W. "Military Roads of the 1850s in Central West Texas." *Yearbook,* WTHA 18 (October 1942).

Woodhull, Frost. "The Seminole Indian Scouts on the Border." *Frontier Times* 15, no. 3 (December 1937).

Woolford, Sam, ed. "The Burr DuVal Diary." *SHQ* 55, no. 4 (April 1962).

PUBLIC DOCUMENTS

Adjutant General's Office. Records. TSA. Letters Rec'd. Office of Field Services. Van Horne to Jones, December 18, 1848.

———. Military Book 27. Marcy to Worth, December 10, 1848.

———. General Correspondence. Reports of Capt. George Wythe Baylor re: Campaigns against Mimbres Apache, 1880–1881. RG 401.

Archivos de la Secretaria de Gobierno, Chih. Regular files. *Legajo 175, 1849:* No. 19, "Concerning campaign against Indians undertaken by the American M. Chevally. Proposal, contract, report of plunder taken, etc."; No. 22, "Concerning proposal of the American David K. Porry [Torrey] for the ransom of captives among the Comanche." Cited on page 455 of Eugene Bolton, *Guide to Materials for the History of the United States in the Principal Archives of Mexico.*

Bexar County [Texas] Clerk's Office. San Antonio. Probate of Ben Leaton's will, 1851.

House Ex. Doc. No. 129, 34th Cong., 2d Sess. Capt. John Pope's Well-Drilling Assignment Along Pecos River.

National Archives. Washington, D.C. Record Group No. 98 [Re: Ben Leaton at El Fortín, Presidio del Norte.]

Sen. Ex. Doc. No. 1, 30th Cong., 1st Sess. Report on Battle of Sacramento. "Doniphan to Jones," with enclosures, March 4, 1847, 495–513, after message from the President in "Report of the Secretary of War."

Sen. Ex. Doc. No. 64, 31st Cong., 1st Sess. "Reconnaissance of Routes from San Antonio to El Paso." 1850. Bvt. Lt. Col. J. E. Johnston, 562.

Sen. Ex. Doc. No. 64, 31st Cong., 1st Sess. 1850. [Richard Howard's work on survey of Texas Colorado River.]

Sen. Ex. Doc. No. 64, 31st Cong., 1st Sess. [Whiting-Smith Expedition.]

Sen. Ex. Doc. No. 92B, 31st Cong., 1st Sess. [Col. Jack Hays's official report to Sec'y of War W. L. Marcy.]

Sen. Ex. Doc. No. 455, 33d Cong., 2d Sess. January 20, 1855. [Parker H. French's 1850 embezzlement of army supplies in San Antonio.]

Sen. Ex. Doc. No. 2, 36th Cong., 1st Sess. 1859–1860. Capt. A. T. Lee, 8th Infantry, Fort Quitman, reporting to General Twiggs, commanding, San Antonio. [Re: Apache raid on fort.]

Sen. Ex. Doc. No. 19, 45th Cong., 2d Sess. [Reconstruction.]

U.S. Census. Schedule I. "Free inhabitants in San Antonio in the County of Bexar, Texas," enumerated on the 21st day of September, 1850.

————. Texas. Slave Schedule. Vol. 1 (1860), *U.S. Census Reports,* 8th Census.

Uvalde County [Texas]. Inventory of County Archives of Texas. Texas Historical Records Survey, WPA, No. 232. Uvalde, 1941.

War Department. Chief of Engineering Office. Letters Rec'd. Worth, Order No. 10, February 9, 1849.

————. General Order No. 5. AGO. March 1, 1861. [Dismissal of Gen. David Twiggs for treason.]

Index

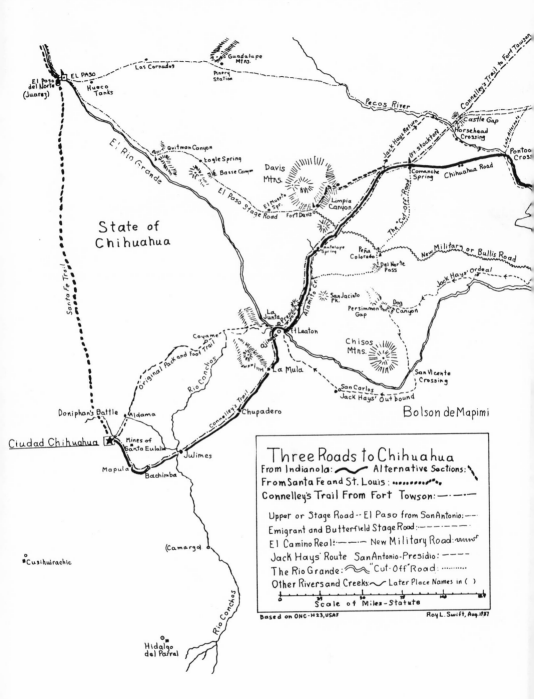